EVERYTHING
you wanted to know about the
COUNTRYSIDE
(but didn't dare ask!)

First published in Great Britain by Merlin Unwin Books Ltd 2022

Merlin Unwin Books Ltd
Palmers House
7 Corve Street
Ludlow
Shropshire SY8 1DB
UK

www.merlinunwin.co.uk

The author asserts her moral right to be identified with this work.
ISBN 978 1 913159 47 4
Typeset in Adobe Jenson Pro in 11pt by Merlin Unwin Books
Printed by IMAK

EVERYTHING
you wanted to know about the
COUNTRYSIDE
(but didn't dare ask!)

Jill Mason
Photographs by David Mason

MERLIN UNWIN BOOKS

ACKNOWLEDGEMENTS

I am extremely appreciative that David, my husband, is a photographer and around 90% of the photographs used to illustrate this book are his. His splendid pictures have contributed greatly by adding visual meaning to my text. Grateful thanks too to my son Andrew, also a keen photographer, who has helped out with several pictures relating to bovine matters and a few others he's taken when he's not busy looking after cattle.

I am also indebted to Wild Knight Distillery, Goat Shed Farm Shop and the Wheelyboat Trust for their help. Several companies have also permitted me to use their own pictures of subjects I would not otherwise have been able to access. My thanks go to Simon Whitehead, Fishtek, DairyFlo, Thanet Earth, Soya UK and *Poultry World* magazine.

CONTENTS

INTRODUCTION

When you're old, time is like a ball rolling down a hill, gathering speed as it goes. And so it appears to be with developments in the countryside. Changes in the last 25 years have certainly gained momentum. I have worked and lived all my life in the countryside and through experience and a natural curiosity I've endeavoured to keep abreast of what has been happening over time. This book contains my observations.

Nearly three-quarters of land in the UK is farmed in one way or another and much of the remainder is managed for conservation. Government funding for the countryside has now swung towards improving the environment, which needs caring for with compassion and understanding. Rural Britain is a complex place in which one action can interact with another, triggering a chain of events, sometimes unintended, that can take generations to rectify.

Agriculture has been swift to embrace the benefits of modern technology which in the last fifty years has taken us beyond imagination. Satellite technology is fitted in many tractors, sprayers and combines; drones are used to survey plantings; and there are robots on farms to tackle weeds, monitor crops and even milk cows! Livestock are identified and information stored electronically in microchips either inserted beneath the skin or embedded in ear tags, collars, anklets or bracelets.

But even though it utilises advanced technology, farming is still subject to an annual cycle of work. On large arable farms this means preparing the ground, sowing crops, applying fertiliser, herbicides or pesticides and then harvesting. Autumn is the time for land cultivation and the sowing of different crops. Meanwhile, livestock and poultry farmers have to attend to their animals every day of the year. Some aspects of their care may be automated and seasonal, but a great deal of it is still very much hands-on. Fieldsports have for centuries played a big part in the countryside, both directly and indirectly, and still do.

Every aspect of farming is affected by the weather. In the last twenty years, thousands of acres have been committed to renewable energy installations to combat climate change, with wind turbines and solar farms now commonplace. Anaerobic digesters can turn animal waste or green crops into biogas.

Those in the countryside today have to be prepared to move with the times but they also cherish their heritage. Many have their roots in the countryside and they share an empathy with the land, as do I.

With fewer people employed in farming, the structure of small country villages has changed. Once home to farmworkers and rural craftsmen, many have become places where urban retirees seek a more peaceful way of life, or visitors come for a holiday.

Hopefully my attempt in this book to explain what goes on in the countryside today, as well as how it functions and some of the facts behind it all, will pave the way to a wider appreciation.

Jill Mason, August 2022

Mixed farming predominates in southern England

FARMING: THE BIG PICTURE

During the Second World War farmers set to work ploughing up every available acre in order to feed a hungry nation. They ploughed up vast areas of bracken, which is poisonous to cattle, and reseeded it with grass. Three million acres of marginal land were brought into production. The farmers did a remarkable job and took pride in their achievement. After the war, the Agricultural Act 1947 encouraged them to continue on that route with guaranteed minimum payments.

In the centuries leading up to this, farming methods had changed little but from the 1940s came a complete revolution in farming. Huge advances were made in agricultural science, technology, machinery and chemistry. It all happened with such speed that no-one was aware of the long-term effects. Factories which had been making weapons of war switched to manufacturing agricultural machinery. The little grey 'Fergie' (Ferguson) tractor revolutionised life for farmers on small farms and Fordson tractors did the same for those on large farms. Combine harvesters and mechanical sugar beet harvesters began to appear. Work horses disappeared. They hadn't needed much room to turn round in a field but large machines did, so hedges were ripped out to make the fields bigger. Artificial fertilisers and synthetic sprays were introduced. DDT was one of these which was highly effective compared with what had been used before but also highly toxic. At the time there was widespread ignorance of the risks its use involved but eventually it was banned in 1984 when there was undeniable proof of the dangers and devastation it caused.

The next major demand made on farmers came in the 1960s when consumers wanted cheaper food. Farmers successfully responded by intensifying their production methods. Scientists discovered how to engineer naturally, by selection, the structure of plants so that dwarf varieties of cereals were developed, in which the plant's energy was channelled into growing bigger seed heads and putting less into the stems. Previously, for instance there had been surplus straw which had to be burned, but shorter stems not only meant less unwanted straw but also the ripening crop was less likely to be flattened by wind and rain before it could be harvested.

GRANTS AND SUBSIDIES

In 1973 the UK became part of the Common Market, now known as the EU, with completely new subsidies offered to farmers by way of the Common Agricultural Policy (CAP). Those European subsidies were geared to increasing production which, in the 1980s, inadvertently led to surplus 'mountains' of beef, butter and grain and 'lakes' of milk and wine through overproduction. In 1992 'set aside' was introduced to take land out of production and which could be regulated to allow adjustments to be made. Permanent subsidies for organic farming were introduced in 1994.

EU grants were paid to landowners regardless of their financial status. This penalised the likes of hill farmers in some of the most remote areas of Britain who had no option as to what and how they farmed.

The Countryside Stewardship (CS) was set up in 2015 providing financial incentives for farmers, woodland owners, foresters and land managers to look after and improve the environment. The emphasis on farm payments shifted from a system encouraging farmers to maximise production, to one based more on

▼ Small farms contribute to preserving the landscape and habitat of British upland areas

basic care of the land. The policy meant that payments were made on acreage, so the larger the farm, the more money it received.

The sheer amount of paperwork involved in farmers applying for government grants and subsidies is mind-boggling. A crucial part of farm management these days is employing someone to sift through all the jargon to advise what would be most advantageous to farm income. The original Country Stewardship scheme manual, published in January 2015 amounted to 94 pages!

The UK officially left the EU on 31 January 2020 with the year-long transition period, during which nothing changed, ending on 31 December 2020. Being outside the EU allowed new trade agreements to be drawn up but with the possibility of trade tariffs being imposed. Importers and exporters faced increased paperwork and red tape while the EU made life as difficult as possible for the UK. After a chaotic start to Brexit, and with the exception of Northern Ireland, within a few months things settled down as everyone began to get used to the new ways in which things needed to be done, although Covid was rife, creating its own problems. 2021 saw many new multi-million pound trade deals being struck around the world, opening up new markets to the benefit of British farmers.

POST-BREXIT VISION FOR FARMING

With the UK's exit from the EU, radical changes in agriculture were introduced by way of agri-environmental schemes. Previously, farmers received taxpayer-funded grants based on the amount of land they owned which discriminated against small farmers. Under the Environmental Land Management Scheme (ELMS), payments will instead be made to farmers to improve the environment, the vision being that there will be more trees, meadows and wetlands and fewer sheep and cows. Under this scheme, which will be phased in over seven years, subsidies will be paid for protecting 'heritage' farm buildings and stone walls, expanding hedges, natural flood management including creating ponds and restoring river bends, landscape recovery, restoring peatland and planting new woods, capturing carbon in soils, cutting pesticides, reducing the use of antibiotics, and improving animal health and welfare. In addition, funding will be made available for equipment and technology such as robots, and for new infrastructure such as water storage on farms. In October 2021 the first phase of the new multi-million pound Farming Innovation Programme was announced in support of ambitious projects which would transform productivity and enhance environmental sustainability.

Some farmers had already been following practices used by previous generations to enhance the health of the soil on their farms, improve the quality of the meat they produce and, in a small way, help combat climate change. With the emphasis now being on improving the environment, farmers will be able to apply for subsidies of up to £70 per hectare for 'actions to improve the health of their soil'.

FARMING IN THE UK TODAY

In 2021, nearly 80% of England, Scotland, Wales and Northern Ireland was farmed, mostly as permanent pasture grassland.

There are currently 14.8 million acres (6 million hectares) of arable land in the UK which is the lowest level since 1945 when the population was below 50 million. This now stands at 68 million but fortunately output has nearly doubled since the Second World War and the general cost of food remains low. Fifty years ago food cost the average household 20% of their salary, now it is closer to 10%. If UK farmers are expected to keep on producing low-cost food, then

continued financial support in the way of grants and subsidies is needed. The alternative is that they will be undercut by foreign imports, which are cheaper because they are not produced to such high welfare and environmental standards.

Farmers have become a victim of their own success. Public opinion today sometimes condemns farmers for doing what was required of them a few decades ago. Post-war technology has greatly improved crop and livestock production, resulting in surpluses in the western world.

In 2020 it was estimated that a fifth of all food purchased by households was binned, an appalling state of affairs when the carbon footprint created by growing it and possibly importing it is taken into account.

Post-WWII farmers were told what they had to do but in present times the way they farm is mostly manipulated by Government grants, subsidies and quotas which 'persuade' them which direction farming takes. The poultry and pig industries are the only ones not directly influenced by these grants.

There is now greater emphasis on conservation and combatting the effects of climate change. Farmers have had to take everything into account and adapt. There are several minor ways in which they can play a part without the need for large investment. While tree

▲ Farming in East Anglia is primarily arable

planting on a large scale and filling a whole field with trees is seen to be the way forward, they can instead plant trees in small, unproductive corners of fields. Or simply by ploughing a sloping field cross-ways rather than up and down, farmers can reduce the risk of flooding.

Post-Brexit a new range of agri-environmental schemes are being introduced, under the heading 'Public Money for Public Goods': the intention is to reward farmers for actions that benefit the environment, such as tree planting, flood management and habitat restoration, rather than for the amount of land under ownership. The new Environmental Land Management Scheme (ELMS) is due to be rolled out in full by 2027 with the intention being that public money should be spent on things which have public value that are not already in place. This includes enhancing our environment and protecting our countryside, better animal and plant health and animal welfare as well as improved productivity; all as part of a move to higher regulatory standards.

British farms already have some of the highest standards in the world.

Advanced technology and naturally improved plant and livestock breeding, brought about by selecting the required characteristics, has increased production by 50% in the last 50 years.

Around 60% of our food is home-produced and more could be grown.

But the land paid a price when mixed farms began to disappear and farmers needed to specialise in order to justify purchasing expensive machinery.

Wheat yields have doubled in three generations and Britain now has very nearly the capacity to be self-sufficient in growing wheat for bread-making. These advancements enable surplus land to be put into conservation schemes.

These schemes will provide funding to farmers and land managers to farm in a way that supports biodiversity, enhances the landscape, and improves the quality of water, air and soil. This balance can continue to be struck despite populations continuing to rise, resulting in an increased demand for food.

Not only is there a basic need for sufficient food to feed the world, but as people have become more affluent in the richer countries, they seek out a wider variety in their diet, many items of which have to be imported because the UK's climate is not conducive to growing them.

RED TAPE

Many farmers still feel they are being slowly strangled by red tape, much of which would be far better replaced with plain, good, old-fashioned common sense. Incomes are falling and health scares affecting humans such as CJD, E. Coli and Salmonella and animal diseases such as Swine Fever and Foot and Mouth Disease have taken their toll on livestock production in the past. The Foot and Mouth Disease epidemic February-September 2001 infected over 2,000

farms. In the aftermath of FMD, many new recording, bio-security and restrictive measures were introduced adding to the heavy burden of red tape already suffered by farmers.

CORONAVIRUS

Then came the Coronavirus pandemic which struck, first in China, in January 2020 and quickly spread around the world. In Britain lockdown restrictions were imposed on 23 March bringing the country more or less to a standstill. Farmers were classed as key workers, being food producers and essential in caring for livestock. They were some of the least affected by Covid regulations as, by the very nature of their work, they were either working on their own or could easily comply with the required social distancing rules.

They faced difficulties as cafes, pubs and restaurants closed down, slashing demand for some of their produce. Livestock and farmers' markets closed. There were cases of milk having to be poured down the drain, because milk production cannot be turned off like a tap. Cows carry on producing milk and still need milking and feeding.

As travel for leisure was banned around the country, tourism came to an abrupt halt. Across the country those farms that had diversified into holiday accommodation were left with no bookings and no additional income, and those who relied on the tourist market to sell their produce were left seriously out of pocket.

For many years, migrant workers, the vast majority from Eastern Europe, have been heavily relied on to harvest vegetables and fruit which can only be picked by hand. It requires skills that even robots cannot be programmed to learn.

Normally 60,000 to 80,000 seasonal workers are needed each year but immigration control only granted 30,000 entry during Covid-19 lockdowns in 2020.

Thousands of British people, having been furloughed, were out of work, potentially making them available when the 'Feed the Nation' and 'Pick for Britain' recruitment campaigns were launched in April 2020 to connect those seeking work with prospective employers. With patriotic enthusiasm 50,000 British people applied but only 6,500 completed interviews of which only 4% lasted the season. Employers were looking for reliable people, like the migrant farmworkers, who were willing to work hard for long hours and who would sign a contract. Very few British were willing to commit themselves to these requirements. Foreign workers are diligent and skilled in the work and, besides being guaranteed the minimum wage, can earn bonuses for working quickly. Produce went to waste.

Growers need to know well in advance what labour is available to them for the coming season, and it needs to be guaranteed so they can plan accordingly. Difficulties continue due to legislation regarding the employment of foreign labour. A lack of skilled butchers and abbatoir workers meant some 35,000 pigs went to waste in 2021 and many sectors of horticulture suffered because of labourer shortages. It proves just how reliant British agriculture is on foreign labour and how disinclined the British are to do that type of work for the pay.

OTHER FARMING CHALLENGES

Unsurprisingly, farming is potentially a dangerous occupation in which to work. British agriculture has the worst rate of fatal injury per 100,000 workers, higher than any other industrial sector. In 2020/2021 41 people were killed in farm accidents. Gigantic moving machinery, overturning vehicles, insecure heavy loads, slurry pits, silos, working at height or with chemicals and large, unpredictable animals all contribute to making farm work particularly hazardous. Very often the casualties were working alone.

Mental health is also of increasing concern. On the face of it, a farming life might appear to be idyllic but there are many stresses associated with it. Financial worry and the sheer volume of paperwork can be aggravated by things beyond farmers' control such as the weather and diseases in crops and animals, which reduce income. Many farmers live an isolated way of life, working long hours on their own much of the time and bottling up their worries. Help and advice is available but farmers, by nature, are independent people and find it difficult to talk about their problems. In 2019 there were 133 suicides among those involved in agriculture. 2020 proved to be an exceptionally challenging year for farmers, as they faced falling sales due to the pandemic and at the same time the UK suffered its worst harvest for at least 25 years following twelve months of extreme weather. A very wet October in 2020 meant that difficulties were encountered in harvesting the potato crop. During the spring 2020 drought, grass had not grown and the silage crop, a very important method of conserving grass for winter livestock feed, was halved. The withdrawal of neonicotinoids as a pest control on crops also presented its own problems.

Global markets affect prices and each year harvests across the world are very dependent on the weather. Shortage of any commodity invariably increases the price of crops which can particularly impact the cost of animal feed.

THE FUTURE

Today there is no place for the country 'yokel'. Modern farming requires highly skilled people to operate hi-tech machinery and manage the large numbers of livestock. It is a necessity to be computer literate for every aspect of farming life.

The average age of farmers is 59, one third are above retirement age and only 3% are under 35. It is increasingly difficult for youngsters to

Isolated farms in the North Yorkshire Moors

have their own farms. Apart from the enormous amount of capital required to set up a business, the leases that are offered are often for only a short period, whereas it takes years in farming before a successful enterprise can become established. There are a number of mostly small farms in the ownership of local councils which provide a foothold for first-time farmers to start up but the number of these is diminishing as cash-strapped Councils sell them off.

THE STATE OF FARMING TODAY

In the 1950s 5% of the population was employed in agriculture but that has all changed due to modern technology.

- about 1.5% of the nation's workforce works on the land although it is they who care for more than 70% of it.
- on average farmers work 65 hours each week.
- only 20% of farms are in excess of 250 acres (100 hectares).

About 70% of farms are smaller family-run farms which may well have been in the same family for several generations. They play a very important role in the countryside, particularly when it comes to upland farms where knowledge of the ground is vitally important. Very often the flocks of sheep on these farms belong with the farm rather than to the farmer. Well over half of farms are owned and the remainder tenanted.

Of the areas classified as agricultural holdings about one third is arable land and the remainder grassland, a proportion of which is classified as rough grazing. Woodland accounts for 13% of land use.

Unlike the Continent, British farms are generally run as individual units whereas in Europe farmers form co-operatives to share costs and capital outlay. Many British estates that come on the market are now being purchased by foreign or city investors, and prices are rising as investors continue to buy up small local farms to add to large ones.

Farming activities were once limited by the climate and suitability of the land. Waterlogged land is now made use of by laying pipes under the soil to drain off excess water into ditches. Soil type also influences farming and interestingly varies greatly in colour across the country. Peaty soil in the Fens is black and fertile. Light coloured sandy soil is impoverished and chalk makes the land appear nearly white. Heavy clay sometimes looks yellow or red and land in parts of Devon appears red due to iron compounds in the soil. Cattle and sheep are kept in uplands and wetter areas where grass grows well. Arable crops are grown in the drier parts of the UK notably in the east.

Now, though, because of grants, subsidies and sophisticated machinery, the scope is much broader. Diversification has become the key word and there are many ways in which to diversify but some prove unprofitable.

Organic produce is much in demand but after the initial boost of government grants to get started, many farmers are now finding it difficult to maintain their organic business. Potentially, under the new ELM Scheme, farmers can continue to earn more money by simply managing the landscape rather than gambling with the uncertainty of growing food.

There is little doubt that the climate has become more extreme and can affect annual returns from both livestock and arable farming. Every aspect of farming is at the mercy of the weather. For example, the so-called 'Beast from The East' which hit Britain in March 2018 bringing heavy snow and bitterly cold 70mph east winds made a lot of extra work for livestock farmers. Sheep in particular were hard hit, becoming buried in snowdrifts, and new-born lambs perished in the cold. Other livestock suffered because their water supplies were frozen solid. 2020 by contrast experienced prolonged spells of drought, heat and excess rainfall which reduced crop yields by 30-40%.

Benign spring weather is of particular importance, a time when seeds are germinating and farmers need plenty of grass to grow to nourish their livestock as well as being preserved as winter feed.

Researchers are evaluating different varieties of grasses and cereals that can adapt or are better suited to the effects of global warming. In arable areas with below average rainfall, such as East Anglia, farmers have constructed reservoirs to store water for irrigation. These are topped up through the winter months with rainfall or water extraction from rivers once they have reached a certain level.

More than 20,000 people employed in agriculture have annually quit working on the land in recent years. Approximately 300,000

workers are employed in the agricultural industry and many live in 'tied' accommodation. Housing is supplied free or for a nominal rent when it is necessary for employees to live near to their place of work in rural and sometimes isolated areas. Accommodation is taken into account as part of their wage deal; in return agricultural workers are expected to be available to work very long hours when required, including weekends. Land work has to be done when conditions are right and livestock requires attention seven days a week. Many landowners now rely on contractors to do the work in preference to employing their own full-time staff.

70% of farms are family-run.

Farming has its own jargon, often very localised, which, like many dialects is dying out. Terms such as 'backend' meaning nearing the end of the farming year are seldom heard. There are more localised terms used in sheep keeping in the north of England than anywhere else, all part of our farming heritage.

The whole structure of countryside communities is changing as fewer people work on the land. The houses agricultural workers once lived in are now occupied by commuters, retirees, used as weekend retreats or rented out. Although work still has to go on in the countryside, there are far fewer people doing it and less general understanding of how and why it's done. Many farm jobs are now done sitting in vehicles and machines, and people become more detached from the land.

Even 50 years ago a quarter of the population had a connection with farming, today that figure is only a fraction of that.

FUTURE LAND USE

The expansion of villages and towns is consuming agricultural land and taking it out of use for farming. Large-scale tree planting projects, seen as one way to combat global warming, will take up land used for livestock or cultivated crops. Science has improved crop yields and increased production from animals so that in theory less land is needed to feed the human population of the UK, but the number of citizens is ever increasing. For the sake of the environment our food needs to be home-grown and produced to the high standards set in this country. Advanced technology means that produce is packed in a way that retains the quality and freshness at the same time as prolonging shelf life. Modified atmosphere packaging (MAP) removes or vacuums out most of the natural air. Oxygen levels are greatly reduced and replaced with nitrogen or carbon dioxide. Milk is pasteurised and homogenised to give it a longer shelf life.

CROFTING

Crofting is a traditional way of farming practised in the Highlands and Islands of Scotland which has been passed down through generations and continues to this day.

A croft is not only a house but also the unit of agricultural land attached to it.

There are over 17,000 crofts in Scotland.

Crofts range from an acre (½ha) to more than 125 acres (50ha) but an average croft is 12 acres (5ha). There are legislative duties attached to the house and land ensuring that it continues to be used for its original purpose. The majority are tenanted. Small groups of crofts, known as townships, are still worked by local people. Most have only a few acres of improved grassland for their cattle and sheep, or land that is good enough to grow a crop, but in addition they have access to common grazing land. Their livestock live a semi-wild existence. Crofters help each other when extra hands are needed to gather

▼ Crofters help each other when it's time to gather their sheep

the sheep for sorting, dipping and shearing. Some still clip their sheep by hand as it leaves the wool slightly longer than electric clippers, thus providing more protection against the often inclement weather.

Earning additional income to crofting is necessary, so often crofters have another job such as fishing or delivering the local mail.

A croft has been described as being a piece of land too big to use as a hobby and too small to be a farm, but crofting means being very much part of the community.

FEEDING THE NATION

The buying power of large supermarkets has a big influence on production and marketing issues. Farmers can't cut their overheads and are of course obliged to pay a minimum wage to anyone they employ, even if they don't properly pay themselves. Additionally they have to comply with strict animal welfare and health and safety standards while trying to compete with imports from countries that pay scant regard to such things.

> *The Red Tractor symbol signifies that food has been produced to an assured high standard in the UK; traceability and accountability are important.*

While some farmers are only in it to make a living, for many others there is much more to their work than that. There is a traditional pride in raising good crops and healthy livestock. There's much more to farming than the amount of money that is made from it.

Britain produces some of the highest quality, best value and safest food in the world but it has to remain competitive. The difficulty is to work out how.

GLOSSARY

ACRE Pre-metric measurement of area equal to .4047 of a hectare

HECTARE One hectare equals 2.47 acres or 10,000 square metres

ORGANIC Produce supplied by farmers registered with a recognised organic inspection body to ensure that the strict standards set for production are met. No chemical fertilizers or feed additives can be used.

DEFRA Department for Environment, Food and Rural Affairs. Formed in 2001 to bring together environmental, rural and food related issues in the UK.

BPS Basic Payment Scheme

ELMS Environmental Land Management Scheme

ES Environmental Stewardship

RPS Rural Payments Agency

CS Countryside Stewardship. Different tiers provide options regarding animal management and environmental benefits funding

FARM ASSURED Producers must conform to one of the farm assurance schemes which ensure that farmers comply with DEFRA recommendations for welfare and legal requirements

FREEDOM FOOD Meat from producers who conform to standards set by the RSPCA. Animal-based protein in feed, with the exception of milk products, and growth promoters are banned and transport times are limited

BRITISH FARM STANDARD Identified by its logo of a red tractor with blue wheels which denotes that the product has been produced in Britain and meets recognised standards

LEAF Linking Environment and Farming is an organisation which works with farmers to improve sustainability combined with education and public engagement projects

FARM PARK A visitor attraction where children can meet, touch and learn about farm animals and birds

THE CROFTING COMMISSION Replaced the Crofters Commission in 2012 as the statutory regulator for crofting in Scotland

CLA Country Landowners Association

NFU National Farmers Union

Highland cattle are hardy enough to live out on the hills all year round

FARMING LIVESTOCK

Just over half UK land is used for grazing or growing grass and the total UK livestock output for 2019 was worth £14.7 billion. The industry is still very important to the country even though in recent years there has been a decline in the amount of meat consumed. Over half a million people are now vegetarians or vegans.

Plant-based diets, while often adopted as an aid to saving our planet, have their drawbacks. A healthy diet needs to include protein, and meat-based protein has to be substituted with plant protein. This comes from soy and other pulses, many of which have to be imported as it's not possible to grow them in the UK on a commercial scale.

One third of the UK population have either cut down or given up eating meat

However, although vegetarianism is on the increase, this has not changed the demand for milk, butter, cheese and eggs, and meat still plays a major role in the diet of the majority of people and is also exported.

For those with environmental causes at heart, meat that comes from animals grazed naturally on unfertilised, species-rich pasture, rather than intensively reared animals fed mainly on grain, is far preferable. Natural grazing applies to a large number of sheep and cattle particularly those raised in the upland areas of the UK.

Where animals are kept for meat production and are grazed traditionally on unimproved pastures, marshland and uplands, it is of great benefit to indigenous plants found within the sward, as well as insects, which in turn are an asset to many species of birds. In summer this

Grazing animals can live where no crops could be grown

is well illustrated by swallows flitting among groups of cattle, catching the surrounding flies and insects stirred up by their feet or attracted to them. Rooks and starlings turn over the cowpats in search of beetles and grubs.

> *The presence of livestock is advantageous to biodiversity.*

BEEF BREEDS

Old breeds of cattle once took four years before they were grown enough to be slaughtered but now the average is about 18 months. From the 1960s onwards, breeders set about improving the quality of established beef breeds by using bulls imported from the Continent. The public no longer wanted so much fat on their meat and Continental breeds were bigger but leaner, with a disproportionate amount of muscling on their rumps where the most expensive cuts of meat come from. Originating in France, the Charolais became popular in the early 1960s; Limousins, also from France, and Simmentals from Switzerland followed in the early 1970s; and in the 1980s massive Belgian Blues appeared. Of these, the Limousin has proved most popular over the years as a beef sire, although our native Aberdeen Angus gives it a run for its money. Herefords too remain popular. Both were once small animals but have now been bred much larger to satisfy supermarket demands and compete with continental breeds.

While these continental breeds and their crosses now play a large part in meat production, there is still a place in farming for the heritage breeds.

> *350 years ago Longhorn cattle were the only breed seen throughout the length and breadth of England.*

They provided milk, meat and acted as draught animals pulling ploughs and wagons.

They are still kept today on a much smaller scale to supply a niche meat market and conservation grazing. Aberdeen Angus, Galloway and, in Scotland, white Shorthorns crossed with Highland cows have proved they can cope with environmental conditions where Continental breeds fail to thrive.

GLOBAL INFLUENCES

Livestock farming is often at the mercy of world events, which can quickly have a huge knock-on effect to demand and supply. Economic uncertainty and varying exchange rate affected prices in recent years. One country's loss is another's opportunity. The Chinese rear and eat a lot of pork and in 2019 a devastating outbreak of African Swine Fever (ASF) in China saw British pig farmers receiving higher prices for their pigs.

GRAZING

Sheep, and especially cattle, play a minority part in global warming but selective breeding has improved the efficiency of cattle to convert vegetation into meat. The climate in the UK is favourable for growing an abundant amount of grass in most areas. Sheep and cattle grazing on it convert the grasses and other plants, which humans are unable to digest, into high nutrient protein. Grass is a complete healthy food for ruminants and little in the way of supplementary feed is required when it is available. It is also preserved in the form of hay, made from dried grass, and silage, made from fermented green grass, to provide feed in winter. Straw from the cereal harvest is also used, occasionally for feed but mostly for bedding.

Pigs cannot live on grass nor can chicken, so, as with intensively kept cattle, they need to be fed on rations manufactured from home-grown cereals mixed with plant protein which has mostly had to be imported. Cereals, even home produced, will have been grown on land that

Silage to feed sheep and cattle in winter is baled so it can easily be transported

required cultivation and the crop will have been treated with fertiliser, pesticides and herbicides. The plant protein mostly comes from soya imported from the US although some may have been grown on land in the Amazon or Congo basins where ecologically important rainforest has been illegally felled.

Sheep and cattle eating grass are more environmentally friendly than pigs and poultry.

MEAT LABELLING

Labelling of prepacked meat can be misleading. It may well be labelled 'packed in the UK' but this does not mean that it was produced here. Livestock farmers are worried because numerous foreign countries don't measure up to the UK's high standards of health and animal welfare. The use of antibiotics is generally more extensive abroad. In the USA growth hormones, at present banned in Britain, are used to make cattle fatten quicker and there are also welfare issues because US cattle are penned together in their thousands in 'beef lots'. There is also concern that American chicken is routinely washed in chlorine to kill any bacteria that might be present, another practice not permitted in the UK. **The Red Tractor Assurance Scheme** logo on food indicates traceability, that it is safe to eat, has been produced in a responsible way and has been farmed, processed and packed in the UK. **RSPCA Assurance / Freedom Foods** producers have to meet even higher standards. Some dairy milk cooperatives, such as Arla and First Milk also require their members to meet higher welfare standards.

ENVIRONMENTAL LAND MANAGEMENT

One of the proposals included in the new Environmental Land Management (ELM) Scheme, is to reduce the number of cattle and sheep in the UK. The effect of this is debatable as, unless the consumption of meat is greatly reduced, it will result in more imports.

There will always be a demand for meat but if the UK doesn't produce enough of its own then it will be imported from countries with standards lower than ours. Consumers will need to bear in mind that in many cases imported produce is cheaper than home produced goods because more corners have been cut and a strain put on the environment.

The ELM Scheme also needs to take into account the positive effect which grazing sheep, and in particular cattle, are to wildlife by increasing biodiversity of the land.

There are pages and pages of government legislation with regard to keeping livestock in the UK concerning their welfare, management and risks to human health.

LIVESTOCK MARKETS

Many meat producers sell their animals under contract, whereby they get a pre-agreed price. However, livestock markets are still places where farmers sell their stock of all different ages. Prices on the day are unpredictable. Market closures because of Covid 19 resulted in welfare and financial issues when animals weren't able to be sold when planned. Further welfare complications were encountered with sheep when pandemic lockdowns prevented the gangs of shearers from New Zealand from coming to this country. They are extremely experienced and quick and for many years have been relied on to shear large UK flocks under contract. Only the best sheep farmers can match them for speed and efficiency; an expert can shear a sheep in a couple of minutes. It was a great relief when they were eventually allowed entry. However, 14 million kilograms of British wool remained unsold as world wool markets closed.

Not only do livestock markets hold regular sales of young, breeding and animals fit for slaughter, they often host farmers' markets and antiques fairs. Seventy years ago many country town markets, both livestock and produce, were held on a certain day each week. Very few of these markets have survived in the arable areas of southern and eastern Britain. But livestock markets, where they are still held, continue to play an important part in the lives of those farming especially in the more remote places.

A farming life is often a solitary one and markets offer the opportunity to exchange ideas, information, views and news as well as catching up with local gossip. Special markets are held for pedigree animals and very often their sale is preceded by being judged. The bidding for these is always in guineas (£1.05) rather than pounds.

County shows also offer farmers the chance to socialise with others who share a common interest. There too, they can show their livestock and the competition can be quite fierce at times. A champion animal or bird not only achieves a better price if it is sold but also enhances its owner's reputation. County shows promote a better understanding among town-dwellers of what happens in the countryside generally.

▼ Livestock markets are not only auctions but social occasions as well

FARMERS AND ANIMAL CARE

Nearly all livestock keepers, whether on a large or small scale, form an attachment to their animals and feel a responsibility for their welfare, even when they are destined for slaughter. Any person caring for livestock must be prepared to work unsociable hours and weekends. Animals give birth, have an accident or suddenly get sick at any time of the day or night. Anyone responsible for looking after them must be prepared to administer to their needs whenever required. Bio-security plays an important part in keeping animals healthy. Contagious diseases can easily spread between farms. Rats are carriers, as are migratory birds. Poultry are particularly at risk and every year outbreaks of avian flu, not a threat to humans, are recorded. The most likely carriers are flocks of starlings which migrate to Britain from Europe every winter.

A good stockman is usually able to sense when one of the animals in his charge is 'not right', even before it shows any obvious symptoms of being sick. Veterinary care of farm animals is costly, and a call-out for a sheep can easily cost more than the animal is worth.

▲ Sheep come under the hammer at market

There are several preventative vaccines and treatments which can be used by the farmer. Experienced stockmen are fully capable of carrying out many of the necessary routine treatments such as worming, vaccinating or administering drugs prescribed by the vet. Inevitably though there are emergencies and the services of the local vet need to be called upon. In the grassland areas of Britain where farm animals still flourish, attending to them is an integral

▲ Outbreaks of serious contagious diseases such as F&M, Swine Fever and Avian Flu necessitate the affected herds of animals and poultry flocks being humanely culled

Supplementary feeding for cattle kept outdoors in winter

part of a rural vet's work helping with difficult births, injuries and diagnosing illnesses. Farm vets still have to do much of their work in difficult conditions that are far from sterile and often out of doors, at all times and in all weathers.

However, much of a vet's work is now routine and includes the compulsory testing for diseases such as tuberculosis. A skin test is carried out to identify any possibility of tuberculosis infection. Blood samples for cattle, when needed, are taken from a vein beneath the tail, and many infections, deficiencies and illnesses can be diagnosed through the blood. To make working with such large animals that are not used to being handled, such as beef cattle, easier and safer, they are driven one at a time into a small pen called a 'crush' where they can be better restrained.

Animals kept outside require up to 20% more food to retain condition, so costs are higher. And if the British public want cheap meat and eggs then intensive systems, as are applied to the pig and poultry industries, are needed to produce it. There are many rules and regulations in place to ensure the highest standards of humane care as possible are maintained, and there may well be improved financial returns if the livestock are fit, well and content.

Traceability within the food chain has become an important aspect of livestock farming. Movements of all livestock have to be recorded and individual lifetime identification of all cattle and sheep is now a legal requirement. This is done by fixing a numbered electronic tag containing a microchip in their ear soon after birth which can then be easily read, visually or electronically, and recorded. Each calf is also issued with a passport. Post Brexit, changes have been made for the identification of cattle, sheep, goats and pigs exported to the EU and Northern Ireland, including ear tags bearing the ISO country code of identification, which has been changed from 'UK' to 'GB'.

HOBBY FARMING

An increasing number of enthusiasts today enjoy hobby farming, maybe with as little as a few acres, keeping some chicken, a few sheep, a couple of pygmy goats and maybe a pig or two. Some go on to be farmers, others want to know that what they are eating is chemical free and produced in a compassionate, wildlife friendly manner. Some want to farm organically, or keep animals as a means of contributing towards their other hobbies, for example a few sheep are often kept to supply special wool for those whose craft is related to spinning, weaving and knitting.

Government livestock regulations still apply, however small the number of animals kept or for whatever reason.

Feed needs to be taken to sheep kept out on the hills in winter

ANIMAL WELFARE

The way in which livestock is kept in the UK meets some of the highest standards in the world. Any procedures carried out are purely intended to improve the welfare of livestock. The Farm Animal Welfare Forum (FAWF) brings together the leading organisations concerned with improving farm animal welfare in the UK.

'Anthropomorphism', crediting animals with the same feelings as humans, is the bane of livestock farmers' lives. Every species of animal and bird have different temperaments and behavioural needs so it is pointless to compare them with those of humans. Animals react to their present situation, they possess no imagination, so the future is of no concern to them. They survive through their natural instincts, learn by association and past experiences and live only for today. Only a few species such as dogs, apes and elephants show any great degree of intelligence. In certain situations dogs show signs of being telepathic and are able to sense their owner's mood. For example hounds and gun dogs seem to be able to tell the difference between days they will be worked and those they are merely exercised, even though their handler follows exactly the same routine each morning before taking them out. Sheep are not known for their intelligence although they know to shelter from the wind or hot sun but that is purely a natural instinct indicating how best to survive. Food, the urge to reproduce and daylight are the principal influences on the behaviour of animals and birds.

Whenever animals are owned by someone, that person has the responsibility of their care whether on farms or in the home. Even though the British are considered to be a pet-loving nation there are thousands of cases of cruelty and mistreatment reported each year. It is not always deliberate though as many owners are misguided in the way they care for their pets. Giving an animal copious amounts of tit-bits to overeat can be as unkind and bad for its health as not feeding it enough. Many pet owners are guilty of this and over-indulgence is certainly not a kindness.

The world treats animals in very different ways. In Britain dogs are pets but they are eaten in China. British cows are a commercial investment but they are sacred animals in India and donkeys in Egypt have to work extremely hard for their living.

In the UK, there is much more attention paid to how farm animals are kept than domestic pets.

There is a vast amount of legislation concerning farm animal welfare. The majority of the population think that farm animals are best kept in natural conditions but this isn't always the case as nature can be cruel. Creatures in the wild are exposed to cold, wet and hunger as well as parasites, infections and the risk of being eaten or injured. If, as some people believe, animals have 'rights', who passes judgement on the owl that preys on the mouse? Whose right is it that needs protecting – the prey or the predator? The choice is a dilemma that also faces many conservationists.

Young lambs look happy gambolling in the sunshine but many born outdoors perish if there was a prolonged cold, wet spell at the time they are born. Weak ones are always at risk of being killed by foxes or having their eyes pecked out by crows. It happens.

ANIMAL WELFARE

Animal welfare is represented in Britain by the Farm Animal Welfare Council (FAWC), a government-appointed body to advise ministers. Its purpose is to oversee the physical and mental wellbeing of farm animals kept on agricultural land and in buildings, at market, in transit and at slaughter houses.

Animal welfare embraces the Five Freedoms:
Freedom from
1) hunger and thirst
2) discomfort
3) fear and stress
4) pain, injury and disease, and
5) the freedom to express normal behaviour regarding space, facilities and the company of its own kind.

The latter causes the most problems. Certainly this requirement is conveniently disregarded by all those pet owners who keep one animal for their personal pleasure. Many animals gregarious by nature. A horse is a herd animal, a dog a pack animal and a budgerigar is a sociable bird that lives in flocks. Is it compassionate to keep them without company of their own kind? Deprived of canine company, dogs are intelligent enough to recognise humans as being very acceptable members of their pack who provide food and comfort.

It is costly to provide farm livestock with more space; housing and land are expensive capital investments. The higher the throughput, the higher the returns and management has to be finely tuned. Government guidelines for stocking levels of animal and birds kept on a commercial scale have sought to keep a balance between the standard of welfare and the cheap food production expected by the consumer. If farm livestock is grossly overcrowded they do not grow or yield to their full potential and therefore become unprofitable. Freedom can lead to deaths of the new born and stress levied on older animals or birds by their companions. Every creature is either territorial if solitary by nature or has a 'pecking order' if gregarious. Both result in fighting to establish dominance. It is often management policy to keep groups together for most of their lives so that they live in harmony with each other; mix the groups and stress results. The way in which farmers manage their livestock is in the way that has proved to work the best for them.

TRANSPORTATION OF LIVE ANIMALS

The media often reports on the transport of livestock. Occasional delays are unavoidable on Britain's overcrowded roads. The Foot and Mouth outbreak in 2001 exposed big failings in the marketing of sheep. Some were being moved on from one market to another within a matter of days and obviously this practice was not acceptable on both welfare and health risk

▲ There are strict regulations regarding the transportation of live animals

grounds. Livestock crammed into trailers is frequently depicted which in the face of it may appear to be cruel but tightly packed animals are far less likely to be buffeted about or fall over and be trampled on. There are strict regulations regarding the transport of live animals. Hundreds of thousands of livestock are transported annually without coming to any harm.

EU legislation set humane standards for animal welfare but it meant many small local slaughterhouses had to close because they were unable to meet the stringent regulations for health and hygiene. Ironically, this now means that livestock destined for slaughter often has to be transported much longer distances.

There are rules in force regarding the provision of food and water for animals in transit and for regular stops. In fact livestock appear to settle down quietly once on the move and most stress is caused to them at the stops when they have to be unloaded and loaded up again which also extends the journey time. Unlike humans, many animals have the ability to rest or sleep standing up.

VEAL

Veal crates were banned in Britain in 1990. This adversely affected the market for newborn calves as did subsequent very public demonstrations over the export of live calves to the Continent. Combined with the BSE health scare, the result was that there was no longer a market for the leaner, male (bull) calves of dairy breeds with the result that many were humanely destroyed at birth. This unpalatable situation was alleviated by the introduction of 'rose veal' in 2008 which created a market for male 'dairy' calves and made eating veal acceptable once again. – *see veal page 35*

To give milk it is necessary for a dairy cow to have a calf every 12 to 14 months.

Checking a heifer's identifying ear tag while a vet takes a blood sample

It is now possible, but more expensive, to select the sex of a calf from the semen used for AI. However, this does not reduce the number of calves born each year to milking cows, and sales of young calves of any kind meet a poor demand. If more are born than the UK has the capacity to rear and there is a demand on the Continent, it is inevitable that some will be exported live and fattened up abroad. Usually young calves are transported in lorries by sea but flying is being looked at as an option to improve welfare through minimising the journey time.

When the choice is between destroying newborn calves or shipping them abroad, making an ethical decision is difficult.

Reducing milk production by keeping fewer cows is not the answer because that would mean importing more dairy products which in all probability would come from countries with lower animal welfare standards than our own.

SURGICAL INTERVENTIONS

Unless animals were to be given unlimited freedom (which would be impossible) certain practices are a valuable aid to welfare management.

All so-called mutilations are strictly regulated by FAWC who recognise the benefit from existing practices.

Castration is probably the most common because it not only means that animals will fatten quicker but it also minimises aggression and unwanted sexual activities. There are three methods which can be used. Most commonly for sheep and quite often for very young calves is the application of an elastic band, applied using an elastrator, round the neck of the scrotum. This has to be done within a few days of birth.

Another method for castrating bull calves under two months old is to use a burdizzo implement to crush the spermatic cord, with recommended local anaesthetic. Surgical castration on older animals has to be carried out by a vet who by law injects a local anaesthetic into the area before cutting the scrotum and removing the testicles.

Today many pigs and sheep destined for early slaughter, being smaller and more manageable than cattle, are often not castrated. However, problems are encountered if they are left to reach maturity and then have to be segregated from the females to avoid unplanned pregnancies.

Sheep are born with long tails but those intended to be kept on lush grass in the lowlands (which makes their excrement more liquid) will be docked soon after they are born. If they weren't, their wool would become soiled and attract flies which lay eggs on the dirty fleece and in turn hatch into maggots which then bury themselves into the flesh beneath. Fly strike, as it is known, is not obvious to begin with and if not detected soon enough, the unfortunate victim literally would be eaten alive and suffer a slow and horrific death. To dock a lowland lamb is more humane than to leave it with a long tail. This procedure is frequently carried out using the same elastic rings and elastrator tool as is used for castration purposes and is done at the same time.

> *Sheep kept in the uplands have poorer vegetation to graze so their tails are not docked so short. Those kept on high ground aren't docked at all because their excrement is dry and a long tail offers them some protection from the harsher weather conditions.*

Nearly all dairy breeds of cattle and some beef are born with horns that begin to develop soon after birth. Cattle have horns for fighting and self-protection. If these weren't removed, they would be a danger not only to humans but also to each other. Calves are 'dehorned' or 'disbudded' when they are a few days old. A local anaesthetic is given and the emerging 'buds' are either burned off with a hot iron or a caustic

▲ A ring in a bull's nose enables it to be handled more safely

▲ A crofter dosing his sheep for worms

substance is used which at this young age causes them little distress and the small wounds very quickly heal. Horned breeds of sheep and goats aren't normally dehorned.

PIG WELFARE

An increasing number of pigs are being kept out of doors. The breeding stock are kept in large paddocks giving them space and plenty to occupy themselves but the young ones born outside do not usually enjoy the same freedom as their parents for very long.

Outdoor pigs still need protection from the sun and prolonged rain which can turn their paddocks into a quagmire. Pigs love digging up the ground with their noses and nose-ringing breeding stock kept outdoors prevents this happening, thus improving the conditions they live in. When a sow is about to give birth she not only makes a nest but also digs a hole in the ground, which is a certain death trap for her newborn piglets. Because she is about 200 times larger than them, they will inevitably be crushed and suffocated when she lies down if they have rolled into the hole she dug. Three or four rings in the top of each nostril are sufficient to stop a pig from digging with its snout.

Objections have been made to putting rings in pigs' noses although oddly it is acceptable for human parents to have an earring put in their baby's ears or a nose ring in themselves which is a very similar procedure.

Farrowing crates in buildings, which limit the sow's movement, are designed to minimise the risk of piglets being squashed. There have been many calls to have these banned but without farrowing crates, production would be lower because more piglets would die or become injured from being crushed, creating welfare issues and raising costs. Then cheap pig meat imported from abroad, where welfare standards are often lower than UK standards, would fill the gap.

In the first few days of their lives it is important that piglets are confined close to their mothers, both indoors and outside, so they don't get lost. Very young piglets sometimes have the points of their canine teeth clipped off so they don't make the sow sore when they suckle, or damage each other when they play fight. Because they like to chew the tassel on the ends of each other's tails, which can lead to soreness, pain and even cannibalism, the tip of the tail is often docked.

STRIKING A BALANCE

It is extremely difficult for the farming industry to find animal welfare solutions that will assuage public opinion and maintain moral standards, while being both practical and economic.

There are 'pros' and 'cons' in everything to do with animal welfare. Even the best systems can fail if they are badly run or there are unforeseen circumstances such as an outbreak of disease, when the movements of livestock are restricted by law. The year 2000 outbreak of swine fever in East Anglia, and Foot and Mouth disease throughout Britain in 2001 created huge backlogs of animals waiting to leave farms.

Rearing programmes rely on a tight schedule for throughput, and animals had to be destroyed on welfare grounds because there was no room left to keep them or no fodder available to feed them.

The vast majority of people working with livestock are compassionate towards their animals and do their best for their welfare but even unpredictable weather can make this extremely difficult at times.

British farmers are some of the most responsible and progressive in the world regarding animal welfare and, unlike many countries, believe legislation and moral standards are an obligation, not something to be ignored. It is not in the interest of any livestock farmer to neglect or mistreat animals. If they are not fit, healthy and contented they will neither fatten nor thrive to their full potential so it is uneconomic not to care for them properly.

A broad view of all animal welfare issues needs to be taken. Judgement should not be made without full awareness of the implications, or based on a few isolated incidents which the media have often taken out of context. UK welfare standards should not just be influenced by public opinion but need to follow practical common sense.

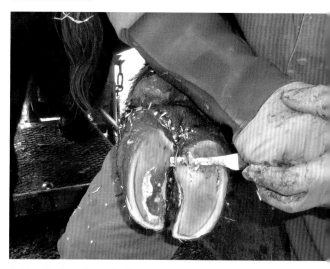

▲ Hoof trimming a bull

A typical farmyard showing l-r feed area, housing, silage clamp and slurry lagoon

CATTLE FARMING

There are nearly 10 million dairy and beef cattle in the UK of which almost a third are kept in the southwest of England. The number of cattle farmers is dwindling because, like every other business, the smaller ones find it increasingly difficult to remain competitive. Many small farmers who were devastated by Foot and Mouth Disease in 2001 seriously thought of alternative ways to earning a living rather than by going back into keeping cattle, and some did give up.

The Milk Marketing Board was formed in 1933 as a producer marketing board to control milk production and distribution in the UK. It provided stability for producers by guaranteeing a minimum price and developed marketing opportunities for milk products. Post war, the benefits of milk were widely publicised. The scheme came to an end in 1994, in part due to pressure from the EU. The dairy industry was set adrift to make its own way.

In 1980 Sainsbury became the first supermarket to sell cheap milk. It sounded the death knell for the milkman and his pints of milk. Now only about 3% of milk is delivered to the doorstep although during Covid lockdowns in 2020, deliveries increased by more than 30%.

TRACEABILITY

Traceability is now very important which requires identification of every animal, usually in the form of an ear tag fastened in each ear. For dairy breeds this has to be done within 36

◀ Calves are identified by two ear tags; an electronic collar enables each individual to be electronically recognised when it visits an automatic feeder

With their well-insulated coats Highland cattle are able to survive the harshest of weather conditions

hours of birth and ideally within 20 days of birth for beef breeds. The primary tag is a large yellow plastic one. In the UK a crown symbol is inscribed on it along with a number identifying which herd the calf was born into and its own unique lifetime identification number. Animals destined for export from Britain to the EU or currently Northern Ireland have to be identified with an ear tag inscribed 'GB'.

A secondary tag in the other ear, often a different size or shape, contains corresponding, and possibly additional, information but may be made of metal or plastic. Since the year 2000, passports have been a legal requirement to identify individual animals and this has to accompany it whenever it leaves the owner's farm, however briefly. Its movements can be traced at all times throughout its life. Passports list the animal's date of birth, its official ear tag number, the ear tag number of its mother, breed and sex. Applications have to arrive with the British Cattle Movement Service within 27 days of birth.

FALLEN STOCK

The disposal of any animals that die on the farm is subject to strict government regulations. The death must be recorded and reported within seven days and if it is over 48 months old, tested for BSE disease. The carcase cannot be buried or incinerated on the farm. The owner is liable for the cost of sending it to an approved site for disposal.

These cattle regulations similarly apply to buffalo.

CASTRATION

The majority of bull calves retained to fatten are castrated although they are sometimes left entire where an intensive system is used, if they are destined for slaughter at 12-14 months of age – see Animal Welfare.

◄ For easy calving, Aberdeen Angus, a native beef breed, are often used to sire the calves of dairy heifers

DEHORNING

It is recommended that a ring is inserted in the nose of bulls that are to be kept for breeding when they are ten months old.

On average about 2,000 farmers a year are injured by their livestock. Cattle with horns can be a danger to humans, and to each other, especially when handled or confined in pens. A few breeds such as Aberdeen Angus, and some strains of others which have been selectively bred, naturally don't grow horns. But horned breeds of calves, either for beef or dairy, are nearly always dehorned/disbudded. This procedure is carried out before they are two months old and can be done by a trained and competent stock keeper with the help of an assistant. It involves administering a local anaesthetic prior to the emerging horn buds being burned off and cauterised with a heated iron. Chemical cauterisation is not recommended. Older animals with developed horns can only be dehorned by a vet who administers a local anaesthetic and uses abrasive wire or a saw to cut through the horns.

BOVINE TB

Routine testing for TB is compulsory in the UK at varying intervals according to the prevalence of TB in the area. In areas deemed as the lowest category, testing is every four years and for those in the highest it is every six months.

More than 27,000 head of cattle in England had to be slaughtered in 2020 because they returned positive TB results.

When a cow tests positive for TB, very strict movement restrictions for cattle are then placed on the farm until further testing has been clear. The rest of the herd cannot be moved or sold and the farm is put into quarantine. If cattle remain quarantined on the farm over a long period of time, it creates numerous welfare issues and any farmer in this situation may be faced with financial ruin. The milk can still be sold for human consumption as it is routinely pasteurised which kills off any bacteria which might possibly be present.

There is evidence that badgers are partly responsible for the spread of bovine TB, so although badgers are a protected species, in high-risk areas culling has been sanctioned.

To date it has not been possible to vaccinate cattle against TB because tests for the disease could not differentiate between vaccinated and infected animals. However, a major breakthrough has been made recently by government scientists and trials are underway to remedy this.

CATTLE PARASITES

In common with all animals, cattle suffer from internal and external parasites. Externally they

Summer grass is a complete food

may become host to mites, lice and ticks which can cause great discomfort and possibly transmit or cause diseases. There is a range of treatments available. 'Pour-on', poured along the spine, or 'spot-on' squeezed onto the top of the shoulders are widely used and easy to apply. Injections are another alternative. These treatments are also effective against flies which are the bane of a cow's life in summer. Additionally further fly protection can be applied by using insecticide-impregnated ear tags and tail bands. These act in the same way as a flea collar on a cat or a dog. Applied in May, the treatment will last for four or five months and provide a measure of relief during the worst period. Various types of screens and electrocution traps are obtainable to reduce fly nuisance inside buildings.

Gut and lung worms and liver fluke are internal parasites that may affect cattle of all ages although the young are more susceptible. There are four methods of treating these - with an oral drench, injection, 'pour on' solution or by means of a bolus. The latter is a large slow-release tablet which is inserted down the animal's throat and swallowed; this will then lie in the stomach and gradually dissolve over a matter of weeks.

Foot problems are not as major an issue with cattle as they are with sheep. Occasionally an animal's hoof will overgrow and require trimming and of course foot care is very important for working bulls.

CATTLE FODDER

Grass is a complete food providing for the basic needs of cattle and it supplies the bulk of their food between March and October. A good rate of growth in early spring is very important to provide an abundance of grass both for grazing and making winter feed. Grass does not grow in the winter months. This is the time when excess grass which was cut and preserved in summer, usually in the form of silage or hay, is substituted.

In addition, supplementary feeding, which might be crushed corn or pelleted concentrates containing additional nutrients such as protein, minerals and vitamins, is given when required to cows in full milk, growing or pregnant animals and those being fattened. Other feed is utilised from by-products arising from human food production. Sugar beet pulp, maize gluten or biscuit waste is often used where available. The brewing and distillery industries both use malted barley and the residues from this are marketed as 'brewer's grains' or as 'draff' if it comes from whisky distilleries.

Much research and analysis is carried out into the nutritional value of rations, including the quality of hay and silage which very much depends on weather conditions during the growing period, the time the grass was cut and the way it was treated afterwards. A well-balanced diet is essential for peak performance. Cattle are often given free access to additional minerals and vitamins which are very important to their health, usually in a solid form as blocks, licks or in buckets.

It is always a great relief when the herd is turned out to grass in the spring, a pleasure shared by cattle and stockmen alike!

FENCING

Cheap electric fencing has replaced much of the barbed wire once found on dairy farms. It is less costly, easily and quickly erected and the risk of stock being injured is greatly reduced.

When milking cows are turned out to grass, electric fencing is often used to control grazing. Dairy farmers use different methods of grassland management. Some 'strip graze' in which the fence is moved daily allowing the cows access to a strip of fresh grass each day. Some use small paddocks which are grazed on rotation. Many others, including beef producers, opt for the traditional method of larger fenced or hedged fields when cattle are moved to a new field only after they have eaten the grass.

REPRODUCTION

Before it produces any milk, a cow has to first give birth.

A young (female) cow is known as a heifer and continues to be called that until she has her second calf.

The gestation period for a cow is nine months and normally she will only give birth to a single calf. She will come into oestrus at any time throughout the year so calves may be born in any month; however to fit in with seasonal growth of natural food, production costs and financial returns most beef calves are born in early spring and dairy calves in late summer. Calving may take place either indoors or outside, with advantages and disadvantages to both.

Beef cattle and dairy cattle are very different animals.

Dairy cow with her newborn calf

BEEF CATTLE

The UK produced 926.2 thousand tonnes of **beef** and **veal** in **2020** with the beef supply chain contributing approximately £2.8 billion to the UK economy.

USA BEEF PRODUCTION

UK beef is produced in a very different way to that in the USA. In the States, many calves begin their lives living free range on ranches. Later they are sent to beef lots, on average for their last five months, where they are fed on grain to finish fattening. Typically they are slaughtered at 15 to 28 months of age. These beef lots house many thousands of cattle in huge open yards, often with no shelter. Three quarters of American beef is produced in this way, and growth hormones are used to hasten fattening.

There are thought to be fewer than a dozen farms in the UK using intensive methods similar to these and in the UK growth hormones are prohibited. Instead beef cattle here are reared in a much more natural way.

UK BEEF PRODUCTION

Many beef calves are born around late February and March. Typically they and their mothers spend from April until October outdoors feeding entirely on grass. Very often a bull is put to run with the cows when their calves are a few weeks old, so natural mating takes place to produce next year's crop of calves. Managed in this way, these are known as *single suckler herds*. Beef breeds do not give nearly as much milk as dairy so one calf is enough for a beef cow to rear. However a dairy breed, if used as a foster mother or 'nurse cow', may produce enough milk to rear up to four calves.

In the autumn the beef calves are separated from their mothers when they are eight to ten months old and either sold as *stores* to other farmers or brought into yards to be fattened.

▲ Simmental Bull, a Continental breed with little fat but less hardy

Because of the inclement weather and wet ground, most British beef cattle are housed in barns for the winter in groups and bedded down with straw. At the beginning of the year the cycle starts over again and the cows are turned out again as soon as is practical. When conditions allow, beef cows of the hardier native breeds may sometimes be left outside all year.

Continental breeds are very popular for beef production because of their conformation, with the Limousin the most popular, although they can be temperamental. Very little fat is wanted on the carcases of beef animals today which is why the Continental breeds are so popular: they produce lean meat and plenty of it. But pure-bred Continentals are less hardy and do not thrive on poorer grazing so are often used as sires to cross with cross-bred or native breed cows.

Smaller native breeds, such as the white-faced Hereford and the all black Aberdeen Angus, still have their place and are sometimes better suited to local conditions. Whichever breed a Hereford is crossed with, the calves will have white faces. Calves bred from a black Aberdeen Angus bull inherit their sire's black colouring and are naturally polled (hornless).

Post-war, these popular native breeds went through a phase of being bred to be smaller, often only waist high to a man. In order to compete with the invasion of much larger Continental breeds, their size has been genetically increased so they are now much bigger. Even so natives are still smaller than Continentals and are often the choice of dairy farmers for crossing with their cows if herd replacements aren't required and especially for heifers, as a smaller calf generally means easier calving. The resultant cross-bred calves are reared in a similar way to dairy calves although they may have increased rations so they gain weight faster. Likewise they may have a summer out at grass before being brought into straw yards for the winter and fattened to be sold directly to wholesalers or at auction in local markets.

VEAL

Some calves are kept to produce veal. Welfare issues which used to be associated with veal production have been addressed – *see Welfare* and concerns are now very much a thing of the past in the UK. White veal meat was originally produced by keeping calves penned individually in very small crates, feeding them only on milk and slaughtering them at under six months. Veal crates were banned in the UK in the 1990s but not across the EU until 2006.

Today veal calves are reared until they are 8-12 months old to produce 'rose' veal which is pink in colour. In addition to milk, their diet includes cereal, hay, other solid food and possibly grass. These improvements have made veal acceptable once again.

> *Rose veal has the great advantage of creating a market for otherwise unwanted dairy bull calves which were previously either sent for export in their thousands or put down at birth.*

The export of live calves was very controversial and there are now strict welfare standards in place and the number has been greatly reduced. In September 2020 the export of live calves was banned in Scotland. In 2021 the UK government announced it was committed to banning the export of live animals destined for slaughter.

DAIRY CATTLE

There are about 12,000 dairy farms in the UK. Figures for 2020 show that milk accounted for 16.4% of total agricultural output and was worth £4.4bn in market prices. Although the number of dairy cows has fallen by 27% since 1996, now down to 1.9 million, they produced 15 billion litres of milk, the highest annual figure since 1990. The average milk yield per cow has increased by nearly 100% since 1975; up from 900 gals (4,100 litres) per year to nearly 1,800 gals (8,150 litres) in 2020.

> *A high yielding cow, at the peak of its lactation, may produce 60 litres of milk a day.*

These figures show how selective breeding, aided by better quality feed rations, has greatly improved output.

◀ Limousins are a popular Continental breed used by beef farmers but they can be temperamental

Dairy breeds are by nature lean, as they are kept to produce milk not get fat. They have been specifically bred to convert the food they eat primarily into milk. The Holstein, preceded by the very similar Friesian, is a breed that has been developed solely to produce milk, with the very best dairy Holsteins achieving up to 12,000 litres in a season's lactation. Both breeds originate in the Netherlands. These very high yielding dairy cows cannot eat enough grass alone to survive, so are reliant on supplementary rations.

There are now 1.9 million dairy cows in the UK and, because of high overhead costs, it is vital that optimum performance is achieved from each animal. The majority are the familiar black and white Holsteins although the Friesian is gaining favour again. Friesians are slightly smaller, have lower feed requirements and, being heavier in build, their calves have better potential to fatten.

The price a dairy farmer receives for his milk is only a fraction of what is charged for milk by supermarkets.

A dairy farmer has had to bear the cost of rearing a calf for two years, before she gives any milk.

REPRODUCTION

Cows come on heat for approximately one day every three weeks all year round.

Dairy heifers (young females) are usually mated for the first time when they are between 15 and 18 months old so they calve when they are about two years old.

Either AI is used or the females are mated naturally by being run with a bull. A naturally occurring hormone called prostaglandin that can be artificially produced is frequently administered to bring young heifers into heat all at the same time, making subsequent management easier.

As there is no assurance that calves from young unproven dairy heifers are worth keeping, a small beef breed such as an Aberdeen Angus or Hereford, for easy calving, is often used because unwanted pure-bred dairy calves are of no value. When the female line is unimportant, the cow can also be bred to a beef breed bull for which there is a better market for the resulting offspring.

Although exceptions are sometimes made, normally it is uneconomic to keep a cow if she does not conceive within a certain time; any that don't are sold as 'barren'.

Dairy cows waiting in the collecting yard for their turn to be milked

ARTIFICIAL INSEMINATION

For many years AI (artificial insemination) has been commonly used in dairy herds, enabling farmers to use semen from the best bulls in Britain, and further afield. Throughout the UK this has greatly improved the quality and output from dairy herds since the 1950s. Semen is collected and divided into 'straws' for AI use which are then frozen in liquid nitrogen and stored, maybe for several years, until required. One straw is sufficient to impregnate a cow and a single collection from a bull can yield enough semen to divide into 200-300 straws.

There is a 50-50 chance that the 'dairy' calf will be a bull calf, for which there is little demand but recently, sexed semen has become available. Although it is expensive and isn't guaranteed to be 100% effective, it is an ideal way to reduce the number of unwanted bull calves born and also to preserve the best blood lines.

Sexed semen is being used more frequently and it is estimated that 70% of dairy farmers are now taking advantage of it.

Several calves can now be bred from one cow at the same time. This involves injecting the donor cow with a substance that will make her produce several 'ripe' eggs when she would normally only produce one. Giving her another injection brings her into oestrus (heat) and by inseminating her three times during the critical period it is possible to fertilise several of the eggs. These are left to develop for about seven days before being removed by a vet, carefully checked under a microscope and then each embryo is either implanted into a surrogate heifer or cow or frozen at this stage and stored for future use. This is an expensive procedure but it does mean that several calves from an *exceptional* cow can be either produced or stored each year, thereby speeding up the process of selecting the best or preserving the bloodline.

It may be argued that the dairy industry is a victim of its own success in selective breeding but escalating costs combined with lower financial returns have forced it to investigate ways of increasing efficiency. Apart from some additional food being needed, it costs as much to keep a cow producing 4,000 litres of milk a year as it does one giving double that amount.

If twins of differing sexes are born, the female is invariably sterile and therefore useless for breeding and will not give milk. She is known as a 'freemartin'.

Because it is so important that a cow or heifer is got in calf, pregnancy tests are routinely conducted. Pregnancy can be determined at any time after about 5 weeks by scanning. A vet is also able to confirm a cow is pregnant after 6 weeks through conducting a manual examination by putting his arm inside the cow and actually feeling the developing foetus. Dairy farmers do not welcome twins; they are often small and can give rise to various complications.

MATURING THE CALVES

Nearly all dairy calves are separated from their mothers after a short time. However, it is vital for the health of the calf that it receives 'colostrum', the first milk produced by its mother, for two or three days after giving birth. This is not only extremely rich and highly digestible but it also contains antibodies passed on from the cow which will, to begin with, provide the calf with some degree of immunity and resistance to bacteria and other harmful bugs, as well as flushing through and activating its digestive system.

THE MILK

90% of dairy herds in the UK are Holsteins. Lower yields from other commercial herds can still prove to be economic if a low cost and streamlined system of management has been adopted.

Commercial herds of native British dairy breeds have now become a rarity and are mainly kept by pedigree breeders. Few traditional dairy breeds are kept solely for milk production although there is still a demand from cream and ice cream makers for the rich, creamy milk of Jersey cows.

The UK is currently very nearly self-sufficient in milk production.

A small percentage of dairy products are imported into the UK but this is offset to some degree by a small percentage being exported.

Some producers choose to have their herd calve in the autumn as they receive a slightly higher price for milk in winter. Others prefer spring calving as it is cheaper to keep the cows on grass. A few like to calve throughout the year so they receive a regular year-round income.

A cow's lactation peaks seven or eight weeks after calving before beginning to gradually decline until after about 10 months she will be giving only a few litres and only being milked once a day. At this stage she will be 'dried off' (stopped from giving milk) by cutting back her food allowance for a short while. As she gets nearer to calving, her food ration is then gradually increased allowing her to build up her reserves so she and her calf are in good condition when it is born and she comes back into milk.

After that, the amount of food a cow receives will vary as to how much milk she is producing. In many cases this means being given supplementary feed, which is sometimes given while they are being milked. This may be fed manually but cows in most large herds wear a collar or an anklet containing a transponder so they are recognised individually and can be fed the correct rations automatically; either in or outside the milking parlour.

As a cow's gestation period is around nine months, to be profitable a dairy cow needs to have a calf every 12 to 14 months otherwise she stops producing milk.

Although some extremely high yielders may be milked three times a day, most herds are milked twice. This means that a herdsperson starts work very early in the morning, usually about 5am, and often doesn't finish until after 6pm or later, but it is sometimes possible for them to take an extended lunch break. Cows of course have to be milked in the same way on weekends and bank holidays so anyone milking cows has to be prepared to work not only long

Once weaned dairy calves are kept in straw yards until they can be turned out to grass in the spring

but also unsociable hours. Small scale farmers often have to do all the work themselves, unable to afford the cost of employing a relief milker, so they are rarely able to take more than a few hours off at a time and holidays are unknown. Besides the long hours, milking is physically demanding, repetitive and dirty work: cows are not house-trained. To lessen back strain, the herdsperson usually works from a sunken pit between two rows of cows; they do not always notice the telltale sign of a raised tail and have to suffer the unpleasant consequences.

SELLING MILK

Once the Milk Marketing Board was abolished in 1994, the all-powerful supermarkets virtually took over selling milk. They stipulated how much they were willing to pay dairy farmers. There followed a spell when keeping dairy cows became unprofitable and many producers were put out of business. When it was realised that if that situation were to continue, there would be a shortage of milk, the amount paid improved as supermarkets signed contracts with dairy farmers guaranteeing a minimum price.

Dairy farmers sell their milk to milk processing companies, some of which are co-operatives, and it is collected from the farm daily or every other day, in large insulated tankers.

Fresh milk is sold after it has been pasteurised, which kills off harmful bacteria; and homogenised, a process which breaks the fat (cream) globules in milk down into extremely small particles so that it is distributed uniformly throughout the milk. It is sold on as fresh milk or processed into long life milk, cheese, butter, cream, yoghurt, ice cream, milk powders, tinned evaporated and condensed milk.

There are a number of 'micro dairies' in the UK who bottle their own milk to sell direct to the customer. About 200 of these sell at the gate, others through local shops, home deliveries or vending machines and there was increased demand for this during Covid-19 lockdowns. Sometimes milk is sold as 'raw' milk which has not been treated in any way, although the distribution of raw milk is illegal in Scotland.

HOUSING CATTLE
Most dairy herds are turned out to grass from spring to early autumn. The rest of the year they are kept indoors; sometimes housed loose in covered straw yards with access to a feed area and mangers but most often in large barns fitted out with cubicles. These are individually sectioned-off compartments which allow each cow its own space to lie down in but narrow enough to prevent it turning round and soiling its bedding. There are 'dunging' passages between the rows. The cows are not tied up, enabling them to move about freely. They have access to areas where they are fed, unrestricted access to water and a 'loafing' area. The cubicle bedding provided may be sawdust, wood shavings, chopped straw or sand and cubicles are fitted with rubber mats for comfort. A few farmers prefer to keep their herds indoors all year and feed them fresh cut grass when it's available. This is known as 'Zero Grazing' and is much followed on the Continent.

The yards and passageways where cattle are housed need to be cleaned out every day using either an automated scraper or one mounted on a tractor. The semi-liquid muck is moved into a storage pit (slurry lagoon) or to where it can be pumped into a large circular storage tank prior to being spread or sprayed on the fields. A system similar to that used for irrigation can be used to apply this valuable source of fertiliser.

MILKING PARLOURS
Modern dairy herds are milked in hygienic milking parlours with raised floors. Some very small herds may still be kept in old fashioned stalls where cows are tied up individually to be milked and stand at the same level as the operator. Where cows are grazed away from the farm buildings in summer, for example on water meadows such as the Somerset Levels, a portable structure known as a 'milking bail' may be used; a generator powering the milking machines. The milk from each cow is first

Individual cubicles where cows are able to rest and relax

collected in a container or large glass jar before it is released into an overhead pipe conveying it to a refrigerated bulk storage tank.

There are several designs of modern milking parlours: in all of them the cows stand approximately 90cms above the operator. The most popular is the 'herringbone' where the operator works from a central pit. A small batch of cows is let in and they stand with their backs to the pit at an angle of 30 to 35 degrees – hence the name herringbone. When they have been milked they exit from the other end. The operator then turns his attention to the cows waiting on his other side, then a fresh batch is let in. Another design is known as an 'abreast' or 'parallel' parlour. It is similar to a herringbone but the cows stand at right angles to the operator who works directly behind them and has to reach forward to attach the pulsating suction cups. Milking each cow takes a few minutes and afterwards the batch of cows exit through doors in front of them.

Some very large commercial dairy herds have invested in 'rotary' parlours or 'carousels' where the cows enter onto a circular raised platform that moves very slowly past the operator who may be working from a central pit or from the outside. The cow exits near to where she entered and another takes her place. On massive dairy units, milking on this scale may be continuous 24/7.

A relatively new innovation is the invention of robotic milking parlours which the cow is free to enter when she chooses and is milked automatically. She is identified by her electronic collar or anklet.

Portable bucket machines remain available for milking individual cows when necessary, such as when they are being kept in isolation; if their milk has to be discarded when they are receiving medication; or if they are taken to a show.

Milking parlour designs have evolved to make milking quicker and easier and sometimes the cows receive part of their food rations while

◄ Herringbone milking parlour

they are being milked. Although in theory it makes the work of a herdsperson easier, it has often meant that one person is expected to milk many more cows. There is also a lot of dung that has to be cleared up each day from the parlour, from the collecting yards where the cows wait prior to milking, and from the dispersal yards where they are let out of the parlour afterwards.

There are now extremely high standards of hygiene in place that have to be met. A refrigerated bulk milk tank is a modern necessity on a dairy farm. Here the milk is agitated, cooled quickly to a temperature not exceeding 4°C and stored until collected by a milk tanker, normally either daily or every other day. It is then taken to a distribution centre before either being packaged and sold fresh or sent for butter, ice cream, cheese making or yoghurt production. Samples are taken each day by the tanker driver which are randomly tested several times a week for the presence of bacteria, traces of antibiotics, to make sure that there is no evidence of blood or water and to do a cell count to detect the presence of

mastitis, a common infection in the udder. If a cow or heifer has been treated with antibiotics or any other drugs, a detailed record has to be kept of the medication used and the milk has to be thrown away both during treatment and for a fixed number of days afterwards. The premises and equipment are regularly inspected.

Dairy farmers face stiff penalties if their milk is found to be contaminated in any way.

THE HERDSPERSON

However large or small a dairy enterprise may be, much of its success is due to the skills of the herdsperson in charge. He or she has the responsibility of caring for herds which can exceed 200 cows in milk. Keeping them fit is vital not only because drugs are expensive but also because of lost revenue from milk which then cannot be sold and has to be tipped down the drain – although there are times when this milk can be used to feed calves. An experienced herdsperson is competent at performing many veterinary procedures such as giving injections, treating foot problems and assisting with difficult births.

▼ Rotary milking parlour

© Dairyflow, Scotland

It is their stockmanship, attention to detail and dedication on which the welfare and therefore profitability of the herd depends.

DAIRY CALVES

While beef calves are suckled by their mothers for several months before they are weaned, dairy breeds are usually weaned at 6-8 weeks old. The calf is normally separated from its mother within 48 hours which reduces stress levels and health risks but it is very important that it will have had some colostrum to start with. Very quickly it will learn to drink straight from a bucket or a container with artificial teats attached.

Nearly all dairy calves, and some beef calves, are reared on milk substitute because it is only half the cost of fresh milk. This comes in powder form and is mixed with the appropriate amount of either warm or cold water and fed once or twice a day, occasionally ad lib, until the calves are weaned.

▶ Milking machines use a vacuum to gently squeeze the milk from a cow's udder

Hand-reared calves are often housed in small pens separate from each other but which allow them the freedom to turn around and generally move about. By this method they can receive individual attention and every calf gets its fair share of milk, hay and concentrate feed (pellets or pencils) which they are also given. Keeping them separated avoids them being bullied or developing bad habits such as sucking one another's navels, a vice that can persist into adulthood. If this pen system isn't adopted, calves may be kept in small groups of similar ages so that they can be fed individually as they put their heads through a 'yoke' (grille). This prevents the greedy stealing from the slower ones and buckets of milk being knocked over.

Feeding calves individually is labour-intensive so larger-scale calf rearers often use a container fitted with multiple teats or install fully automatic computerised calf-feeding machines. The calves are kept in batches in straw yards and each one is identified by wearing a collar transponder. They are limited to the amount of milk they receive individually in 24 hours but are free to visit when they want. The number of feeds and amount they've consumed is automatically recorded. Their milk allowance is increased after the first week

A single suckler cow rears its own calf

and they have access to hay and concentrates. When they are about six weeks old the amount of milk is gradually reduced until they are fully weaned at eight weeks.

Despite the fully automated system, the calves still need regular care and attention from a conscientious stockman to keep them fit and in good health, with particular attention to hygiene. Calves need to be kept in clean, well-ventilated and draught-free conditions. The buckets or containers of the milk fed to them need to be kept scrupulously clean. Scours and respiratory ailments such as pneumonia are normally the biggest threats to a calf's health.

WEANING

After dairy calves are weaned at around 2 months old, they are usually 'loose housed' in straw bedded yards or barns, in groups of similar ages, until they are 4-6 months old. While kept indoors they will continue to be fed on concentrates and good quality hay or silage. They are usually turned out to grass from April until October before being brought inside again for the winter. Occasionally, in drier areas, yearling stock may be left outside for their second winter.

Although it is a requirement that calves are ear tagged soon after birth to provide identification, dairy cattle are also often freeze branded with a number on their rump before entering the herd. Freeze branding uses an iron that has been immersed in liquid nitrogen or dry ice. It is applied for less than a minute and destroys the pigment-forming cells in the hair follicles so that white hair grows back. This causes little pain and allows the identifying number to be seen from a distance, although it does not work well on cows that are predominately white!

Young calves soon learn to drink from a bucket

GLOSSARY

BULL Entire male

STEER/BULLOCK Castrated male reared for beef

COW Mature female

CALF Newborn male or female

HEIFER Young female up until the time she gives birth to her first calf

STIRK Young male or female cattle

STORE A young animal reared for beef that is sold on to another farmer or a dealer to grow further or be fattened

FAT STOCK Livestock ready to be slaughtered

CULL COW A cow that is no longer profitable to keep either because of age or health issues

DRY COW A cow that is not in milk

SUCKLER COW A beef breed cow rearing its own calf

NURSE COW A cow used to suckle other cows' calves – foster mother

POLLED A breed that naturally doesn't grow any horns

FREEMARTIN A female calf that is born twinned with a male and is invariably infertile. Applies only to cattle

BULLING A heifer or cow that is on heat

AI Artificial insemination

OESTRUS, HEAT Period of ovulation when mating can take place

SERVE Mate

GESTATION Period of pregnancy

MAIDEN Animal that has not previously been bred from

BARREN Infertile

EMPTY Not in calf

COLOSTRUM Very rich milk produced by an animal for a few days after giving birth

BEASTINGS Another name for colostrum

BAG Another name for an udder

QUARTER A cow has four teats and the udder is divided into four separate quarters

LACTATION Period a cow is producing milk, 10-11 months on average

STEAM UP Increase feed rations prior to calving

DRY OFF Cease milking so that a cow stops producing milk

CRUSH A small, strongly built pen for restraining an animal

PARLOUR Building in which cows are milked

UNIT Milking machine

CLUSTER Vacuum cups on milking machine that fit onto the teats; an intermittent squeezing action releases milk from the udder

DISBUD/DEHORN Remove horn growth, normally done in the first few weeks before the horns develop

FREEZE BRAND Permanent identification carried out by applying liquid nitrogen which turns the marked hair white

EAR TAG Plastic or metal identification tag, sometimes electronic, inserted in the ear

TRANSPONDER Contains a microchip where information is stored. Used in ear tags, collars or anklets on cattle

FLY TAG Chemical fly repellent tag inserted in the ear.

BULLDOGS A spring closing and self-locking grip that clips onto the nasal septum of fully grown cattle and is used to increase control over the animal

CALVING JACK A device to aid a difficult calving by gently pulling on the legs of the unborn calf

TURN OUT Give access to grazing outside

STRIP GRAZE Allow animals access to a small area of grazing. Electric fencing is normally used and is moved daily across a field to provide fresh grazing

ZERO GRAZING Keeping cattle permanently housed and feeding them fresh cut grass

HAY Dried grass

SILAGE Mown grass or maize that partially ferments while stored and ultimately provides palatable fodder

STRAW The dried stems of cereals. Barley can be used for feed but wheat and oat straw are only suitable for bedding

CONCENTRATES Supplementary food containing necessary nutrients such as protein and vitamins compressed into pellets, pencils, nuts or cake

LICK Solid mineral or nutrition block

ELECTRIC FENCE Thin single strand wire fence electrified by a battery that is charged either by a small windmill, solar panels or a transformer

CATTLE GRID An alternative barrier to a gate consisting of a shallow pit covered with evenly spaced heavy duty metal bars. An effective method of preventing cattle and sheep straying where roads crossing open areas of grazing are unfenced.

TB Bovine tuberculosis

BSE Bovine Spongiform Encephalopathy, also known as 'Mad Cow Disease'. It is a neurodegenerative disease of cattle which can be transmitted to humans through infected meat. In 1995 the human variant, Creutzfeldt-Jakob Disease (CJD), led to the deaths of 177 people from eating infected meat. Four million head of cattle were slaughtered in an effort to contain the outbreak. This incident resulted in a ten-year worldwide ban on British beef and much stricter regulations regarding the preparation of carcases for consumption

A dog and a quad bike are vital parts of a modern shepherd's equipment

SHEEP FARMING

One third of the UK land area is upland terrain, most of which is only suitable for sheep grazing. For hundreds of years small, hardy breeds have evolved which are able to utilise this grazing and withstand the harsh climate. The Badger Face Welsh Mountain sheep are probably the oldest of British breeds with their origins believed to date back to the 1st century. Herdwick sheep, 95% of whom live a semi-wild existence on the Cumbrian Fells, are thought to have been introduced by Norse settlers during the Viking invasions between the 8th and 11th centuries. Soay are small, primitive sheep which originate from the isolated island of the same name in the Outer Hebrides. Soay means 'Sheep Island' in the Norse language so it is thought they also date back to Viking times.

Originally sheep were kept on a commercial scale principally for their wool. In medieval England, wool became big business and many landowners grew rich from producing it. The reason why there are so many disproportionately large medieval churches in small villages across the country is because landowners who became wealthy selling wool had them built as status symbols.

Fleece quality varies greatly with the breed and the majority which are the coarser ones are almost worthless and can only be used for making carpets. The finer ones are of more value.

With the introduction of man-made fibres in the mid-20th century, demand for wool fell dramatically and today the average value of each fleece does not cover the cost of the shearing.

Demand for British wool of any sort is minimal and since the majority is used for carpet-making, the covid pandemic restrictions in 2020 brought about a collapse in sales as hotels, restaurants, conference centres and cruise liners, where demand is greatest for floor coverings, ceased trading. Wool can also be used as insulation. Ironically the popular 'fleece' clothing material today has nothing to do with a sheep.

Nearly all sheep in Britain are now kept primarily for meat production.

There are an estimated 33 million sheep and lambs in the UK of which nearly half are breeding ewes.

Traditionally ewes are put to the ram on Guy Fawkes Day and will lamb on April Fools' Day but many lowland farmers now lamb their sheep earlier in March.

The majority of lambs are sold for slaughter when they are around six months old so total numbers fluctuate throughout the year. Pre-Brexit, UK farmers exported a third of the lamb they produced, much of it to the EU. Now with the additional opening up of markets in the Middle East and Japan, exports amounted to £436 million in 2020.

- 90% of British lamb meat comes from animals grazing naturally on grass or moorland

- More than 90% of Welsh lamb is exported to the EU and the Middle East.

- Sheep are sold as lamb if they are marketed in the year of their birth (or in the year

following its birth if the lamb is born after 30 September). After this it becomes known as a hogget and will be marketed as mutton.

BREEDS OF SHEEP

There are about 90 different breeds and recognised crosses of sheep in the UK which have evolved to suit the diverse terrain. Sheep breeds can be roughly divided into three tiers, lowland, hill, and upland. Some breeds have horns on both sexes, others only on the rams but most of the lowland breeds have none at all. Many of the sheep kept in Britain are what are known as 'half-breds' which means a direct cross of two pure breeds. These have been deliberately crossed to possess the best attributes of the two breeds selected.

Sheep over 15 months old are no longer lambs but hoggets and their meat is mutton.

A new breed known as 'Easy Care' sheep has become popular with some small-scale and larger sheep farmers. It was originally developed in the 1960s by selectively cross breeding Wiltshire Horn sheep, a native breed that naturally sheds its fleece, with other breeds. Easy Care sheep are low maintenance, produce excellent meat yields, good lambing ratios and do not require shearing. Since the price received for wool does not cover the cost of shearing, having a breed that doesn't need clipping is an added bonus.

Some breeds are very local to an area, such as the Herdwicks which are found only in the Lake District, Swaledales in the north of England, the Welsh Mountain in Wales and Scotch Blackface in Scotland. Some hefty Continental breeds have become popular for crossing with native breeds of sheep, notably the Texel, Charolais and Beltex.

◀ The Texel is a Continental breed used widely in fat lamb production, in other words, for eating

Many flocks are now lambed indoors but some hardy breeds are still left to lamb outside

A popular breed in the north of England is a 'Mule' which is a cross often between a blue-faced Leicester ram and a purebred hill ewe, usually a Swaledale.

All our native breeds have been evolved over the centuries for their capacity to thrive in the many different environments in which they are expected to live. Sheep are one of the most adaptable species of animal in the world, able to exist in arid deserts and on the tops of mountains.

Hill and upland breeds are mostly small and slow maturing but are able to withstand the rigours of the open hills and mountains. They can thrive on poor grazing and provide the main source of income for hill farmers. Hill sheep live a fairly wild existence on wide expanses of land. They are sometimes brought in for shearing and dipping or confined in fields for a week or two when the rams are first put in or when the ewes lamb – but for 10 or 11 months of the year they roam completely free on the hills and fells. It takes a gang of people and dogs several hours to round them up and get them off the hills. Hill farms usually only have a few acres of what is known as 'in bye' land close to the farm where the sheep can be penned for a short time, and the rest of the time they spend on the hills. In late summer silage or hay is made on these 'in bye' fields.

HEFTED SHEEP

Sheep possess a strong herding instinct and those loose on the open hillsides naturally divide into groups and live in certain territories. This is known as 'hefting' or 'heafing'.

When a hill farm changes hands, the resident flock of sheep are usually included with the sale.

The offspring of these hefted sheep naturally learn from their mothers which part of the moor they live on, a knowledge that has been passed down through generations of sheep. There is a hereditary instinct to stay within these invisible territories which prevents a flock wandering aimlessly over vast expanses of hill and getting lost. The loss through Foot and Mouth disease in 2001 of so many of these hefted sheep flocks caused great concern to hill farmers as it was feared that a natural system, which had worked so well for hundreds of years, would die out.

Hill farmers often help each other out at busy times when their sheep have to be gathered in, such as for shearing, dipping or weaning. It's no easy task when they roam hundreds of acres and can easily hide in rocks, gullies or bracken. Under these conditions, good working dogs are invaluable to the shepherd. Hill sheep are often the only way of utilising the impoverished soil of the British uplands, although grouse shooting and deer stalking can also provide an income in those places where the conditions are right.

Upland sheep may need as much as 10 acres (4.05 ha) of rough grazing to sustain a ewe and her lamb while lush lowland pastures can be stocked with up to 5 sheep per acre (.405 ha).

GRAZING FOR ECOLOGY

Sheep are tidy grazers and nibble the grass very short. They have front teeth only on the bottom jaw and a hard pad on the top. They eat quickly and then regurgitate the cud (grass) when they are resting, in a similar way to cows. It is then chewed again thoroughly before being swallowed. Many conservationists make use of the sheep's neat grazing habits to create ideal, cropped ground conditions for certain species of flora and fauna. Their droppings are evenly distributed and can add fertility to the soil.

HILL AND LOWLAND SHEEP MANAGEMENT

After they have had three or four crops of lambs, hill ewes are often sold to lowland sheep farmers where they continue their productive lives in less extreme conditions. Here they may last until they are up to eight years old. Usually it is their teeth that fail, becoming broken and making it impossible for them to feed properly.

Many lambs are weaned off hill sheep flocks in autumn and sent to the lowlands to fatten or overwinter on grass, unsprayed stubbles or arable crops. East Anglia is a popular area for this as stubble turnips sown directly after harvest and sugar beet waste left on the fields, is utilised. Sheep are often '**folded**' over turnips by restricting their access to small areas using electric fences, which are then moved to give access to a fresh area. As many as 100 sheep may be kept like this per acre (.405 ha). In-lamb ewes are often sent to the lowlands for the better quality grazing and a gentler climate.

Providing winter keep for sheep enables arable farmers to supplement their income and enrich the soil while providing a service to hill farmers. Sometimes lambs are sent as '**keepers**' where payment is made per head or per week and then they are returned to their owner's farm. If no winter grazing it available and they are not big enough for slaughter, they are sold as '**stores**' at September lamb sales and bought by dealers or other farmers to fatten. Besides feeding on roots '*keep*' sheep are used to tidy up grass in cow paddocks after the cows have been brought indoors for the winter.

With a few exceptions, sheep come into oestrus in late summer or early autumn. One or two of the lowland breeds such as the Dorset Horn will come in much earlier than this.

The larger lowland sheep are first to lamb in early spring as the climate is kinder but in the uplands, where winter weather drags on, ewes might not be lambed until well into April or even May.

Most sheep farmers now have their ewes routinely scanned, ideally between 70-90 days into pregnancy, to determine whether they are pregnant and, if so, how many lambs they are carrying. This is a great help in determining what level of feed needs to be provided. Obviously a ewe carrying twins or triplets will require a higher level of nutrition to ensure well-developed

Fodder crops are often grown in arable areas as winter keep for sheep from elsewhere

lambs and a good milk supply. Sheep can then be divided into different groups and rations can be worked out accordingly, thus saving money by unnecessarily providing supplementary food. Ewes carrying more than one lamb are also likely to need more attention.

Farmers intending to produce lambs for the Easter market will lamb ewes as early as Christmas.

Although the grass will not be growing if lambs are born midwinter, and they will need additional feed, the cost is offset by obtaining Easter prices. The black-faced Suffolk is a very popular breed for producing quality fat lambs both from lowland flocks and by crossing with hill sheep breeds.

Lowland farmers normally choose to start lambing in March so that the new growth of grass will help ewes to produce plenty of milk and the lambs will have plenty of grass to fatten on, throughout the summer. A single, fast growing, well-fed lamb can be ready for slaughter as early as 12 weeks but most lowland farmers prefer to have twins even though they are slower growing.

When talking about a lambing percentage of 175%, shepherds mean that they have had 175 lambs from a hundred ewes. Early lambs are sold as fat lambs straight off the ewe but the main crop are separated sometime in July or August. They are weighed regularly and are ready for sale when they weigh about 80-90lb (36-40kg) live weight providing they are fat enough – although it is possible for them to get too fat. Experts can tell by feeling a lamb's back through the wool at the base of the tail whether it has the correct 'finish'. Carcase weight is approximately half the live weight and the greatest demand is for carcases weighing 35-46lb (16-21kg).

Ewes are not generally bred from until their second year, when they will be at least 18 months old.

TUPPING

Ewes whose lambs have been weaned are moved back to poorer grazing so that their milk dries up, before being turned onto better grazing a few weeks before the rams are put in. This system is known as '**flushing**' the ewes. Being on a rising plane of nutrition helps improve fertility.

Prior to turning the rams in, many shepherds clip the wool short around the ewe's hindquarters to facilitate mating. Sometimes a vasectomised ram, known as a **teaser**, will be run with the ewes beforehand to stimulate them to come into oestrus. One mature ram will mate with up to 50 ewes in lowland flocks but a lesser number out on the open hill for here it takes more time for him to find those that are receptive. AI is rarely used in sheep. Ewes are on heat for about two days and have a 17 day cycle. The gestation period for ewes is approximately 150 days (five months) and the rams, or tups as they are also known, are put in according to which day lambing is planned to commence. Coloured paint (**raddle**) is frequently put on the ram's chest, or a crayon held in place by a harness, so that the ewes are marked on the rump when he mates with them. Raddling provides a visual indication that can be seen from a distance. The colour is often changed after three weeks or so, to identify those that have been served later or not tupped the first time.

Scanning, ideally 80 days after tupping, will reveal the number of lambs a ewe is carrying. A few weeks prior to lambing, those carrying more than one lamb will very likely be given supplementary food to ensure they keep in good condition, have plenty of milk, and their lambs are well developed.

One mature ram will mate with up to 50 ewes in lowland flocks.

LAMBING

Most sheep farmers now lamb their flocks in large sheds or barns, a section of which is temporarily divided into pens. The ewes are kept in groups but once they have given birth are often penned individually for a short time with their lambs to make sure they bond with their offspring, and have sufficient milk to feed them. Weather permitting, after two or three days, they are then turned out together into fields with the rest of the ewes that have lambed. Once lambing is completed the barns and sheds can be used for other purposes later in the year.

OUTDOOR LAMBING

Some flocks, especially in the north, are still lambed outdoors and the weather can have devastating consequences. Lambs do not usually come to much harm when it is cold so long as it is dry. It is the cold combined with prolonged rain or drifting snow which causes the damage,

▶ Scottish Blackface Ram

▼ Rams are marked on the chest with a crayon to indicate which ewes have been mated

and weak lambs don't stand a chance. Simple shelters made out of straw bales and hurdles may be provided and stone walls give a measure of protection from the wind.

Some farmers put specially designed polythene jackets on the young lambs which stay on for a few days and are biodegradable.

LAMBING DIFFICULTIES

Lambing is an extremely busy and tiring time. Farmers need to be vigilant, as birthing difficulties are frequently encountered with large sheep which have multiple births. Most frequently it is because lambs are not in the correct position of having their two front legs and head presented first when they begin to arrive. Sometimes the legs of twins get muddled up inside the uterus or a lamb is abnormally large. Farmers much prefer if a ewe can give birth naturally or if necessary shepherds can cope with problems themselves but occasionally a vet's assistance is needed. Weak lambs also require extra care. On farms with large flocks requiring attention 24/7, contract labour, sometimes in the form of agricultural or veterinary students, is often employed for a few weeks to ease the strain during the lambing season.

About 15% of newborn lambs die before weaning due to trauma at birth, lack of mothering, disease, weather and predation.

It is common practice for the navel of newborn lambs to be dipped in iodine to prevent infection. Temporary numbers are painted on the sides of lambs so they can be identified with their mothers, invaluable early on when they are kept in large groups and a lamb may become separated from its mother, enabling them to be easily reunited.

FOSTERING LAMBS

It's estimated that 5% of the newborn lambs who die are lost each year due to predation, with the smaller breeds being most at risk. Their lambs make easy prey and if a ewe has twins it is very difficult for her to defend both. Foxes, crows and ravens are the principal offenders.

Inevitably there are occasions when a ewe is unable to feed her lambs. Ewes only have two teats so if she has triplets, which is not uncommon, she is only likely to be able to feed two of them. Lambs that have lost their mothers or are not getting sufficient milk are fostered onto another ewe when possible, although this isn't always easy to do. If her lamb has been born dead then another lamb can be immediately rubbed in the amniotic fluid of the dead lamb, whose scent creates an immediate bond; otherwise the ewe will reject any lamb that she doesn't recognise. Another age-old ploy if a ewe has lost her own lamb is to skin her dead lamb and fit the skin over one that needs to be fostered. The hope is because it has a smell she can identify with, she will be fooled into thinking it is her own.

Failing a successful adoption, the lamb will need to be hand-reared. In local dialects there are various names given to all ages of sheep and in the case of these bottle-fed lambs, they are known as orphan, sock, sickie, cade, pet or poddy lambs.

It is extremely important that new born lambs receive the first milk (colostrum) which besides being a rich source of energy and containing a laxative that gets the bowels working, also contains antibodies against disease that are passed on through the milk.

DOCKING AND FENCING

For welfare reasons, hill lambs do not have their tails docked. Those kept at intermediate levels may have half of their tails removed and the tails of those on lowland grazing are docked quite short so that their wool does not get soiled by their softer droppings from the lusher grazing and attract flies. Both castration and tail docking has to be carried out during the first few days and most often the rubber ring method, which cuts off the circulation, is used for both. Castration may be avoidable if lambs are destined for slaughter below six months of age. There are strict regulations covering castration and tail docking and if it's not carried out early on then it has to be done by a veterinary surgeon using an appropriate anaesthetic. There is ongoing discussion about pain caused by these procedures but in the case of rubber rings applied at a very young age, this is minimal.

However, there can be serious welfare issues if sheep on rich grazing are not docked. The wool can get badly soiled on which flies then lay their eggs. Fly eggs hatch into maggots within 24 hours which soon burrow their way through the wool to the skin and begin feeding on the sheep's flesh. This is not obvious to begin with if the wool is long and can very easily go unnoticed for several days resulting in great distress for the sheep. If left untreated the result is a horrific, lingering death. If the wool has grown long around their hind quarters and fly strike is likely to become an

issue, the wool is clipped off to keep them clean. This is known as 'crutching' or 'dagging'.

Lambs destined for the early markets in spring are often **'creep fed'**. Supplementary pelleted food is provided in a trough surrounded by hurdles or fencing which denies access to the ewes but allows smaller lambs to pass through. This system is also sometimes used to allow lambs access to fresh grazing ahead of the ewes.

Hill sheep on high ground are not fenced in. Those at intermediate levels are often kept in by stone walls which are constructed to have a small gap at intervals in the base to allow small animals and birds or even young lambs to pass through. These go by various names in different parts of the country.

Where a permanent fence is required in the lowlands, strong, large meshed, galvanised wire netting is put up but where temporary fencing is needed electrified, lightweight mesh is used.

▼ Herdwicks living semi-wild on the Fells need to be gathered in occasionally as below

Another popular method of sheep fencing is the use of three separate strands of thin electrified wire. This is very quickly erected using an apparatus mounted on a quad bike or barrow pushed by hand. All types of electric fencing are supported with insulated metal or plastic posts. Power is provided by a battery using mains electricity reduced through a transformer, or a battery possibly charged by a small wind turbine or solar panels.

IDENTIFICATION

Since 2015 it has become a legal requirement that all sheep must be identified electronically by nine months of age with an ear tag inscribed with the letters UK and the registered flock number. Since the beginning of 2021 those intended for export from Britain to the EU or Northern Ireland have to be identified with an ear tag inscribed 'GB'.

It is a further requirement that adult sheep over 12 months have a secondary tag, inscribed with an individual identification number. Most legal requirements applied to sheep are also applicable to goats. Farmers and those whose sheep run wild on the hills may also use a tattoo in the ear for identification The old fashioned way of marking ownership by putting notches in sheep's ears is also still often used. Each farm has its own code, thus easily confirming who sheep belong to. These are known as **lug marks**. It is common practice with horned sheep that an identification mark is burned into one horn, which is a painless procedure, and sometimes sheep are marked with coloured tape round one horn. Hill famers often also mark their flocks with **'smit marks'** on the fleece by using a daub or two of paint in identical places on their sheep's bodies. This enables them to be identified from a distance. Odd sheep sometimes get muddled up with a neighbouring flock on the hills and this makes distinguishing them apart quick and easy.

▲ Corresponding numbers are painted on the sides of young lambs so they can be identified with their mothers

SHEARING AND WOOL

Lambs are not sheared in their first year. Mature sheep are normally sheared (clipped) in May or June, hill sheep a month later. It is very important on welfare grounds that adult sheep are sheared each year, even though the farmer is faced with being out of pocket. Apart from the obvious problem of over-heating there is also a serious risk of 'fly strike' when flies are attracted to wet, greasy or soiled wool. Different sheep have different grades of wool varying from the really coarse texture of Herdwick and Hebridean to the finer and more valuable fleeces of Cheviots and Shetlands. The UK produces about 22,000 tons of wool each year and the majority of UK sheep owners are required to register with British Wool before they can market and sell their fleece wool. Owners of four or less sheep are exempt from this requirement.

The returns for low grade fleeces do not even cover the cost of shearing and the coronavirus pandemic in 2020 brought about a collapse of what were already meagre prices. Wool, over the decades, has been displaced by artificial fibres which is reflected in the drop in price paid for

▲ Crofters help each other out clipping their sheep by hand which leaves a slightly longer fleece to protect them against the weather

▲ Much of the shearing is done by well equipped contractors

wool. The best quality is used for clothing and knitwear while the lesser goes into making carpets and mattresses.

With hobbyists showing a resurgence of interest in spinning and weaving, a few new breeds have appeared to supply the special wool required. Some native breeds are renowned for their quality wool, notably the Blue-faced Leicester, Downland breeds and the Cotswold.

Many sheep farmers employ contractors to do the shearing. Normally gangs of experienced men and women come over from New Zealand from May to July to do this and travel around the country using their own equipment. They are very skilled at shearing and can each clip up to 400 in a day. Others in the gang expertly roll up the fleeces. The weather can prove to be a problem as sheep need to be dry when they are sheared otherwise the fleece deteriorates when stored. It is only possible to do the shearing on wet days if the sheep have been penned indoors beforehand to dry off. Lowland sheep that are brought inside for the winter are sometimes sheared prior to being housed.

Some farmers were forced to burn their fleeces because there was no sale for them but this is now illegal. Unwanted fleeces are very difficult to dispose of, requiring specialist treatment before they can be sent to landfill, composted or turned into fertilizer and this involves more expense. Other uses are currently being sought for the poorer grades of fleece such as house insulation and as mulch for gardening use.

HEALTH PROBLEMS

Sheep suffer from a variety of harmful external parasites which, depending on the area, present a major problem to sheep keepers. But these can be prevented to some extent with routine treatment. Ticks suck the blood and carry a disease known as **Louping ill**; and also **Lyme disease** which affects humans. Heavy infestation can result in the death of young lambs as well as grouse and is debilitating to deer. Dipping sheep to protect them was once compulsory but is no longer. However, many farmers still dip their sheep as it helps not only with tick control but also other parasites such as scab mites and from **fly strike**. Dipping is carried out a few weeks after shearing and the sheep have to be kept submersed for at least a minute. The dip is a formulation of insecticide and fungicide. The toxic chemical organophosphate was cheap and effective but withdrawn in 1999 because of the highly dangerous side-effects it was having, particularly on the people using it. It was replaced with other, much safer chemical compounds. An alternative to submerging the animal is for it to pass through a shower unit; or to use a 'pour-on' treatment, applied along the spine; or a 'spot on' similar to that used as an insecticide for domestic pets.

Intestinal parasites are another ever-present problem for sheep farmers. Routine dosing (**drenching**), administered as an oral medicine using a 'gun' designed to deliver the correct dosage, is carried out for lambs. Regular moves of sheep to fresh pasture can help break

the reproductive cycle of these parasites. Ewes are usually dosed prior to mating and again just before they lamb. **Liver fluke** is a problem in certain areas and can also affect cattle, goats, deer and rabbits. Grouse on high moors can become severely debilitated from infestations of strongylosis worms and ticks they pick up from sheep. Several species of birds and other wild animals indirectly gain some protection from parasites through the regular treatment of sheep.

Sheep are also inoculated against various diseases. Lowland ewes are vaccinated against clostridial diseases about four weeks before lambing and protection is passed on to new born lambs for up to six weeks through the ewes' milk. At some time during the ensuing few weeks, lambs receive a multi-dose vaccine which

▶ Sheep are dipped or otherwise treated for external parasites or skin problems

▲ Worming is a necessary part of sheep management

protects them from as many as eight diseases for several more months.

Sheep are notorious for having bad feet. Lameness is one of the symptoms of Foot and Mouth Disease and in 2001 it was difficult for hill farmers, who don't have such close contact with their sheep, to identify possible infections. Sheep kept on stony ground wear their hooves down but those on lowland pastures tend to develop soft overgrown hooves and can suffer from lameness caused by bacteria living in the soil or bedding. Lowland shepherds have to pay regular attention to the feet of their flocks. Long grass can also cause sores between the cloven hooves, particularly in wet weather.

Any overgrown hoof must be pared away with a sharp knife or specially designed cutting tool, and treated. The principal causes of lameness are contagious bacterial infections known as '**foot rot**', which affects the hoof; and '**scald**' which affects the area between the two parts of the cloven hoof. Individual cases can be treated using antibiotic aerosol sprays but many shepherds routinely pass their flocks through a foot bath containing a diluted solution of formalin or zinc sulphate both as treatment and prevention.

A sheep kneeling down to graze is often an indication of it having sore front feet.

SHEPHERDS' TRADITIONS AND PEDIGREE BREEDS

The shepherd's year traditionally begins in autumn. At this time of year lambs are separated from their mothers. Young sheep are selected for breeding stock and the rest sold or put on better grazing to fatten. Breeding ewes are checked over, the condition of their teeth and udders being most important. Any not fully fit will be sold.

There are a number of sheep farmers who specialise in keeping pedigree sheep. Ram lambs bred from these can make good prices in the autumn sales. Suffolk and Texel are probably the most popular sires for early fast-growing lambs although some other continental breeds are also gaining in popularity. In the north of Britain rams from breeds such as the native Blackface and Cheviot, whose lambs are hardy enough to survive the rigours of the uplands, are much sought after. Across the country, shows are held in late summer often combined with a sale. It is common practice among farmers showing hill breeds of sheep to colour their wool in the belief it will help catch the judge's eye. Usually it is light brown or dark grey colouring but in the case of Hardwicks, a dark red pigment is favoured.

▲ The fleeces of breeding sheep destined for sale are sometimes coloured, for effect

In the Western Isles of Scotland, as well as Shetland, there is still a demand for wool from local breeds to make the traditional Fair Isle and Shetland knitwear and, of course, the renowned Scottish tweeds. Most famous is Harris tweed which carries its own iconic 'orb' trademark. This certifies that it has come from virgin wool and been dyed and spun in the Outer Hebrides before being hand woven and finished by the islanders in their own homes, where there are about 150 handlooms still in use.

SHEEP MILK

A few farmers in the UK have diversified into keeping sheep for milk production. The most popular is the East Friesian, a breed originating in Holland. British Milksheep and Lacaune are other dairy sheep breeds. Ewe's milk is very rich and in an 8 to 10 month lactation period a ewe

can produce 125 gallons (570 litres) or more. Ewes are milked twice a day with specially designed milking machines as they only have two teats whereas a cow has four. Their milk is used to make cream, yoghurt and artisan cheese.

Because sheep's milk has a much higher fat level than cows, about 40% less volume is needed to make a pound of cheese.

Dairy sheep require a high level of nutrition. The actual cheese-making is a complicated procedure which, by law, has to have very high standards of hygiene. It has a niche market attracting prices.

NOVELTY SHEEP

Sheep are sometimes kept for functional and decorative purposes, especially in parks surrounding stately homes. Their manner of grazing produces a short, even sward that gives a most attractive lawn-like appearance to the grounds. Breeds such as the Jacob with its double set of impressive horns and black and white markings can add an extra dimension to the landscape. A novelty breed appearing in the UK recently is the attractive Zwartbles sheep, originating from the Netherlands, black with a white blaze, white feet and a white tip to its tail, as well as the eye catching Valais Blacknose from Switzerland.

GLOSSARY

EWE A mature female sheep

RAM A mature entire male sheep

TUP A ram

TUPPED EWE One mated with a ram

TEASER A vasectomised entire ram

TEG, HOGG or HOGGET Sheep in its first year between January and its first shearing

SHEARLING Sheep between its first and second shearing

GIMMER, THEAVE, CHILVER Young female sheep between its first and second shearing which has not yet had a lamb

WETHER A castrated male sheep over two years old, often sold as mutton

YELD An older ewe that is not in lamb

TWO-TOOTH The age of a sheep is told by its incisor teeth. One with two permanent front teeth is approximately 18 months old

FULL MOUTH At four years a sheep will have a full mouth of permanent front teeth

BROKEN MOUTH Ewe which has missing or damaged teeth but is otherwise fit and able to survive where the living is easy

DRAFT EWES Older ewes, often 4-6-year-old hill ewes that can no longer withstand the harsh conditions but which can still be sold for breeding in the lowlands

CULL EWE A ewe which has reached the end of its productive life and is destined for slaughter

IN LAMB Pregnant

CADE LAMB Bottle fed

FAT LAMB A lamb ready for slaughter

STORE LAMB A lamb which needs more time before it is fit for slaughter

MUTTON Meat from a sheep over two years old

MULE A crossbred sheep popular in the north

KEEP SHEEP Sheep kept by another farmer on a temporary basis, often taken off the marshes or hills for the winter

SHEAR or CLIP Remove wool by cutting close to the skin

DAGG or CRUTCH Remove soiled wool from the hindquarters of a sheep

DRENCH Administer liquid medicine orally

DIP Immerse sheep in a chemical compound to eliminate sheep scab and other parasites including ticks, lice and blowfly. Now often replaced with pour-on or injectable insecticides

FOLD Move sheep over a small area at a time

FLUSH Increase food rations prior to mating or lambing

RADDLE Coloured paint or crayon put on a ram's chest to identify the ewes he has mated with

COUPED or CAST A sheep which has rolled onto its back and is unable to get up

FLY STRIKE Attack from flies that lay their eggs in the wool. These hatch into maggots which eat into the flesh

HEFT An unfenced area on open hillside grazed by a particular group of sheep

EAR TAG A permanent identifying metal or plastic tag clipped into the ear, carrying an electronic chip for traceability

EID Electronically Identified (ear tag)

SCAN An ultrasound scan used to detect pregnancy and the number of foetuses

FEED BLOCK Supplementary food provided for sheep in the form of a compressed block

LICK A food or mineral block used to supplement the diet which the sheep lick

CREEP FEEDER A feeding trough with narrow bars which allows lambs access to supplementary feed while denying larger sheep entry

Outdoor piglets are confined to their nursery to begin with to keep them safe

PIG FARMING

Pigs are descended from the European wild boar and were domesticated 9,000 years ago.

There are eleven native breeds of pigs in the UK and all are considered to be at risk of extinction. Many crossbreeds and hybrids, which have been selectively bred to be more prolific and quicker growing, are now used for commercial purposes. But there are breed enthusiasts keeping pedigree pigs who take pride in maintaining and showing native breeds. It is vital for the future of the industry that a nucleus of pure native breeds is preserved because their genes may have an important part to play in the future.

In the past, when nothing was ever wasted, a pig was the householder's waste disposal unit. Being omnivorous, pigs will eat anything: household and garden waste, by-products from brewing and cheese making and maybe even a chicken that had died. Most farm cottages had a sty in the garden, often built alongside the privy, in which a young pig would be installed to fatten through the summer when food was plentiful. Slaughtered in the autumn it was said that the only part which couldn't be used was its squeal. Most of the meat would be salted and smoked to preserve it through the winter.

In cider-making parts of the West Country, pigs would be turned into the orchards to clear up fallen apples and in Hampshire they would be turned out in the New Forest to eat acorns, a custom which is still practised to a lesser extent and known as **pannage**. In the 1900s when every village held an annual fete, 'bowling for the pig' always proved to be a popular money-spinner, the prize a live piglet, which sometimes needed to be transported home on the bus! Today the prize is more likely to be a joint of pork.

There are currently about 10,000 pig farmers in the UK.

Pig production is one of the few aspects of British farming that is not subsidised directly by the British government.

Consumer demand is for cuts of meat with little fat so careful selective breeding has

Aerial view of an outdoor pig breeding unit

engineered hybrid breeding stock that will produce plenty of young pigs that are long and lean. As these will not breed true to type, the original breeding stock has to be replaced every three or four years. An industry that relies on buying in hybrid breeding stock obviously requires a regular supply of healthy animals and there are farms that specialise in producing these.

Producers with contracts to supply supermarkets are ensured a market for their products, but they have to meet strict guidelines laid down by the buyers and are open to frequent inspections regarding the health and management of their stock. The onus is on the producer to guarantee a quality supply as and when it is required. Approval also has to be given before producers can qualify for the premium offered by being part of an Assured Scheme.

Our love of pork, bacon, ham, sausages and pork pies means that about 10 million pigs are slaughtered each year in Britain. The majority of British pig meat is sold fresh as joints with little going for processing. Of the 1.7 million tons of pig meat consumed in the UK annually, more than half is imported, the majority from the EU.

Surprisingly, the UK also exports pig produce, including offal and ears, China being one of the principal customers.

Pigs are highly intelligent, adaptable and social animals. Living naturally, a pig is omnivorous and will forage and root for food, eating a wide range of vegetables, fruit and roots. They are also carnivorous and will eat meat including carrion. Contrary to their reputation, pigs are clean animals but they do like wallowing in mud, often to keep cool in summer. They rely on their fat for insulation but are not able to sweat and can overheat in summer, even suffering from sunburn.

60% of farmed pigs are confined indoors while 40% are now kept outdoors.

There about 400,000 sows kept commercially for breeding. Young sows are known as '**gilts**' and are first mated when they are about 8 months old.

Pigs can only be kept on light land that is free draining – this is predominately found in arable areas on the eastern side of England.

OUTDOOR PIG FARMING

Outdoor pigs have become very much part of crop rotation, as the land benefits greatly from the straw and manure associated with outdoor units from pigs which are left on the same ground for one or two years. Sandy soil is low in nutrients and outdoor pigs kept in this way improve soil quality and make it possible for four consecutive years of crop-growing to follow. Although labour and feed costs are higher, and moving the whole unit to fresh ground every couple of years is a mammoth task, as well as being an expensive part of outdoor pig management, there is not the need to invest in expensive buildings. Outdoor production methods appear to be more acceptable to the consumer and most outdoor units supply the quality assured schemes operated by supermarkets. They all meet stringent rules imposed as part of this system of marketing.

The outdoor system is more complicated than indoors as batches of pigs are rotated round different parts of the field. Small groups of sows are kept together in paddocks fenced with two or three strands of electric wire; these fences do not need to be very high because pigs make no attempt to jump over them. They have access to large straw-bedded huts for shelter and have the space to forage in their environment and generally behave naturally. The pigs are fed pelleted food which is dispensed from a tractor-drawn trailer, either by pouring it into troughs or occasionally hurling large pellets out into the paddock. This keeps the pigs occupied by having to search for them all, although rooks, crows and seagulls scavenge the food and are at risk of carrying and spreading diseases which might affect pigs. Feed hoppers are also sometimes used. Water is supplied through individual drinkers or sometimes in large troughs big enough for the pigs to lie in. The area around these gets very muddy which the pigs enjoy wallowing in.

FARROWING

The gestation period of a pig is approximately three months, three weeks and three days. A commercial breeding sow will average 2.4 litters a year.

As a group of sows near the end of their pregnancies they are moved into paddocks with smaller individual huts known as 'arks'.

Thousands of pigs are now bred and reared outdoors

▲ Commercially bred outdoor piglets are weaned when they are about four weeks old

Each sow is free to choose which one she wants although arguments do occur when two want the same hut! When they have sorted out amongst themselves who will have which hut they proceed to make a nest out of the straw provided before giving birth, normally to 10-14 babies. Once she has farrowed (given birth) a low barrier is placed in front of the hut which she can step over but which confines her piglets inside for the first 2-3 weeks. Some sows can be quite aggressive in protecting their young so the stockman has to be very careful each time he goes to check on them inside their respective huts.

Breeding sows are kept outside in groups

The piglets are weaned at about 26-28 days and subsequently kept in weaner groups until they are 12-13 weeks old. They may either be kept in specialist weaner accommodation on the field and then moved into indoor finishing units or moved straight into permanent buildings. About 60% will be kept on straw, the remainder on slatted floors.

Less than 3% of pigs spend their entire lives outdoors; they are slower growing and will therefore need to be kept longer making them more costly to rear.

Fattened pigs are slaughtered for pork at about six months, when they weigh approximately 250lb (115kg) but are kept longer if the carcase is intended for processing, ie sausages etc.

There is a top limit to the size of pigs that can be handled in standard abattoirs and processing units.

Once their litters have been weaned, the group of sows will be moved to another paddock. After about five days they will come into oestrus (season) again and be served by one of the boars running with them. Sows are left in with the boars for about 10 weeks to make sure they get pregnant.

A small group of boars, maybe four, will be reared together and remain together for the rest of their lives. This way they establish a hierarchy (pecking order) and will rarely fight over the sows they are run with. Outdoor boars are seldom dangerous but those kept indoors can be quite vicious.

A commercial breeding sow will average 2.4 litters a year.

Although outdoor pigs have plenty to occupy them, they still like to chew on objects – behaviour that is, perhaps wrongly, attributed to boredom with intensively kept pigs indoors. Most outdoor pigs are kept in areas of the country where the soil often contains a liberal amount of stones or flints, which hold a certain attraction for pigs who will spend many hours chewing on them, rather like a human chewing gum. The reason for this behaviour isn't clear.

The outdoor system appears to be much more humane but is not without its challenges. Rearing costs are higher and wet weather can make pig welfare a major problem even on the lightest of land. In winter, because pigs dig up the ground, pens can become a sea of mud and only by building up the straw in huts to a higher level are the pigs able to find anywhere dry to lie. Prolonged spells of bitterly cold weather can freeze up the entire water systems meaning that water has to be carted to the paddocks and dispensed by hand. Strong winds can damage huts and a very dry spell can result in a lot of dust.

INTENSIVE INDOOR PIGS

Whilst rearing piglets intensively follows much the same pattern as for outdoor systems, there are times when indoor management can be easier, and even more humane, than outdoor units. Meal is fed in preference to pelleted food. Considerable numbers of pigs, kept in large fully-automated sheds, can be looked after by one skilled person.

The use of stalls, in which sows were permanently confined and tethered, was completely banned in Britain in 1999 but is still in use in some foreign countries.

Pigs relish wallowing in mud whenever the opportunity arises

The only permitted constraint of pigs at present is that sows may be kept confined in farrowing crates from a few days prior to giving birth until the litter is weaned. Solid floors are used for some designs, and slats for others which might be of plastic, cast iron, steel, coated mesh or concrete. Commercial sows have large litters and there is a high risk of tiny newborn piglets being trodden or laid on. The risk is minimised by providing them with space to move away from the sow and they will often choose to lie well out of danger under a heat lamp if one is provided in this area.

Farrowing crates also protect the safety of stockpersons, as sows are very large animals and can be protective of their new litter. Most intensively kept sows in the UK farrow in crates, but a few producers use indoor pen systems which do not confine the sow.

Once her piglets have been weaned, the sow is put back in a group and mated again and the cycle is repeated. Artificial insemination is often used, as well as ultrasound scanning to confirm pregnancy.

Young pigs kept intensively are divided into age groups and are housed unrestricted in sheds with either slatted floors or a strawed area with a dunging passageway. A pig has clean toilet habits and will not soil its bedding if it can avoid doing so. Group housing gives pigs more freedom to move and socialise but is open to problems with aggressive and bullying behaviour.

NOSE RINGS etc

Tail docking to prevent piglets nibbling one another's tails and teeth trimming were once a routine part of piglet management but can now only be carried out as a last resort when there is no alternative way of avoiding welfare issues. Castration is no longer a routine part of commercial pig production.

Adult pigs kept for breeding in outdoor units often have a ring or rings put in their noses to discourage them from digging up the ground. Sows are fitted with two or three small ones in the tops of their snouts while boars (like bulls) have one larger one put through the membrane dividing the nostrils. Although the single ring is not so effective against rootling in the ground as the smaller rings, it prevents any risk of injury during the pre-mating ritual involving the boar prodding the sow's body with his snout.

IDENTIFICATION

It is not a legal requirement to permanently identify pigs until they are 12 months old unless they are sent for slaughter, moved to any type of market or to a show or exhibition. An identifying ear tag inscribed 'GB' is required for any pigs exported from Britain to the EU or Northern Ireland.

Those intended for slaughter must be identified by means of a metal ear tag or have been double 'slap marked' which is a form of tattoo. This is done by using a metal plate with small pins on it which are then pressed on an ink pad and quickly slapped onto the animal's shoulders – one mark either side. A tattoo inside the ear is also acceptable. Plastic ear tags are used to identify breeding stock. A temporary paint mark is permitted if young pigs need to be moved between holdings.

By law, a license is required for pigs to be moved to other premises other than a slaughterhouse.

BIOSECURITY

Outbreaks of disease, and there are a number that both indoor and outdoor pigs are susceptible to, are always a high risk. Biosecurity is of great importance as the repercussions of any highly transmittable infectious disease are felt across the entire industry, not only financially but also in the form of pig movements within the country. Foreign exports of livestock and meat are also affected.

Pigs kept in fields attract wild birds which potentially pose a health risk, so it is more difficult to successfully contain an outbreak of disease in free range systems than intensive ones. Pest species are also a greater problem outdoors than indoors: straw-filled outdoor shelters provide a comfortable home for rats who share the bonanza of free food with flocks of jackdaws, crows, rooks and feral pigeons. They are joined by flocks of starlings whose numbers in winter are swelled with birds from the Continent which may be carrying diseases. In regions where fox numbers are not controlled, these too soon discover an easy living can be had from raiding farrowing huts and stealing young piglets. All these pests add significantly to the overall costs.

Swine Fever, the most infectious disease to affect pigs but which poses no threat to human health, rampaged across East Anglia in August 2000. Through a strict regime of slaughtering and biosecurity policies, it was successfully contained in the region. Even so, thousands of pigs were culled and hundreds of farms affected.

It was a major crisis for the pig industry and only months later, in early 2001 a routine inspection found signs of Foot and Mouth Disease in pigs at an Essex abattoir. It was subsequently believed that the highly infectious virus, which mainly affects cattle, pigs, sheep and goats, had already spread to 57 farms nationwide in the days prior to it being confirmed, causing further farming devastation.

African Swine Fever is a new potential threat which spreads very quickly and results in high mortality rates although it does not affect humans. There is no treatment or preventative treatment for pigs and 100% mortality can occur within ten days of infection. In 2019 there was a serious outbreak in China which swept across Asia. In the summer of 2020 some cases were identified in Germany following reports of it having been seen in wild boar on the Polish/ German border. Contingency plans are in place should it ever reach Britain. Preventing this devastating disease reaching our shores highlights just how important biosecurity measures are.

As in every aspect of animal husbandry medication is not given to pigs unnecessarily because it is expensive but, as with all other livestock, there are certain preventative treatments that are beneficial both financially and for the wellbeing of the animal. Whatever

The opportunity to scrounge free food attracts starlings to pig fields but they can be carriers of disease

drugs are used, there is a statutory requirement that detailed records are kept and withdrawal periods prior to slaughter adhered to.

Pig welfare has improved in recent years and even under intensive systems, the UK maintains a much higher standard than many other countries.

PET PIGS

Because of the high risk of spreading diseases such as Foot and Mouth or Swine Fever, all pigs kept as pets, even if only one, are subject to the same regulations as any herds of pigs.

Before purchase, a County Parish Holding Number (CPH) must identify the place the pig will be kept and it must be registered with the Animal and Plant Health Agency (APHA) as soon as the pig arrives on the new owner's premises. The animal must be legally identified, accurate records kept of all its movements and any veterinary treatment it receives.

Pigs cannot be moved anywhere without a licence and a 'walking licence' needs to be obtained from APHA if it is intended to take a pet pig for walks. To minimise the disease risk there are certain places that are 'out of bounds' for pet pigs, so an approved route needs to be agreed on.

The law also forbids the feeding of any waste food, kitchen scraps or food that has come from a domestic or commercial kitchen.

WILD BOAR

In the mid-1970s, a few farmers in southern England began importing wild boar from Eastern Europe to farm for meat. By 1994 there were around 40 farms keeping wild boar and by the year 2000 some 4,500 wild boar were being kept. Some escaped or were released in 1999 and a further illegal release of 60 occurred in 2004. Classified as feral, there are now several pockets of wild boar living across the south of England and they have also become established in Dumfries and Galloway. It is estimated there are between 2,500 and 3,000 living wild and their

▲ Wild boar were first bred in captivity for meat in the 1980s but since then escapees have become a serious pest in some areas

numbers are increasing rapidly. One particular area for concern is the Forest of Dean where in November 2018 the population was estimated to be more than 1,600. Wild boar are large animals which can cause a lot of damage to woodland, crops and gardens and there is a high risk of them spreading disease to domestic pigs. Under the Dangerous Wild Animals Act 1976 a licence is required to keep them. It is legal to shoot wild boar as a means of controlling numbers, as long as certain requirements are met. As yet, there is no close season although morally sows should not be killed when they have young.

GLOSSARY

BOAR Mature male pig

SOW Mature female pig

DRY SOW Not giving milk in the period between weaning and farrowing

GILT Young female pig that has not had a litter

SERVE Mate with

FARROW Give birth to

WEANER Young weaned pig up to approximately 12 weeks

GROWER Also known as a rearer or finisher. A pig over approximately 12 weeks until reaching slaughter weight

HYBRID Mix of breeds

AI Artificial Insemination

FMD Foot and Mouth Disease affecting cloven hoofed animals

Farmyard hens behaving naturally

POULTRY FARMING

INTRODUCTION

Chicken is the most popular meat in the UK, outselling beef, lamb and pork combined. An estimated one billion chickens are produced annually in Britain for the table, 42 million kept for egg production and over 8 million as breeding stock. Ducks, turkeys and geese amount to another 25 million birds.

The vast majority of chickens kept today are hybrids specifically bred for their purpose.

Hens for commercial egg production are usually brown in colour and those for meat production (called broiler chickens) are nearly always white.

Generally speaking, white feathered chickens with white ear lobes lay white eggs and those that

Hamburgh bantam, bantams are miniature versions of chicken

▲ Buff Cochin cockerel: a rare breed kept by poultry fanciers

have brown feathers and red ear lobes lay brown eggs. There are more than a hundred different breeds of chicken which vary greatly in size, the colour of their plumage and the colour of their eggs. Bantams are miniature versions of these breeds. There are poultry fanciers dedicated to preserving the native breeds once common across Britain before intensification took over and it is worth visiting a poultry show just to see the variety of poultry that are kept. It is now compulsory to register as a poultry keeper with the Animal and Plant Health Agency (APHA) if more than 50 birds are kept on the premises.

Poultry chicks can feed themselves as soon as they hatch. They are covered in fluff when they first hatch but their feathers develop very quickly. Once fully grown, they naturally moult once each year in late summer, shedding their old feathers and growing new ones, looking quite scruffy for a few weeks while this is happening. The combs of healthy birds are red although may appear paler in winter. Chicken don't sweat but in hot weather disperse heat through their combs; if they get excessively hot they pant.

POULTRY HEALTH

Stocking densities, management controls and many other factors are strictly regulated and inspected from time to time.

Over 90% of meat poultry farms are Red Tractor Assured meeting strict standards of animal welfare, safety, hygiene and traceability.

Freedom Foods (RSPCA approved) and organic farming organisations lay down their own sets of rules. Every poultry keeper has to be familiar with the regulations in place for his own operation and keep meticulous records. Biosecurity is of great importance in maintaining the health of poultry in the UK, particularly in winter. Some poultry meat, especially in the form of portions, is imported and, as with eggs, home-grown products have far higher standards than foreign imports in production, hygiene and welfare standards.

Avian flu is a disease of wild birds and most years there are outbreaks amongst poultry in the UK coinciding with the arrival of migratory birds. It is not of any danger to humans but is highly contagious among birds. Winter 2021-22 saw the worst recorded outbreak with 115 cases, necessitating the culling of millions of poultry. Avian flu is of particular threat to any poultry kept free-range as there is a high risk of them coming into contact with migratory birds.

In an area where avian flu has been confirmed, an order is put in place that free-range poultry must be confined indoors and not moved in an effort to contain the outbreak. This is very difficult to comply with because housing for any free-range system is not designed for this and of course to retain free-range status, hens cannot be confined indoors for longer than twelve weeks and the quarantine time period may well exceed this. There is a high risk that the health and welfare of poultry will be compromised when restrictions are imposed.

Migratory birds in winter such as starlings are often responsible for the spread of Avian Flu

Although feeding, lighting and heating may be automated, as with all livestock, the ultimate results are down to the quality of the person who is responsible for looking after them. Observation, attention to detail, conscientiousness and experience not only add to the profit but also greatly to the birds' wellbeing.

HATCHING AND REARING

All birds hatch from eggs and this in itself is a complicated procedure.

Obviously parent stock is needed, but not in equal numbers in terms of sex because one male bird will mate with several females. Breeding birds must be kept in conditions where this act can comfortably take place, namely a solid-floored area, usually inside large sheds with automated feeders, drinkers, lighting and ventilation systems. Plenty of nest boxes need to be made available so that eggs are laid in a clean and safe environment.

These are collected regularly and then checked. Dirty ones are either dry cleaned or washed in a sanitising fluid. The eggs are often fumigated as well before being stored in a cool place prior to being dispatched to hatcheries.

Here they are checked again and put into trays, pointed ends down. The trays are then slid into trolleys and fumigated before being stored at a temperature of about 55°F (13°C) for up to a week. The embryo inside the egg will not begin to develop at this temperature. It is only after the trolleys of eggs are wheeled into '**setters**', machines which provide a controlled environment, that development starts to take place. Inside the setter, the temperature is kept fractionally below 100°F (37.6°C), the air is circulated, the trays are regularly tilted from one side to another, and a certain level of humidity is maintained inside the machine. All these functions are controlled automatically.

Chicks hatch in 21 days and ducks, geese and turkeys take about 28 days.

From time to time a sample of eggs will be passed over a bright light, known as '**candling**', so that development of the chicks inside can be monitored and this also shows up any eggs which are 'clear' which means infertile and these are removed. A few days before the chicks are due to hatch, the eggs are taken out of the setters and transferred to a '**hatcher**'.

The eggs are then placed on their sides in chick-proof trays. The temperature inside the hatcher is marginally lower and humidity slightly higher than in the setter. Trays of eggs are not tilted once they are inside a hatcher.

These last few days inside an egg are critical for a chick as it has to perform an amazing feat in which it rotates to have its head under one of its tiny wings and uses a small 'tooth' on the top of its beak to chip right the way round the shell about two thirds of the way up from the pointed end. It then needs the strength to force the lid open and scramble out of its prison, a process which takes many hours.

At all stages of the embryo's incubation, humidity plays an important role, for there needs to be an air sac in the top of the egg to allow the chick to manoeuvre and breathe during hatching. If there has not been enough moisture, the chick will be small and under developed, if too much it will have grown too big and probably be deformed. When the chick eventually struggles free it is very wet and weak but given a few hours more inside the warmth of the hatcher it will soon gain in strength and change into the familiar fluffy chick or duckling. Because of this essential drying off period, freshly hatched chicks are known as 'day olds'.

Cleanliness of the eggs and equipment is vital throughout because the moist warm environment which is needed to hatch eggs also provides ideal conditions for bacteria and other nasty 'bugs' to rapidly multiply. Many of these can easily penetrate the shell and infect the chick hatching inside or gain entry into its body through contact with its wet navel immediately after it has hatched.

SEXING THE CHICKS

Chicks can be sexed when they are day olds: male chicks can be a different colour to females which makes sexing easy; experts can tell the difference by carefully inspecting the rear end of each chick; and sometimes it is possible to tell the difference by the length of the tiny wing feathers. If they've not been sexed they are sold as '**as hatched**'. For table poultry, both sexes are

▼ Newly hatched broiler chicks. All poultry chicks can feed themselves as soon as they hatch

reared but obviously only females are retained for egg laying. Unwanted day old male chicks are usually gassed or humanely killed by some other method and used as food for predator species such as birds of prey or snakes kept as pets, or in wildlife centres and zoos. Breeding flocks require both sexes but only at a ratio of one male for between four and eight females.

TRANSPORTING DAY OLDS

Day olds are transported in cardboard or plastic chick boxes, often for long distances which causes them no harm. These boxes are specially designed to hold a fixed number of chicks and are lined with either wood wool or shredded newspaper. Filled to capacity they retain the chicks' own body heat, keeping them warm enough, while providing adequate draught free ventilation. Because day old chicks still have some unabsorbed egg yolk inside them (the part of the egg which provided their nutrition before they hatched) they are able to survive for many hours, even a few days, in transit without food or water,

▲ The tips of chickens' beaks are trimmed to prevent them hurting each other when kept in confined spaces

although obviously the sooner these are provided, the better. Inevitably a few chicks die between the fifth and seventh day. These are known as '**starve outs**' and are weak chicks that, for one reason or another, have failed to eat or drink. Until this age they will have been able to survive on the remains of the egg yolk inside them.

Before a chick is a week old it is a normal part of management for those destined for commercial egg production ie: layers and those kept free range, to have the pointed tip of the top beak trimmed which is carried out using an infra-red beam. Only a little is removed and it does not grow back. It is a natural instinct for a bird to peck at things including each other; blunting the beak prevents them from damaging their companions or pulling out their feathers, which can lead to cannibalism, for the rest of their lives. Those destined for meat (broilers) don't usually have their beaks trimmed because they reach slaughter weight at approximately 5-6 weeks of age – basically they are too young to develop bad habits. Ducklings and goslings are not beak trimmed.

EARLY WEEKS

The majority of chicken, ducks and turkeys spend the first few weeks of their lives in large environmentally controlled deep litter sheds, just as their parents did. They are kept warm by specially designed radiant gas heaters called '**brooders**' which they settle beneath when they get cold. Alternatively some rearing houses use electric heaters or are space heated to the necessary temperature. A temperature of 35°C (95°F) is needed for the first few days. This is thermostatically controlled and gradually reduced as the chicks grow older. Natural light is excluded from within the shed and artificial light is provided as required on a time switch.

Vaccination of laying and breeding birds is carried out when the chicks are a few days old, often administered in the drinking water, giving them protection against certain diseases for life.

Bedding on the floor is usually either wood shavings or chopped straw or a mixture of the two; it is very important for the young bird's health and welfare that it is kept dry. Poor air flow can result in high humidity within the shed which in turn can lead to a build-up of ammonia from damp compacted litter; as can badly adjusted drinkers. Under the right conditions a chemical action takes place between the bird's droppings and the litter which works it into a fine, dry composition.

Poultry feed is manufactured in three basic forms: a meal; crumbs (which are usually fed to young chicks); and pellets of varying sizes according to the size of the chick. As the young birds grow, the composition of their food rations is altered to take into account their changing nutritional needs. Food conversion rates, the equation relating to weight gain or eggs produced from the amount of food consumed, is continually improved through selective breeding. Genetic selection has made huge changes to the poultry industry since intensification (or factory farming as it used to be called) evolved in the 1960s. The reproduction cycle of poultry is comparatively short, ie 3-4 weeks for an egg to hatch and about six months to maturity but development of a strain to lay even more eggs or grow faster is ongoing. Intensive research into nutrition as well as breeding and disease has produced hybrids that consistently meet with the high standards required.

Light patterns play a very important part in the bird's growth and maturity rates and windowless houses with artificial lighting mean that adjustments can be made accordingly. It is only after the first few weeks that rearing methods radically change depending for which purpose the birds are destined.

EGG PRODUCTION

Approximately 42 million hens are kept in the UK for egg production making the country nearly 90% self-sufficient; the balance is made up with imported eggs. A few home-produced eggs are exported. Public demand in this country is for brown eggs and less than 1% produced are white, which usually go for processing.

13 billion eggs are eaten each year in the UK, an average per person of nearly 200 in one form or another.

Hundreds of thousands of eggs are packed each day, creating the opportunity for full and part-time jobs for local people living in rural locations.

British eggs are stamped with the British lion symbol and the use-by date, which is three weeks from when they were laid, although they can be safely kept for some time after that in a refrigerator. Compulsory regular tests for salmonella are conducted although producers

▲ British eggs are stamped with the lion logo

are exempt from these if fewer than 350 hens are kept and the eggs sold directly to the consumer, most often through farm gate sales. The British Lion symbol also means that the laying hens have been vaccinated against salmonella.

There are three different systems of keeping laying hens in the UK – free-range, enriched cage, and barn.

The issue of animal welfare has become of greater importance in recent years and as a result more than half of eggs sold now come from free-range hens. Some are produced using the barn

system. The use of cages is diminishing and it has been proposed that they be banned after 2025. There is a government code of practice in place on how laying hens are kept and higher standards have to be met for the Red Tractor and RSPCA Assurance Schemes.

Whichever system is going to be used, flocks of hens kept for commercial egg production are usually reared in sheds in a similar way to broilers from day old until 16 weeks. Sometimes these are partly slatted and occasionally the birds may have been raised in wire cages.

Laying hens are only kept until they are approximately 16 months old. During this time, they will have laid about 300 eggs.

As layers' productivity declines, they are replaced. Some are saved from slaughter by the British Hen Welfare Trust which re-home intensively kept hens that are still capable of laying plenty more eggs. They may appear to be a bit tatty when they arrive but they very quickly grow new feathers.

Nutrition is extremely important for both layers and table birds, to ensure good growth and production and also general health. A bird's nutritional needs alter at different stages in its life so the correct balance of vitamins, minerals and protein needs to be adjusted throughout to maintain body condition and maximum food conversion rates.

Light stimulates growth and also egg production. Whichever system laying hens are kept under, artificial light is used to replicate the equivalent of 14-16 hours of daylight.

There are two groups of hybrid laying hens: lightweight ones which are usually white in colour and lay white eggs; and heavier ones which are predominately brown and lay brown eggs. There is no difference in the nutritional

◀ Small producers often sell their eggs by the roadside

◀ Domestic breeds of chicken are descended from wild Jungle fowl

FREE-RANGE SYSTEM

Free-range laying hens arrive on farms when they are about 16 weeks old, shortly before they begin to lay. They are generally predominately brown in colour and lay brown eggs. They have the tip of their top beak trimmed when they are very young as there is still the risk that, even though they are kept free-range, they might feather peck.

Vaccination is given against several diseases including salmonella. This is particularly important for free-range hens because, unlike chicken in laying cages, free-range hens are exposed to possible diseases through direct contact with their own excreta and from infections transmitted by wild birds. Bird flu is transmitted by wild birds, with an increased risk at migratory times, so an influx of starlings from the Continent might well cause outbreaks. When avian flu is identified in poultry, free-range poultry must by law be confined under cover for 12 weeks, which may well be extended should further outbreaks occur.

Other pests and diseases which can affect poultry are more difficult to prevent and treat because they live in the soil which is impossible to disinfect thoroughly. Medication for poultry is often administered in the drinking water, but when it is raining, free-range chicken can find an alternative water source outside thus reducing their intake of medicine.

Free-range birds are kept in various sized flocks. Some may be very small while large enterprises may house thousands of free-range birds in big sheds or barns, similar to those used for intensively kept layers, but from which they have outside access.

Once outside, the free-range hens are confined to grass paddocks with high wire netting fences to keep them in and electric fences to help

quality of either brown- or white-shelled eggs. Larger brown hens cost more to feed but when they have reached the end of their productive lives, the carcase value is marginally better and there is greater demand for brown eggs.

Cockerels are only ever kept with hens for breeding purposes; they are never put with hens producing eggs for human consumption.

Food consumption and labour require–ments are higher for free-range poultry and, on average, egg production and quality is lower. The cost of producing free-range eggs is about double that of hens kept indoors and even more expensive if the birds are subject to strict organic standards.

The number of laying hens kept free-range is increasing as consumers are becoming more aware of welfare issues and are prepared to pay premium prices. Many of the major retailers no longer sell eggs from caged birds and a few supermarkets now only stock free-range eggs sourced only from UK farms.

▲ Free-range layers: but they only like to go outside when the weather is clement

keep them safe from predation. There are many regulations regarding their welfare including a maximum stocking density of 2,500 birds per hectare. The RSPCA Assured Scheme sets even higher standards and under Soil Association standards for organic egg production, the standards are even higher with the flock size restricted to a maximum of 2,000 birds kept at a stocking rate of 1,000 birds per hectare.

Whatever size their accommodation, the food of free-range hens is administered indoors, either in tube feeders which are filled daily or in automated chain-supplied troughs, and their water is from nipple drinkers. Most of the floor space is slatted with a droppings collection pit beneath; the shed is also equipped with plenty of perches, a dust bathing area and a plentiful number of nest boxes. These are often lined with 'astroturf' and designed so that the eggs roll away. The eggs are collected regularly either by hand, or by conveyor belts in the largest sheds. Some systems are designed so that the nest boxes automatically close at night by slowly tilting at a set time and are opened again early in the morning. This prevents hens from sleeping in them and fouling the nest box and it also empties out any dry dirt. It is very important that conditions are kept clean as dirty eggs have to be discarded.

▶ A broody hen will sit on a clutch of eggs until they hatch

OUTDOOR ACCESS

When free-range pullets first arrive at a laying unit they will be kept shut inside for a few days to get them acclimatised to their new surroundings. Because they have been reared intensively in sheds, they are not used to green grass, wind and rain, wild birds and vehicles and are very tentative about venturing outside through the pop holes when they are first allowed out. They are allowed access outdoors only during the hours of daylight.

Hundreds of birds regularly going in and out of the shed can quickly make the entrances very wet and muddy. Often there is a covered veranda area over the access pop holes and a mixture of sand and gravel or a mesh is used in front of them. This allows the hens to have some shelter without going inside and also helps to keep the interior cleaner and drier.

Conditions inside the building that house free-range hens are not a lot different to birds kept intensively under the barn system.

Hens dislike going outside in heavy rain or snow, in which case they become tightly packed inside.

Laying hens kept organically have more space allocated to them. Even given the option to get away from their companions, chicken don't appear to mind that much if they're crowded together. The open entrances, even though small, allow draughts, and the largest sheds provide most comfort to the birds because of their accumulated body heat.

Keeping free-range chicken is very labour intensive. Frequent egg collections, especially in the smaller non-automated sheds, is time-consuming but very necessary. Predation is a hazard faced by free-range hens, not only from foxes but also badgers, mink, large birds of prey, stoats and dogs. Free-range chicken naturally settle down indoors for the night but as it is not possible to drive hens, they can only be shut inside when they choose to go bed when it's getting dark (which is very late in summer) and have to be let out again early in the morning. If this is not done they are at high risk of falling victim to foxes who kill by reflex and may account for a hundred or more deaths in one night. A determined fox is quite capable of negotiating the protective high wire netting and electrified fencing.

A free-range chicken's life might not always be as idyllic as it seems.

BARN SYSTEM

Laying hens are also kept intensively in barn, perchery or occasionally deep litter systems. They have no access outside but although kept at a high density they are free to move around inside the large buildings and, to some extent, behave naturally. Perches are provided for roosting as well as material to dustbathe and forage in and tiers of nest boxes.

Poultry kept indoors can be given ideal conditions with regards to temperature, lighting and availability of food and water. Any medication given in the water supply is easy to administer.

Lighting is limited to about nine hours a day for the first month after which it is increased to stimulate the hens to lay. If they are given too much light too soon, they quickly come in to lay but produce small eggs which they will probably do for the rest of their lives. By waiting until the hens are about 20 weeks old, having gradually increased the light to 16 hours a day, they can be expected to produce plenty of good quality eggs.

Hens normally reach full lay at 20 to 22 weeks of age and peak at about 24 weeks although the best quality eggs will be laid when the hens are about 32 weeks.

▲ Layers kept in the barn system

CAGE SYSTEM

Pullets leave rearing units when they are close to laying. Small battery cages, housing approximately ten hens, have been banned in the UK since 2012 and replaced with colony systems by which 40-80 hens are housed in much larger cages in three or four tiers. These are installed in large sheds which are windowless but very well ventilated. These cage colonies have a high standard of welfare, curtained nest boxes, perches and an area where the birds can scratch enabling them to exhibit their natural behaviour. Although the hens are confined in a relatively small area this is an improved way of keeping caged laying birds than previously.

Because they are kept on weldmesh wire floors they do not come into contact with their droppings as these fall through onto a revolving belt which carries the excrement outside into storage pits. This can be spread straight onto the land. Because the hens have no direct contact with any excreta, they are cleaner and are at less risk of contracting diseases, many of which are passed from bird to bird through contact with contaminated droppings. The disease risk factor in chicken kept in laying cages is low. Providing

there is adequate ventilation, respiratory ailments are not common. If any problems are encountered it is normally due to the weather – either damp fogs or exceptionally hot oppressive days when the air temperature outside is no cooler than that inside. Even so, chickens are remarkably resilient birds and can cope with most things. Very cold weather is not a concern because body heat given off from the birds themselves ensures that the shed is always warm inside.

A unit of 70,000 layers may well be producing more than 50,000 eggs a day.

Vaccination for some diseases providing lifetime immunity is carried out when the birds are very young.

Food is dispensed automatically. Often a coarse meal is fed so that it keeps the hens occupied longer. Egg yolk colour is determined by the food so maize or grass meal is often included in the rations to ensure a rich colour. Water is provided through nipple drinkers.

When they are laid, eggs roll out of the front of the cages, away from the hens, onto a belt which prevents them from getting damaged or dirty. This belt automatically conveys them from the laying shed to the egg packing department.

▲ Commercial egg packing unit

Several full or part time workers are employed to pack the eggs.

Apart from regular checks to make sure that everything is working properly, each cage has to be inspected thoroughly every day. If a chicken has died or looks sick it is removed immediately. Profit margins are so tight that it is vital there are no hitches in production.

When a flock of layers needs replacing, the building and all the equipment is thoroughly cleaned and disinfected before the new batch of birds arrive.

Fewer than half of British eggs now come from caged hens and while their welfare has been improved, a complete ban on their use is proposed for 2025.

It may not appear to be a very happy life for hens kept in cages but they display few signs of stress and good results would not be obtained if the hens were under pressure. It doesn't take much of an upset to put hens off lay. There is little competition for food and water, lower risk of disease and no threat from predators. In whatever conditions chickens are kept, a hierarchy always exists. The fewer birds that are kept in a group, the less bullying there is likely to be.

EGG HANDLING

On reaching the packing room, each egg is passed over a bright light to check there are no blood spots inside or that the shell isn't cracked. They then continue over a grader where they are sorted by weight into different sizes. Any dirty eggs are removed and the rest packed into cartons moulded from recycled paper pulp fibre or plastic, ready for dispatch. These first quality ones go directly to supermarkets or are sent to wholesalers in trays which usually hold 30 eggs in each. Dirty eggs need to be washed in a sanitising fluid or dry cleaned and cannot be sold for consumption in the shell. Instead they will be sent to processors and end up being used by bakeries and food manufacturers.

TABLE CHICKEN

Broiler chicken (ie those for eating) which are raised intensively grow incredibly quickly and are ready for slaughter from six weeks onwards, depending on the weight required and the conditions they are kept under.

About 20 million broiler chicken are killed every week of which 20% will have been reared in the east of England where the industry is concentrated.

Very few table chicken are reared on free-range or organic systems which require outdoor access for part of their lives and a minimum slaughter age of 81 days for the latter. Kept under free-range or organic conditions, broilers take nearly twice as long to attain killing weight, making the feed, management, and labour costs incurred extremely high; few customers are prepared to pay for this.

Almost all chicken destined for the table are reared intensively in large sheds. Broiler chicks arrive on site in plastic chick boxes when they are one day old, directly from specialist hatcheries.

Broiler chicken are bred to be white feathered as traces of dark feathers are deemed to look unsightly when the bird is prepared for the table.

Free range organic broiler chickens: they are reared for a minimum of 81 days

Only rarely does a coloured one appear, a throwback to some distant ancestor from which the modern, fast growing, well-fleshed strains have been developed. Sometimes the chicks will have been sexed but generally they arrive 'as hatched'. Heat is thermostatically controlled and they always have light. Ventilation is either automatic or controlled manually by the stockman. Depending on the size of the sheds, up to 45,000 chicks may be put in each one.

To ensure the chicks find food and water quickly, vital for their wellbeing, corrugated paper may be laid on top of the litter for the first few days. Crumbs of food are sprinkled on this and extra water provided in flat dishes.

After this the chicks will have gained strength and quickly found their food which is supplied automatically in a trough which encircles the shed. They will also have discovered water in nipple drinkers that they have to peck at to get a drink. It is very important that the litter is kept dry and with this type of drinker, there is no spillage.

Broiler chicks are not normally beak trimmed or have any other devices fitted in their beaks to stop them feather pecking for it is not generally a problem – they are slaughtered at 5-6 weeks, before they develop bad habits.

Antibiotics are used only if there is a serious outbreak of disease requiring treatment but never on a routine basis. Over the last seven years their use in the poultry meat sector has been reduced by more than 80%. There are very strict standards in force in Britain regarding medication and there is a statutory withdrawal period prior to killing, ensuring there is no possibility of residues remaining in the meat.

Unlike some countries, artificial growth promoters in broiler chicken are banned in the UK.

A broiler will reach 4lb (1.8kg) live body weight (the minimum acceptable size) in about 38 to 40 days. The average weight is 2.5kg. Young chicks when they are first put in the sheds have plenty of space and it is only during the last few days that they appear to be seriously overcrowded although there is legislation regarding the amount of space provided.

Many poultry units adopt an 'all in, all out' policy in their sheds. When contracts demand larger birds, a batch is reduced by selection. About one third of the largest will be taken out allowing more space for the ones that are left to grow bigger. This may be repeated 2 or 3 times until the remaining chicken are about 52 days old and weigh 6.25lb (2.8kg) the maximum size required to sell.

Poultry being sent for slaughter are usually caught in the dark to minimise stress. Although there are now machines which catch broiler chicken by a gentle sweeping action, most of them are still caught by hand. Normally a gang of four or five people begin work very early in the morning. Modern handling facilities mean that the crates they are put in for transportation can be taken inside the shed. With lights dimmed, the birds can be handled with minimum disturbance and stress and the modules loaded immediately onto a waiting lorry using a small fork-lift.

After the shed is emptied it is thoroughly cleaned, disinfected and fumigated between batches. As with all livestock, hygiene is paramount. The litter is either used as a fertiliser on the land or as fuel in the new generation of environmentally friendly biomass units or power stations where it is burned to produce steam which in turn powers turbines to generate green energy. The ash residue is then used as fertiliser.

Once the shed has dried out it is then prepared for the next arrival; the whole process usually takes about a week.

Some bigger companies employ relief staff so those caring for the poultry can take a day off a week. The routine for smaller concerns is that the stockman works every day caring for a batch of chicks until they are gone, maybe for six to eight weeks. He or she then has several days off before the next batch arrives.

WELFARE

Very young chicks need a lot of attention. Even when they get bigger, the person caring for them has to be on call 24 hours a day, never going far from the site in case there is a breakdown of equipment or some other emergency.

One person may be expected to manage up to 150,000 broilers at any one time and it is a big responsibility.

Apart from the previously mentioned losses occurring in the first week, deaths are rarely due to disease or poor stockmanship. They are most frequently due to the incredible growth-rate achieved from selective breeding and specialised food rations. Broiler chicken have been developed over the years to satisfy the consumer who wants the plumpest chickens for the least amount of money. If these aren't supplied by competitive broiler units in Britain then they will be imported from abroad where welfare,

Modern unit with green poultry sheds and bulk food storage bins

▲ Broiler chicken approaching the age they are slaughtered

health and hygiene standards are unlikely to be as high as they are in this country.

To meet this demand for cheap meat, legislation is in place to make the mass production of broilers in the UK as humane as possible at every stage although obviously it is far from ideal.

TURKEYS

All turkeys originate from the black wild turkey from North America and have no association with the country with which they share their name.

Research and selective breeding have developed a fast-growing, reasonably priced table bird which has become popular at other times of the year besides Christmas.

15 million or so turkeys are produced annually for the table, 10 million of which are normally sold for the Christmas trade.

Female (hen) turkeys are more compact and do not reach the proportions of the much larger males (stags). Because of selective breeding over the years a huge range of sizes have become available. Mini turkeys reach approximately 8lbs (3.5kg) at about 12 weeks of age, but the most popular choice are hen birds weighing between 10 and 15lb (4.5 to 7kg) when they are 20 or so weeks old. Stags can be grown on for several more weeks and are marketed at 18 to 40lb (8kg to 18kg) but can reach maximum weights of 45 to 50lb (20 to 23kg). These giants are cut up and used for processing. Turkey 'crowns' have become increasingly popular with British cooks. These consist of the whole breast on the bone minus the legs, thighs and wings which are sent for processing.

Turkeys raised specifically for the Christmas trade are usually killed between 5-10 December and left to hang in chilled conditions.

The name Bernard Matthews is synonymous with turkeys. It was he who, in the 1950s, pioneered the development of turkeys for the table. From very humble beginnings in Norfolk, the company now employs more than 2,000 people rearing and processing more than 7 million turkeys a year. 40% of all turkeys are reared in the East of England.

This maturing greatly improves the flavour. Some commercial turkeys reared for the table are kept outdoors or in open-sided 'pole barns' but most are reared intensively in a similar way to broiler chicken. The majority are hybrids which are white in colour and have been bred to have a high proportion of breast meat. Besides being sold fresh for the Christmas market, some are frozen and a small number are sent for processing.

A few producers specialise in old traditional breeds such as the Norfolk Black and Broad Breasted Bronze breeds, which are usually reared outdoors. These have black plumage, are slower growing and less compact than hybrids and are sold fresh as free-range. Being reared outdoors puts them at extra risk of diseases transmitted by migratory wild birds. Outbreaks of avian flu in early December 2020 resulted in tens of thousands of turkeys having to be culled only a few days before they would have been slaughtered for the Christmas market.

Difficulties mating

The reason turkeys are costlier to produce than chicken is not their inability to grow as quickly but the prolificacy of the breeding stock. Because of their disproportionate body size, modern turkeys bred for the table are generally unable to mate naturally so fresh semen has to be collected from the stags and used to

Broad Breasted Bronze Turkey

artificially inseminate the hens. This is carried out once a week during the laying season and is obviously a very labour intensive and time-consuming chore.

Breeding stock are usually housed in 'pole' barns which have open sides covered with small mesh wire netting to exclude pests such as rats and birds and are littered with straw. Stags and hens are kept separately and the laying season extends from April to August. A variable regime of artificial lighting stimulates, maintains and extends egg production. This is used to bring the hen turkeys into lay a little sooner than they would naturally have done. Nest boxes are provided at ground level and eggs are collected at frequent intervals to avoid damage and ensure they are as clean as possible.

Most producers achieve up to 100 turkey eggs from each hen during the 18 week laying period.

Some of the bigger companies who require birds for year-round processing extend egg production a further month and obtain about 120 eggs from their stock. It is more economic to replace breeding stock each year than to over-winter them. Sometimes hens are kept for a second year but they do not lay so many eggs.

Day old chicks, which have often been sexed, arrive from specialist hatcheries and are reared like broiler chicken in environmentally controlled sheds usually on wood shavings. After a few weeks, those destined for rearing in 'pole' barns or under a free-range system will be transferred. Occasionally young turkeys are purchased from a rearing unit when they are four weeks old and no longer require supplementary heat. These are known as poults.

Sometimes turkey chicks are beak trimmed when they are a few days old or kept in subdued lighting to avoid feather pecking. Preventative drugs are sometimes included in the food rations for the first few weeks as a precaution against disease. The risk of leg weakness, once a common problem with commercial turkeys, has now been greatly reduced through improved diet and selective breeding.

A fully automated environment makes it is possible for one skilled man to rear tens of thousands of turkeys but a very high standard of stockmanship is needed to avoid problems.

GEESE

Goose is not in great demand in the UK so consequently little research and genetic improvement has been done. For centuries it was the most favoured bird in Britain for celebrating special occasions. It was the regular choice of many families at Christmas until the 1960s when turkey began to take over as favourite. Goose however is regaining some of its previous popularity as a traditional Christmas dinner.

Geese reared for the table are white hybrids descended from the wild greylag goose. About 250,000 are produced for the Christmas trade, many of which are reared outdoors in grass paddocks. Besides their normal food rations geese will also graze grass when given the opportunity. Demand is for birds weighing between 3.5kg and 6.5kg oven ready. Although they grow quickly and can be ready for table when about 12 weeks of age, most are kept until they are about 24 weeks old. The most stringent organic body, the Soil Association, stipulate a maximum outdoor stocking rate of 600 geese per hectare and a minimum slaughter age of 140 days.

While young birds fatten relatively quickly, goose meat is still expensive to buy, due to the cost of keeping the parent stock and low egg production. The females lay a limited number of eggs during spring and summer, only producing between 30 and 80 eggs during this period. One male (gander) is needed for four or five hens. They need to be put together at least two months before mating begins in the spring but once bonded they can be kept as a 'set' for several years within a larger group.

Geese are cleaner to keep than ducks and are relatively disease-free.

Goose fat has become very popular for roasting potatoes and the feathers and down can be used for filling pillows and duvets. In spring, goose eggs can sometimes be found offered for sale at farm shops and markets.

DUCKS

Ducks, as with all commercial poultry in the UK, have been the subject of selective breeding which has produced a placid, white feathered, fast-growing table bird and prolific breeding stock. Pekin hybrid ducks are the preferred breed for commercial meat production and Gressingham duck, evolved from crossing wild mallard with Pekins, account for more than half of table ducks produced each year. About 15 million duck are reared annually, mostly for the restaurant trade. Although they are good layers there is very little demand for ducks' eggs to eat. They are rich, but there is a recognised risk of salmonella transmission so cleanliness is essential at all times for egg production, whether for human consumption or for hatching.

The preferred way of keeping ducks for breeding is in controlled-environment, intensive housing similar to chicken. Ducks are known for their love of water so a separate slatted area is provided where they are watered, so their bedding keeps dry.

Breeding ducks do not need swimming water to mate but a plentiful supply of fresh cool drinking water is a necessity. For breeding purposes one male (drake) needs to be kept for every eight females.

About 90% of table ducks are reared in East Anglia, the majority intensively indoors in sheds

Geese reared outdoors for the table

on chopped straw or weld mesh. Because of their messy habits, they may be reared on weld mesh for the first four weeks and then transferred onto straw to finish. Ducklings grow rapidly and at 7 to 10 weeks old weigh 4.5lb to 7.5lb (2kg to 3.5kg).

Free-range ducks spend the first three to four weeks of their lives being reared under similar conditions before being allowed access outdoors from the shed.

The light sandy soil in parts of East Anglia is ideal for rearing free-range ducks out of doors during the warmer months. Put out when they are about three weeks old, by which time their feathers are well developed, they only require rudimentary shelter because fluff and later their feathers are naturally oily and in the summer months give sufficient protection from the weather.

The ducklings are put out in groups of about 200 in well-grassed runs at a specified maximum stocking density of no more than 2,000 per acre (5,000 per hectare). Organic standards however specify a stocking rate of no more than 2,000 per hectare.

The ducks are fenced in with low mesh fencing; this is all that is needed to keep them in as they cannot fly.

Additional electric fencing may also be used as a precaution against predation. Outdoor ducks are very vulnerable to attack from predators, particularly foxes, which can cause serious losses. Younger ducklings are also at risk from rats and marauding black-backed gulls. The pens must be moved onto fresh ground between batches to avoid a build-up of disease in the soil.

As with free-range chicken, production costs are high and management can be very difficult at times. Economic success depends on the consumer's willingness to pay a higher price for duck that have been reared outside.

◀ Ducks destined for the table are often reared outside in the summer; they do not require shelter or a pond but they do need a plentiful supply of drinking water

QUAIL

Diminutive quail are the only game bird reared for meat and their eggs were once a popular delicacy for the rich. Today quail are still kept commercially to cater for the niche market. They are reared in a similar controlled environment as broiler chicken and are ready for table at about 40 days old when they weigh approximately 7ozs (200 grams). They are susceptible to respiratory diseases so require a very high standard of management.

Quail mature quickly and will come into lay at approximately 10 weeks of age. A ratio of one male to five females is kept for breeding in a flock system. Hens lay about 200 eggs during the course of a year. Fertile eggs are not required for human consumption so quail kept for egg production do not have males kept with them.

GLOSSARY

BARN/ PERCHERY Large enclosed intensive shed system for laying hens equipped with perches, nest boxes and dust bathing area.

DEEP LITTER Large enclosed shed system where poultry are kept intensively on a chopped straw or wood shaving littered floor. Used for breeding stock, rearing poultry, meat production and also occasionally for laying hens.

FREE-RANGE System of keeping laying hens which allows them limited access to grass paddocks. Also sometimes used to rear broiler chicken, ducks, geese and turkeys.

CAGES A system by which groups of laying hens are kept in wire mesh cages. With this system hens are housed in big cages inside large, environmentally controlled, windowless sheds. The cages are designed in long three tiered rows. Food and water is supplied automatically and the nest box floors are slightly sloped enabling the eggs to roll out. Small battery cages were banned in the UK in 2012. The larger enriched laying cages which replaced them allow more space per bird and provide perches, nest boxes and dust bathing facilities.

EGG INCUBATION The time it takes for a chick to hatch from an egg.
Quail 18 days.
Chicken 21 days
Partridge 23 days
Pheasant 24 days
Duck 28 days
Goose 30 days
Turkey 28 days

CANDLING A bright light is shone through an egg making it possible to detect cracks in the shell, blood spots or development of the chick within.

CLUTCH A nest of eggs

BROOD A group of young chicks

INCUBATOR Equipment for keeping eggs or chicks in a warm space

DAY OLD A newly hatched chick

POULT Term used to describe the period of growth between a chick losing its fluff and becoming mature; applied to young game birds and also often to turkeys.

PULLET An immature female chicken.

P.O.L. Point of lay. The stage at which hen birds will be approaching the age to lay their first egg; about 16 weeks for a chicken.

BROILER Chicken raised specifically for meat production

TUBE FEEDER A circular hanging feeder holding 15kg or more with a trough around the bottom.

NIPPLE DRINKER Small water dispenser activated by a bird pecking at the valve on the tip.

BEAK TRIMMING The removal of the tip of the top beak at between 3-10 days of age to prevent feather pecking and cannibalism. Only a small part is removed and this causes little distress to the chick. In poultry this only has to be done once as the beak does not grow again. It is principally used as a management tool for hens kept for laying. Once known as de-beaking it gave the false impression that the top beak was cut right back. It used to be carried out using a red hot blade but now an infrared beam is used instead to blunt the sharp tip of the bird's beak which only takes seconds. Its use is controversial but it can greatly improve the welfare of poultry, whichever system they are kept under, as it is a natural instinct for a bird to peck at things and each other.

Garrons are still used on some Scottish estates to transport shot deer off otherwise inaccessible hills

HORSES AND PONIES

For centuries oxen were used as draught animals to plough the land and pull wagons until they were gradually replaced with heavy horses. By the end of the nineteenth century oxen were redundant and steam engines had appeared on the scene to plough large fields. In the main, heavy horses were not replaced by tractors until after the Second World War. It took a man and a team of two horses a day to plough an acre of land, walking eleven miles in the process. Tractors were far quicker and a lot less work and they didn't need an hour of tending each day before and again after they finished work!

Many stalwart workers of yesteryear, such as the shepherd's pony and the garron, have been replaced by ATVs (all-terrain vehicles). Garrons are Highland ponies which are used to carry shot red deer off the hill in Scotland and there are a few estates in Scotland that still maintain this old tradition.

Only a very small minority of the 850,000 horses and ponies in Britain are kept solely for working purposes.

The vast majority of horses and ponies are kept solely for their owner's personal pleasure, whether it is for riding, driving or racing or merely as pets. It is now mandatory in the UK for every horse, pony and donkey to be microchipped and to have an equine passport, with a unique registration number and record of the owner's name, even if they never leave the place they are kept.

A horse or pony can live more than 30 years but not all remain fit or are fortunate enough to be kept in retirement after the end of their usefulness. Some end their days in horse sanctuaries but others are slaughtered in approved abattoirs and processed for pet food or human consumption overseas. In the UK there are greatly improved standards in animal welfare and strict rules are in place. There are abattoirs which are fully licensed to slaughter horses and ponies and far fewer live animals are now exported to the Continent.

SHOEING HORSES

If they are regularly ridden or worked, horses and ponies need to be shod. Their hooves are fairly soft and if shoes are not put on they can easily become worn down or damaged. A lame horse cannot be used for anything.

In normal use, horseshoes need replacing about every six weeks.

The farrier specialises in shoeing horses a practice which dates back more than two thousand years, brought to England by invading Roman soldiers who had learned that putting iron shoes on their horses' feet protected them from lameness. When donkeys and oxen were used as draught animals these too were shod. Oxen, which have cloven feet, had two half-moon shaped pieces of iron fixed to each hoof.

Shoeing is a highly skilled job and requires more than four years served as an apprentice to learn the trade and a thorough knowledge of the anatomy of a horse is also taught. Some physical horse problems can be solved with specially designed shoes.

This formal training is required under the Farriers (Registration) Act 1975. Successful apprentices are awarded a Diploma of the

▲ A farrier trimming a horse's hoof

▲ Shoes are checked when they are red hot but this causes no pain to the horse

Worshipful Company of Farriers (DipWCF). The highest qualification that can be achieved in farriery is Fellowship of the Worshipful Company of Farriers (FWCF).

Horses' hooves, like our fingernails, keep growing but there is no feeling in the outer

QUOITS

The game of 'quoits' dates back to the 14th century and originated from competitions to see how many horseshoes could be thrown over a peg stuck in the ground.

edges. It causes no pain when the shoes are fixed in place with nails. If a horse is not ridden or worked then it is unnecessary for them to be shod although their feet will still need to be kept regularly trimmed by a farrier.

Horseshoes are applied when they are red hot. While one is being heated in a forge, the farrier trims the outer hoof as well as the horny triangular centre part, known as the '**frog**', which acts as a shock absorber. The shoe is hammered into shape on an anvil and 'tried', the hot metal leaving an outline on the newly-pared hoof. Any necessary adjustments can then be made. Finally the shoe is quenched in a water trough before being fixed in place with nails hammered into the shoe and at an angle through the lower wall of the hoof. The sharp protruding ends of the nails are then cut off. Although the smoke and stench of burning hoof makes it appear quite traumatic, the procedure is painless and the majority of horses quietly accept being shod.

Horses always used to be led or ridden to the local forge, or smithy as it was known, to be shod. Shoes were formed from a bar of iron and individually made. Now horses are attended to in situ by mobile farriers bringing their equipment in the back of a van. Horseshoes are now available ready-made so only minor adjustments are required and they can even be put on cold. Studs are sometimes fixed into the shoes if the surface is slippery. Plastic shoes are occasionally used and racehorses are shod with lightweight aluminium shoes for racing.

There are about 850,000 horses in Britain and the equestrian industry employs approximately 200,000 people. The economic value of consumer spending across a wide range of goods is estimated to be £4.7 billion. Horses need feeding, stabling, veterinary attention, shoeing, blankets and tack. Their owners require specialist clothing, hats, boots and transport for their animals. Unless horses are turned out in a field, as hardy ponies sometimes are, their care is costly and time-consuming. They also need to be kept fit either by regular exercise or with the help of a mechanical 'horse walker'. This is a device with a central tower from which radial

Exmoor ponies roaming free on Exmoor, the breed was facing extinction following WWII

Dartmoor ponies live wild on Dartmoor

arms extend and to which horses are attached individually. A 'walker' is designed to take several horses, leading them round in a circle following each other. The speed and timing can be regulated and it is also useful for horses recuperating from injury or to allow them to cool down after strenuous exercise.

RIDING FOR THE DISABLED

Many find it satisfying to own a pony or horse. Even very young children can enjoy riding and here the diminutive Shetland finds its niche. Disabled children can find riding extremely stimulating, giving them a freedom otherwise denied them. The charity 'Riding for the Disabled Association' (RDA) has nearly 500 centres all over the UK where horses and ponies are kept for the benefit of people with a disability. Over 25,000 disabled children and adults join in fun activities like riding and carriage driving. Qualified coaches at the RDA provide therapy, fitness training, skills development and opportunities for achievement with the help of 18,000 volunteers.

As children grow, there is a wide choice of breeds or crosses to suit their size. In fact in Britain a breed of horse or pony can be found to suit every purpose. Donkeys are no longer common although they are sometimes kept as pets or companions for another horse or pony

and they can still be seen at the seaside giving rides to children.

Ponies are hardy, resilient and sometimes strong-minded, rather like terriers. They are an excellent choice for those who do not have much spare time or money, who enjoy the occasional ride out.

Livery stables will care for an owner's horse or pony. For those who can't afford to own a horse, riding stables offer the opportunity to hire an animal as well as providing tuition. Pony trekking holidays are another way the occasional rider can enjoy their hobby.

BREEDS OF PONIES

There are several breeds of ponies native to Britain. The sturdy little Shetland, as its name implies, originates from the Northern Isles off Scotland. Stocky Fell ponies, Exmoor and Welsh Cobs and the lighter framed Dartmoor and New Forest ponies are all unique to their areas. Some of these breeds can still be found roaming free in their natural habitats. Dartmoor and New Forest ponies run wild and each autumn are rounded up and the unwanted foals and yearlings sold at special sales. Some find homes as children's pets but a few end up being slaughtered. This traditional method of management is probably the only way in which some of the native breeds can be conserved

▲ A New Forest pony browsing on holly

as there is not enough grazing to support the additional annual crop of young stock. When stallions are allowed to run free with the mares it is inevitable that many will conceive.

RECREATIONAL RIDING

There are numerous Pony Clubs for youngsters across Britain which hold gymkhanas offering a chance for children to ride competitively. Numerous mounted games are played and jumping over fences is always popular. For older riders, events include show jumping competitions, or dressage, which involves intensive training to display the obedience and suppleness of the natural movements of a horse.

Eventing combines these disciplines with a cross country course over natural hazards and solid fences testing all-round fitness and ability. Eventing competitions are often held over three days with dressage on the first day; a cross country course, which includes a set distance covered on roads and tracks, on the second; followed by show jumping on the last day.

The hunting of foxes and hares is now banned but it has been replaced with trail hunting. This enables many people to still enjoy the opportunity to watch hounds work and to ride out in different parts of the countryside with an added purpose for being there.

The main sport played on horseback is polo. It was once a game only enjoyed by a privileged few but the number of polo clubs in

◄ Fell ponies are a breed native to Cumbria and were once used as pack animals

the UK has increased significantly making it more accessible.

Carriage driving either for leisure or competition is another popular hobby and many breeds including native ones can be used for this purpose.

Trotting has never become as popular in Britain as it is in the States except with the travelling community. Specially bred horses with an unusual gait that enables them to trot extremely quickly while pulling a lightweight cart, can sometimes be seen.

Some horses and ponies are kept just for showing as perfect specimens. These are led around the show ring to be judged although some classes, such as child's pony or hunter, may require the animal being ridden, in which case the rider will be as immaculately turned out as his or her mount.

WORKING HORSES AND PONIES

PIT PONIES

At one time there were estimated to be up to 200,000 horses and ponies working down British mines. Their numbers peaked following

▲ Many children first learn to ride on a Shetland pony

the Mines Act of 1842, which banned the employment of women and boys younger than 10 underground. The ponies spent their entire working lives down the mines. It was a hard life for them and the miners who worked alongside them. It wasn't until 1994 that the practice of stabling them underground came to an end.

The last two working pit ponies in Britain were retired in 1999.

Coloured horses are very popular with the Romany community

MILITARY HORSES

They are working horses used for displays and ceremonial occasions. The Household Cavalry, based at Knightsbridge, carry out ceremonial duties on State and Royal occasions while The Royal Horse Artillery, whose headquarters are in Woolwich, also pull the First World War gun carriages.

The British Army today has more horses than tanks.

Army horses are treated to a fortnight's summer holiday in the countryside away from the busy London streets.

POLICE HORSES

Police horses are highly trained, much respected and are mostly employed in crowd control. Mounted police are better able to assess situations from their elevated position, and are also able to access places which a vehicle can't as well as carry out crowd control.

There are thirteen mounted police units in Britain.

HEAVY HORSES

In 1910 there were more than a million horses working on farms, most of which were heavy horses used for agricultural work. At the outbreak of the First World War in 1914, half a million horses of all types were requisitioned by the War Office which virtually emptied the countryside of any horse fit enough to be of use.

But by the 1950s, cart horses disappeared at an alarming rate. It wasn't long before the Scottish Clydesdale, the French Percheron, the East Anglian Suffolk and the massive Shires from Middle England were facing extinction. Fortunately there were enough interested people who recognised this threat and preserved these

▲ Sowing potatoes the old fashioned way

magnificent animals. Better still they ensured that these horses were still capable of doing the work for which they were originally kept, thereby also safeguarding the dying skills of the old horseman.

Thanks to a few dedicated enthusiasts our three native breeds of heavy horses, Shires, Clydesdales and the Suffolk Punch, have been preserved but are now mostly kept as a hobby. They can be seen working at shows or organised ploughing matches. A few can still be found employed in agriculture or forestry, hauling brewers drays, pulling carriages along sea fronts or on ceremonial occasions. There is grave concern for their future as even keeping one is an expensive hobby and their numbers are decreasing.

Percherons are black or grey and, although they have deep bodies and short legs, are very active but normally placid.

Clydesdales originated in Lanarkshire and are usually black, bay or brown with a lot of white on their face and legs, running up to the underbelly. One of their most outstanding qualities is the strength of their legs and particularly their feet.

Shires are most often seen either pulling wagons (this striking breed is a favourite of the breweries) or doing farm work. They are the largest of the heavy horses, in fact the largest in the world, ranging from 17-19 hands (approximately 6ft or 2.75m) tall and weighing 1,800 to 2,400 pounds (over a tonne). A distinctive feature of Shires is their feathered (very hairy) legs below the knee. Shires can be of any colour and these gentle giants often have white feet and a blaze on their foreheads.

Suffolk Punches are very broad in the body and have short legs with no feathering to which mud can cling. Suffolks are always a shade of chestnut but a white star on the forehead is acceptable. The breed is the oldest in Britain, dating back to the 16th century. The ancestry of every Suffolk horse alive today is said to trace

▲ Using a horse is an environmentally friendly way of extracting timber

back to a horse called 'Crisp's Horse of Ufford' which was born in 1768. During its commercial working life the Suffolk 'Punch' was very much a breed local to the eastern counties of England but this area was one of the first to become agriculturally mechanised and numbers fell rapidly. In 1966 only nine foals were born. Even now there are only 300 breeding mares with 30-40 youngsters being registered annually which makes the Suffolk very much at risk as a breed.

The two breeds native to England are thought to have evolved from Tudor war horses. Very strong horses were needed to bear the burden of a man in armour.

▼ Working the land with horses: a Suffolk on the left teamed with a Percheron

◀ A pair of Suffolk horses competing in a ploughing match

PLOUGHING MATCHES

Each autumn, across the country, ploughing matches are held with classes for heavy horses. They are each allocated a strip of land to plough. It is a fantastic sight to watch a pair doing the work they were bred for as well as seeing the care and pride their handler takes. The single furrow has to be absolutely straight and the plough carefully adjusted to turn the soil over so any surface debris is buried. Some owners work their horses in ordinary harnesses but others display yet another

skill in the way they turn their horses out. Many hours beforehand are spent braiding straw and ribbons in the mane and cleaning leather and brass harness so it gleams in the autumn sunshine.

The horsemen of old knew many ways to get the best out of their animals and it's good that a few dedicated enthusiasts still retain their knowledge and practice, their skills.

THE RACING INDUSTRY

By far the largest part the horse plays for millions of people is on the racecourse. The British Horseracing Authority (BHA) is the regulatory authority for horseracing in Great Britain.

The racing industry generates £3.45 billion and supports 85,000 jobs.

Indirectly, racing is financially supported by countless men and women who have never been closer to a horse than their television screen or local betting shop. Millions of pounds are spent every year in Britain on gambling.

▼ Clydesdales at a ploughing match

▲ Point-to-Point races are organised by local hunts for amateur riders; they originated from races being held between marked points which were often church steeples

It is estimated that important National Hunt meetings like the three day Cheltenham Festival in March, the Grand National at Aintree and the famous Epsom Derby and Royal Ascot summer meetings on the Flat generate £100 million pounds in betting money at each event.

There are approximately 14,000 thoroughbreds in training, directly providing employment for more than 6,000 people including 550 licensed trainers and 450 jockeys.

While training racehorses remains traditional in many ways, it also embraces modern technology to legitimately improve performances. Most training facilities use automated 'horse walkers' to help exercise their horses and many of the larger ones have hydrotherapy pools.

At the bottom end of the racing scale are Point to Points which are organised by local hunts under the supervision of the Jockey Club. These races are only open to amateurs and horses that have been out hunting: it is the bedrock on which the sport of steeplechasing has been built. Horses are only eligible to run if the owners and jockeys are members of or subscribers to a recognised pack of hounds. Point-to-point horses are required to have had a certain number of days out hunting with the pack to qualify. A hunter certificate has to have been issued by the Master of the pack to verify the horse in question has met this requirement.

Owners do not have to be incredibly wealthy to own a racehorse although having them professionally trained does not come cheap.

FLAT RACING, STEEPLECHASE OR HURDLES

Horses that run in either hurdle races or steeplechases are older horses that have either been specially bred, made their mark as point-to-pointers or are those that do not have the speed to have made the grade over shorter Flat race distances. These rejects can prove to be useful animals as they mature and learn the new game but most males by this age will have been castrated and have no future value at stud. While Flat racers begin racing when they are two or three years old, those that are bred for jumping are usually about four before they are raced over hurdles and even older before they tackle bigger steeplechase fences. Not only do

▲ A string of racehorses returning from exercise on the Warren Hill gallops in Newmarket

they need a certain amount of natural ability to be successful, they also need stamina as well as speed enough to win over the longer distances. These qualities can be inherited so their breeding is of great importance.

Prize money for races run on the Flat generally far exceeds that offered for hurdle races or steeplechases.

Although the National Hunt season extends almost throughout the year, officially beginning in May, there are very few meetings during the summer when the ground is too dry and hard. Meetings occasionally have to be cancelled in winter if the course is frozen, snow-covered or waterlogged. For major jump meetings, the course may be covered when temperatures are below zero to prevent the ground from freezing. Jump racing is often regarded as the poor relation to Flat racing but it really comes into its own between November and early April which is why it is known as the 'Winter Game'.

Flat racing on the other hand gets underway in March and continues until November. In summer, Flat race meetings sometimes take place in the evenings, in addition to afternoon ones. There are a handful of Flat meetings during the winter on synthetic all-weather racecourses such as Lingfield. Fibresand and Tapeta are used as synthetic surfaces but Polytrack, a mixture of silica sand, polypropylene and recycled rubber coated with wax, is the most favoured.

An enormous amount of care is taken on grass courses to provide a safe surface. Good drainage prevents the going becoming too 'heavy' and irrigation is used to stop it becoming too firm. On race days, if necessary, some of the divots (holes made in the ground made by the horses' hooves) are filled in by course attendants after each race.

STUD-VALUE

A horse that consistently wins top quality Flat races can accumulate a substantial amount of prize money and also be worth a phenomenal amount for breeding purposes. A top-class stallion is worth millions of pounds and is usually retired from racing and sent to stud when he is 3 or 4 years old.

He can sire more than 50 foals a year, continuing to do so for 15 to 20 years.

If his progeny prove to be successful, his services can remain fully booked at a very high price throughout his lifetime. The Jockey Club has never allowed the use of artificial insemination for thoroughbred racehorses.

► Two-way traffic in Newmarket

Every thoroughbred racehorse is micro-chipped for identification purposes. Under British Horseracing Authority (BHA) rules *'In order for a horse to be eligible to race under Rules or in Point-to-Points they must also be registered with a unique name, which will remain with them for life. This is to distinguish each horse from others in a race and allows bloodlines and pedigrees to be more easily traced. A horse will also need to be registered with a unique name if it is to be used for breeding purposes'.*

Weatherbys assist the BHA by providing administration and data on their behalf. They are responsible for keeping all the records and have held the General Stud Book register since 1791.

Newmarket is the headquarters of the racing industry and the whole town revolves around the racehorse. Famous stable yards occupy prominent positions and lesser ones are tucked away in the back streets. Horse walkways are built alongside pedestrian pavements and there are rider-operated traffic lights where horses need to cross busy roads to exercise on the 3,000 acres of heath training grounds, known as the 'gallops' and also several synthetic training areas. There are several other major training centres in the UK notably at Middleham and Malton in Yorkshire and Lambourn in Berkshire. These are places where racehorses can be exercised on old established gallops where the turf provides good conditions underfoot, rarely too wet in winter or too firm in summer.

TRAINING A RACEHORSE

Racehorses are extremely well cared for. Preparing one to race is a matter of slowly building up fitness. It is a gradual process starting first with walking then trotting and finally cantering to reach a peak. National Hunt horses are also schooled over fences, and swimming provides excellent therapeutic exercise. Racing stable routines are rigid with an early morning start when the first 'lot' are ridden out. After breakfast a second lot will be taken out and stables and tack thoroughly cleaned. A stable lad or lass is expected to look after two or three horses and probably ride them out to exercise although the services of some experienced outside riders or jockeys may be called upon to assist with the exercising.

◄ This larger-than-life statue, close to the National Stud in Newmarket, was unveiled in 2000 to mark the Millennium

▲ Newmarket is the headquarters of the British racing industry and the whole town revolves around the thoroughbred horse

Racing stables are busy places and visits during the day are likely from the vet, the farrier and sometimes owners. Most days during the season, horses from the larger stables are taken to race meetings, sometimes far away or even abroad.

Horse care, in common with working with any other livestock, isn't a 9-5 job. Racing involves getting up early and working in the evening but there may be an opportunity for some staff to take a couple of hours off in the afternoon, before the late feeds and other chores are taken care of. The trainer or his Head Lad will also have a look round last thing at night to make sure that all is well with the horses. Out of the racing season, some horses may go back to their owners for a holiday and enjoy the pleasure of being turned out to grass. Day-to-day pressure on stable staff is not so intense then.

Thoroughbred flat racers usually only have a short career although there are exceptions. Males (colts) are not castrated and any that have excelled will be retired when they are 3 or 4 years old because of their value for breeding. The females (fillies) are not only judged by their achievements but also by their bloodlines so, even if they haven't been outstanding on the course, they can still prove their worth at stud.

Ex flat race horses may be sold on for National Hunt racing or for personal use such as for hunting or eventing. Smaller ones may even make good polo ponies. Colts not retained for breeding are usually castrated. It is inevitable though that some may have to be put down if they cannot be rehomed.

Many racehorse owners from the Middle East enjoy thoroughbred racing in the UK enough to have training stables and stud farms here. It is therefore hardly surprising that they also get pleasure from racing their native Arabian horses. Several race meetings are held each year specifically for these.

Arab horses are renowned for their stamina. Endurance racing is increasing in popularity which involves this elegant, ancient breed covering distances of up to 100 miles to fully test their famed qualities of soundness and stamina. They are allowed several breaks during the race in which their physical condition is carefully monitored by vets to make sure they are not becoming over-stressed.

STUD FARMS

The thoroughbred breeding industry contributes £425 million to the British economy and supports 19,000 rural jobs. The Newmarket area has many stud farms in the vicinity, and there are numerous others dotted around the country, breeding the next generation of racehorses. Some are small, providing a hobby for an owner while others are huge enterprises, many of which are foreign-owned.

Approximately 5,000 thoroughbred foals are bred in Britain every year for racing.

The National Stud at Newmarket, owned by the Jockey Club, is the showcase for British Thoroughbred breeding. Some top-class stallions are based there and on certain days it is open to the public. For every racehorse foal born, an enormous amount of research and planning has gone into choosing a sire that will complement its mother's qualities and strengthen her weaknesses.

BROOD MARES

Breeding (brood) mares that have not previously been mated, and those sent from abroad to be served, are kept in an isolation unit on arrival at a stud for 2-4 weeks to eliminate the risk of infection.

A mare naturally comes into season in spring and summer for about five days during a three-week cycle. Pregnancy lasts for eleven months and on average a mare at stud would normally be expected to have a foal in two years out of three.

In the early 19th century 1st January was declared the official birth date for all thoroughbred foals, irrespective of the actual date when they were born. This means that a foal born at Christmas, most unfairly, is considered to be one year old on 1st January despite being only a few days old. Breeders therefore aim to get their mares in foal in late winter and early spring by getting them mated between mid-February and no later than the second week of July.

A veterinary examination determines whether a mare is ready for mating and a **'teaser'** is used to gauge her acceptance level. Separated by a boarded frame or gate, she and the substitute stallion are introduced to each other and her reactions observed. It is only when she shows her readiness that a mare is introduced to the selected stallion.

Today mares are usually kept at their owners' private studs to foal. With the ease and luxury of modern transport they can be **'walked in'** (transported) to the stud to be served.

The services of a top stallion are phenomenally expensive and many studs offer a guarantee of 'no foal no fee' within a certain time.

Twins are most unwelcome and if they show up when the mare is scanned two to three weeks into her pregnancy, it is possible for an experienced horse vet to dispose of one of the embryos. Scanning is carried out again after about four weeks and again at eight to make sure everything is in order. As thoroughbred mares and their offspring are very valuable, when mares are near their time to foal, a groom stays up with them every night. Signs of the birth being imminent are waxing of the teats and a rise in body temperature. There are devices that measure this rise and trigger an alarm but they are not entirely reliable, so most studs still prefer to have somebody in attendance.

Modern stud farms usually have purpose-designed maternity units. These have veterinary facilities, special sitting up rooms for the groom and CCTV surveillance within the unit which is also connected to the Senior Stud Groom's house. As soon as a foal is born it is immediately checked over, its navel is treated with an antiseptic agent to safeguard against infection and it is encouraged to suckle. Bonding with its mother is vital as are the health benefits it receives through the mare's first milk (colostrum). A thoroughbred foal needs to grow quickly and hand rearing on the bottle is never very successful. If the mare is unable to feed her offspring then, if at all possible, a foster mother is used which may be of any breed.

The foal needs to be registered in the official Stud Book and its markings and coat patterns, as individual as a human fingerprint, noted as identification. Micro-chipping is also now used as a permanent and reliable record of its identity.

EARLY MONTHS

It is very important that a foal is well handled in the first few months of its life. To begin with mother and baby are turned out for a few hours each day, weather permitting, into a sheltered grass paddock that has been specially sown with a palatable mixture of grass, herbs and other nutritious plants. Deep rooted ones absorb beneficial trace elements from the earth beneath. Limestone/chalky areas are favoured as sites for studs because the foals do particularly well on this type of soil.

Droppings in the paddocks are picked up daily with a suction machine to reduce the risk of infection from parasites such as worms. Grass soon becomes an important part of a foal's diet. Analysis of the soil and herbage is carried out so any mineral or vitamin deficiencies can be rectified when supplementary feeding is introduced at about two or three months.

Racehorse foals are weaned at about five to six months old depending on their condition. Immense care is taken with their health: they are vaccinated against tetanus (which horses are very prone to) and equine flu. Mares and foals are both also wormed regularly. Foot care is of particular importance for a horse cannot run if it has anything wrong with its feet or legs. Foals need to have their hooves regularly trimmed and any slight problems or defects in the legs or feet can often be remedied by the way in which an expert farrier pedicures the feet. Brood mares are not usually shod unless there is a medical reason to do so but their feet also need to be kept in shape. For safety reasons, stallions usually only have front shoes fitted because it could be dangerous should they kick out with their hind feet. Careful attention has to be continuously paid to their hooves and they are also regularly checked by a farrier.

Thoroughbred mare and foal on a stud farm

HORSE SALES

Thoroughbred horse sales begin in September, Tattersalls in Newmarket probably being the most famous. Sales are usually held over several days, often in the evenings after racing. Britain is renowned for the quality of its thoroughbreds and the sales attract wealthy buyers from around the world. Foals, yearlings, horses in training, older horses and brood mares change hands, some for phenomenal prices. Wealthy individuals from the Middle East have shown great interest in horse racing for decades and thanks to their involvement in this country, with both racing and breeding, the industry has gone from strength to strength. Many of the best stallions they own have remained at stud in Britain when they could so easily have been sent abroad.

Not all foals and yearlings go through the sale ring; a lot are retained by their owners before being sent directly to trainers when they are rising two years old where they are broken-in prior to being raced.

STUD STALLIONS

Valuable breeding racehorses lead a cosseted life and the stallions are no exception. One man is usually employed to look after two stallions, with some extra assistance. The individual temperaments of each stallion have to be taken into account. Such valuable, strong, highly strung, intelligent and sometimes temperamental animals require sympathetic handling at all times.

Stallions at stud are not often ridden although they need to be fit enough to mate with two or three mares a day during the five month covering season from mid-February until mid-July. Exercising begins in earnest in October and includes daily lunging (exercising on a long rein in a circle around the handler) and walking. Not only does taking stallions for a daily walk around the countryside help get them physically fit, it also stimulates them mentally; boredom can be a threat to their stability. Some studs also believe that spending a few hours outside, running loose in their own paddock enables stallions to exercise themselves and gives their lives an added dimension. Tread mills and mechanical 'horse walkers' are sometimes used for exercise but do little in the way of stimulating them mentally.

At the end of the covering (mating) season, stallions are rested and allowed to relax for three or four months before being prepared again for the next season. Diet also plays an important part in their wellbeing and each senior stud groom has his own recipe for success.

Thoroughbreds, whether in training or at stud, are subject to continuous veterinary observation. The slightest hint of anything amiss detected by the stable lad or lass looking after the animal, the trainer, head lad or stud groom, is immediately acted upon. Blood tests are regularly conducted, swabs and physical examinations are commonplace. Facilities at top stables and horse veterinary centres are superb and the amount of care and attention racehorses receive is unparalleled, putting many aspects of human health-care to shame.

Studs, training establishments and racecourses dot the British countryside, particularly in England, and of course the Irish are renowned for their affinity with the racehorse. Many top jockeys, especially National Hunt ones, originate from Ireland.

Only about 5% of thoroughbreds in training ever win a race and very few become famous.

It is the owner's belief that one day one of their horses will be a winner, and the willingness of the punter to part with their money that keeps the industry going. Both the racing and breeding industries provide much-needed employment in rural areas and have a direct impact on the rural economy.

GLOSSARY

HORSE Over 14 hands high

PONY Under 14 hands high

STALLION Entire male over 4 years old

COLT Entire male under 4 years old

ENTIRE A male that has not been castrated

GELDING Castrated male

MARE Female over 4 years old

FILLY Female under 4 years old

FOAL Under one year old

YEARLING Aged between one and two years old

JACK Male donkey

JENNY Female donkey

DAM Mother

SIRE Father

HAND Measurement of height equal to 4 inches (10.16cm) eg 16 hands high is 5 feet 4 inches (163cm) at the withers.

WITHERS Shoulders

COB Small stocky horse of no defined breeding

GARRON Highland pony used by deer stalkers in Scotland

DRAUGHT/HEAVY HORSE Cart horse

BAY Brown horse with a black mane, tail and lower legs

ROAN Horse whose main colour is flecked with white

PIEBALD Horse with black and white markings

SKEWBALD Horse with brown and white markings

PALOMINO Horse with a cream coloured coat and a paler mane and tail

FARRIER Person who cares for a horse's feet, a blacksmith

BREAK Train a young horse to be responsive and used to being ridden

TACK Equipment for a horse eg saddle, bridle etc

SCHOOL Practice

LUNGE Exercise on a long rein in a circle around the handler

HORSE WALKER A mechanical way of exercising which is also sometimes used to assist with rehabilitation following injury

GAIT The pattern of steps taken

PACE The four paces of a horse are walk (slowest), trot, canter and gallop. It can also mean the rate at which a horse runs during a race

SOUND Fit and healthy

RIDING STABLE Place where horses or ponies are kept for hire or tuition is given

LIVERY STABLE Place where owners can pay to have their horses or ponies kept for them

AT LIVERY Kept in livery stables

GYMKHANA Show where children ride in competitions

INDOOR SCHOOL Barn used for riding tuition

RACING AND STUD

BHA The British Horseracing Authority is the regulatory authority for horse racing in Great Britain

JOCKEY CLUB Governing body for British racing and also the owners of 15 English racecourses and the National Stud at Newmarket

NATIONAL HUNT Racing over hurdles or fences

STEEPLECHASE Race over fences

POINT TO POINT Race meeting over fences for amateur riders organised by Hunts under the supervision of the Jockey Club

BUMPER Flat race for amateur riders

ALL WEATHER COURSE Artificial surface for flat racing

HURDLE Portable low flimsy obstacle

FENCE Permanent substantial obstacle usually constructed from birch boughs and sometimes topped with gorse or fir branches

PADDOCK Parade ring at a racecourse or small enclosure on a stud farm

PACEMAKER Horse entered in a race to set the pace they go

MAIDEN Horse that has not won a race or a female that has not been bred from

STRING Group of racehorses

YARD A trainer's stables

HEAD LAD The person responsible for the day to day running of a racing stable

TRAVELLING HEAD LAD The person responsible for racehorses in transit and at race meetings

STUD FARM A horse breeding establishment

SENIOR STUD GROOM The person responsible for the day to day running of a stud farm

STAND AT STUD Term used when a stallion is kept for breeding purposes

COVER Mate with

TEASER Stallion used to ascertain whether a mare is ready to be mated

BROOD MARE Mare kept for breeding

FOAL AT FOOT Mare with a young unweaned foal

Seed drilling is becoming more ecologically sound

ARABLE FARMING

The farming year traditionally begins and ends around the time of Michaelmas, the last week in September. This is particularly relevant to the arable farmer who by then has harvested most of his crops and is about to sow the seeds for next year's.

Nearly all farmers use a system of rotating crops. Some, such as legumes, put nitrogen back into the soil while others take it out. Crop rotation has been practised for hundreds of years and is a well-recognised management tool. Not only does changing the crop preserve the structure and fertility of the soil but also helps to prevent a build-up of pests and diseases. In recent years arable crop yields have improved greatly as plant breeding scientists have bred varieties which are more productive and have increased disease resistance.

Taking care of the soil is vital if it's not to become merely somewhere for the roots of growing crops to be held and their nutritional needs supplied completely artificially. But loss of living organisms, organic matter and compaction all reduce the fertility.

Continuous farming can deprive the soil of organic matter if it is not replaced. Once, when nearly every farm wintered cattle in barns or kept pigs, this was rectified by spreading straw-based farmyard manure on the land before it was ploughed. Livestock, the providers of the old fashioned 'muck,' have disappeared from many farms. Growing green crops such as mustard and buckwheat has been used by organic farmers as a natural way of replenishing and stabilising the soil and is now being used more widely. Unwanted straw from cereal crops is often chopped as part of the combining process. This is then ploughed back into the ground helping to increase organic matter in the soil and maintain its fertility.

A good level of organic matter in turn creates a healthy ecosystem of living organisms which combine to improve the health of the soil.

There are 29 species of earthworm in the UK and they contribute to the maintenance of healthy soils by eating organic matter and minerals and making compost which enriches the soil.

Their underground tunnels also help fields absorb more water and improves drainage, to buffer against flooding. Direct drilling crops (not ploughing or cultivating the land first) helps maintain beneficial micro-organisms, bacteria and fungi within the soil which, in turn,

improves its structure. Crops grown in poor quality soils are weaker and more susceptible to being attacked by pests and engulfed by weeds.

It is thought that increasingly poor soil condition is a major factor in limiting crop yields. The extremes of weather in recent years have aggravated the situation. Heavy rainfall results in soil being lost through erosion and it also suffers more from compaction and waterlogging.

Arable machinery

Farm machinery gets bigger and more sophisticated, and is usually leased or contractors employed. Huge tractors are now fitted with tracks to reduce compaction and enable them to get on fields even when the ground is wet, which means that land work can continue except in exceptionally bad conditions.

In large-scale arable farming, tractors and self-propelled machines are equipped with air-con, fridges, 2-way radios, computers and GPS. Satellite technology is being adopted to make farming activities more efficient. Data received provides specific information on soil conditions and crop health. Infra-red light refraction can also be used to monitor the health of the crop to determine which applications, and at what level, need to be applied. Global navigation satellite systems enable the machine to steer itself and are programmed to work the land with precision. The insides of cabs on large tractors now resemble the cockpit of an aeroplane! Technology and telemetry has become so advanced that fault-detecting electronics installed in agricultural machinery, similar to that in F1 racing cars, can relay information back to a central hub. If the fault can't be fixed remotely this makes it possible for the technician to arrive on the farm to repair it before the machine has actually broken down!

Combine harvesters can now cost over £750,000 and are only used for a couple of

◀ Grants are available to plant conservation headlands around fields of cereals

▲ Combining wheat

months of the year. Top of the range combines are able to cut a strip 40ft (12.2m) or more wide.

Weed 'wipers' which work by brushing a herbicide onto unwanted plants which are higher than the crop are sometimes used. They only kill plants they make contact with.

Top of the range for high-tech sprayers are machines with booms 30 metres wide which can be automatically folded back along the sides when not in use.

HAY AND STRAW BALES

Loose hay and straw is compacted into bales which vary greatly in size depending on their intended use. As mechanical means of handling have been developed, large round bales have become popular for hay. Large rectangular bales, known as Hestons, which are easier to stack and equal to about 20 conventional, small, oblong ones, are often used for straw, although smallholders and horse keepers favour the small bales which can be manoeuvred by hand.

▶ Baling straw

CROP DISEASE MANAGEMENT

There are many diseases which can affect agricultural crops. Management and biological control may play a part but some soil-borne pests and diseases are combatted by using seed that has been treated with a systemic dressing which is absorbed into the plant before it is sown. This reduces the need to spray crops, at a later stage.

BEE-HOSTILE SPRAY BANNED

The use of neonicotinoids, also known as 'neonics', was banned in 2018. Bees are very

▲ Round straw bales: an alternative to the plastic wrapping should soon be available

important for pollinating crops, without which, plants will not bear fruit or seeds, and neonics kill bees, which are already under threat. Neonics were used to combat yellow virus disease, spread by aphids in sugar beet and kale, and flea beetle attack on rape. The biggest risk to bees came from rape as the neonics remains within the crop at flowering time and were ingested through the pollen and nectar. Sugar beet, a crop that doesn't flower during its growing cycle, carries a relatively low risk of harming bees. Since the withdrawal of neonicotinoids, no substitute has proved effective and farmers are encountering reductions in yields which seriously affect their returns.

Both sugar beet and rape are very important crops which grow well in the UK: 50% of our sugar is home grown. If there is a reduction, for any reason, in the amount that farmers are able to grow each year it will inevitably lead to higher imports. Having to import such products at a time when agriculture is trying to reduce its own carbon footprint does nothing to support this ideal especially when the countries involved might well be using treatments banned for use in the UK, such as neonicotinoids.

For weed control, pre-emergence herbicide sprays are often applied soon after the crop has been sown and before it comes through. Artificial fertilizers are usually applied direct to the crop in liquid or granular form.

SINGLE-USE PLASTIC AND FLEECE

One of the most ecologically harmful threats on farms comes from the single use of plastic and fleece. Plastic is used to wrap silage, to cover crops, for irrigation purposes, to transport feed and fertiliser in bags and package liquids. Plastic mulch and fleece is used widely by the horticultural industry to provide protection and improved growing conditions for a range of vegetable and salad crops. Some of the plastic now used in horticulture is biodegradable. Not so, though, for the huge amount used for covering or wrapping bales. Plastic is cheap, strong and waterproof. It is something farmers would like to be able to manage without but currently there is no alternative. Since 2006, legislation prevents them from burning or burying it. All agricultural plastic can now only be disposed of through an organised operator, a service for which the farmer has to pay. It is very difficult to recycle after it has possibly become contaminated with soil, pesticides and fertiliser.

ECO SUGAR BEET PRODUCTION

Recycling and finding a green use for waste products has come to the fore in the fight against climate change and there is no better example of an industry implementing these principles than the British Sugar Company in their four factories. The process of refining sugar from locally grown sugar beet creates several by-products all of which are put to good use. Their waste is virtually zero.

Soil washed off the beet is screened and sold as topsoil, extracted stones as an aggregate and lime residue as a soil improver. The discarded beet pulp and molasses go for animal feed; it

Removing stones to ensure a fine seed bed in which to sow a root crop

is the drying of this that results in plumes of steam which look like smoke being emitted from the chimneys.

The factories are powered by a combined heat and power system producing both steam and electricity. These are utilised to the maximum and modern power plants in two of the factories produce an excess of electricity which is fed into the National Grid system. In 2016 an anaerobic digestion plant opened at the Bury St Edmunds factory using pressed sugar beet pulp to produce renewable energy.

The Wissington factory in Norfolk is the largest and most modern in Europe and also produces bio-ethanol fuel. In 2000 44 acres (18ha) of glasshouses were constructed adjacent to the factory which utilised surplus heat and carbon dioxide produced to grow tomatoes. In January 2017 these were replaced with medicinal grade cannabis plants to produce cannabidiol oral solution (CBD), a drug used for treating epilepsy.

NEW ARABLE TECHNOLOGY

There is a wide variety of crops grown in Britain, some of which are only suited to particular areas. Sometimes this is because of different soil types, and sometimes because of climate. Farmers maximise the potential from each crop to the best of their ability, out of the necessity to remain profitable and competitive as well as personal pride.

Larger arable farms are kept busy the whole year round with cultivations, drilling (sowing) a succession of arable crops, caring for them and then, later in the year, harvesting them. Cereal crops are valuable and the harvest, between June and September, is weather dependent and the busiest time.

When conditions permit, combine harvesters will be in action from as soon as the dew has dried off in the morning until it comes down again in the evening which may mean working halfway through the night.

Grants are now paid to farmers to leave stubbles after harvest untouched through the winter. If the land isn't required immediately, some farmers sow a green crop as 'green manure' which can be ploughed in later to improve the soil structure. Deep 'mole' ploughing, if needed, is done

◀ Neat rows of newly emerged young corn

out in one action. Seeds are nearly always sown individually and in straight lines, thanks to modern technology, the spacing depending on the crop grown. Usually rows are deliberately missed at measured intervals to leave tracks or 'tramlines' enabling sprays or fertiliser to be applied accurately over the field by large machines without causing damage to the crop.

The most valuable cereal crop is wheat, and plant scientists have developed strains that do not grow very tall, as the straw is of little value.

on heavy land to help drain the ground prior to any other cultivation (preparation of the ground).

Most fields were once ploughed, an action which turns the soil completely over, burying the weeds and crop residue. It is now thought that minimal cultivation is better for the health of the soil and instead, a tractor-mounted implement known as a cultivator, which has large tines that are dragged through the soil, is used to break up the land. Further cultivations are carried out to break down the soil to a fine tilth before the next crop is drilled. Given the right conditions these operations may be combined and carried

Many farmers in recent years have adopted minimal cultivation systems and others a no-till policy by which they leave the ground untouched and sow the seeds directly into it as a way of reducing greenhouse gas emissions and costs. Precision drills are used to sow crops such as maize, beans and sugar beet. These evenly distribute the seeds in the soil, one at a time, with great accuracy. For decades sugar beet needed to be hoed by hand to thin out the plants and remove weeds. Precision drilling makes thinning out unnecessary and weeds can be hoed mechanically with a tractor using a mounted inter-row hoe.

In low rainfall areas, irrigation is used for some crops in times of drought

A crop of wheat flattened and subsequently ruined by heavy rain

While the majority of crops are for food production some are grown especially for seed.

THE ARABLE YEAR

There is a seasonal order in which crops are sown. The first to be drilled after harvest is usually grass which can become established before cold weather sets in. Stubble turnips are sometimes sown directly into uncultivated stubbles as these grow very quickly and will provide fresh green winter feed for sheep. Oilseed rape is sown early, with rye and winter barley following on and then winter wheat and beans by which time in many areas the ground will be too wet for tractors to get on it.

Weed seeds such as poppies can lie dormant in the ground for many years until the soil is disturbed.

After a mid-winter lull, a few drying days in late February and March will see spring wheat, barley and oats being sown. March is also the time when sugar beet and fodder beet are sown, as well as peas and potatoes. Last of all in late spring are the more susceptible linseed (flax), maize, and any other crops which cannot tolerate hard frosts.

By May, when the last of the arable crops have been sown, grass is nearly ready to cut for the first crop of silage and fertilising and spraying crops needs to be done. Hay is usually made in late June or July by which time in southern England winter barley will be quickly ripening. Oilseed rape will also be nearly ready although this is sometimes desiccated (sprayed with a herbicide to kill the plant) to hasten ripening. Other crops continue to be harvested until mid September and even later in the north.

And so the year has passed and the growing cycle begins all over again. Nearly all the crops, with the exception of grass, are annuals and need to be replanted each year.

Overheads in farming are high. Fertiliser is an expensive necessity, for without it plants would be puny and non-productive. However, more attention is being paid to lowering the use of sprays both because of costs and because of public concern over their safety; increasingly they are being used more sparingly.

Growing alternative crops is being explored, especially high protein ones. Meat and bone meal in livestock feed was prohibited because of the BSE health risk so it meant that alternative protein sources had to be found: protein is to animals what fertiliser is to plants. Fish meal is an excellent substitute but fish stocks are already threatened. Soya bean is high in protein but has to be imported, so experimental soya crops are now being grown in this country. The lupin is another plant that may potentially prove to be useful.

WEATHER

Progressive arable farmers are motivated to explore and exploit every possibility that comes their way in order to make a living from the land. The one thing they have no control over is the weather but it plays a key part in the successful growing and harvesting of most crops. In 2020, farmers suffered from the unusual and extreme weather pattern. The previous autumn and winter were mild and extremely wet meaning that barley and winter wheat could not be sown. Farmers made up for it by sowing spring varieties. Then more than two months of record high spring temperatures followed with virtually no rainfall. Yields in some places were down by as much as a third.

Wheat suitable for milling gives the most lucrative returns but only if it is top grade.

In most years, cereal growers' costs are increased by having to artificially dry the grain to a level where it can be stored safely and the quality is acceptable to the buyer. If not dry enough, the heaps of grain get warm and mould grows rendering the crop worthless.

Premium prices are paid for malting barley.

Straw, like hay, must not be baled unless it is properly dry. If damp, it will heat up when the bales are stacked, become mouldy or even be subject to internal combustion.

ROOT CROPS

SUGAR BEET

For centuries Britain imported sugar from British colonies in the West Indies where sugar cane flourished. It wasn't until the early 1900s that sugar beet was grown in Britain; the first factory was opened at Cantley in Norfolk in 1912. Production rapidly increased until

▲ Sugar beet seedlings

levelling out in the 1970s at about 480,000 acres (195,000ha) but new varieties and improved farming practices have now reduced this area to around half that. There are now about 3,000 growers in England producing approximately 8 million tonnes which is converted into 1.4 million tonnes of sugar annually. Of the original 18 sugar beet processing factories only four remain: one in Nottinghamshire and three in East Anglia.

The sugar beet industry supports about 9,500 jobs in farming, processing and transportation. British sugar is grown within roughly a 30 mile radius of the four remaining factories: Bury St Edmunds, Wissington, Cantley and Newark, and marketed under the 'Silver Spoon' label.

Sugar beet is grown under contract ensuring an agreed price per entire crop. This means that in a very good growing year, when the crop is exceptionally heavy, it is guaranteed that any surplus will be purchased but probably at a very low price. An average of 80 tonnes of beet per hectare are harvested between October and March.

Sugar beet can only be grown in soil that is free-draining because of the big machinery needed to harvest it.

Rhizomania is a disease that affects only sugar beet, but scientists have now bred rhizomania-resistant seed which has greatly improved the situation for farmers. Selective plant breeding has increased yields by 25% in the last ten years but sugar beet is also subject to a yellow virus disease spread by aphids which is very difficult to control.

SUGAR BEET YEAR

Sugar beet seed is precision-drilled in March or April. Harvesting begins in late September and continues until the end of February. This harvesting period is known as the '**Campaign**'. Enormous machines complete the harvesting work in one operation. First the green leafy tops are cut off and discarded to one side, the roots are then eased out of the ground onto a rotating turbine or slatted elevator which allows dirt and stones to fall through. The beet is then either stored in a bin on the machine to be emptied later or dropped straight into a trailer driven alongside. The green tops are incorporated back into the soil to provide much-needed organic matter. Alternatively cattle or sheep may be turned into the field to eat them along with any pieces of roots that remain in or on the ground which they find very palatable. In north Norfolk beet tops are often left on the fields for the thousands of migratory pink-footed geese to feed on through the winter.

Most farmers like to have the beet transported to factories as soon as possible after it is lifted, having tipped it into a heap in a place where lorries have easy access to load up. Occasionally the beet is unloaded in a long line rather than a large heap and a special machine moves along the line and loads them onto lorries. Loads can only be taken into the factory by permit, ensuring a constant supply. Later in the season, when there is a significant risk that the ground may become waterlogged or frozen, farmers lift any remaining sugar beet and store it in 'clamps'. Big bales are often used to form a barrier around three sides and if prolonged sub-zero temperatures are forecast

Harvesting sugar beet

Loading sugar beet onto a lorry

the top may be covered with plastic sheeting or more straw as insulation.

The existing four sugar beet factories are advanced manufacturing plants which operate 24 hours a day, 7 days a week during the five or so months they are open. The 1.4 million tonnes of sugar they produce contributes about half the amount consumed in the UK each year.

When the sugar beet arrives at the factory it is sampled for its sugar content, which averages about 17%. It is then washed so that soil, stones and other debris are removed. Once inside the factory the large roots are sliced before passing into large vessels where they are 'diffused', a process like brewing tea in a teapot. The 'cossettes' (slices) are mixed in hot water at 70°C for about an hour which extracts sugar from the slices. The juice so formed is then purified by mixing with milk of lime and adding carbon dioxide gas. The resulting lime solids are then filtered off, carrying much of the impurities with them. Then the juice goes through an evaporation process to concentrate the solution which is either stored or goes on for further processing.

The actual crystallisation process operates in vacuum pans where more reduction takes place before tiny sugar crystals called 'seeds' are introduced to form a nucleus on which larger crystals will form. This mixture of syrup and sugar crystals is then spun in a centrifuge to separate. The crystals are then washed and dried ready for storage while the syrup is processed twice more to extract as much sugar as possible before being discarded to be used as animal feed.

NOTHING WASTED

From the refining process, 500,000 tonnes of dried beet pulp animal feed is marketed annually. More is used as fuel for an anaerobic digestion plant. 300,000 tonnes of a liming product is another which is used on the land as a soil improving agent. When beet is washed after it arrives at the factories 200,000 tonnes of soil and 4,800 tonnes of stones are retrieved which are sold as top soil and aggregates. Surplus heat and carbon dioxide produced in beet processing are put to good use in greenhouses, and surplus electricity is fed into the National Grid system. British Sugar also manage their factory sites for wildlife and biodiversity.

The British Sugar 'Silver Spoon' label markets the white sugar products manufactured from British sugar beet such as granulated, caster and icing sugar. Sugar is also supplied directly to factories producing cereals, sweets, jams, ice cream, cakes and biscuits etc.

POTATOES

About 80% of potatoes eaten in the UK are home grown, with 5-6 million tonnes being produced annually on approximately 300,000 acres (120,000 hectares). The acreage grown is around half of that fifty years ago but output remains the same.

There are about 500 varieties of potatoes but only 80 of them are grown commercially; each has its own distinctive texture and flavour.

Early varieties do not crop so heavily and are not suitable for storing but maincrop potatoes average over 16 tonnes per acre (40-50 tonnes per hectare). Large acreages are grown in the drier, free-draining areas of Britain, predominately on the eastern side of England and Scotland.

Some potato varieties are multi use but others are grown specifically for one purpose, for example crisps or frozen chips.

Enough potatoes can be grown on one acre of land to produce half a million crisps.

The potato farming year

Land is prepared in early spring and formed into ridges, any stones are sifted out and deposited in the dips between the ridges. The tops of potatoes are susceptible to frost damage so planting times vary according to the area. Early varieties are usually planted in March and occasionally covered with plastic to protect them from frost damage. Main crops follow on after. The **chitted** (sprouting) tubers are planted quite deeply, one at a time, by a tractor-drawn machine manned by one or two people whose job it is to keep a check on the proceedings. Several young potatoes grow from one tuber. The tops grow tall and green with either white or purple flowers, depending on the variety, appearing in July or August. If

Potato harvester which sieves out the soil and stones

the tops (**haulm**) are green when the crop is ready to be harvested, the leaves have to be cut off or sprayed to kill them. The growth on main crop varieties, which are not harvested until later in the year, dies off naturally. The earliest of all potatoes are ready in early June, even though they are still immature. But the high price new potatoes command makes a lower yield acceptable. The bulk of potatoes are lifted between September and the end of November when the skins have set and they can be stored safely. In wet autumns it is sometimes impossible for the heavy machinery to get on the land and the crop is destroyed if the ground gets frozen. Huge self-propelled machines lift the potatoes out of the ground and transport them upwards into trailers via a slatted conveyor which sieves out the soil and removes stones.

They still need to be sorted by hand to remove any debris and damaged ones. Sometimes this is done on the field by workers sitting at the rear of the harvesting machine, or it can be done when the trailers unload at the barn where they will be packed or stored. Rejected small or damaged potatoes are used for livestock feed.

Potatoes grown in bulk can be stored for several months inside large, darkened, environmentally controlled buildings.

Nearly all potatoes these days are harvested by machine although the old fashioned method of 'spinning' them out of the ground with a small tractor-drawn implement is still used where they are grown on a small scale. These are then picked up by hand. It is best if they can be left to dry before being gathered but potatoes cannot be left very long because they soon turn green when exposed to light and should not then be eaten.

STUBBLE TURNIPS

Stubble turnips are similar to vegetable turnips and are often sown after harvest directly into the stubble. They are fast growing and both the green tops and roots provide fodder for sheep in late autumn and winter. They are confined to a small part of the field with an electric fence to start with and, when they have cleared that, the fence is moved allowing them access to fresh ground. This system is known as 'folding' and droppings from the sheep add fertility to the soil.

SWEDES AND MANGOLDS

Swedes and mangolds (sometimes called mangelwurzels) are grown in some areas for winter stock feed. Swedes are also used for human consumption.

FODDER BEET

Fodder beet are grown in a similar way to sugar beet but are used specifically for stock feed. They are probably the highest yielding forage crop grown for livestock in the UK, yielding around 20-30 tonnes per acre (50-75 tonnes per hectare).

CEREAL CROPS

There are several uses for grain grown in the UK. Best quality oats, barley and wheat are all grown for breakfast cereals. Wheat is milled and used for bread making and sold as flour for biscuit and cake making. Barley is used in the brewing and distilling industries. Inferior grades of all three are used for livestock feed.

Cereal crops are sown in straight lines which are obvious when they first germinate. In summer when fully developed they gradually turn from green to a pale, dull yellow as they begin to ripen.

Timing is critical when harvesting cereals. They need to be at a stage when the ears of corn are fully ripe otherwise the grain will be too damp to store. If left too long it will fall out onto the ground. The weather for combining has to be dry as combine harvesters do not work efficiently in damp conditions. The moisture content in grain from cereal crops needs to be about 14%

otherwise it will deteriorate in storage. It is often higher than this when harvested and then needs to be artificially dried. The temperature of the heaps of grain needs to be regularly checked. Temperatures above 15°C increase the risk of fungal growth as well as insect and mite populations developing and grain quality quickly deteriorates.

Barley straw is sometimes used as fodder but the majority of straw is used for animal bedding in barns, stables and pig sheds or huts. Some goes for bio-fuel and chopped straw is sometimes used as bedding for horses, poultry and small pets.

Basket-makers use straw and house roofs are often thatched using long wheat, or occasionally rye straw but this has to have been cut using an old fashioned binder and tied into sheaves so that it is in pristine condition.

WHEAT
The grain at the top of the upright wheat stalks does not have 'whiskers' although a few varieties have short ones. The best quality wheat is either used for breakfast cereals or milled into flour for use in the bakery trade.

When growing conditions permit, Britain is able to produce almost the entire quantity of milling wheat required for baking bread, biscuits, cakes etc annually.

In 2008 contracts were introduced to sell bread wheat direct to supermarket bakeries. **Durum**, which looks more like barley, is a variety of wheat grown specially for making pasta.

Lesser quality is known as **feed wheat** and is processed for use in livestock rations or fed as whole grain to poultry or game birds. Wheat has the highest protein of all cereals and by-products from the milling process such as **bran** can be used for either human or animal consumption. The straw is only suitable for use as livestock bedding.

Wheat yields approximately 3-3.5 tonnes per acre (8-9 tonnes per hectare) and nearly 5 million acres (2 million hectares) are grown in the UK each year, mainly in England. Because of adverse national weather in 2020, the wheat crop was 40% lower than average.

BARLEY
The grain on the stalk has long barbed whiskers, individual seeds are encased in a fibrous cover and when ripe the heads knuckle right over.

Barley

Wheat

The best quality is known as **'malting barley'** and used in the brewery and distillery trades for making beer and whisky. By-products from these processes, called brewers grains, or **draff**, are utilised as cattle feed. Inferior quality barley goes for livestock feed and is often crushed and used to fatten cattle. The straw also has some value as feed for cattle, often treated with molasses to make it more palatable and nutritious.

Winter barley can be expected to yield up to about 3 tonnes per acre (8 tonnes per hectare), spring sown barley less. Over 2.5 million acres (one million hectares) is grown annually in the UK mainly in England and Scotland.

OATS

The dainty seed heads droop down on individual stems and do not have any whiskers. Any that do are an unwelcome weed known as **wild oats.** These are removed from crops either by using a selective spray or sometimes by hand (**rogueing**) if there is only a light infestation or when the crop is being grown for seed.

Oats are not so commonly grown as wheat and barley but Scotland is famed for them especially in porridge. The best quality oats are used for milling and breakfast cereals and the rest for livestock feed. It often forms part of the rations for sheep and horses. Like barley, the straw has some value as animal feed. Approximately 420,000 acres (170,000

Oats

hectares) are grown annually, mainly in England and Scotland, yielding at about 2.2 tonnes per acre (5-6 tonnes per hectare).

RYE

Similar in appearance to barley but usually taller, rye is used for milling and breakfast cereal production, with the remainder used for animal feed. It is not grown extensively but in recent years rye has been grown specifically to supply anaerobic digester plants producing green biogas. The fully grown plant is cut while still green before farmers get busy with cereal grain harvesting. 50,000 acres (20,000 ha) and rising are now being grown specifically as biomass and this figure is likely to increase.

Rye

TRITICALE

This is a hybrid cereal created through crossing wheat and rye. Only about 35,000 acres (14,000 ha) are grown each year in the UK and the grain is used in livestock rations. It is sometimes grown as a game cover crop on shooting estates and has potential for being another source of biomass to produce green energy.

QUINOA

Not, strictly speaking, a grain crop although it is often referred to as one. It originated in South America and is considered to be a health food. Attempts have been made to grow it commercially in the UK since 2014 although on a limited scale. It is of particular interest to organic farmers.

FORAGE CROPS

GRASS

This is grown as feed for livestock, either grazed directly or cut and preserved for winter use. Many different species of native perennial grasses cover our hills, downs, fells and marshes providing natural grazing for sheep and cattle. Cultivated varieties are found in lowland fields which are faster growing and more lush. Some **leys** (grass fields) are left in for several years while others are regarded as annuals. Rye grass is very quick growing and is often planted as a silage crop from which three or four cuts may be taken in a year before it is ploughed up.

HAY

Making hay is the traditional method of preserving grass for winter use. It is cut and left to dry in the fields between July and September.

The best quality hay comes from the oldest meadows which comprise a mixture of grasses and other plants.

Best quality hay can command top prices as feed for horses. However, whichever the field it comes from, good hay can only be made in good weather. With the fickle British climate this is a gamble for farmers as the weather needs to remain dry for several days: hay has to be turned two or three times before it is fit to store.

After the grass has been cut it needs to dry quickly and is turned, spread out (**tedded**) and then put into rows before being baled. It needs to be thoroughly dry before it can be baled; sun and a gentle breeze are the ideal conditions. A light shower is a nuisance but an extended period of rain not only makes more work but seriously damages the quality of the hay crop and renders it useless. Baled hay needs to be protected from the weather and stored undercover.

SILAGE

Silage is a comparatively modern way of storing winter feed for livestock through a natural fermentation process. It is made from a green crop, usually grass or maize, which has been cut and allowed to wilt for a day or so.

There are two ways in which silage can be stored.

- It is either picked up with a self-propelled forage harvester which chops it and loads it into a trailer before being taken back to the livestock unit. Molasses is sometimes added.

Preparing a seed bed using a tractor fitted with tracks to avoid compacting the soil

There it is piled loose in a large pit, known as a '**clamp**', then compacted tightly to eliminate the air by driving a heavy tractor to and fro over it. It is then sealed over with plastic sheeting which is often weighted down with old car tyres. One problem associated with this method of making silage is the effluent which leaks out from the compressed and fermenting grass and is difficult to dispose of. Should it pollute a water course, it can be very damaging to the environment. Many people find the smell obnoxious. A new method is to store silage in a long plastic tube known as an AgBag.

- A new, less environmentally-damaging system has revolutionised the production of good quality silage for livestock. Instead of being stored loose in a clamp, after it has been left to wilt for a short time, the silage is baled which compacts and seals it into big bales. These are then tightly wrapped in plastic and can be individually stored safely outdoors. The bales are too heavy to handle by hand but transporting and handling is very simple by tractor. Many farms, whether big or small, now use this method. The downside is disposing of the plastic wrapping.

Silage needs to be left to naturally ferment for at least four weeks before it is fed.

Properly made silage will remain in good condition for many months and is a nutritious food for livestock, and modern techniques make it a more reliable source of winter feed than hay. After it has been analysed, supplementary feed rations can be adjusted to take the quality of different silage crops into account. Silage is mostly fed to cattle, while hay remains a valuable feed source for calves, sheep and horses.

HAYLAGE

Haylage is grass that is grown and cut in the same way as for hay but left to dry for a shorter time

so it has a higher moisture content. Like silage, it is baled and the bales are tightly wrapped immediately afterwards to preserve the quality.

LUCERNE (ALFALFA)

A deep-rooted perennial which grows well in dry areas. It has a blue/purple flower and is cut green to be used for hay or silage.

CLOVER

A perennial with a white or red flower. It is not often grown but can also be used for either hay or silage.

KALE

A popular autumn/winter frost-hardy green feed for dairy cows, which are usually only allowed access to a fresh, narrow strip each day so that the crop is not damaged by being trampled on. Kale is also sometimes grown for game cover when it may be left in situ for a second year. This, apart from saving costs, also allows seeds to develop after it has flowered in spring which are particularly attractive to many small farmland birds.

MAIZE

Maize is grown across the country to make silage for animal fodder and, increasingly in the last few years, as fuel for anaerobic digesters. Because of this, demand and therefore production, has rocketed. In 2020 about 450,000 acres (183,000ha) was grown.

In appearance, maize looks very similar to sweetcorn although the crop is bulkier and grows thicker and taller, reaching over 6 feet (2 metres) in height.

It has two or three cobs on each stalk and makes nutritious winter feed. It is harvested for silage in a similar way to grass, usually with the whole crop being chopped when it is cut and put in a clamp in September when the plant

Tractor-drawn and self-propelled crop sprayers are used for spraying insecticides, pesticides, fungicides and other preventative treatments on crops.

is naturally beginning to dry off. Before that happens though the farmer sometimes makes a few pounds extra profit by cutting a configuration of tracks through it to create a 'maize maze' for the public to find their way around!

Maize grown as biomass fuel for anaerobic digester plants is also cut in September or October and transported straight off the field to the AD plant.

Maize is also frequently grown on shooting estates in strips or small blocks to provide food and shelter for pheasants and partridges. Millet is occasionally planted with it, the small seeds of which are very attractive to both game and other smaller birds.

PULSES

BEANS (FIELD OR TIC)

There are many varieties which can be sown in the autumn or spring, usually into ground that is ploughed but not cultivated to a fine tilth as it is for other crops. The plant is very closely related to the broad bean grown by gardeners. It is harvested after it has turned black in late summer and begins to die off. Beans, when they are harvested, yield about 2-3 tonnes per acre (5-8 tonnes per hectare). The majority of the 460,000 acres (185,000 ha) grown in 2020, are in England. In the UK field beans are crushed and used for animal feed but there is also a market for them in North Africa and the Middle East for human consumption.

PEAS

There are many varieties of peas and although some are grown commercially as a fresh vegetable others are used for animal feed. For this the plants are left in the field to dry off naturally before harvesting. The separated peas are then crushed. There has been a significant increase in dry peas grown which, when harvested, yield up to 2.3 tonnes per acre (6 tonnes per hectare). About 126,000 acres (51,000 ha) of peas for harvesting dry are grown annually, mainly in England.

SOYA BEAN

One of the prime sources of protein for both animals and humans is soya which is not grown on a wide scale in Britain although experimental crops are being tried by a few farmers with limited success. The plant is similar in appearance to a 'dwarf' or 'french' bean grown by gardeners and the beans need to be dried after harvesting.

CHICKPEAS

Another experimental crop. Farmers who made the decision to grow less rape because of the difficulty of controlling flea beetle are looking at other crops to grow in its place. Some farmers are looking at chickpeas which are the key ingredient of hummus and need to be dried before use. With the increasing number of vegetarians and vegans there is increasing demand for both soya and chickpeas, the bulk of which are currently imported.

LUPIN

This is another experimental crop appearing in the British countryside. Lupin is grown for its seeds which are high in protein for animal feed.

MISCELLANEOUS CROPS

OILSEED RAPE

This is a member of the mustard family whose tiny seeds develop inside pods. It is the crop which creates a patchwork of bright yellow fields across the countryside when it flowers in April and May, and is dreaded by those who suffer from asthma and hay fever. The majority of rape is grown in England particularly in the east of the country.

Rape is usually ready to harvest from July onwards, and is often cut or sprayed with glyphosate to dry it off prior to combining. There is only a short window when the crop is at its best to harvest before the pods burst open and the ripe seed drops out and falls to the ground. The coarse stalks are baled and used for producing green energy or shredded by the combines at the time of harvesting and spread back on to the field.

Oilseed rape yields about 3 tonnes per hectare and about 850,000 acres (345,000 ha) were grown in 2020.

In 2018 the EU banned the use of neonicotinoids because there was growing evidence that it was harming domesticated honey bees and other pollinating species of wild insects. Since its withdrawal rape crops in the UK have been badly affected by flea beetle, a pest which can decimate the plants. Rape yields were down by a third in 2020. Neonicotinoids were applied as a seed dressing to protect against cabbage stem flea beetle. Now, because of the high risk of serious damage to the crop without this protection, farmers have substantially reduced the amount of rape being grown. This results in more having to be imported coming from countries which, in all likelihood, are using products that are illegal in the UK.

The small seeds are dried, stored then crushed to extract the oil which is used for cooking and in margarine, salad dressings etc, for livestock feed, biodiesel fuel and industrial lubricants.

▼ Field of rape in flower

▲ Linseed fields create a beautiful pale blue patchwork landscape across England in early summer

Because of the situation, rape growers are experimenting with natural ways of deterring flea beetles. One method being tried is sowing it more thinly along with a crop of buckwheat which it is hoped might disguise the rape plants, reducing attack by flea beetle at the time when they are most vulnerable. The use of treated human sewage incorporated in the soil in the form of sludge, is another way being tried to deter attacks. This not only has some value as a fertilizer but is strong smelling which, it is hoped, flea beetle will avoid.

MUSTARD

Mustard is planted in late spring and looks very similar to rape but is susceptible to frost. It is normally grown for game cover or to be ploughed back into the soil as a green manure and, on a small scale, for culinary use.

LINSEED (FLAX)

Linseed adds colour to the landscape for a short time in early summer but only when the sun comes out.

Its pretty blue flowers burst open only to close up again when the sun disappears.

Linseed is one of the oldest cultivated crops but only around 66,000 acres (27,000ha) are grown in the UK. It is a small delicate plant growing only about 18 inches (half a metre) tall. Some varieties can be sown in autumn, others in spring. The seeds of linseed are tiny and yields are well under a tonne per acre (less than 2.5 tonnes per hectare). They are used in the human health food sector and oil is extracted for industrial use. More than 40% oil can be extracted from the seed and it has many uses including the manufacturing of paints, varnishes, printing ink and linoleum. The residue left from the extraction process is compacted into high protein 'cake' for use in livestock rations.

There are also varieties of linseed that are grown for their stalks which are sometimes chopped and used for animal or poultry bedding: light to handle, super absorbent, not dusty and rots down quickly after use. However, the fibre is mainly used to manufacture linen, high quality paper such as that once used for bank notes and more recently for car interior mouldings. Because of its excellent insulation value, flax straw is now also being used in house construction.

HEMP

Industrial hemp has enormous potential as a crop but because of complicated requirements, only about 2,000 hectares are grown in the UK. Although it is a member of the cannabis family, industrial hemp is of no use for producing narcotics because the cannabis content is very low. Legislation has recently been amended and hemp is now recognised separately from other cannabis species. Even so there are a number of regulations that have to be complied with to stay within the law and growers in the UK have to obtain an approved Home Office licence before it can be grown.

Hemp is sown in spring, is very quick-growing and environmentally friendly. The fibres are used for making paper, rope, textiles, clothing, biodegradable plastics, paint, insulation, biofuel. In recent years the majority of UK-grown industrial hemp has been used in the building and construction industry. The seeds are used for food, oil, health products and animal feed.

GLOSSARY

ANNUAL A crop that completes its life cycle in one year or less

BIENNIAL A crop that is sown one year and harvested the next

PERENNIAL A crop that will keep producing for more than two years

LEY Area sown with grass

STUBBLE The remaining stalks left in a field after a crop has been cut

FALLOW Land that is ploughed but left without a crop being planted

BREAK CROP A rotational crop grown that helps to prevent a build-up of disease, replenish certain nutrients and may add organic matter to the soil

ROTATION System of management where crops are grown in a certain order

LEGUME Pod-bearing plant such as pea or bean

BRASSICA A member of the mustard family which includes a large number of plants including kale, rape and swede

HAY Dried grass

SILAGE Fresh grass that has been compressed and left to partially ferment

STRAW Dried stalks of cereals

EAR Grain bearing head of cereal

AWNS The 'whiskers' on ears of cereals

BINDER Old fashioned horse or tractor drawn implement that cuts and ties cereal crops into sheaves

SHEAF Old fashioned method of harvesting cereals where they were cut and tied into small bundles

STOOK or SHOCK A group of sheaves, usually eight, stood together and left out in the field to finish drying

LAID/LODGED Standing crop that has been flattened, usually resulting from heavy rain

ROGUEING The pulling up by hand of unwanted plants, usually applied to removing the weed known as wild oat from cereal crops.

BALE Hay, straw or grass compressed into round or rectangular shapes and fastened securely with string, mesh or plastic

TOP DRESS Spread fertilizer on to the ground

PESTICIDE General term for herbicides, fungicides and insecticides

FUNGICIDE Chemical that destroys fungal diseases of plants

HERBICIDE Chemical applied to kill plants

INSECTICIDE Chemicals that destroy insect pests on plants

SELECTIVE SPRAY Herbicide that kills certain plant species while leaving others unharmed

DESICCATE Spray with the herbicide glyphosate which quickly kills every plant

LIGHT LAND Free draining soil such as sandy types.

HEAVY LAND Water retaining soil such as clay

LOAMY LAND Fertile soil which is a mixture of clay, sand and silt and the ideal soil type for growing most crops. It retains sufficient water without becoming waterlogged, as is the case with heavy land, and does not dry out quickly like light land.

HEADLAND The ground forming the perimeter of a field

TRAMLINE Evenly spaced gaps left in a crop the exact width of the machinery wheels. Used as a management tool to make spraying and fertilising easier

COMBINE Large self-propelled machine that cuts crops and separates the grain from the stalks

SPINNER An implement that dispenses seeds or fertiliser over a wide area

PLOUGH A tractor-drawn implement that slices through the soil and turns it over as it does so

MOLE PLOUGH An implement that cuts deep into the ground and leaves a mole's tunnel effect to improve drainage

LAND DRAIN Pipe installed beneath the soil to drain off excess water into ditches.

FURROW The number of blades on a plough or the narrow channels it leaves in the soil

PRESS An implement attached to a plough which levels and compacts the soil

TILTH Broken down condition of the soil in the preparation of a seed bed

DISCS A tractor-drawn implement that consists of round discs used to break up lumps in the soil

CULTIVATOR A tined, tractor-drawn implement that breaks up the soil

ROTOVATOR A tractor-powered implement that breaks down the soil into a fine tilth

HARROW A tractor-drawn spiked implement for levelling the soil or 'combing' grassland

ROLLER A heavy tractor-drawn implement for compacting the soil or grassland , either having a flat surface or comprising solid rings

DRILL A tractor-drawn implement for the precision sowing of seeds

SPRAYER An implement, either tractor-drawn or self-propelled, for the precise application of liquids. Used for crop protection as well as applying fertiliser

BOOM The fold up 'arm' of a sprayer

CLAMP A large heap of a root or fodder crop such as maize or grass

GAME COVER Crop grown to provide food and shelter for pheasants and partridges, very often a mixture of seed-bearing plants

CHITTED The new growth on seeds or plants. Potatoes are deliberately exposed to the light prior to being planted to encourage growth in order to hasten development

Specialist plant breeding and management has resulted in very high yielding crops of tomatoes
© Thanet Earth

HORTICULTURE CROPS

INTRODUCTION

3.5 million tonnes of fruit and vegetables are grown annually on 378,000 acres (153,000 ha) of land in Britain. Horticulture is very labour intensive and the industry employs approximately 40,000 full time workers augmented by a large number of seasonal workers.

About 56% of vegetables and 16% of fruit consumed are grown in the UK.

The number of vegans has quadrupled in the last 15 years and organic fruit and vegetables are often their first choice. The fastest growing sector is vines for wine making.

The Covid-19 pandemic which hit the UK in the spring of 2020 benefitted some sectors of horticulture. People were forced to cater for themselves at home. This happened at the time of year when home-grown salad products were just coming onto the UK market and sales boomed as retailers adjusted to increased demand and in many cases offered home deliveries. As the lockdown period progressed into summer, vegetables became readily available and many companies that had previously supplied hotels and restaurants turned to supplying boxes of mixed produce direct to customers.

NEW DEVELOPMENTS

There are several large producers who have acres of land under glass producing salad crops. State-of-the-art greenhouses provide ideal microclimates in which they are grown as well as having fully automated systems which can be remotely controlled, in some cases using a mobile phone. The largest glasshouse complex in the UK is Thanet Earth in north-east Kent, which opened in 2008 and covers a remarkable 220acres (90ha). The crunch comes, however, when the crops need picking because this can only be done by hand and it is very difficult to find sufficient labour.

A range of coloured fruit and vegetables are now obtainable although they are still a niche market. Black tomatoes, bright pink mushrooms, yellow beetroot, blue potatoes, orange cauliflowers and red lettuce, celery and sprouts can now be discovered on supermarket shelves. Orange is no longer the only colour of a carrot. They now come in shades of red, yellow, purple and white. Many new colours of vegetables are in fact historic: purple carrots were being grown in Egypt in 2,000BC but in the 16th century the Dutch used mutant seed to change them to the orange we're familiar with today.

Scientific research into plant breeding continues to improve the quality and disease-resistance of plants. Combined with good management, the resulting uniformity of a crop can be very impressive. Any vegetable gardener will fully appreciate how difficult this is to achieve.

The commercial growing of vegetable and fruit crops is scattered across the British countryside wherever conditions suit the crops but there is very little horticulture in Wales. All root crops need to be grown on light, free-draining land, firstly because in early spring a fine seed bed has to be worked in which to sow the seeds and secondly, heavy machinery needs to be able to get on the ground in autumn and winter to harvest the crops. For this reason a lot of vegetable crops are grown in East Anglia and the East Midlands. The rich, black soil of the Fens makes it one of Britain's prime vegetable-growing areas and there are many packing stations scattered throughout the area.

Kent is famous for its orchards, particularly for its cherries. The West Midlands is known for its apple orchards and Somerset for its cider. Greenhouse produce, salad crops and soft fruit are grown extensively in many parts of England. Cheap imports have reduced the amounts grown in this country although this situation may well change post Covid-19 and Brexit.

THE ROLE OF SUPERMARKETS

Top quality produce found on supermarket shelves is normally supplied by growers under contract. It is in the supermarkets' interest to deal with big suppliers, reducing their administration and other costs while ensuring consistent quality and availability.

However, this puts the producers under enormous pressure as they have to invest heavily in expensive equipment with no guarantees that the whole crop will be used, nor for what

◄ Asparagus is sometimes protected with polythene to ensure an early crop

price. Waitrose are unique in having their own 4,000 acre (1,600ha) Leckford Estate in Hampshire, the produce from which supplies their supermarkets.

Large supermarkets are powerful. They notify their contracted growers of their requirements and the price they will be paid for it. The harder part is for the growers. They have to estimate what acreages of the crop they need to grow to fulfil the order. They need to care for it in such a way that it is ready for harvesting at the agreed time and is of the high quality demanded.

When seasonal products, such as lettuces, cannot be grown in the UK at certain times of the year (usually winter and early spring) the grower under contract is expected to supply the goods by sourcing crops from abroad.

Spain is an ideal place to grow salad crops with a warmer climate than Britain, and relatively close in terms of transport costs. But in some instances crops such as parsnips have even been sourced as far afield as Australia to ensure a constant supply for the supermarkets during early summer when they cannot be grown here.

TRANSPORTATION

Even though produce may have come from the other side of the world, it can still reach the British consumer in perfect condition. It is sealed in special 'modified atmosphere' plastic bags which release the harmful gases that hasten degeneration while retaining other gases which maintain the produce in good condition for as long as 28 days. This type of packaging is seldom used in Britain except when it may be necessary to hold produce over, such as at Christmas time. Most perishable fruit and vegetables grown in this country arrive at the supermarket within 24 hours of being picked or harvested. The exceptions such as potatoes, onions and apples can be stored for several months in a controlled environment without deteriorating.

Producers not directly contracted to supermarkets sell to wholesalers who then distribute to smaller shops and traders, which means that the produce might not be quite so fresh by the time it reaches the customer. The increasing

Fruit crops can be ruined by a late frost when the trees are in blossom

▲ Crops of lettuces require irrigating twice weekly during dry weather

number of farmers markets provide a useful outlet for many smaller growers and by selling direct off the farm they cut out the middle man.

WEATHER AND SOLUTIONS TO IT

The weather, as ever, is the bogeyman. Other than growing crops in greenhouses or plastic tunnels, where the environment can be controlled, there is little that can be done to combat unseasonal UK temperatures and rainfall.

Fleece

Covering early outdoor salad and vegetable crops with plastic or spun horticultural fleece in spring provides a relatively cheap solution. Horticultural fleece, made from polypropylene, was invented in France in the 1980s and has since become widely used as protection for a variety of early crops. It is lightweight, permeable, lets in the light, insulates the plants and retains warmth in the soil thus speeding up growth. It also offers protection from wind, rain, frost, birds and to some extent insects. Fleece is laid on the ground immediately after the crop is sown from a roll mounted on a tractor and put in place by hand. It is possible to wind up the used fleece and, if handled carefully, it can be used for a second season if considered to be cost effective to sort and clean it. An alternative

is to send it for recycling and there are companies across the country that deal with discarded farm plastic waste. It is manufactured into pellets that are recycled to make plastic wood which can then be used for a variety of agricultural uses including fence posts and pig huts. Otherwise agricultural fleece and plastic has to be dumped in landfill sites as it is illegal to burn it. While fleece has so many benefits, the downside comes in disposing of it afterwards. Efforts are being made to create biodegradable fleece.

Both plastic and fleece are normally removed by mid-May when the weather should be milder although a hard frost later in the month can cause severe damage to some crops.

Irrigation

Another problem likely to face growers raising crops outdoors is lack of rainfall and drought. Many vegetable and fruit crops, particularly in the drier parts of Britain, are likely to need irrigating.

Carrots and parsnips need a soaking at least once a week, lettuces twice and potatoes require an astounding inch (2.5cm) of water each week.

Such irrigation can be supplied by many methods from the simple rain gun which swishes water from side to side while slowly dragging itself across the field to sophisticated computerised systems delivering a fine mist to the more delicate plants. For many years water for agricultural use has been abstracted, under licence, directly from rivers or underground boreholes.

The drought years in the early 1990s put a severe strain on the country's water resources and the Environment Agency began to take a close look at the feasibility of allowing crop irrigation to continue on their 10-year licensing system and the revenue received from it. Many growers realised that their licenses to abstract water may not be renewed when they expired, so rather than put their crops in jeopardy they began to build reservoirs on their farms and lay a network of underground pipes to reach parts of their land where irrigation might be needed. These reservoirs are topped up in autumn and winter, under Environment Agency supervision, from rivers once they exceed a minimum height. This is an excellent way of preserving unwanted excess winter rainfall until the summer time when rivers are naturally low. Most of the reservoirs have been constructed on crop-growing farms in the East of England which is the driest part of the UK.

Extreme Weather

Extreme weather later in the year also causes problems. A prolonged wet spell in autumn can make it impossible to harvest potato crops. But potatoes are unable to withstand severe frosts so cannot be left in the ground. A few weeks of hard winter weather, when the ground is frozen solid, can make picking brassicas or harvesting carrots or parsnips almost impossible.

Polythene and straw laid on top of the rows provide some insulation for root vegetables and helps prevent the soil from freezing. It can also delay unwanted growth when spring arrives with its warmer temperatures. Laying this, though, is a costly undertaking and is a dilemma that growers face as it may well prove to be a waste of money in mild winters. While the straw can be ploughed back into the ground and will improve the soil structure, disposing of the polythene is an issue.

DISEASE AND PEST CONTROL

There are stringent government regulations relating to chemical use, and supermarkets are extremely strict over what treatments can be used, and when.

Regular inspections and testing is carried out to ensure that no residues remain in produce by the time it reaches the consumer.

There is always great public concern regarding the use of sprays, and farmers would much prefer not to need to use any at all because they are costly not only to purchase but also to apply. Crops are regularly monitored for the presence

Planting a field with lettuce plants is labour intensive

Harvesting leeks by hand

of pests and traps baited with pheromones are used to catch a sample of insects and moths in order to identify potential problems.

Pesticide use is decreasing as the chemicals have become more efficient and through selective breeding, plants have been bred to be more pest and disease resistant. A few treatments are approved for use on organic farms.

Commercial trials with natural plants such as garlic, which can act as a barrier against insect pests as well as diseases, have promising results. For example, traps are set out amongst pea crops to monitor moths that can cause devastation within the pod, or flies whose larvae can end up as maggots inside carrots. By checking the traps regularly it is possible to know whether the crop is likely to be at risk from the presence of these pests and act accordingly.

While consumers express their grave concerns about the use of pesticides, many would be horrified to find maggots in carrots and peas, slugs and aphids on their lettuces and caterpillars in their cabbages and cauliflowers which would be commonplace if sprays weren't used.

LABOUR CHALLENGES IN HORTICULTURE

Another major problem that large growers are eternally faced with is that of recruiting sufficient labour. Only 11% of seasonal workers in 2020 were from the UK.

Although there are now hi-tech machines to do most jobs there is still a great need for manual workers in the horticultural industry. Lettuces have to be cut by hand. In the field they are placed in cups on a huge machine known as a '**rig**'. A gang of workers do the cutting while another team will be on board the rig trimming, wrapping and packing. They put 10 lettuces into each crate and handle maybe 3-4,000 crates a day.

There may be as many as four of these rigs working in the same field at any one time.

Salad onions are pulled by hand, the roots and tops trimmed and the outer skin removed before being bunched together with two elastic bands. Celery is gathered in a similar way to lettuces, first cut by hand before being placed on the rig where each head is washed, trimmed, packaged and put

NATURAL PEST-CONTROL

The application of beneficial nematodes is a comparatively new, non-chemical, biological treatment for crops and is an asset to organic growers. Nematodes are microscopic worm-like creatures that act as parasites on other insects. There are thousands of different kinds; some can be damaging while others can be used to advantage when applied as they seek out and kill the larval stages of harmful soil-dwelling insects. Specific nematodes target individual species of pests by first entering the pest larvae and injecting it with bacteria, causing death. They will then eat the dead body, multiply, and immediately start searching for a new host. If they can't find one, they themselves die.

into a crate. Cabbages, cauliflowers and leeks are also cut by hand and packaged on a rig.

Greenhouse produce, tomatoes, cucumbers, peppers, soft fruits, flowers etc have to be very carefully picked by hand to avoid damage and consequently are very labour intensive. Thousands of people are employed in packing stations sorting, packaging and despatching fruit and vegetables often working around the clock on a shift system.

Only about 25% of the cost of production of greenhouse produce is in the actual growing, the other 75% is accounted for with packaging, labour and transport.

WASTED PRODUCE

There is a huge amount of waste of horticultural produce because what is not quite perfect is rejected by supermarkets. Sometimes produce that isn't top grade might be sold to wholesalers and appear on markets stalls. Alternatively it goes for processing to be sold canned or frozen or used in ready meals. The latest 'war on waste' initiative is using what would have gone for

animal feed or been dumped as fuel for anaerobic digester plants, producing eco-friendly power.

Why do supermarkets insist on only offering immaculate produce? There is probably nowhere else in the world which offers such consistently high quality and safe products as those found on UK supermarket shelves. In real terms many horticultural goods still cost less now than they did several years ago. Just as they are with livestock production British standards are normally higher than elsewhere, even within the EU, which adds to overall costs of the producer.

CROP PRODUCTION

Root vegetables need to be grown in soil that is free of stones. This allows the roots to grow perfectly and eliminates the risk of damage to machinery used to harvest the crop.

Soil preparation begins soon after Christmas when the ground is ploughed; it is then ridged up. Tractor-drawn stone picking machines work their way very slowly along the ridges sifting the soil and depositing stones into the deep furrows in between. Potato tubers are mostly planted deeply, directly into the ridges because the developing potatoes must not be

Laying polythene over newly sown carrots for an early crop

Harvesting carrots with the fronds left on

exposed to light. If they are, they turn green and become unusable. For other crops the soil is either levelled out or formed into raised beds about a metre, in some cases two metres, wide which buries the stones sufficiently deep enough not to affect the development of the roots. The seeds are then sown in rows. In some cases cereal seeds might be sown with them to provide some protection and stabilise the soil, preventing the smaller seeds from being blown away. The cereal growth is then sprayed off with a selective herbicide once the desired crop is established.

Much research has gone into plant breeding; scientists have made giant strides with regard to disease resistance and productivity. F1 hybrids have been developed as the result of crossing two different varieties to produce a third which combines the best attributes of both.

Commercially grown vegetable seeds are usually treated to protect them from pests in the ground and sometimes 'pelleted' - ie coated with fertiliser as garden seeds occasionally are. Most of the sowing is done with 'precision drills' that plant the seeds out evenly so they do not compete for space, thus eliminating the need to thin the crop. Drilling of carrots, parsnips and onions begins in January or February and the early crops are usually covered with strips of agricultural fleece or polythene sheeting to protect them from the weather and encourage fast germination. The fleece is designed to allow water to seep through while protecting the crop from wind and the cold. The covering is removed in early May when the crop is well established but there are difficulties with disposing of it because it cannot be recycled and is not easily used again. Parsnips continue to be sown until mid-May and carrots until mid-June.

ROOT CROPS

To improve the quality and prevent damage to machinery used to harvest them, all root crops for human consumption need to be grown in stone-free soil.

CARROTS

Carrots are now available in a variety of colours, purple, yellow, white, other than the standard orange but this is a case of this popular root crop turning full circle. Carrots first appeared in Britain in Elizabethan times having originated from Holland where the original red, purple, black, yellow, and white varieties were hybridised to create today's bright orange.

On average each person in the UK eats about 100 carrots a year.

Approximately 700,000 tonnes are grown on 22,000 acres (9,000 ha) in the UK. Harvesting begins in mid-June and continues almost throughout the year. Later crops intended for winter use are often covered with straw to protect them from frost so they can still be harvested in hard weather when the ground might otherwise be frozen.

There are two types of huge, self-propelled, multi-row harvesters used to gather commercially grown carrots. One lifts them by pulling them out of the ground by their tops, known as '**top lifting**'; early in the season this is often carried out at night to ensure their freshness. The other method for later main crop carrots uses a 'share harvester' which slices off the tops and eases them out of the ground with a blade. They are carried up an elevator before being tipped into a trailer and then taken straight from the field to factories or packing stations where they are washed and packed.

Carrots reach supermarket shelves within 24 hours of being lifted.

The carrot grower contracted to supply the produce is given an order late in the afternoon, which is confirmed the following morning and he is expected to deliver the goods that same afternoon. This means that people employed on the farms or in the packing sheds may have to work shifts, even sometimes through the night.

Each pack is sent out 10% over its marked weight to allow for any dehydration that may occur before it is purchased.

PARSNIPS
Parsnips are lifted by machine and handled in much the same way as main crop carrots. Harvesting begins in late July and continues through until mid-April. Although more frost-resistant than carrots, some late parsnip crops are covered in straw for the same reasons.

Parsnips need to be kept moist after lifting. If they are allowed to dry out the skins turn yellow making them look unattractive.

Only about 50% of the crops of carrots and parsnips make the required top grade, the remainder is used for processing or animal food.

Swedes and turnips for human consumption are grown on a much lesser scale and may also be grown for livestock fodder. Turnips are

Harvesting beetroot June-October

frequently sown directly into stubbles after harvest as winter food for sheep which eat both the tops and the roots.

BEETROOT

Grown and harvested in a very similar way to carrots, the beetroot seed is sown in March and April and the crop harvested from June to October. It is either sold fresh in bunches with the tops left on or vacuum packed. Some is sold in jars pickled in vinegar or is sent for further processing.

COMMON BULB ONIONS

These are either grown from seed, transplanted seedlings or 'sets' which are small immature onions grown the previous summer and kept dormant for a period of time. When planted, they resume growing into mature onions. Sometimes onions are sown in autumn to provide an early crop the following year but the majority are planted in spring for autumn harvesting. When onion seed is sown, it might be necessary on very light land to grow some cereals or incorporate a small amount of straw to stabilise the soil until the crop has got established.

Main crop onions are dug up by machine, which slices the tops off and lays them on top of the ground for a short while to dry before being loaded onto a trailer. On reaching the storage barns they are sorted, dried and stored in a similar way to potatoes.

Red onions are also popular for their milder flavour and are often used in salads because of their attractive colouring.

SALAD CROPS

TOMATOES

Approximately 92,000 tonnes of tomatoes are produced annually in heated greenhouses but this is only a fifth of the total sold in the UK. High energy costs have always been a stumbling block in growing glasshouse produce in the UK but renewable energy has made this more workable. Modern greenhouses are designed to be as energy-efficient as possible and sometimes utilise surplus heat, carbon dioxide and rainwater from another manufacturing source. Larger and larger glasshouse complexes are being built each year so home production is increasing. The biggest greenhouse complex at present is Thanet Earth in Kent, an industrial-scale unit that covers 220 acres (90ha) and uses high technology which allows total control of climatic conditions inside.

Thanet Earth produces 30 million cucumbers, 24 million peppers and 400 million tomatoes annually which are all picked by hand and packed on site.

Two other giant glasshouses, one near Norwich in Norfolk and the other near Bury St Edmunds in Suffolk have recently come into production. Covering 40 acres (16ha) and 32 acres (13ha) respectively they are at the forefront of carbon efficiency and renewable energy use. Sited next to Anglian Water's water treatment facilities, heat is extracted from the sewage works and through the use of renewable energy, carbon emissions are reduced by 75%.

HYDROPONIC GROWTH

Commercial tomatoes are usually grown hydroponically (using water not soil) in large troughs. The plants are first rooted in a recyclable fibre block with an opening in the base and as they develop, the roots are left exposed. Nutrients the plants require are fed into the water and, as the plants grow, they are trained vertically up wires. It's possible for them to reach 50 feet (15m) in height. In optimum growing conditions one plant might produce up to 40lb (18kg) of fruit. Lighting is controlled to replicate summer conditions all year round.

▲ Salad crops are grown extensively under glass in England © Thanet Earth

Inside the glasshouses friendly insects are released as natural predators to eradicate pests and, most importantly, worker bees or bumblebees are released to pollinate the plants.

Peppers and cucumbers are grown in a similar way.

LETTUCE

From the beginning of March onwards, lettuce plants, which have been started off in greenhouses, are planted outdoors. Iceberg and Little Gem are the most popular varieties. Using plants purchased from other commercial growers rather than growing from seed is the most popular method. All the lettuces in a crop are cut at the same time, for economic reasons.

Fleece or porous plastic is usually put over early crops in March and left on for five or six weeks. Planting is normally carried out on a weekly basis to ensure a continuous crop for harvesting from the second week of May until mid-October. The whole process of cutting and packing is carried out on the field by a gang of workers. As soon as possible after the lettuces have been cut and packed on the rig, they are taken back to the factory where they are vacuum cooled to a temperature of about 4°C and kept chilled to maintain them in perfect condition.

On a lesser scale, lettuce is sometimes grown in polytunnels or greenhouses. There is also increased interest in 'vertical farming' to produce salad crops artificially. This is a soil-less method of growing plants in trays stacked one above the other using rainwater with added nutrients and artificial heating and lighting. Seven times

Harvesting and packing lettuces using a self-propelled rig

more can be harvested than from the same area of polytunnels but the downside is that energy costs are very high.

SALAD ONION

The seed is sometimes drilled in August or September under polythene so that early picking can begin in late March the following year. Onions are hardy enough to survive the average British winter. For a continuous supply, sowing resumes in February, weather permitting, and continues until July. Picking continues until mid-October. Gangs of people are employed for the laborious job of pulling, preparing and bunching. Sometimes floodlights are erected in the fields so that work can continue through the night if it is necessary to fulfil orders.

CELERY

Mainly grown in the fenland of East Anglia, celery is cut by hand and washed, trimmed and packed on huge self-propelled rigs similar to those used for lettuces. Contracts are made between growers and supermarkets and the celery is cut according to their requirements.

Harvesting peas for freezing with a 'viner'

Often this means working from early morning to late at night. Large growers who are contracted to supply celery all year round rely on casual workers.

The massive celery-harvesting rigs, weighing more than 30 tons, are sometimes transported out to Spain to continue with the harvesting there through the winter, a massive undertaking.

OTHER CROPS

LEEKS

Leeks are harvested between November and May and a total of about 34,000 tons are grown on 5,000 acres (2,000ha) annually in the UK. A machine similar to that used for processing lettuces in the field is used. The pickers manually pull the leeks and cut the tops off before they are trimmed and packed on the rig.

PEAS

Peas for freezing are sown in the spring, inspected regularly and their growth monitored. The season is short and they are harvested as soon as they are at their best which, ideally, is during a 24-36 hour time slot. Samples are tested for tenderness before the decision is made to start harvesting a field. Large machines called **'viners'**, are used to cut and shell the peas. These cost £500,000 each and are only in use for six to eight weeks of the year. Tractors and trailers transport the peas immediately to a processing plant where they are cleaned, packed and frozen within two and a half hours. Around 86,000acres (35,000 ha) of vining peas are grown in the UK annually. Birds Eye is the leading producer, growing 45,000 tonnes each year and there are three million peas in every tonne! Selective plant breeding has created strains that are prolific with pods that all mature at the same time.

BRASSICAS (CABBAGES, SPROUTS)

As with lettuces, it is more economic to grow brassicas from plants supplied by specialist growers rather than to grow them from seed. They are normally planted out in the spring ready for harvesting in autumn and winter although some varieties of cabbages, calabrese and cauliflower are gathered throughout the summer. Harvesting any kind of greens during the winter when they are wet or frozen is unpleasant work, some of which inevitably has to be done by hand. Cabbages, broccoli and cauliflower are harvested in a similar way to lettuces by gangs of workers who cut them ahead of large slow-moving self-propelled machines. They are placed on a conveyor belt which carries them inside where they are sorted and packed.

For many years sprouts were picked by hand, a thankless task in the cold and the wet.

Fortunately there are now machines that strip sprouts from the main stalk on which they grow.

▲ Cutting asparagus during the short season

BRITISH ASPARAGUS

These are grown on light land and the tender shoots grow quickly and need to be picked daily by hand before they grow too big. They are taken to packing sheds, sorted, washed, bundled and refrigerated prior to delivery. The season is a short one, usually beginning in late April or early May and traditionally ending on June 21st. As with every sector of horticulture, cutting and packing asparagus is not a job that appeals to many British workers so foreign labour has come to be relied upon.

There is only a very limited time when asparagus is at its best.

COURGETTES

Courgettes are grown outdoors and cannot tolerate cold temperatures. Once established in late spring the courgettes develop quickly and are picked by hand. To supply the size preferred by consumers, this has to be done frequently otherwise they rapidly develop into marrows.

DWARF GREEN BEANS

These are usually imported but can be grown in this country. They are normally picked by hand although a unique, specially designed machine was trialled in 2020 when Covid-19 restrictions resulted in a drastic reduction of migrant labour being available. It is possible that this machine might be able to replace 200 hand pickers and green beans will be grown in the UK on a larger scale.

SWEETCORN

This is very similar to maize but is available for only a very short season when it is at its best in late summer. It is usually handpicked.

RHUBARB

While many country cottages have a rhubarb patch, the majority of Britain's rhubarb crop comes from what is known as the 'Yorkshire Rhubarb Triangle' – an area between Wakefield, Leeds and Bradford. Here it is traditionally 'forced' to grow prematurely in sheds, in the dark, so that it can be harvested in late winter. Elsewhere it is grown in fields for the canning industry and harvested in spring.

FRUIT

SOFT FRUIT

Virtually all soft fruit in the UK is picked by hand and typically labour costs account for half the cost of production. Each variety only has a short season and gangs of pickers, very often Eastern Europeans, are employed. Large fruit farms grow several different varieties or species of plants, which allows an extended picking season. Communal accommodation for pickers is often provided. The shelf life of soft fruit is short as it quickly deteriorates once picked; so in order to keep customers supplied it needs to be picked continuously while it is available.

Blackcurrants destined for the jam and drink industries are the only soft fruit to be harvested by machine. It mechanically shakes the plant and gathers up the fruit at the same time.

Strawberries and raspberries are grown mostly in the south and east of England although there are several big growers in the east of Scotland.

Since the early 1990s, soft fruit has increasingly been grown in polytunnels. Strawberries are now often planted in raised troughs using a hydroponic (water-growth) system rather than soil or on benches in grow bags. Before that they were grown outdoors in fields with straw laid along the rows to raise the fruit off the ground and keep it clean and safe. Blackberries, currants and blueberries are normally grown outdoors.

Growers of soft fruits on a commercial scale need to be close to their handling facilities and have labour on hand when it is needed. Strawberries and raspberries have to be picked by hand. Blackcurrants are grown outdoors and, although they can harvested by machine, those that are destined to be sold fresh also have to be handpicked.

Growing soft fruit under cover, either in polytunnels or glass houses, has greatly extended the season, making British strawberries available from April through to October. When grown outside they were only obtainable in June and July.

ORCHARDS

Orchards are mainly in the southern half of England, notably Kent, which earned the title of 'The Garden of England'. The Worcestershire area and its surrounding counties are another noted region and of course Somerset is famed for its cider apple orchards. 90% of British cherries are grown in Kent.

Alarmingly, nine out of ten traditional orchards have been lost since the 1950s and of those remaining, a third or more are in a neglected state.

▲ A heavy crop of apples goes to waste

Apples, pears, plums and cherries were once grown extensively but are now in serious decline. A few years ago many orchards were grubbed out when there were EU grants to do so. Others have been abandoned because they became uneconomic. Orchards are very good for wildlife. Bees depend on early orchard blossom and the crop's success is subject to their pollination.

Unpredictable British weather has always made fruit production difficult. Late frosts in May, when the blossom is out, can devastate the future crop. Although heaters can be placed in orchards and be lit to protect the flower from frost damage, the cost is unlikely to be justified because of low prices received for the fruit.

Brogdale Farm near Faversham is home to the National Fruit Collection of over 3,500 varieties including apples, pears, cherries, plums and bush fruits.

Fortunately enthusiasts are endeavouring to preserve as many varieties as possible even though most heritage varieties are not economically viable.

Commercially grown apples are put to many uses. They are used for cider making, apple juice, for cooking and eating raw. The latter have to be picked by hand, work often done by seasonal foreign workers. 1.6 billion apples were gathered in this way in 2020. They are then taken to packing sheds where they are washed then passed through computerised equipment which records images of each fruit and separates them into different sizes and grades. The apples can then be stored in environmentally controlled sheds for many months before being packed for sale. Sometimes apples are also available to buy as 'Pick Your Own' from the orchard.

There are 800 native varieties of apples, some over 400 years old, although only ten are still grown on a commercial scale.

Gala are the country's most popular eating apple and Bramleys for cooking.

Those destined for making cider or turning into juice, where quality is not a priority, are often mechanically gathered using a tractor-drawn machine. This shakes the trees causing the apples to fall to the ground and is followed by another machine which sweeps them up and loads them into a trailer to take to the processing unit where they are pressed.

HOPS

Hops have been grown for centuries for use in the brewing trade and have always been associated with the county of Kent in England. Once grown widely across the country, commercial production is now confined to the West Midlands and south-east England. There are still 50 major UK hop growers.

Each of the 34 British hop varieties has a different flavour.

The most celebrated are Fuggles and Goldings although commercial brewers often use higher-yielding modern varieties. Hops are sometimes grown on a small scale by the makers of craft beers.

The hop plant is a perennial that dies back in winter. Green shoots appear from the rootstock in spring, the plant grows quickly and the stems, or **'bines'** as they are known, can reach 26ft (8m) in length within three to four months. They are wound or trained up strings attached to a framework of poles and wirework about 20ft (6m) above the ground. The flowers, which are actually seed cones, are ready to harvest in September and afterwards need to be dried. They may be about 80% moisture content when first picked which needs to be reduced to 10%.

There are now machines that pick the hops. In the past, in the south-east of England and the West Midlands the hops were hand-picked then dried in distinctive buildings known as oast houses. The fields where they were grown were known as 'hop gardens' or in the West Midlands as 'hop yards'. Dried hops weigh very little and could be transported in very large hessian sacks known as **'pockets'** or **'pokes'**.

Until the 1950s less well-off women and children from London would move down to Kent for their annual three weeks 'summer holiday' of hop picking. Accommodation in huts was provided for them. Their menfolk would continue working in London during the week and travel by train to visit their families at weekends. It was their annual escape to the country, the only time they exchanged urban life for a taste of rural living and the hop growers were very dependent on their labour.

Less than 2,500 acres (1,000 ha) of hops are now grown annually in Britain, most being imported.

MISCELLANEOUS HORTICULTURE
NURSERIES

The boom in TV gardening programmes has led to an increased interest in many kinds of plants and shrubs and gardening is traditionally a great British hobby, with sales of seeds and plants on the increase.

Specialist growers and nurseries supply these either directly to the customer, often by mail order, or indirectly through garden centres. Most annuals and tender plants have to be grown in heated greenhouses or plastic tunnels in order to be ready when the customer wants them to make a colourful display in summer. Many are imported. Pre-Brexit, about 55,000 lorry loads a year arrived from the Netherlands alone. It is possible now though that UK growers will be looking to reduce their reliance on imports by growing more themselves. Many bi-annuals, perennials and hardy shrubs can be grown outdoors.

FLOWERS AND BULBS (TULIPS, DAFFODILS etc)

Daffodils and tulips are grown mainly in the east of England particularly around Spalding in Lincolnshire. The growing fields are planted with bulbs in the autumn where they are left to flower in the spring and are a spectacular sight. Daffodils and tulips are sometimes grown outdoors to be picked as flowers but most are cultivated for sale as bulbs. The West Country, with its milder climate, is noted for its very early daffodils and the Scilly Isles has a long history of growing early blooming daffodils: it is their main industry.

All the flowerheads on bulbs grown to be sold for planting are cut off while in bloom to improve the quality. After the foliage dies back later in summer, the bulbs are lifted, dried, sorted and packaged and are often exported.

A large proportion of fresh flowers are imported into the UK although they have now become expensive. As a result more are being grown in this country and a vast enterprise in Lincolnshire has recently been established which produces 85 million tulips a year in climate-controlled greenhouses. Fresh flowers have to be perfect and need to be picked by hand, so there is often difficulty in finding sufficient labour to do this. Gladioli are grown outside in this country and picked while still in bud either by hand or with a special machine.

With the government's commitment to plant millions more trees before 2025 to combat climate change, there is huge potential for nurseries to supply these young trees. Many will otherwise have to be imported with the accompanying risk of disease and generation of carbon emissions.

HERBS

There is increasing interest in herbs both fresh, dried and as oil. The uses of herbs in natural health and beauty treatments and in cookery are on the increase.

Harvesting parsley with a small machine

▲ These tulips are being grown commercially for the bulbs not for the flowers

There are 400 different herbs and growing them has become big business in recent years with many varieties now being grown on a commercial scale.

Once again, the East of England is a primary area. Colman's, not only famous for its mustard but also the variety of sauces produced in jars, bottles and packets, was based in Norwich for more than 160 years. The original factory closed in 2019 and moved to a new site at Honingham a few miles away, albeit on a smaller scale. Mustard seed is harvested with a small combine harvester in a similar way to rape, to which it is related.

Crops for processing such as parsley and mint can be cut with a small machine similar to that used for cutting silage grass before being transported by tractor and trailer to factories.

Many herbs to be sold fresh have to be picked and sorted by hand requiring a large labour force.

Herbs have an increasingly important value for alternative medicines, remedies, cosmetics and aromatherapy use. Herbs are also very useful to organic producers. Some can be used to provide natural treatments for health problems in both plants and animals, while others make valuable organic fertiliser. Garlic is particularly useful as it is a powerful antibacterial and anti-fungal agent.

NICHE PRODUCE

On a smaller scale there are enterprising individuals who have found other horticultural niches which they are able to fill. There are a few pumpkin growers who supply the demand at Halloween. There are flower growers who cultivate niche varieties of flowers which are not grown on large scales to sell as fresh cut or to dry the petals to sell as biodegradable confetti.

In 2017 British Sugar's 45 acre glass house at Wissington in Norfolk, which utilised surplus hot water and carbon dioxide produced by the process used to extract sugar from sugar beet, switched from growing tomatoes to growing medicinal cannabis plants. These cannabis plants are used to make the medicine cannabidiol (CBD) oral solution known as Epidyolex that is used to treat a life-threatening form of epilepsy in young children.

Genetically modified rape is grown extensively in some countries but not in Britain

GENETIC MODIFICATION

Modern scientists discovered a shortcut in selective breeding when they finally unravelled the mysteries of chromosomes, followed by genes. It was in 1953 in Cambridge that Mr Watson and Mr Crick identified the structure of DNA, which carries the genetic code.

For centuries growers and farmers have practised genetic engineering naturally, by way of selective breeding of plants and livestock in order to continually improve crop management, disease resistance, growth rates and yields. This helped keep an ever-increasing population fed. Farmers improved the milk yields and growth rate of their livestock through cross breeding, to develop different strains. Attention was also paid to improving crop yields.

It wasn't until 1970 that scientists discovered how to move DNA between unrelated organisms.

It changed the world forever. This was the moment when the public began to realise the previously unimaginable implications and expressed grave concerns over which directions future experiments would take. Instead of the genetic engineering of plants being confined to using natural pollination which would only work between similar species, scientists could now introduce what they consider to be desirable traits not only from other plants but also from fish, animals, etc. This is probably the most alarming aspect.

Tobacco was the first genetically modified (GM) plant produced in 1983 and in 1990 the first GM cereal was grown.

The commercial growing of GM crops remains banned in the UK.

Straw is an often unwanted by-product from growing cereals so short-stemmed varieties were selectively (not GM) bred and the disposal of surplus straw was no longer a problem. However, if modern GM technology could be used, crops could also be bred to be drought-resistant which would help farmers in this and particularly developping countries. It is very easy to be critical and complacent when living in a wealthy and wasteful society. However, people who live in many African countries unable to produce sufficient food and on the borderline of starvation no doubt have a completely different opinion and would probably welcome GM crops if they helped to alleviate their plight. Probably the biggest benefit in Britain would be the growing of GM crops which were herbicide tolerant and resistant to virus and insect damage. GM crops would greatly reduce the use of sprays which are at present of such great concern to the consumer.

GENETICALLY ENGINEERED ORGANISMS

Many other countries, some of whom we import food from, grow Genetically Engineered Organisms (GEOs) including carnations, chicory, cotton, flax, maize, oilseed rape, papaya, potatoes, sugar beet, soy bean, squash, sweetcorn, tomatoes and tobacco. Also being grown are rice and bananas which have been genetically modified to provide high levels of vitamin A to counter blindness, malnutrition and other diseases in children living in underdeveloped countries. Although 'golden rice', as it is known, was developed two decades ago, there are still many places where it has not been approved even though it potentially offers great health benefits. It has, though, been authorised for use in Australia, New Zealand, China and parts of North and South America.

More deadly diseases are spread by mosquitoes than any other insect.

Genetically modified mosquitoes are being bred in an attempt to combat malaria, dengue fever, yellow fever, zika and several other diseases transmitted by mosquitoes.

In theory, by mixing genetically modified ones with those in the wild they will interbreed and the resulting offspring will die off before reaching maturity. There are plans to release 750 million into the Florida Keys in 2021/2022 with the first 20 million having been released in May 2020. Millions of others have already been released in Malaysia and the Cayman Islands. However, ten years ago GM mosquitoes were

▲ GM maize is grown in many countries but not the UK

◀ Potatoes have been genetically modified to resist attack by Colorado beetles

COLORADO BEETLE AND POTATOES

The Colorado beetle is a common pest in some countries causing much damage to crops but GM potatoes have now been developed that are resistant to attacks by this pest. One naturally occurring organism in the soil excretes a substance which is harmless to humans but toxic to insects. This has been isolated and used for many years as a pesticide for crops. However, when researchers were able to isolate the gene responsible for the toxin they were then able to insert it directly into the plant which enabled it to generate its own insecticide within its own tissues, hence potatoes that won't get eaten by Colorado beetles.

released in Brazil but recent research has shown that the experiment has not gone according to plan as some of the offspring, which were thought would die, are actually surviving and breeding.

The potential for the beneficial use of genetic modification is enormous but the long term effects of GM have yet to be evaluated.

As always, with such a far reaching innovation there is the potential for more sinister uses.

Although Britain has played a leading role in developing biotechnology there are no plans to grow GM crops on a commercial scale until a full assessment has been made. More needs to be known about the impact they have on the environment in the countries where they are at present being grown. Experimental trials on a small scale however are being conducted on several sites across the UK.

There is obviously a need for caution and very strict controls regarding the use of GM crops but a broad view needs to be taken. If their development could feed the hungry, reduce the need for so many sprays and artificial fertiliser, enable food plants to adapt to climatic changes or if plants could be used to produce medicinal drugs and even be bred to absorb impurities from contaminated land, the potential for good may well outweigh the bad.

GENE EDITING

Having been denied the use of genetic modification, UK plant scientists are now exploring the possibility of gene (or genome) editing which is a relative new development.

This alters a species' own genes without permanently adding any new genetic material. It is different to genetic modification because scientists are working with what already exists, not trying to introduce genes from other sources.

> *Put simply, gene editing involves removing genes whereas genetic modification involves adding genes from a different living organism.*

Gene editing could help in the control of pests and diseases by not using synthetic and sometimes toxic substances. Genetic engineering has already produced amazing results using animals and micro-organisms to manufacture medicines such as insulin, interferon and human growth hormone as well as vaccines. A substance called rennet is a necessary element in the manufacture of cheese. It could only be found in calves' stomachs and had to be extracted from them after the calves had been slaughtered; now thanks to genetic engineering it can be produced artificially in laboratories.

Gene editing in a laboratory is the same as the traditional breeding techniques which have been practised for centuries, but it is far quicker.

If gene editing were to be accepted, it would reduce the cost of food production. Hardier and more nutritious varieties could be grown and the changes would make it possible to grow gluten-free wheat and disease-resistant fruit and vegetables.

Consultation on the future of gene editing of crops in England was launched in January 2021 and accelerated in 2022 when Britain's food security was threatened by the war in Ukraine.

▼ Genetically modified soya beans are widely grown in other countries including North America and Canada © Soya UK

Coastal marshes are ideal for raising beef organically

ORGANIC FARMING

Organic farming is a natural method of farming that avoids the use of synthetic pesticides and artificial fertilisers for growing crops. The use of genetically modified material is prohibited as is the routine use of drug and antibiotic treatments for rearing animals.

The organic movement began more than 30 years ago and there are now about 6,000 operators in the UK. It reached a peak in 2008 but this was followed by a gradual decline. In 2020 there was a growth of 12.6% in sales in the UK's organic market which contributed £2.79billion to the economy.

More than one and a quarter million acres (half a million hectares), 2.7% of the total agricultural area in the UK are registered for organic food production, nearly two-thirds of which is in England. 63% is permanent grassland and 8 % is used to grow cereals.

Because of the standards that have to be met, organic yields are between 20% and 40% lower than crops grown intensively.

Organic standards are certified here in the UK by The Soil Association or another approved organic body which have very strict requirements that have to be met before a producer can be certified or continue as an organic producer. Certificates are only issued after the enterprise has been inspected and the Soil Association are satisfied that activities meet organic standards. Thorough annual inspections are carried out and detailed stock, management and financial records have to be kept.

No system of farming has higher levels of animal welfare than farms working to Soil Association organic standards.

It is not only the products that have to comply with specifications but also the soil has to be looked after in a way that meets requirements.

It takes two years to convert to an organic system.

A processing licence is legally required where on-farm processing is carried out to ensure that the rigorous standards are maintained regarding labelling, record keeping, hygiene etc.

As the British population becomes increasingly aware of health and ecological issues, there is an ever-increasing demand for organic products, in meat, fruit and vegetables. Because of our seasonal climate, stringent legal requirements and the fact that crop care is more labour intensive, organic produce is inevitably more expensive. Increased affluence has meant that some shoppers can now afford to choose the organic option.

Financial aid is available for farmers wishing to change but it is a gradual process and few large farms have gone over entirely to organic growing.

Nearly half of the land used for organic farming utilises unimproved grassland such as hills, moors, water meadows and marshes. This land has not been contaminated with chemicals in the past and lends itself readily to an organic system for rearing livestock. It is also very good for conservation, as restricted stocking levels mean that native plants and grasses in these areas are not damaged by overgrazing.

Virtually all organic meat and eggs are produced in Britain but some dairy products have to be imported as well as a large proportion of organic cereals, fruit and vegetables.

To qualify as being organic animals must have been born and managed on an organic holding to full organic standards throughout their lives. Animals that may be bought in, such as calves, must originate from organic holdings.

Organically raised livestock must have access to natural light and air and be able to conduct their basic behavioural needs. Farrowing crates for pigs are prohibited as are cages for poultry. Herbivores, pigs and poultry species

▼ Seaweed has a use as organic fertiliser

must, in normal circumstances, be allowed permanent access to pasture. Breeds have to be selected that are suitable to local conditions, so indigenous breeds and strains of livestock are the recommended choice. Poultry kept free range for meat takes longer to reach killing weight.

> *Organic standards for table chicken require outdoor access for part of their lives and a minimum slaughter age of 81 days.*

Organic turkeys have a specified minimum slaughter age of 100 days for females and 140 days for males.

Fodder to supplement grazing and other foodstuffs must contain a high proportion of organically grown material for animals and poultry to be certified as organic. Cereals are only grown organically in the UK on a small scale and most have to be imported, adding to the feed costs.

Animal welfare standards are very high and natural methods of producing livestock are used wherever possible. Disease management is based on preventative measures but, inevitably, animals at some time in their lives may become sick and need medication. Natural remedies are becoming more widely used but if all else fails then specified drugs and antibiotics may be administered as a last resort but have to have an extended withdrawal period, longer than is normal, between the end of treatment and human consumption of the meat, milk or eggs produced.

A diverse range of aquatic species are also being farmed organically which include several different fish species, shellfish such as mussels and oysters, and seaweed.

Trout and salmon are produced organically with the latter finding a good export market on the Continent.

Organic food production aspires to be self-sustaining, mainly by applying crop rotation to improve the fertility and structure of the

▲ Aphids can be problematic for organic farmers

soil. Different crops have different nutritional requirements and one that has taken a lot of nitrogen from the soil will likely be followed by a crop of legumes (peas, beans or clover) that release nitrogen back into it. Animal manure and plants such as mustard can be ploughed back into the soil to improve both the fertility and texture. In some instances it is permitted to use certain naturally occurring substances such as rock phosphate, lime, potassium, copper and magnesium.

ORGANIC PEST CONTROL

Any seeds or plants that are bought in must have been grown organically. No synthetic herbicides are allowed so weed control has to be by other methods. Enriched soil not only increases the crop yields but also weed growth. Crop rotation

Home-grown organic vegetables are often sold direct to the public at farmers' markets

plays a part in minimising weed growth but the main weapons are mechanical tools or weeding by hand.

Synthetic insecticides and fungicides are also banned so natural methods of pest control have to be employed. Grass banks, known as beetle banks, may be developed in fields to provide a breeding ground for various beneficial bugs and beetles that prey on pests damaging to crops such as slugs, caterpillars, greenfly and other insects.

Beetle banks are also of recognised value to general conservation. Naturally occurring substances such as sulphur and even some that are toxic can sometimes be used for disease and pest control. Current research using garlic is proving it to be a very effective tool in the fight against both pests and diseases. Once again crop rotation plays a key role.

Organic production is labour intensive, and the organic industry is reliant on seasonal foreign workers and students who are often brought into the country on work permits from Eastern Europe. If it wasn't for these willing and hardworking people, organic produce would either be less available than it is now or more expensive than it already is.

MARKETING ORGANIC PRODUCE

Having gone to such lengths to grow organic produce to such a high standard there is obviously an important need to market the results efficiently. Increasingly a broader range is appearing on supermarket shelves and in health food shops. Other marketing schemes are being developed locally to ensure a higher financial return by dispensing with the 'middle man' and reducing haulage costs and pollution. There have always been a few farm shops and market stalls but more recently farmers' markets have sprung up all over the country. These can sell only local produce and have become a useful outlet for organic farmers while giving town people the opportunity to buy fresh locally grown food and at the same time aiding the rural economy. Another system of marketing used increasingly by organic producers is known as a 'Box Scheme' whereby boxes of fresh seasonal food are assembled and delivered directly to subscribing customers.

Farm shops sell a variety of locally-grown produce

FARMING DIVERSIFICATION

Nearly 70% of UK farmers have diversified in one way or another, of which 37% involve non-farming activities and with investment in renewable energy topping the list.

Farm shops now sell a broad range of local goods; other farmers regularly attend farmers' markets to sell their produce. These are thriving and are brilliant for bringing the countryside back into towns. Usually held once a month, numbers have almost trebled from 1,200 to 3,500 in the last 15 years. Farmers markets sell only locally made or grown produce and enable farmers to come into direct contact with their customers, allowing town and country to meet and talk, enabling a more personal experience of the British countryside for town-dwellers than they would have filling a supermarket trolley. Vending machines are appearing at some farms

▶ Forward-looking pig farmers have diversified into making their own products

◄ An enterprising way of generating additional income

making home produced, locally sourced, fresh, chilled and even frozen produce available to consumers, often 24 hours a day, 7 days a week.

LEISURE

The countryside is increasingly becoming a place for leisure. New golf courses are appearing although these require a substantial long-term investment.

Some areas are rich in aggregates (gravel, rock, minerals etc). Where these have been quarried it creates large holes in the ground which can eventually be attractively landscaped and developed into lakes to provide a further income from fishing or water sports activities.

Riding schools and livery yards make horse riding available not only for local people but for holiday-makers as well. Sometimes stabling can be provided for those wishing to bring their own horse or pony with them. There are nearly 700 miles (1,100km) of dedicated bridleways in Britain.

Other rural leisure activities that can be accessed on farms include shooting, off-road driving, survival skills training, orienteering and paint ball games.

'Open farms' attract visitors who are always keen to see young animals and have a ride on a tractor and trailer. Providing wildlife viewing and photography opportunities are now big business. Animals such as badgers, which were often considered a nuisance to farmers a few years ago, can now generate an income in return for the small cost of erecting a viewing hide. Wildlife parks, sanctuaries, woodlands and places for marriages and burials are being opened up to the public in rural areas.

For decades Bed and Breakfast has been offered on farms and this is expanding. Many farmers have more recently invested in converting their old redundant buildings – cow sheds, stables and barns, into self-catering holiday lets. Some have made them into small business units to rent.

For a long time camp and caravan sites have been another sideline. These are still as popular as ever and have become much more upmarket with the advent of 'glamping' which is growing rapidly in popularity, whether in a yurt, tepee, shepherd's hut or even a treehouse. Glamping 'pods' are glamorous wooden huts often built in the shape of a gypsy caravan. Electricity is normally connected and in some cases there might well be the added bonus of heat and running water, even perhaps an en-suite bathroom.

Diversification is keeping the countryside alive and has awakened interest in some of the countryside skills that looked at one time as though they would disappear.

CHEESE MAKING

This is one of the most favoured branches of farm diversification.

It is thought that the process of making cheese was discovered accidentally thousands of years ago when our ancestors used bags made from ruminants' stomachs, which naturally contained rennet, for storing or transporting milk.

The rennet caused the milk to curdle and has been used ever since, although a vegetarian substitute is now available. Rennet can also be sourced from slugs and snails. Cheese has been made in the UK for two thousand years. Until the process became automated, cheese-making was women's work.

More than three billion litres of milk are now used annually to make cheese in the UK, amounting to half a million tonnes.

Four pints (4.5 litres) of fresh milk makes about one pound (450g) of hard cheese or two pounds (900g) of soft cheese.

There are more than 700 named cheese varieties made in the UK. Some are mass produced while many others are artisan cheeses. Manufactured on a small scale by dairy farmers, this form of diversification is thriving. Most cheeses take their names from their connections to local areas with Cheddar, from Somerset, the most popular.

▼ A number of farmers have embarked on cheese making using home-produced milk from their cows and goats

WENSLEYDALE CHEESE

The Wensleydale cheese recipe was brought to Yorkshire from France by Cistercian monks 800 years ago. Originally it was made from sheep's milk but converted to cow's milk in the 1800s. The Wensleydale Creamery, which is open to the public, currently produces 4,000 tonnes of cheese every year from locally sourced milk. In 1992 it was faced with closure but was saved by a management buy-out and now employs more than 200 people and contributes in excess of £13 million to the local economy. Wensleydale cheese was awarded Protected Geographical Indication status (PGI) from the European Commission in 2013. This ensures that Yorkshire Wensleydale is produced in the designated area in accordance with the time-honoured traditional recipe.

The semi-hard, blue-veined Stilton cheese has also been awarded protected status. It originated as a cream cheese and was being made in the village of Stilton, Cambridgeshire,

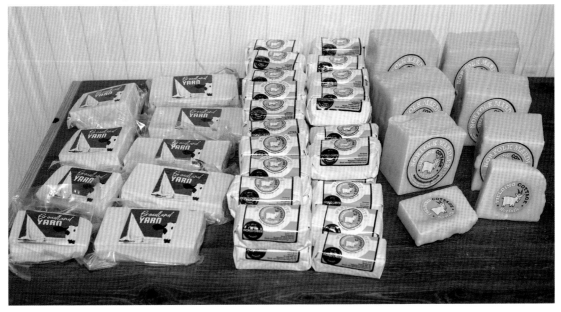

certainly by the early 18th century. Since 1996, Stilton has held European Protected Designation of Origin (PDO) status, one of 65 products in the UK to do so. Stilton cheese can only be made in licensed areas of Derbyshire, Nottinghamshire and Leicestershire, and producers have to follow traditional recipes that have been in existence for generations.

Some farmers have diversified into producing cheese from goat and sheep's milk and even water buffalo. The latter's milk is very rich and can be used to make mozzarella cheese.

There are a number of dairies selling home-produced milk to the public, usually in glass bottles which can be reused. About 200 producers sell raw (unpasteurised) 'green top' milk direct to consumers, either at a farmers' market, at the farm, or delivered. Home-produced yoghurt and ice cream are other side-lines which can also be purchased by the public.

DRINKS

Wine There are now approximately 700 vineyards growing grapes in the UK (about 540 of which are being managed on a commercial scale) with 200 or so open to visitors. In excess of 2,000 people are employed in the UK wine industry with more than 170 in wine production. In 2019, vines were being grown on more than 8,500 acres (3,500ha) of land, four times greater than twenty years previously. Originally only white wine was produced in the UK but now some growers are making red.

Wine production is benefiting from climate change, warmer than average weather in recent years improving grape yields and wine quality. Grapes are picked by hand, usually only in a short window during October. Extra help is sought locally and from family members.

The majority of vineyards are in the south of England, mainly producing sparkling wine but it has been proved that grapes can even be grown in Scotland. English wine is becoming more popular as the quality improves and some have won international awards. Obviously crop production varies from year to year but 2018 proved to be a record year for the UK when 15.6 million bottles were produced. Wine is a fast developing market going from strength to strength. Potentially there is room for expansion with grants available.

Gin and Vodka have become artisan products made from locally sourced ingredients. Both provide a quick turnover. There are now more than 440 gin distilleries, and UK vodka production is expanding.

Beer In the last decade the number of micro-breweries has rapidly increased as craft beers, known for having bold, hoppy flavours, have gained in popularity.

There are now well over 2,000 independent UK brewers.

◀ Some farms have invested in making gin or vodka on a small scale using home-grown or locally sourced ingredients

Artisan brewers are free to experiment and put their individual stamp on craft beer with an emphasis on flavour and quality.

Cider has been made for centuries and there were many orchards, some of which still exist, specifically growing cider apples. Recently there has been a renewed interest in cider. New orchards have been established in various parts of the country by artisan cider makers. These producers also often market other products such as apple juice and perry which is made from pears.

CROPS

Some farmers have diversified by putting a few acres aside to grow soft fruit and orchards for the 'Pick Your Own' trade, while others deliver 'veg boxes'. There is a renewed interest in herbs and some species such as camomile and lavender are grown commercially to be manufactured into essential oils. Pharmaceutical companies continue research into the use of plants in medicine, offering potential demand for bespoke crops to be grown.

Fresh flowers for cutting are being grown on some farms and even edible flowers. Sometimes flower petals are dried to make biodegradable confetti.

Around 85% of the fresh cut flowers sold in Britain are imported.

▲ Growing crops on a commercial scale for garden bird food can prove to be lucrative (Sunflowers shown here)

More and more cut flowers are being produced at home. Because of Britain's unpredictable weather, to ensure consistent high quality, these are mostly grown indoors. One grower in west Norfolk has developed a business producing in excess of 32 million stems of cut flowers annually. Grown under six hectares of glasshouses and polytunnels, the company is able to supply supermarkets 52 weeks of the year.

- Wild flowers are also being grown for seed in response to the demand created by new farm environmental schemes to restore natural bio-diversity. This includes annual flowers for growing in cornfields.

▼ Lavender is grown for its oil

- Where the soil is suitable, spring bulbs, mostly tulips and daffodils, are being grown to sell as bulbs. Some daffodils may be picked for sale in bud but mostly the flowers are cut off and the bulbs left in the ground until the leaves have dried off before being harvested.
- Fields of sunflowers, millet, quinoa or other seeds are cultivated to supply the huge demand for garden bird food or can be crushed to make cooking oil.
- Grass turves for sports stadiums and gardens are 'farmed' in places where conditions are right. Special seed mixes are sown and the process is carried out over a period of 14 months.
- Oil seed rape is widely grown as an agricultural crop and there are about 70 farmers who have invested in equipment to press the seed and extract the oil. This they bottle, sometimes creating their own flavours, and sell at farmers' markets, food festivals and in local shops.
- Warmer weather in the UK is tempting some farmers to experiment with crops not normally grown in this country such as lentils, soya and wasabi which have previously been imported.

- Eight million Christmas trees are sold each year and some farmers have diversified to grow these. To be saleable, the trees need to be the right shape, in good condition and not overgrown with grass or brambles, so require a lot of attention. There are several different varieties and a 6ft Christmas tree takes around 10 years to grow.
- A very fast-growing strain of willow is being grown to produce biomass as ecofuel for the new generation of environmentally friendly power stations. Elephant grass is also being grown for this purpose. In the south-west of England there are trials to discover if growing eucalyptus is a feasible option, for biomass and firewood.
- Seaweed has great potential and has long been used around the west coast of Britain as a cheap source of fertilizer for the land. Recently it has been realised there is potential for farming seaweed. There is also demand for it as a 'superfood' as well as for cosmetic and pharmaceutical purposes, and as a possible source of biomass that can be turned into green energy.

ANIMALS

Petting farms and farm parks, many with cafés, play areas and tractor and trailer rides and are a good way of introducing young children to farm animals.

Bees are vital for the pollination of flowers and hence crop production. They proceed from flower to flower, drinking the nectar and accumulating pollen on their back legs. Pollen is produced by male plants and is needed to fertilise female plants in order for fruits and seeds to develop. As bees visit different flowers, they inadvertently deposit a little of the pollen, thus fertilising female plants.

◀ Bees are needed to pollinate crops in order to ensure a crop of fruit; some beekeepers operate on a commercial scale producing honey

They take the nectar and pollen back to their hives where, with the help of other bees, it is mixed together before being cached in the honeycomb which had previously been made by young bees. Wax excreted from their glands dries and forms flakes which older bees chew to make pliable before forming it into hexagonal cells. Bees have a way of communicating with others in the hive as to where the nectar source can be found.

Beekeepers always try to ensure that sufficient food is left for the bees' requirements although there may be occasions when additional sustenance in the form of sugar syrup is needed.

Locally produced honey can often be purchased in farm shops and farmers markets.

There are now about 450 professional beekeepers producing honey on a commercial scale in the UK. Individually they may have up to 700 hives which are moved in succession to sites where a crop is in flower, the owners of which benefit from the bees' pollinating activities. Early in the year it may be orchards or fields of rape and in late summer heather moorland. The flavour and colour of the honey varies according to whatever the bees have been feeding on.

Bee numbers have been in decline but they play a hugely important role in our countryside. As people become increasingly health conscious and environmentally aware, beekeeping could prove to be very profitable. Much of the honey consumed in the UK is currently imported.

In 2015 an apprenticeship scheme was put in place to reignite an interest in beekeeping.

Maggot farming has always been carried out on a small scale to supply bait to the million or more UK fishermen. The maggots are reared in temperature- and humidity-controlled rooms from flies which lay their eggs on the meat or fish provided. The eggs are transferred to a hatchery where after hatching, they are fed fish or poultry and take five to seven days to become a fully-grown maggot. Different colours are produced through dying the food supplied.

Worm farming Gardening experts and environmentalists have awakened an interest in worms which are as important to soil quality as bees are to crop growing. In the UK there are 27 species of worm, 10 of which are commonly found in agricultural soil.

Several commercial worm farms have been set up to supply demand.

Insect farming Insects have huge potential as a valuable source of protein for inclusion in fish, pet and animal food, a lot of which is at present sourced from soya and fishmeal.

Three million tonnes of soya is imported each year, mostly for animal feed, and it does not have good green credentials.

Fishmeal is only sustainable if it is sourced as a by-product of the fishing industry but demand outstrips supply and 6 million tons of fish (25% of global fishing) are caught from the sea worldwide each year to produce it. Around 4 to 5 tons are required to manufacture one ton of dried fishmeal. Many of the targeted species of fish are in serious decline. About half of the protein-rich fishmeal is fed to farmed fish and the rest to livestock. Alternative sources of protein need to be found and insects are a distinct possibility.

There are already insect farms on the Continent, many of which are in the Netherlands. The 'Ynsect' company in France is expanding and looking to be producing 100,000 tons annually of insect products. Some insect farms breed crickets and black soldier flies but Ynsect concentrates primarily on mealworms which are raised on an industrial scale in vertically stacked tiers of trays. Mealworms are the larval form of a species of darkling beetle which breeds prolifically. The larvae take 1-4 weeks to hatch from eggs and after 8-10 weeks reach 1.5inches (4cm) in length. The larvae are fed on organic by-products from the food and drink industry and also produce frass (fertilizer) as a useful by-product. They are usually sold dried.

Breeding insects on a large scale for protein in fish, animal, pet, and possibly even human food, offers a new branch of countryside diversification in the UK, although set-up costs are high.

The feasibility of this scheme moved a step closer in 2020 when the UK government backed such a project with a £10 million funding package. The facility will be used to raise black soldier flies, the larvae of which feed on food waste, and can be processed into sustainable insect protein.

LIVESTOCK

Breeding wagyu beef has recently become a new direction for diversification. Wagyu are a strain of slow-growing Japanese beef cattle noted for having a finer meat texture and higher levels of fat interspersed within the muscle, known as marbling. The British Wagyu Breeders Association was established in 2014 and there are now customers who are prepared to pay premium prices for the superior eating quality of wagyu beef.

Deer farms have been established to supply quality venison and produce breeding stock. Demand for venison is increasing. Red deer are the species usually kept. Initially, a substantial outlay is required for fencing at least 7ft (2.1m) high.

As Red deer have only been domesticated for a few decades, genetically improving the stock is in its early days. Farmed Red deer remain, for the time being, akin to their wild counterparts. Calves are born in late spring and normally ear tagged when they are weaned at five to six months

of age. Red deer have a mating season, known as the '**rut**', from late September to early November. The gestation period is about 33 weeks. Stags are very large animals which during the rut can be dangerous, so it is common practice to remove their antlers (a painless procedure) which re-grow each year.

Deer farming is similar in many ways to beef farming and increasingly herds are being housed in barns during the winter months.

Wild Boar are farmed as they prove popular with consumers in search of meat with a more distinctive flavour. Wild boar are extremely powerful animals which need heavy duty fencing at least 5ft (1.5m) high and buried into the ground to a depth of 18 inches (45cm) because they are able to use their snouts to dig their way out.

The keeping of farmed wild boar is controlled under the Dangerous Wild Animals Act 1976 which means that a licence has to be obtained from the local authority. Becoming increasingly popular is the meat of 'iron age' pigs which are the product of crossing a wild boar with a domesticated breed.

Rabbit farms exist on a small scale to produce meat. Meat rabbits are predominately white in colour and have been genetically bred to grow very quickly.

Goats were once often seen tethered in the countryside but these days are now mostly kept in herds or as companion animals. Goats share many similarities with sheep. They naturally have a mating season in autumn; the gestation period is about 150 days with the young being born in spring. They must be ear tagged for identification before they are nine months old. Some farmers keep goats commercially for their milk, sold fresh or made into cheese. A goat can produce 500 litres in a lactation and will continue to produce milk for a longer period than a cow. Goat's milk has health benefits and can be better tolerated by some people than cow's milk.

A few farmers breed goats especially for meat with the Boer goat, introduced from South Africa in 1987, the most popular breed. Male kids from dairy herds can also be reared for meat. Surprisingly, considering the number of ethnic minorities who live in Britain, there is no great demand for goat meat here.

Certain breeds of goats, as well as sheep, are also kept for their fine wool which is often used for spinning by their owners. Angora and cashmere fibres come from goats and command very high prices.

▲ Boer goats originated in South Africa and are a breed used for meat production for which there must be a potential market in today's multi-racial Britain

Llamas and Alpacas from South America appear very out of place in the British countryside but some farmers are looking to them to earn some extra income from selling their wool. Their young are known as 'cria'.

▲ Alpacas have not only become popular as pets but also for their high value fleeces

There are about 45,000 alpacas registered with the British Alpaca Society. Apart from raising valuable stock for breeding, they are kept for their wool, which comes in 22 recognised colours, and also for novelty uses such as trekking companions, pack animals and even ring bearers at weddings! Their meat is very lean with low cholesterol and fat content. It is widely consumed in South America but not yet in the UK.

Llamas are larger animals and are also kept for their wool but have not proved as popular as alpacas. There are about 2,000 in the UK. A few farmers have tried keeping one or two llamas as protection for their sheep. They are always alert, so act like bodyguards and will not hesitate to chase away a fox or a dog, should they perceive it to be a threat to the flock.

Ostriches and Emus Two other exotic animals that have appeared on British farms in recent years are the ostrich and its cousin the emu, although they do not seem to have made much progress in commercial ventures. They are kept primarily for their meat but the feathers have a value and their skin can make leather. Oil from the birds is claimed to be very good for treating skin irritations and other discomforts.

Guinea fowl are also being bred to supply restaurants.

Game birds There is a large demand for game birds to supply the shooting industry. Many are reared each year and supplied as eight-week-old poults ready to be transferred into large release pens. Big UK game farms normally supply the market but in recent years some game farms have looked to contract out, under supervision, the rearing of chicks from day old to eight weeks, which opens up an opportunity for farmers who have a few acres of land and some spare labour in late spring. Rearing game birds could dovetail in with other farming activities.

▼ Some farmers have taken on contracts to rear pheasants for commercial game farmers

OTHER ANIMALS BRED FOR PETS

The trend in recent years has been for people to look at keeping unusual pets, which has enabled some astute farmers to make good money from diversifying into breeding them from the outset.

They first discovered there was a market for Kunekune, Potbellied and Micro pigs but there are strict regulations about keeping them for pets.

Pygmy goats have become fashionable to have as pets.

With its white fluffy wool and black face and legs, the cute Valais Blacknosed sheep has gained popularity. They can become very tame, behaving more like a dog, and make good pets. Their wool though is coarse and poor quality, but breeding Valais Blacknosed sheep has proved to be a lucrative diversification for some sheep farmers.

Sunset over the Wildfowl and
Wetlands Trust at Welney in Norfolk

LANDOWNERS AND MANAGERS

An alarming amount of land disappears from the countryside each year as housing estates and new towns are built, industrial sites developed and new rail links, roads and motorways are constructed.

Land is an attractive investment particularly to overseas investors and pension funds. Land values are almost 50% higher today than they were a decade ago and huge amounts of UK land is now in foreign ownership. The top 50 landowners currently control approximately 12% of Britain's landmass.

- The Forestry Commission – *see page 183* – is the UK's largest public landowner with 2.2 million acres (900,000 ha).
- The National Trust, together with National Trust Scotland, comes second.
- The Ministry of Defence, the Crown Estate and the RSPB come third, fourth and fifth.

Britain also belongs to many other people. There are traditionally wealthy families who own large private estates but many other estates are now in the hands of foreign investors and institutions such as insurance and pension companies. Completely at the other end of the scale are small family farms, crofts and smallholdings.

COMMON LAND

There is also common land which is generally assumed to be owned by the general public, but this is not the case. Common land is owned by someone, often a local council, an individual or by the National Trust, but the public usually has the right to roam on it and in some cases use it for other activities. Commoners' rights date back more than a thousand years. Some householders still have certain ancient rights attached to their property allowing them to graze livestock, dig peat or collect firewood. Commoners in the New Forest also have rights of 'pannage' allowing them to turn out pigs in autumn to feed on the fallen acorns and beechnuts.

We are very fortunate in the UK to have access to such a large proportion of our countryside. With that goes responsibility by way of not causing any harm to it, not leaving behind litter and generally respecting and appreciating it. In the more remote areas walkers and riders need to bear in mind that help is not always close at hand and often there isn't a signal for mobile phones.

THE NATIONAL TRUST

The National Trust (NT) is a charitable organisation founded in 1895 by Octavia Hill, Sir Robert Hunter and Hardwicke Rawnsley to 'promote the permanent preservation for the benefit of the Nation of lands and tenements (including buildings) of beauty or historic interest'. As a registered charity it is renowned for its work in restoring and maintaining many stately homes throughout Britain which have been gifted to the National Trust. Most of the Trust's properties are accessible to the public and it is a privilege for both British and foreign visitors to be given the opportunity to witness, first-hand, the opulent aristocratic lifestyles of our ancestors.

The National Trust is the second biggest landowner in Britain and also owns parts of the coastline and countryside as well as many pubs and farms.

Despite having over 5.6 million members, and millions of non-member visitors annually, there is nowhere near sufficient income generated to cover the upkeep costs of the properties. It is the extra money received from gifts, donations and legacies that enable the Trust to undertake essential maintenance and restoration work, as well as to purchase new properties.

Legacies bequeathed to the Trust often specify how the money is to be used.

The Trust employs 14,000 staff across England, Wales and Northern Ireland, including seasonal workers in the form of foresters, gardeners, wardens, administrators etc. These

Tarn Howes in the Lake District owned by the National Trust offers an easily accessible walk

The National Trust owns more than 90 fell farms within the Lake District National Park

are supported by a huge task force of more than 50,000 indispensable voluntary workers. Before the covid pandemic in 2020, visitor numbers had reached more than 26 million a year but the National Trust's covid closures and restrictions hugely reduced income, from non-member visitor entrance fees, gift shops and restaurants. These estimated losses were said to be £200 million, which has meant that cutbacks have had to be made.

The National Trust's purpose is to preserve places of historic interest and natural beauty for the benefit of the nation. The smallest place it cares for is Hawker's Hut on the north Cornwall coast which is a very small dwelling built in the mid-19th century from driftwood with a turf roof and partially set into the hillside.

The Trust is also responsible for 610,000 acres (250,000 ha), mostly countryside deemed to be of natural beauty, which covers nearly 1.5% of the total land mass of England, Wales and

Northern Ireland. The land is farmed by 1,500 tenant farmers.

More than a quarter of the Lake District is owned by the National Trust.

Some financial assistance is offered to their tenants but they have to conform to certain methods and specifications as to how they manage their farms. The National Trust issues licences, at its discretion, for various leisure activities to take place on land it owns. Field sports and pest control are strictly regulated.

Holiday cottages owned by the Trust are available to let in some parts of the country.

 National Trust Scotland

The National Trust for Scotland was formed in 1931 and owns and manages around 130 properties and 180,000 acres (73,000ha) of land, making it the third largest

Ownership of Glen Affric is shared between the National Trust for Scotland, Forestry and Land Scotland and a number of private owners

NATIONAL TRUST COASTLINE

The National Trust also owns or protects roughly one fifth of the coastline in England, Wales and Northern Ireland amounting to 780 miles (1,260 km). This includes St Michaels Mount off the Cornish coast and Brownsea Island off of Dorset. The Giant's Causeway in Northern Ireland is the most visited.

land manager in Scotland. In its ownership are castles, ancient small dwellings, historic sites, gardens, 46 Munros (mountains over 3,000 feet (915m) in height), more than 400 islands and islets and significant stretches of coastline.

National Trust for Scotland has a membership of 380,000 and employs over 500 full-time workers, about 750 on a seasonal basis plus an army of volunteers. A million and a half people visit NTS sites each year.

The familiar oak leaf and acorn logo of the National Trust is a reminder everywhere of the importance many aristocratic families in Britain have attached to the preservation of our heritage. Many properties have been gifted to the National Trust and some former owners continue to live in part of them.

The upkeep of such properties is enormous but their future is safeguarded in the care of the National Trust for future generations to visit and admire. The properties attract many visitors from abroad.

MINISTRY OF DEFENCE

The Ministry of Defence (MoD) is one of the largest landowners in the country with an estate spread over approximately 4,000 sites equal to nearly 2% of the UK's land mass.

Huge tracts of land were requisitioned for training purposes at the beginning of WWII. The MoD now owns approximately 543,000 acres (220,000 ha) of land and foreshore in the UK (either freehold or leasehold) and in addition also holds rights of access over a similar sized area. Much of this is agricultural land and farmers have to comply with MoD requirements.

Training areas and ranges occupy over 80% of MoD total area.

Air bases are very often in rural areas providing employment for a significant number of local people and contributing millions of pounds to the local economy.

Designated public access is encouraged on parts of MoD estates but there are often restrictions on times and areas when access is available. It is imperative that warning signs are heeded, as there is a safety risk for those who stray from the waymarked routes. Anything discovered that looks suspicious must not be touched and should be reported. It is important to take notice of raised red flags advising of danger as well as warning signs and notices.

A booklet *Walks on Ministry of Defence Land* provides information and advice for walkers. Alternatively up-to-date local information can be downloaded from the MoD site www.gov.uk/guidance/public-access-to-military-areas

The MoD owns some of the most unspoiled areas in Britain. There has been no urban development, intensive farming or use of agrochemical sprays; it seems almost as though time has stood still there. About half is designated as SSSIs. Parts also come under some other form of environmental protection or are within National Parks. MoD policy is to strike the balance between the military needs of the Defence Estate and environmental and conservation considerations. It works closely with

▲ Many MoD training grounds are unspoilt and a haven for plants and wildlife

local and national conservation groups as well as English Heritage, and their equivalents in Wales, Scotland and Northern Ireland, regarding the preservation of historic buildings and ancient monuments, some of which are included in Heritage Open Days. There are nearly 800 listed buildings and 72 scheduled monuments on MoD land, some of which are included in the Heritage Open Days initiative when buildings of architectural interest are opened to the public.

▼ The MoD preserve places and churches of historic interest on their land

Much of the MoD land has been left relatively untouched for more than 80 years providing a sanctuary for many species of our native flora and fauna.

Large military training areas are relatively untouched by modern farming. Part of Salisbury Plain (150sq miles) has not been ploughed for over 80 years and encompasses a large expanse of open downland. Stanford Training area in South Norfolk covers 30,000 acres (12,000ha) of heath, woodland and farmland. Otterburn is the UK's largest firing range covering 93 square miles (242sq kms) of the southern Cheviot Hills and accounts for nearly a quarter of the Northumberland National Park. Sennybridge Training Area is in mid Wales and covers approximately 37,000 acres (15,000 ha) which is mainly a flat upland plateau.

◀ MoD Lulworth Range Walks

FOXGLOVE COVERT

Foxglove Covert, located at Catterick Garrison in North Yorkshire, was created by the Royal Scots Dragoon Guards soon after they returned from the First Gulf War. In 1992 they converted a disused training area into a wildlife haven comprising several habitats. Contained within its 100 acres are semi-natural woodland, heathland, flower-rich grassland, streams, ponds and wet meadows which support 2,600 different species. Foxglove Covert was designated as a Local Nature Reserve in 2001.

Conservation on the Defence Estates is given high priority. A magazine *Sanctuary* is published annually and reports on the MoD's involvement and achievements, both in Britain and abroad, with regards to preservation of flora and fauna as well as their archaeological sites. With the aim of encouraging positive conservation work, the MoD 'Sanctuary Award' recognises the commitment of groups or individuals to sustainability, energy saving, wildlife conservation, archaeology and environmental protection throughout the Defence estate.

A 'Silver Otter' trophy is awarded each year to the best conservation project on MoD land.

Future MoD policy is to reduce the overall size of the estate, in particularly by selling off land which is surplus to requirements. Investment is urgently needed for the improvement of accommodation for military personnel.

WATER COMPANIES

There are ten Water Companies in England and Wales responsible for supplying safe water and the disposal of sewage. In Scotland, Scottish Water has a similar responsibility as does Northern Ireland Water which is the second largest landowner in Northern Ireland. Between them, British water companies own 424,000 acres (172,000 ha), including hundreds of reservoirs, which they actively encourage the public to use.

Some of the largest sites have visitor centres and facilities for canoeing, wind surfing and other water sports, camping and cycling. Almost all welcome walkers, fishermen and bird watchers, the latter being well catered for by the provision of hides. The waters are stocked with brown and rainbow trout; tickets to fish are available for the season, the day or even an evening and on some reservoirs, boats can be hired. The fishing season normally begins towards the end of March and continues until late October. Sometimes it is extended for rainbow trout. Each reservoir has its own regulations and a limit on the size of the catch, which is usually a generous one. Many are leased to angling clubs.

The ten Water Companies in England and Wales are:

South West Water which owns 50 waters, some of them quite small, in Cornwall, Devon and Somerset for the public to enjoy.

Wessex Water Services includes Dorset and appropriately has its headquarters in Bath.

Southern Water Services spans the commuter belt counties of Kent, Sussex and Surrey and has four main sites of interest to the general public.

Thames Water Utilities is the largest water company serving over 7 million people and dealing with the waste from many more. It owns 39 wetland sites and 365 sewage works, and offers some very important urban sites for wildlife and leisure activities. Staines reservoir is divided by a causeway and can be seen when flying out of Heathrow. Floating solar panels on the Queen Elizabeth II reservoir at Walton-on-Thames generate green electricity.

▼ Derwent Reservoir and the surrounding land in Derbyshire is owned and managed by Severn Trent Water

Anglian Water Services own one of the largest reservoirs, Rutland Water, which offers many facilities and is a favourite haunt for birdwatchers.

Severn Trent Water provides water to over 7 million people and receives more than 5 million visitors a year.

United Utilities Water plc (formerly North West Water) is the largest landowner of all the water companies, having 180,000 acres (73,000 hectares) in its care which include moorland, huge tracts of woodland and many farms.

Yorkshire Water Services has some of the most scenic sites in Britain.

Northumbrian Water also offers superb scenery and interesting wetland sites.

Welsh Water (Dwr Cymru Cyfyngedig) has 58 reservoirs, many of which are open to the public.

▲ Haweswater in Cumbria is owned by United Utilities and supplies 25% of the North West's water

THE ENVIRONMENT AGENCY

The Environment Agency (EA) was formed in 1996 to act as a guardian. It incorporated what was the National Rivers Authority (NRA) together with Her Majesty's Inspectorate of Pollution and Waste Regulation Authorities and some units from the Department of the Environment. In England it is divided into 14 areas. Its priority is to protect people and the environment including every aspect of the care and control of water resources including:

Flood defence. The EA provides flood warning and flood defences for people and property from rivers and the sea and operates a 24 hour emergency phone line. EA sea defences extend to thousands of miles. Inland, work is carried out to control erosion of riverbanks and other water ways by suitable protective measures, monitoring, for instance, whether cattle drinking from rivers cause damage to the banks.

Site management. There are over 1,000 sites that are managed for recreational use such as sailing, angling and walking. Education, the provision of information and the conservation of natural sources, animals and plants are all included, as is the surveying of rivers and the management of the Thames Barrier.

Management of water resources. EA planning provides a balance between water supply and demand. Income is generated from licences issued for fishing and boating, water abstraction, discharging waste into the air or water, the transportation and disposal of solid waste. Major funding is also received from the levies paid by local authorities for building and maintaining flood defences and grants from central government.

Waste management. The prevention and control of pollution is conducted to improve standards of waste disposal and to reduce it through recycling. All waste disposal by both water and on land is strictly monitored and controlled by the Environment Agency.

The EA netting a village pond in order to monitor fish stocks

Fishing and fisheries. The EA actively encourages fishing for all, especially in urban areas, where they are working to improve stillwater fisheries (ponds and lakes) and to create new ones. Over one million licences are issued each year for rod angling and net fishing and advice is offered to owners on improving habitat. The EA regulates the movement of all fish, fry and ova to and from fisheries (rivers, canals, drains and still waters).

It's against the law to move fish without a permit. Mandatory health checks have to be made prior to release, to minimise the risk of spreading disease, parasites and the introduction of non-indigenous species.

Action is also taken over poaching, pollution and where fish have been killed or died. The EA is responsible for maintaining, improving and developing salmon, sea trout, non-migratory trout and coarse fisheries, their habitat and the quality of the water. They are rigorously monitoring the situation whereby farmed salmon, which have escaped in large numbers from farms in

◄ The EA are responsible for keeping rivers free flowing

Scotland, have invaded rivers and are putting our native wild (Atlantic) salmon at risk.

Some rivers are responding well to improve–ments and are recovering from pollution including the Tyne, Mersey and the Thames. When water quality allows, areas are stocked with coarse fish from the Environment Agency's national fish farm in Nottinghamshire. In 2019 it produced more than half a million (520,475) fish for restocking.

Navigation. Small sailing craft or water vessels for use on rivers and canals in Great Britain have to be registered with the Environment Agency. A licence is required to use craft of any kind on nearly all of British inland waterways.

Canoeing is a contentious issue. Of England's 42,700 miles (68,700kms) of inland waterways in England, only 1,400 miles (225,000kms) can be paddled uncontested.

NATIONAL PARKS

National Parks are protected, relatively undeveloped, areas of beautiful scenery, wildlife and cultural heritage which allow access to the countryside for everyone. The first to be created was the Peak District founded in 1951 and most recent is the South Downs in 2011 which is the most densely populated.

National Parks came into being with an Act of Parliament in 1949. In England they are funded by central government. People live and work within National Parks and anyone can visit at any time free of charge. Each National Park is looked after by an organisation called a National Park Authority which includes members, staff and volunteers. They don't actually own much of the land or infrastructure, most is in private ownership, but they work in conjunction with other organisations such as the National Trust,

Snowdonia National Park

RSPB, Wildlife Trusts, Forestry Commission, English Heritage, Nature Scot and Natural Resources Wales.

> *There are 15 National Parks in Britain. Currently there are none in Northern Ireland although the Mourne Mountains are under consideration for National Park status.*

Each one is looked after by its own authority which has its own policies and arrangements but their statutory purpose is to conserve and enhance the natural and cultural heritage of the area and to promote understanding and enjoyment of the special qualities of the national park by the public. Scottish National Parks have two additional purposes: to promote sustainable use of the natural resources of the area and to promote sustainable economic and social development of the area's communities.

NATIONAL PARKS IN BRITAIN

Ten of the National Parks are in England: they are the **Norfolk Broads** (117sq mi), **Dartmoor** (368sq mi), **Exmoor** (267sq mi), **Lake District** (912sq mi), **New Forest** (219sq mi), **Northumberland** (410sq mi), **North York Moors** (554sq mi), **Peak District** (555sq mi), **Yorkshire Dales** (841sq mi) and **South Downs** (628sq mi).
Three are in Wales – the **Brecon Beacons** (519sq mi), **Pembrokeshire Coast** (243sq mi) and **Snowdonia** (838sq mi). National Parks in England are government funded.
Since the year 2000 two National Parks have been established in Scotland. The **Cairngorms** (1,748sq mi) in 2003 and **Loch Lomond** and the **Trossachs** (720sq mi) in 2002. Since 2005 the Freedom of Right to Roam in Scotland allows access to most land and inland waters subject to certain conditions.

The National Park Authority doesn't permit wild camping, camp fires or BBQs on any land they own. However, within them there are many options for accommodation from camping barns, camp sites, youth hostels, holiday lets, traditional B&Bs and luxury hotels.

NATIONAL NATURE RESERVES AND OTHER NATURE RESERVES

National Nature Reserves are designated as key places for wildlife, geology and natural features. Marine Nature Reserves (MNRs) have a similar status in marine environments.

There are 224 (NNRs) in England owned or managed through agreements with Natural England, 76 in Wales (National Resources Wales) and 43 in Scotland (Nature Scot). Combined, these reserves extend to 680,000 acres (275,000ha). There are 47 similarly protected areas in Northern Ireland coming under the jurisdiction of Northern Ireland Environment Agency. Several freshwater areas are statutorily designated for their nature conservation value, in which case there is cooperation with the Environment Agency regarding their care and management.

There are nine NNRs within the Cairngorms National Park in Scotland that extend to 65,000 acres (26,000 hectares). The smallest is a one acre (0.4 hectare) meadow in Cumbria.

Most have some permitted public access and receive millions of visits each year. Certain restrictions apply to photographing or causing possible disturbance to protected species of wildlife. Applications for a licence to do so are made to Natural England or its UK counterparts as appropriate.

Programmes of walks, talks and educational days are organised throughout the country at selected NNRs.

Conservation activities on nature reserves very often involve native breeds of animals local to the area. Ponies, cattle, sheep, goats, pigs and even water buffalo graze in different ways which can be used to restore specific habitats. Conservation often calls for the elimination or reduction of invasive flora and fauna when above acceptable levels.

A surprising number of nature reserves are on industrial land reclaimed by nature, such as old quarries, coal mines and disused industrial sites.

All over the UK, in city, town or country unofficial hidden wildlife havens can be found. Not officially recognised as nature reserves, little fragments of land are sometimes discovered in churchyards, roadside verges and railway cuttings. They were all originally created to suit human needs, but have evolved to become places where wild creatures and plants thrive. Old neglected orchards make ideal wildlife habitats by contributing to the ecosystem with

lichen and decaying wood for insects, flowers in spring for bees and apples as winter feed for birds and animals.

In Greater London there are a number of large Victorian cemeteries, each with their own conservation initiatives. They act like green oases amidst an urban desert, as places of remembrance but also sanctuaries for wildlife. Kensal Green Cemetery extends to 72 acres (30ha) and Brompton and Highgate Cemeteries to 37 acres (15ha) each.

 giving nature a home rspb

ROYAL SOCIETY FOR THE PROTECTION OF BIRDS

The Royal Society for the Protection of Birds (RSPB) of England, Wales and Scotland is the UK's fifth biggest landowner and Europe's largest wildlife conservation charity. It was formed in 1889 by Emily Williamson, who had become gravely concerned about the fashion for adorning ladies' hats with plumes which meant that vast numbers of birds were being killed solely for their feathers. At the beginning, the Society consisted entirely of women.

The RSPB now has 1.1 million members and thousands of volunteers assist the staff employed.

Their work includes monitoring, protection and conservation projects for the preservation of birds.

The RSPB owns more than 320,000 acres (130,000ha) throughout Britain, of which 50,000 acres (20,000ha) is farmland. In the UK the RSPB owns more than 200 nature reserves covering a wide range of habitats aiding the conservation of more than three-quarters of our most threatened

◀ Leverets sheltering under a gravestone in a country churchyard during a storm

The RSPB manages over 200 reserves spread widely across the UK. This one is Balranald on North Uist

bird species. Many of the reserves have hides enabling visitors to view the birds more closely. Some also have cafes, shops and visitor centres displaying a wealth of information.

The RSPB is the country's leading protector of birds and influential over many of the conservation decisions that are made. Despite the organisation being very critical of the way landowners manage land for grouse shooting, they joined the Buccleuch Estates and four other bodies in conducting a ten-year experiment on an established grouse moor at Langholm close to the Scottish border. The Langholm Moor Demonstration Project ran from 2008 to 2018 and the conservation of hen harriers was the principal reason the RSPB became involved, as grouse are one of hen harriers' favoured prey.

THE CROWN ESTATE

The Crown Estate is one of the largest property owners in the UK. It belongs to the reigning monarch and is known as the sovereign's public estate.

The Crown Estate's holdings are extensive with agricultural land and forests amounting to nearly 2 million acres (792,000 ha). Four Crown Estates extending to 37,000 acres (15,000 ha) are in Scotland. The famous Balmoral Estate is not one of these but is owned privately by the Royal Family. 5,000 acres (2,000 ha) of Crown Estate land is owned in Greater London including eight London Parks and many buildings.

Crown Estate is neither government property nor the monarch's private estate.

The Crown Estate also owns approximately half of the foreshore around England, Wales and Northern Ireland and the majority of the seabed for a distance of 12 nautical miles out from the coast. Within this perimeter, some is leased to offshore wind farm companies for which an income is received.

The Crown Estate is managed by the Crown Estate Commissioners.

COUNCIL-OWNED LAND

English councils own about 4% of England's land amounting to 1.3million acres (half a million hectares). Motorways and major A roads are the responsibility of Highways England, Transport Scotland and the Welsh Government Highway Authorities. Responsibility for the upkeep and litter removal of other roads and verges rests with local authorities. The maintenance of roadside hedges and trees falls to the owners/occupiers of adjoining lands.

Councils own golf courses, allotments, road verges, nature reserves, some farmland and land for recreational purposes. There are about 300 Country Parks funded by local authorities.

Golf courses

Many golf courses are municipally owned. Within Greater London 130 golf courses cover 11,000 acres; nearly half of this area is owned by councils. Nearly one million people play golf.

Allotments

During the Industrial Revolution times many men and women moved from the countryside, where they had been relatively self-sufficient, to find industrial work in factories and mills. Conditions were appalling and fresh food scarce and expensive.

An Act of Parliament in 1908 placed an obligation on local authorities to provide sufficient allotments for workers to grow fresh food. After the First World War, land was made available to all, in towns and cities and even large villages with those who had endured the hardship of serving their country given priority, and at that point there were about a million and a half allotments, about five times as many as there is today. Post WWII lifestyles changed, cheap food became available and growing your own lost its attraction but, with the recent trend towards healthy living and sustainability, demand for allotments is increasing. A standard

Allotments are in much demand

full-size allotment is 300 sq yards (250 sq metres) but half-sized ones can sometimes be rented.

Local nature reserves

Councils are able to set up Local Nature Reserves (LNRs) to protect wildlife and habitats of all kinds which usually feature something of local interest.

Councils have control over the land within an LNR, either by owning or leasing it or by agreement with the owner. Many are close to towns and cities where they offer a greater number of people the opportunity to take an active interest in nature and their natural heritage.

- Sefton and Wirral Councils own nearly 30,000 acres (12,000 ha) of foreshore which includes sand dunes and salt marshes.
- Sheffield and Bradford Councils have more than 7,800 acres (3,150 ha) of moorland.
- About 16,700 acres (6,750 ha) of downland belong jointly to Brighton & Hove and Eastbourne Councils.

There are now over 1,280 LNRs in England, covering almost 98,000 acres (40,000 ha), 75 in Scotland and more than 65 in Wales. LNRs have a lower level of protection than National Nature Reserves although some are in a higher category, designated as Sites of Special Scientific Interest.

Country Parks are public green spaces on the edge of urban areas, designated for town people to freely visit and enjoy recreation in the natural, rural atmosphere found in the countryside. They also offer educational opportunities for local school children.

Country Parks were first established under the Countryside Act 1968. Most are owned and managed by Local Authorities and extend to 108,000 acres (44,000 ha). There are around 250 recognised Country Parks in England and Wales, which attract some 57 million visitors a year, and a further 40 or so in Scotland. More are being created. They vary enormously in size, habitat and facilities available. In some there is a charge for car parking. Sherwood Forest in Nottinghamshire is one of the most popular.

The Seven Sisters Country Park is made up of 700 acres (280 ha) of chalk cliffs, within the South Downs National Park and includes downland and the coastal cliffs of the Seven Sisters and Beachy Head which is owned by Eastbourne Borough Council.

County Farms At least 44 councils in England are in possession of small County Farms which they lease to tenants.

The number of County Farms has been in decline for decades and, across England, land usage has plummeted from approximately 425,000 acres (172,000ha) in 1977 to only about half that in 2017. Many were sold off to fund privatisation and council spending. The remaining County Farms still provide an opportunity for many young and first-time farmers hoping to set up on their own and these holdings give them a foot on the ladder to enter into farming.

In England there are now about 2,500 County Farms covering 215,000 acres (87,000ha) with Cambridgeshire having the highest number. In Wales 144 holdings extend over 11,400 acres (4,600ha) of land.

Roadside and trackside verges County Councils are owners of the verges which stretch from the highway as far as a ditch, fence or hedge so they vary greatly in width.

Roadside verges are some of the richest sites for wildlife and plants in the UK.

For safety reasons, on A and B roads a 4ft-wide (1.2 metre) strip along the edge of verges is cut twice yearly. Other more minor roads are likely to be cut only once. Vegetation remaining beyond this is usually left untouched unless there are trees or ditches which might need attention. Where there is a specially recognised conservation site, councils occasionally make exceptions to their cutting regime and mowing is delayed until later in the year. Roadside verges can provide a haven for wildlife especially if the adjacent land is prairie farmed with huge expanses of a single crop. They create mini nature reserves where a large variety of plants and insects survive with minimal interference throughout the year.

> *Many verges are species-rich and include remnants of ancient meadows bounded by old hedgerows and mature trees.*

During spring and summer, close examination of roadside verges will often reveal a wealth of flowers which naturally grow wild in the area. Some of these, such as teasels, will later set seed and provide winter food for many little birds.

County Councils try to manage their roadsides with conservation in mind. They have made it a policy recently to sow wild flower seeds in the verges of newly constructed roads, producing an annual show of comparatively rare plants such as cowslips, that would not normally have grown there. Berry-bearing shrubs such as guelder rose and rowan are sometimes planted to provide winter food for some species of birds. Apart from the benefits to wildlife these all make what might be an otherwise drab landscape more interesting and varied.

Motorways are the responsibility of Highways England, the Welsh Government and Transport Scotland. Verges and banks of motorways are left virtually undisturbed and act as a sanctuary for wildlife. Kestrels can often be seen hovering beside motorways searching for mice and voles which thrive in the rough unkempt grasses. New motorways often have

small trees and shrubs planted on the banks which contributes to biodiversity. Ponds are sometimes constructed to collect surface water run-off. Despite some pollution, they very soon become wildlife habitats in their own right.

Railway embankments Our railways extend to 20,000 miles (32,000km) of track, much of which runs through the countryside. Network Rail is responsible for managing railway embankments and also some other unused railway land. The sides of the tracks, embankments and rock cuttings remain virtually untouched. In the days of steam, sparks from the engines would sometimes set light to the vegetation beside the track, a problem still occasionally encountered by our heritage railways. These are nearly all charitable trusts although some of the rolling stock may be owned by various individuals or voluntary groups. Most of the work running and looking after them is carried out by volunteers.

NATURAL ENGLAND

Natural England (NE) was established in 2006 as an amalgamation of the Countryside Agency, English Nature and the Rural Development Service. Natural England is sponsored by the Department for Environment, Food & Rural Affairs (DEFRA) and is the government's adviser for the natural environment in England assisting with the protection and restoration of our natural world. Agencies carrying out similar work in the other nations are Natural Resources Wales, NatureScot and the Northern Ireland Environment Agency.

Natural England employs 2,000 staff divided into 12 regional teams who are responsible for identifying and designating areas as SSSIs (Sites of Special Scientific Interest) and NNRs (National Nature Reserves).

It generally monitors and advises (taking on managerial responsibilities when needed) the management of biologically sensitive areas of all kinds throughout the country. NE works with many thousands of landowners and agents and in partnership with such bodies as the Crown Estate Commissioners, Forest Enterprise, the Ministry of Defence and many other non-governmental organisations. Research is carried out to help endangered species and grants are distributed for management conservation. NE acts in an advisory capacity to the government and its agencies. All political parties are aware of how important it is for people and nature to have a healthy environment.

SITES OF SPECIAL SCIENTIFIC INTEREST

Sites of Special Scientific Interest (SSSIs) are conservation areas where some of the most important habitats, species and geological features can be found. They are areas of land and water considered best to represent our natural heritage in terms of their flora (plants), fauna (animals), geology (rocks) and geomorphology (landforms) or a mixture of these natural features. Many are also designated as National Nature Reserves. Responsibility for assessing and monitoring the condition of SSSIs lies with either Natural England, Scottish Natural Heritage, Countryside Council for Wales or Department of the Environment and Heritage Service (DoENI).

Of special concern is that 80% of old heathland has disappeared. And 97% of the natural fenland, which once covered Lincolnshire, Cambridgeshire, Norfolk and Suffolk, has been lost to farming.

There are nearly 7,000 SSSIs listed in the UK which vary greatly in size and are mainly privately owned. 7% of land in England is SSSI, 12% in each of Scotland and Wales and 8% in Northern Ireland, covering an approximate total of 10,000 square miles. The smallest is a horseshoe bat roost in the roof of a barn and two of the largest are the Wash at 153,000 acres (62,000 ha) and the Humber Estuary at 91,400 acres (37,000 ha).

The 44 acre Boughton Fen SSSI nature reserve in Norfolk is common land registered to Boughton Parish Council

NATIONAL TRAILS

National Trails, waymarked with the distinctive acorn symbol, are long-distance walks through some of the very best landscapes the UK has to offer. They not only offer scenery but also wildlife viewing and the opportunity to experience some of the UK's amazing history and culture.

The shortest National Trail is the Yorkshire Wolds Way at 79 miles (127 km). Some sections of National Trails can be ridden by cyclists or horse riders. They are administered by Natural England and Natural Resources Wales and there are 16 in total (13 in England and three in Wales), covering around 2,500 miles (4,000 km). The first to be designated as a National Trail was the Pennine Way in 1965.

The Scottish National Trail is a 537 mile (864km) long-distance trail between Kirk Yetholm in the Scottish Borders and Cape Wrath in the far north of the Scottish Highlands. In Scotland, long-distance trails are called Scotland's Great Trails and are administered by Nature Scot, formerly known as Scottish Natural Heritage. These trails are clearly waymarked and range in length from 25 miles (40 km) to 210 miles (340 km). In total there are 29 routes which provide 1,900 miles (3,000 km) of trails.

ENGLAND COAST PATH

The England Coast Path has been opened in sections and is shortly due to be completed. It will go all the way around the coast of England and will become the longest coastal path in the world at around 2,795 miles (4,500 kilometres). National Trails have been created by linking existing footpaths, some of which have become incorporated into the England Coast Path.

THE ULSTER WAY

The Ulster Way is a Long-distance Path in Northern Ireland. It is a 625 mile (1000 km) circular walking route, one of the longest in the United Kingdom and Ireland.

WILDLIFE TRUSTS

The Wildlife Trusts are a charitable organisation made up of 46 local Wildlife Trusts with a combined UK membership of 850,000. Together the Trusts own around 243,000 acres (98,500 hectares) of land which includes 26 farms managed for wildlife. Wildlife Trusts care for 2,300 nature reserves. The idea to purchase land to create nature reserves was first discussed in 1912 and came to fruition in 1926 when the first independent Trust was formed in Norfolk.

THE WOODLAND TRUST

The Woodland Trust was formed in 1972 and is a non-profit-making company and registered charity. Its objectives are the creation, protection, and restoration of our native woodland heritage. It is the largest woodland conservation charity in the United Kingdom and owns over 1,000 sites covering more than 61,000 acres (24,700 ha). A third of this is ancient woodland.

The Woodland Trust has planted 43 million trees since it was founded and is still planting today. The public are allowed access its woods.

WILDFOWL AND WETLANDS TRUST

The Wildfowl & Wetlands Trust (WWT) is a wildfowl (ducks and geese) and wetland conservation charity of international importance in the United Kingdom. It was originally founded in 1946 by the ornithologist and artist Sir Peter Scott. It has ten reserves around the country with viewing hides, shops and cafes, as well as educational facilities and programmes. WWT manages 7,500 acres (3,000 ha) of wetlands, has 200,000 members and one million visitors each year. Volunteers work alongside permanent staff, helping to monitor wildlife of all kinds and maintain the habitat. The majority of wildfowl are migratory and spend the winter in Britain, arriving in late autumn and departing in early spring. For this reason, WWT centres are busiest in winter. Wetlands are a haven for many different species of plants, birds, amphibians and insects throughout the year.

GOLF COURSES

There are about 2,600 golf courses in the UK extending to an estimated 310,000 acres (125,000ha). Ownership is divided between members, local councils, the Crown Estate, private and corporate bodies.

THE HORSE RACING INDUSTRY

The racing industry contributes £4billion to the economy. Public access is often permitted to parts of the racecourses. 15 are owned by the Jockey Club and 16 by Arena Racing Company. In addition there are a large number of stud farms and training stables. These are all on grassland that is never ploughed and most often on chalky soil. Newmarket in Suffolk is the headquarters of the racing industry and has two large race tracks, 50 training stables and 60 stud farms in the vicinity. The town is home to over 3,500 racehorses. Newmarket racecourse celebrated its 350th birthday in 2016.

There are 60 racecourses in the UK, usually close to towns, which cover tens of thousands of acres of land.

THE CHURCH OF ENGLAND

The Church Commissioners own 105,000 acres (42,000ha) of land across England and Wales, including 32,000 acres (13,000ha) of forestry in Scotland, as well as thousands of properties. The Church of Scotland owns 12,500 acres (5,000ha) of glebe (church) land.

THE CANAL AND RIVER TRUST

Since 2012, canals in England and Wales have been managed by the Canal and River Trust, a charitable organisation which looks after 2,000 miles (3,200km) of waterways, nearly 3,000 bridges, more than 1,500 locks and 335 aqueducts. The government-owned body Scottish Canals is responsible for those in Scotland.

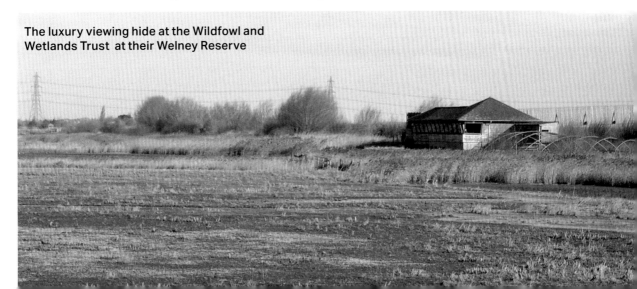

The luxury viewing hide at the Wildfowl and Wetlands Trust at their Welney Reserve

The New Forest was an ancient royal hunting ground

FORESTRY

The area of woodland in the UK is estimated to be nearly 8 million acres (3.21 million ha) covering 13% of the total land area.

Forestry encompasses 10% of England, 15% of Wales, 19% of Scotland and 9% of Northern Ireland.

Large areas comprise commercial pine mono-culture. Tree planting is seen as a way of combatting climate change and 33,000 acres (13,700 ha) of new woodland was created in the UK in 2019-20. In 2021 the government announced aims to plant 74,000 acres (30,000 ha) of new forests across the UK during the current parliament's term in office.

Today forests have become important not only in the commercial world but also for the role they play in conservation, combatting global warming and recreational purposes. There are lucrative grants available for tree planting but careful thought needs to be given as to where trees are planted. If it is in areas which are of little use to agriculture and which have not been cultivated, it may well be counterproductive. Having been left undisturbed, the land is likely to be rich in bio-diversity, and disturbing the soil will release the carbon which is already stored. This is particularly applicable to peatland which is to some extent protected. If the wrong species of trees are planted in the wrong place they can do more harm than good.

Community Forests have existed for nearly thirty years and been planted in and around our largest towns and cities. These woods are on the doorsteps of urban populations where locals can go to connect with the wider landscape, and these trees improve the local air quality, thereby tackling air pollution, climate change and establishing places for nature. In December 2020 the government announced a new £12.1 million fund to plant over 1,250 acres (500 ha) of trees in ten community forests in England over a period of five months.

50 MILLION TREES

The government's target is to plant 50 million trees by 2025. These are grown from seed by specialist nurseries and planted out when they are 1-3ft (30-100cms) in height. These young trees are known as **'whips'**. The problem is that there is nowhere near enough being grown in this country to fulfil the requirement. Instead, a large number will need to be imported adding polluting carbon emissions from the transportation and the risk of disease being brought in.

Forests vary greatly in size ranging from these small urban woods to Kielder Forest in the north of England which extends to 250 square miles. A few decades ago the forests of Britain provided a living for many people. Today, thanks to mechanisation, only about 16,000 are employed in forestry.

More than 11 million tonnes of wood are harvested annually in the UK but this is less than 10% of the timber used here.

Britain's timber industry is finding it difficult to remain competitive with cheap imports from Sweden and the Baltic States. Approximately 85% of all wood products are now imported from abroad including an increasing amount of wood pellets for fuel from North America and Canada. There was an unprecedented demand for timber in 2021 as a result of the covid pandemic.

Woodland is divided into two categories – softwoods and hardwoods – and their management techniques are very different. Over half the woodland in England consists of native, broadleaf/deciduous hardwoods (trees that lose their leaves in winter), and all are privately owned. They are regarded as a long term investment, because hardwood trees are slow growing and not even thinned out until they are 30 or 40 years old, most likely being at least a hundred before becoming mature and ready for felling. Oaks in particular can live for centuries. Leading contenders for the oldest are the Bowthorpe Oak in Lincolnshire with a girth of over 40 feet (12.30m) and the Marton Oak in Cheshire with a girth measuring 46 feet (14m). These are both estimated to be over 1,000 years old. Slightly younger, but probably the most famous, is the

◄ Several species of birds like these Kestrels nest in holes in trees

33 feet (10m) girth Major Oak in Sherwood Forest, purported to have provided shelter for the legendary Robin Hood.

HARDWOODS

Only 2% of Britain's woodlands today are classified as ancient, which means continually forested since 1600. Most of the broadleaf and mixed woodland today was planted and preserved by wealthy landowners for the pursuit of fieldsports, at first for the hunting of deer and foxes and, since the mid 19th century, for pheasant shooting. Many parts of the British landscape, its woodlands and its parks, remain much the same today as when they were fashioned by those people a century or two ago.

The emphasis is now on conservation, and with the availability of financial grants, various new plantings of broadleafed trees have appeared in the last few years. Hardwood saplings are planted approximately 10ft (3m) apart in straight lines and individually

▲ Ready for planting - young saplings, stakes and plastic guards

protected against rabbit, hare and deer damage by fencing, wire surrounds or, more commonly, plastic tubes or guards. The plastic tubes are not environmentally friendly because carbon is produced in their manufacture and the tubes are left to disintegrate into microplastics which are harmful to the environment and wildlife. Now aware of the danger, alternative tree guards to plastic are urgently being sought.

Weed growth is controlled mainly by spraying with herbicides, and attacks by insects and disease have to be dealt with using pesticides.

The trees, which will eventually grow very big, are intentionally planted close together, often with a mix of species, so that they shelter one another and grow straight. After about 30 years, they are thinned out leaving the remaining ones to mature into fine specimens. Often a few evergreens such as holly and laurel are included in these new woods to provide a varied and sheltered habitat for wildlife.

◀ Wooden stakes are used to support hardwood saplings

SOFTWOOD CONIFER WOODLAND

The remaining UK woodland is planted with softwoods with a small percentage of hardwoods mixed in as a conservation measure. Softwoods consist of conifers – evergreen, cone-bearing, needle-covered trees, which grow quickly even in areas where it is impossible to cultivate any other crop.

Planted in regimental lines, their dark canopy eventually eliminates the growth of all plants beneath them and repels wildlife. Soft pine needles carpet the ground and the species of creatures that live on the edge of these forestry blocks are very different to those that once lived on the open moorland.

In the 1960s the timber industry was booming and as a result many of what were once open moorland and hillsides, particularly in Scotland, are now covered with blocks of conifers.

Most soft wood plantations are the responsibility of the Forestry Commission in England; Forestry and Land Scotland or Scottish Forestry in Scotland, Natural Resources Wales and Forest Service Northern Ireland.

The wood from commercially grown coniferous trees has many uses including construction, fixtures and fittings as well as furniture. It is also pulped and used in the manufacture of panel board, chipboard, paper and paperboard. But growing huge tracts of one species (monoculture) has generally been replaced with a more sympathetic approach, aiming to promote conservation and diversification for the benefit of wildlife. Wide woodland rides and clearings not only encourage wildlife and a variety of plants but also act as firebreaks. When a section is clear-felled, the occasional dead tree is left standing for the benefit of insects and birds. Once a conifer has been cut down, no part of it will grow again.

About 60% of the conifers planted in Britain are Sitka spruce; the remaining 40% include Douglas, Scots and Corsican Pine as well as Larch which is the only conifer in Britain to shed its needles in winter.

Harvesting Conifers

Approximately 10 million tonnes of soft wood timber is harvested annually on a rotational basis. Young conifer trees are grown in nurseries from seeds collected in the forests. When the seedlings have become established they are planted out either in fresh ground prepared by ploughing into ridges or areas that have been felled. Often these new plantations have to be protected from hares, rabbits and deer with wire netting fences. At the beginning, many plants such as bramble and birch invade the open

◀ Foresters using chainsaws have to wear special protective trousers, boots, helmets and gloves

▲ Up to 600 trees a day can be felled, stripped of branches and cut into lengths by this incredible machine

ground and need cutting back or spraying so that the young conifers are not overwhelmed by this unwanted growth. However, the trees grow rapidly and soon smother the undergrowth. At this stage they are **'brashed'**, in which the lower branches are cut off. They are then left untouched until they are thinned after about 20 years. The remaining trees are left to grow straight and strong until they are ready for felling when they are mature, at between 40 and 70 years old. When all the trees in a block of forestry are cut down, it is known as **'clear felling'**.

Gigantic computerised machines are now used to fell conifers and have mostly displaced the men who used to do the felling with chain saws, and before that by hand. These machines work very quickly cutting down the trees, and they also remove all the side branches and saw the trunks into the exact required lengths. One minute is all the time it takes for each tree. One of these super-efficient giants can do the work of 25 men. In remote areas such as parts of Scotland, where job opportunities are very limited, this has caused serious economic problems to many isolated rural communities which had relied on forestry work. Other large machines load the timber onto trailers, take it to a roadway and stack it in piles. From there it can be loaded onto lorries. From the time the trees were planted until the time they reach the processing plant, they may well not have been touched by hand!

Roots from the felled trees are dug up and placed in rows. Formerly they were left to decompose naturally but now, where possible, a big machine grinds them into wood chips which can be used for horticultural purposes or as biomass fuel for power stations, with the ash being returned to the land. Disposing of the roots in this manner greatly reduces the risk of fungal diseases being spread to newly planted trees.

▼ Collecting up the felled timber

THE FORESTRY COMMISSION

The original Forestry Commission was a non-ministerial government department responsible for the management of publicly owned forests, and the regulation of both public and private forestry. It was set up in 1919 to restore Britain's woodlands which had been decimated by the demand for wood for trenches during the First World War. At this time only 5% of the land area remained covered in woodland. The Forestry Commission were able to cheaply procure thousands of acres of low quality land which was of little value to farming but was suitable for growing conifers.

The Forestry Commission is now the largest landowner in Britain and is responsible for protecting, expanding and promoting the sustainable management of woodlands. One major activity is scientific research, some of which is carried out in research forests across Britain. Recreation is also important, with several outdoor activities being actively promoted.

The Commission is made up of three parts: '**Forest Services**' who are the government's expert forestry advisors, '**Forest Research**' who deliver internationally renowned forestry and tree-related research to England, Scotland and Wales; and the national organisations who manage the nation's forests. With devolution in 2013, changes were made to the structure of the Forestry Commission and it has rebranded

▲ A few hardwoods, including beech, are planted on the edges of Thetford Forest's conifer plantations

itself and split nationally. The Commission's forests in Wales were transferred to Natural Resources Wales. In Scotland, Forestry and Land Scotland was established in 2019 to own and manage Scotland's National Forest Estate and that same year, England's portion became known as **Forestry England**.

Northern Ireland Forest Service had already been formed separately in 1998. Combined, these departments either own or manage just over a quarter of all British woodland equating to 2.2 million acres (0.86 million ha).

Natural Resources Wales (NRW) is a Welsh Government-sponsored body which became operational from April 2013 when it took over the management of the natural resources of Wales. It was formed from a merger of the Countryside Council for Wales, Environment Agency Wales, and the Forestry Commission Wales, and also assumed some other roles formerly taken by Welsh Government.

Forestry and Land Scotland (FLS) is responsible for managing and promoting land predominantly covered in forest that is owned by

▲ Scotland was once covered in forests such as this

the Scottish Government on behalf of the nation. The FLS co-exists with Scottish Forestry, which is responsible for regulation, policy and support to landowners.

Forestry England cares for more land and trees than any other organisation in England. It is responsible for 1,500 of the nation's forests and supplies the country's largest volume of sustainably sourced timber. Forestry England conserves flora and fauna habitat on their sites as well as providing over 1,800 miles (nearly 3,000km) of walking, running, horseriding and cycling trails as well as other recreational facilities. 230 million visits are made each year and with an ever-increasing interest in rural pursuits, it is very important that visitors are fully catered for.

There is right of public access to more than half of the different areas of Forestry Commission land. Many sites have free carparks and particular attention is paid to way-marking forest trails and tracks which radiate out from them.

There are various visitor centres scattered around the UK to which there is free access although a charge is made for car parking. 13 are in England, 8 in Scotland, 5 in Wales and 7 in Northern Ireland. At these, apart from various trails, there are often information centres, picnic areas, cafés, toilets, play areas, bike hire, and maybe even a shop. Some trails around visitor centres are wheelchair-friendly. Educational projects include 31 forest classrooms. Other facilities on offer to the public are camping sites, self-catering log cabins and touring caravan sites.

Fieldsports are strictly regulated on all Forestry Commission land; game shooting and deer stalking is permitted in some areas. Other sports welcomed include drag hunting (following a scent trail laid by man with hounds or bloodhounds), husky racing, horse endurance racing events, car rallying, orienteering, and many more.

Thetford Forest is the largest man-made forest in England extending to nearly 50,000 acres (20,000 ha) and attracts 1.5 million visitors annually.

There are over 700 ancient monuments on Forestry Commission land. Most of the conifer plantations have been planted since the end of the First World War (1918) and many encompass ancient monuments, the ruins of old crofts and other sites of human habitation.

THETFORD FOREST

Prior to being purchased in the 1920s the poor, sandy soil of Thetford Forest in Norfolk was open heathland. Dotted throughout the forest, hidden away in small clearings, are little flint cottages. These were once the homes of warreners whose working lives revolved around caring for and protecting wild rabbits kept for their fur on the dry heaths. This formed the principal industry of the local area and two factories were built in Brandon (Suffolk) to process the skins. Train loads of rabbit meat were regularly sent to Cambridge and London.

The Forestry Commission is also responsible for large areas which are not forested including some used for agriculture and grazing as well as areas of mountain and moorland. Here the woodland habitat, plants, birds of prey and wildlife in general are their responsibility.

Wildlife rangers are employed to care for and protect the forests. Their duties involve education, maintenance, wildlife and environment protection. Other rangers are responsible for controlling pests such as deer, rabbits and grey squirrels, all of which in excessive numbers can cause serious damage to young plantations.

Around the country much work is carried out conserving our native red squirrels. Reintroduction has been attempted in Thetford Forest (Norfolk), once a stronghold for them, but with little success. Small pockets survive in a few other locations and there remains a modest

▼ Thetford Forest was planted on heathland after the First World War

◀ The seeds of foxgloves can lay dormant for decades until trees in some dense plantations are felled

SPECIES OF TREES AND THEIR USES

COPPICING AND OTHER USES

Until the early 20th century, the coppicing of deciduous trees was a fundamental part of woodland management and created a huge diversity and richness to the wildlife habitat within a wood. Certain species of trees would be cut back to within a few inches of the ground, whereupon the '**stool**', as the resulting stump is known, soon throws out new shoots that grow thicker and taller in each successive year. Many species were harvested regularly in this way including hazel, willow, sweet chestnut and hornbeam

A newly coppiced area is suddenly opened up to the light and, miraculously, plants such as primroses and foxgloves suddenly appear, having lain dormant beneath the shadow of the leafy canopy for many years. Coppicing is now often carried out by conservationists to improve the diversity of habitat.

The production of charcoal was also carried out within broadleaf woods. Large iron cylinders with lids allowed a slow, controlled burn of the wood inside, producing lumps of charcoal, a product of great importance to industry long before barbecues were invented.

All broadleaf trees can be used for firewood and also for processing as wood pulp. When they are thinned out or when older trees are felled, the smaller diameter trunks and branches are usually sold for these purposes. However the large mature trunks of most familiar woodland trees are used for specific purposes and some are quite valuable. Sadly the elm has all but disappeared from the British countryside because of Dutch Elm Disease spread by the

population in Scotland. Where road casualty rates are high, rope bridges have been erected above busy roads enabling them to cross without having to come to ground.

At the beginning of the 20th century woodland was as important to our forbears as farmland, and utilised in much the same way. Native broadleaf species were used for specific purposes with very little going to waste. Firewood was in greater demand than it is now and small diameter stem and branch wood was cut into lengths and stacked to dry out in accessible places. This is known as **cordwood** because it is sold by the 'cord', a cubic measurement of 4ft by 4ft by 8ft (1.22m x 1.22m x 2.44m). Wood burning stoves have become increasingly popular in the last 30 years and have been installed in many homes. This has seen an escalating demand for logs but, because of concerns over pollution, recent legislation in England has banned the use of fresh cut (green) wood which has high moisture content. Only dried, seasoned wood can now be burned which is less polluting, but more expensive. Similar legislation is likely to be put in place for Wales and Scotland.

Elm-bark beetle but others listed below are still commonly found although, for some, their future is also under threat from new diseases and pests.

ASH is probably the best for firewood and is used for wood turning and making handles for such things as axes and hammers; it is also used for veneer, furniture and planking. Ash is a popular choice for sports items such as hockey sticks, skis and cricket stumps but worryingly our ash trees are being threatened by disease.

ASH DIEBACK

It is predicted that Ash Dieback, first confirmed in the UK in 2012, will eventually kill 95% of our ash trees. It is a fungus, the spores of which spread by being blown in the wind. It will be a sad day should ash become extinct for they are such versatile trees which can be found growing in many parts of our countryside.

BEECH has a multitude of uses including turnery, joinery, furniture-making, flooring and manufacturing plywood. It also produces excellent charcoal.

BIRCH although generally considered to be the 'weed' of woodland, still has its uses. It is suitable for furniture production and making toys and handles. Before plastic became commonly used, most brooms and besoms were made from birch as well as bobbins, spools and reels for the Lancashire cotton industry.

Many of the jumps used in National Hunt racing and Point-to-Points are constructed from birch and the bark is sometimes used in tanning leather.

HAZEL, of all the trees and bushes that grow in a wood, is the most useful to country folk. Its familiar yellow catkins herald the arrival of spring and, if squirrels don't get there first, the nuts are a tasty delicacy in late summer. By rotation small hazel plots were coppiced every 6 -12 years. Gardeners use hazel for pea sticks, bean poles and plant supports; short, angled pieces can be used to peg down wire netting; and if they are straight, the longer lengths can be turned into walking sticks. Hazel is used for the shafts of those with fancy handles.

▼ In times past wood was burned slowly to make charcoal which was used in industry

Thatchers use it to make short 'spars' which hold in place the reed or straw; 3,000 may be needed for one roof. Hazel is also used to make wattle fencing and hurdles; untrimmed lengths are tied into 'faggots' for use as sea; and river defences and barrel hoops are made from it.

HOLLY is a popular choice for turning and carving and also makes a strong walking stick.

HORNBEAM is used for flooring, turning, carving, mallet heads and for making the action in keyboard instruments such as pianos.

OAK is often over a hundred years old before it is mature and this slow-growing tree can live to a very great age. The oldest specimens in the UK are believed to be over 1,000 years old but sadly oak is also now threatened with disease.

Up to 2,300 species of birds, mammals, invertebrates such as caterpillars and spiders as well as fungi, not to mention various bacteria and other micro-organisms, are dependent on mature oaks.

They provide nourishment, shelter and places to breed. Given the right conditions one can produce 50,000 acorns in a year which several species of wildlife feed on. Oaks sometimes naturally regenerate from acorns that jays and squirrels have buried. Acorns are poisonous to horses, cattle and dogs but not to pigs and deer.

An oak's great strength means that the wood is used for such things as beams, fencing, gate-posts, boat building and sea defences as well as veneers and furniture. The bark is frequently used for tanning leather and smoking fish.

POPLAR, distinctively tall and slim, is often grown as wind breaks in exposed areas but the wood from this tree is put to very lowly purposes. Before the advent of cheap plastic

▲ Jays assist with oak planting by burying acorns

and disposable cigarette lighters, poplar was used for making matches and the wafer-thin 'chip baskets' and punnets in which soft fruit was sold. Now it is turned into vegetable crates, wood wool and plywood.

SWEET CHESTNUT, familiar for its prickly-cased nuts roasted at Christmas, is commercially grown in some areas to be made into pale fencing and fence posts. Sweet chestnut is cut on a 20-year cycle but this practice is becoming increasingly rare as more and more products are being imported from France. Small plots were sold at auction to be coppiced (cut) during the winter months and then processed during the summer in the woods close to where it was cut. Plots in an area were harvested in rotation. As with hazel, new shoots quickly grew from the 'stools'. Wildlife habitat was greatly enhanced by the rotational clearing of patches within larger woods. Sweet Chestnut can also be cut again after only 2 or 3 years if it is used for making walking sticks.

SYCAMORE is used for flooring, furniture, turning and veneer.

WALNUT and WILD CHERRY are some of the most valued timber in Britain, both being used for high quality veneers and decorative purposes and they make beautiful furniture. The wooden stocks (**butts**) of best quality rifles and shotguns are hand-crafted out of walnut.

WILLOW has several varieties native to the UK which are capable of growing in otherwise unproductive, low-lying, wet ground often found beside rivers and streams. Willow is fast growing and one variety is famously used for making English cricket bats. This is harvested when it is about 20 years old. Another hybrid variety, which grows extremely quickly, is used as a source of biomass to supply green energy power plants. After planting, it is cut back a year later to make it bush out and then harvested every two years. Willow is also used in industry and, in the past, was used to make artificial limbs; it doesn't make very good firewood as it spits.

For thousands of years willow bark has been recognised for its qualities in relieving pain, and aspirin is derived from it.

YEW trees live to a great age although in many cases the main trunk divides into separate sections. Originally yew was the wood of choice for making longbows but now it is valued by cabinet and furniture makers and for carving, turning and making musical instruments.

Yew is often found growing in graveyards, possibly planted there in the first place because their green foliage and red berries are highly poisonous to livestock and it was hoped this would deter folk from allowing their animals to access churchyards. The yew tree growing in Fortingall churchyard in Perthshire is believed to be up to 3,000 years old, making it one of the oldest trees in the UK.

Willows growing in Essex for cricket bats

Hooded crows, locally known as 'hoodies,' are found in Scotland

PEST AND PREDATOR SPECIES

Even the most avid animal lover hates the thought of sharing their home with a rat. It is recognised as a pest because of its habits and disposed of accordingly. A fox is the equivalent of a rat to a poultry keeper. A cat can be a much-loved pet but away from its home will follow its natural instincts and can soon become a pest in certain situations.

There are professional pest controllers and in the countryside gamekeepers wage war, where legally permitted, on most species of pests. Training for the use of all aspects of pest control must have been undertaken, particularly in the handling of toxic substances.

It is in the interests of gamekeepers to protect their game birds from predation because their jobs depend on there being sufficient game to meet their employers' requirements. Much of the breeding success of grey partridge and grouse depends on how efficient gamekeepers have been in culling

predators. By protecting their game birds they are also helping conserve several other species which were once common but are now under threat such as lapwing and curlew. So, additionally, farmers, landowners, bird conservationists and authorities are also benefitting.

The origins of many fieldsports arose through the necessity to control pests such as rabbits, hares, foxes and pigeons, turning the chore into an interesting, challenging and satisfying task.

Many pest species are opportunists and have thrived because of the excessive wastefulness now so common in Britain. Foxes, magpies, crows and seagulls have learned that it is easier to live on scraps discarded in litter bins, or thrown out of car windows than it is to hunt for food. There is a serious risk of disease for them, as well as pets and humans, when they are attracted in high densities to urban areas and their health deteriorates as a result of an unnatural diet. The food for a fox is meat and occasionally wild berries not chips and Chinese takeaways!

Invasive plants can also be classified as pests. The worst is probably bracken which is very invasive and the spores of which are carcinogenic. In the past it was cut for animal bedding in places where straw was not easily available. Farmers and conservationists now attempt to control the growth by continued cutting with a brush cutter or crushing it with a tractor-drawn roller. It is extremely difficult to eradicate, even using sprays, as the root system creeps underground.

Another plant that is problematic in the countryside is common ragwort which grows in grassland and across Britain. Attractive to butterflies and other pollinators, it is poisonous to animals in its dried state.

The Wildlife and Countryside Act 1981 is the main legislation protecting all animals, plants and habitats in the UK.

New legislation came into force in January 2021 concerning the number of pest species included in the conservation category. It is not necessary to apply for general pest control licences but, by law, it is a requirement to abide by their terms and conditions when undertaking licensed acts. The new legislation provides the legal framework to allow for the killing of certain species for the purposes of conservation of wild birds, flora and fauna, protecting public health and safety and to prevent serious damage to crops and livestock. A special licence can be required to cull certain species.

The only species it is permissible to shoot at night are foxes and rabbits.

Snares and traps must be of legally approved designs, which are as humane as possible. Spring traps must not be set out in the open and are designed to kill outright. Cage traps catch animals alive so that they can be disposed of humanely or relocated. Shooting is also covered by various regulations.

It may be distasteful to some but, ever since humans first interfered with nature, they have had to take responsibility for managing it. Controlling pests is part of that.

Only one terrier can be used to evict a fox from its earth and its exit must not be impeded in any way. Two dogs may be used to flush a fox above ground but a pack can no longer be used. No pest species are destroyed without there being a genuine reason to do so. As the population increases there is more and more pressure on wildlife and their habitat in the shrinking countryside. Some species of animals and birds would disappear without predator control. It is inevitable that man has had to become involved not only for the convenience of humans but also to maintain a balance in the countryside.

MAMMALIAN

FOXES

Foxes are predators and of all pests are probably the most damaging to wildlife. It is thought there are between 350,000 and 400,000 foxes in Britain during the autumn and winter and this number at least doubles in spring with the arrival of cubs. These are born underground in an 'earth' and tended by both parents, until they are a few weeks old and weaned.

Although they do some good by feeding on rodents and rabbits, they are non-selective and can cause serious devastation to all ground-nesting birds and young hares. Significant losses occur when domestic livestock is attacked. Poultry and newborn lambs in upland areas are most at risk.

Many a farmer, gamekeeper and conservationist has found bodies scattered around where a fox has been on a killing spree, and in towns, a cat is fair game to a fox.

Urban Foxes

The majority live in rural areas but more and more are finding an easy living in towns and cities especially in southern England. This has led to a completely unnatural existence for they have learned to scavenge on discarded food and that put out for pets, as well as themselves, by well-meaning people.

It is thought about 150,000 of the fox population now live in our towns and cities.

The highest estimate of urban foxes is Bournemouth with approximately 23 foxes per square kilometre followed by 18 foxes per square kilometre in London. Densely populated, their health deteriorates, partly through living on an unnatural diet and partly because, being in such close contact, diseases are quickly spread between them. One of the worst is Sarcoptic Mange, a skin infection caused by microscopic mites which burrow beneath the skin causing intense irritation and the animal much suffering. It easily transmits to dogs and less commonly to

▲ Foxes are predators which can be exceedingly destructive to wildlife and poultry as they continue to kill by reflex, not just through hunger

cats. Without veterinary intervention, a once attractive fox can soon be reduced to a sad, pathetic sight when its hair falls out.

Town foxes that have been rounded up at night and those that have been 'rescued' are often released into the countryside by well-meaning people, where they spread any diseases they are carrying to healthy animals living in the wild. Urban foxes that are not used to hunting for themselves stand little chance of survival and they endure a slow death due to starvation. There may appear to be plenty of rabbits and birds about to provide food but they are extremely clever and very difficult to catch. Foxes are territorial and those already established in the wild do not welcome strangers into their midst, and urban foxes not only have to learn to catch their food but also to capture and hold a territory in which to hunt. Raiding young lambs and domestic poultry is often the only way that urban foxes can find food.

No doubt people are well intentioned but it is a misconception that it is kinder to release a fox into the wild rather than humanely destroying it in the first place.

Fox control

Although a number of foxes are killed on the roads, those that remain pose a severe threat to the wellbeing of the countryside and it is extremely important that their numbers are controlled. Under the Hunting Act 2004 it is no longer permitted to hunt them with packs of hounds. This method has been the only realistic option in many upland parts of Britain where shooting or snaring is impossible. The foot packs of Cumbria once provided a vital service to fell shepherds, particularly at lambing time.

Foxes are nocturnal animals and shooting is most often carried out at dusk or after dark either using a rifle fitted with thermal imaging or night sight or from a vehicle in conjunction with a high-powered spotlight. Lurchers are occasionally used to chase and catch foxes using a powerful light to locate them. Only one terrier can now by law be used underground to bolt a fox which has to be shot and then only under certain circumstances.

Snaring is subject to strict legislation regarding the type of snare, the way it is used and the fact that it must be checked at least once a day. Trapping is only permissible if large baited cage traps are used. It is illegal to gas or poison foxes.

Few people would wish to see them exterminated but the harm they are responsible for should never be underestimated.

RATS

There are two species of rats in the UK: the Brown and the Black. The latter is now very rare and confined to a few dockland areas which it originally occupied in its millions.

It is estimated that rats destroy 20% of the world's harvest and were it not for continuous warfare against them this could also well be the case in Britain.

They inhabit both urban and rural areas and one pair of rats can result in 800 offspring in 12 months.

Being mainly nocturnal, few people are aware of just how many there are and in what close proximity they live to humans. The rise in takeaway food outlets has benefited the rat enormously. They cause serious damage to wildlife by taking eggs, chicks and even adult birds. A huge amount of destruction is caused to crops in storage and to property, particularly in winter when rats vacate their outdoor living places such as banks and hedges to seek the comfort of living indoors. Wherever there is food provided for livestock, rats are likely to be

▼ Rats are a serious pest through carrying diseases and causing much damage to crops in storage

found in residence nearby. Gnawing is another considerable problem. Rodents have teeth that are continually growing and the only way this can be checked is by gnawing which causes damage to pipes, wood, plastic and many other objects.

They spread diseases and Weil's Disease (leptospirosis) is easily caught by humans through contact with rat urine.

While many townspeople welcome foxes to their gardens, few wish to share them with rats.

Almost any method can be legally used to kill rats.

It is extremely important their numbers are not allowed to reach an uncontrollable level. The use of guns, traps, gas, ferrets, dogs and poison are all legitimate. Poison (rodenticide) for rats can be bought over the counter but obviously great care has to be taken with its use. It is very important that the bait is kept topped up for several days until it no longer disappears, for rats can otherwise build up a resistance to the poison and three-quarters have now developed a genetic resistance. This is of serious concern as it makes continued control with existing treatments extremely problematic.

Where there is a heavy infestation, such as in field banks and buildings, one method used is to smoke them out and use terriers to dispose of them, which they do very quickly with one bite.

There are millions of rats in Britain, numbers increased by 25% in 2020 with the population reaching an estimated 150 million.

MICE

These are another extremely common pest both in towns and the countryside causing damage to foodstuffs mainly by contamination with their excreta and also damage to packaging and property by chewing. Control is usually by trapping or poisoning. Bank voles can be destructive to plants.

CATS AS PREDATORS

Estimates vary between there being eight to eleven million cats in Britain, a proportion of which are feral.

Cats, like foxes, are predators and they decimate wildlife. They are, by nature, ruthless, non-selective killers and often the death of their prey is a painful, protracted one. Cats play with their victims before killing them, sometimes not bothering to eat them afterwards.

It's estimated that 55 million birds in Britain every year are killed by cats.

Some cat owners who are totally opposed to hunting foxes with dogs prefer to turn a blind

House mice can also be very destructive in outbuildings

► Feral cats predate birds and small mammals

eye to the habits of their cats. They defend their choice of pet by saying the animal is only doing what is natural to it – but they wish it wouldn't. They are themselves participating in the destruction of wild animals and birds by keeping a cat and failing to recognise the harm to wildlife one can cause. Cats don't discriminate between common and endangered prey.

In 1997, between April and August, the Mammal Society conducted a survey where the owners of nearly one thousand cats recorded the species and numbers of items their cats brought home. It showed an alarming range of animals, birds, reptiles and amphibians, which, if extrapolated, means the total number of creatures caught by cats may amount to 300 million each year. Recorded species included chicks and birds up to the size of a partridge, rats, mice, shrews, voles, squirrels, slow worms, grass snakes, lizards, frogs (a particular favourite), toads and even bats. An average of 16.7 prey items were recorded for each cat during the five month period.

Wildlife is particularly vulnerable to predation by cats between March and August and if this could be reduced it would make a significant improvement to survival rates, possibly reducing deaths by 100 million during this critical time. Wearing collars with bells appears to be inefficient but a survey by the British Trust for Ornithology showed that the use of sonic collars, which emit a regular signal, significantly reduced the amount of predation on birds, showing a decrease of 65%. Most mammals are nocturnal and the number caught could be reduced by keeping cats indoors at night. The cat is the only domestic animal for which the owner has no legal responsibilities. However, legislation is being introduced for compulsory microchipping.

The farmyard cat has its use in controlling rats and mice and may adapt to living in the wild but house cats dumped in the countryside from towns often do not manage to survive for long.

Feral cats (those that have gone wild and have no apparent owner) can be legally controlled by shooting or cage trapping.

Cats are protected by welfare laws regarding cruelty and ill treatment and the domestic cat is also protected by the 'Property Act'. But cat owners should take into account their moral obligations regarding the preservation of wildlife.

GREY SQUIRRELS

Grey squirrels are a very familiar sight and the estimated UK population is 2.7 million and increasing. They are native to North America and were first introduced to Britain in 1876, released into the wild in Cheshire. Between 1902 and 1929 hundreds more were deliberately released across the country. By the 1950s it became apparent that they were devastating the population of native red squirrels and, despite an attempt to control numbers, grey squirrels continued to thrive and there are now only a few areas in England and Wales where Red squirrels can still be found. Grey squirrels are the equivalent of a tree climbing rat but, because they

▲ Grey squirrels carry a disease known as squirrel pox to which they are immune but is fatal to red squirrels. Legislation makes it illegal to release them and if they are caught they must be destroyed

are more attractive in appearance, are more likely to be tolerated. However, control is important because they cause extensive damage to trees by stripping the bark and eating fruit or nuts. The annual cost in England and Wales as a result of bark stripping is an estimated £37 million. Young broadleaved trees, in particular hornbeam, oak, beech and sweet chestnut are mostly attacked when they are between 10 and 40 years old.

Grey squirrels take eggs and chicks from nests and cause considerable damage by chewing. Control is by shooting, trapping or destroying their nests (dreys).

MINK
These are another unwelcome introduction from North America, first imported for fur farming in 1929. The industry boomed in the 1950s but is now banned in Britain. The first wild colony became established in Devon and was recorded in 1953. Since then, due to escapes and misguided releases, mink have spread the length and breadth of Britain and there are tens of thousands now living in the wild. They are ferocious killers which are having a devastating impact on our wildlife by threatening animals and birds near the waterways where they live.

Mink have played a major part in the decline of water voles which have now disappeared from more than 90% of their former sites.

Their population has decreased from eight million in the 1960s to fewer than one million now. Moorhens are another species to have particularly suffered mink attacks and domestic livestock including small animals, poultry and game birds are also victims. Mink are not easy to catch and gamekeepers, water managers, farmers and conservationists are continually trying to trap them by using humane cage traps set on floating rafts, which catch them alive and unharmed. In the last few years researchers believe that the mink population has begun to decrease, perhaps due to increasing numbers of otters resulting from successful conservation measures.

STOATS AND WEASELS
They are ferocious hunters native to Britain. There are no weasels in Ireland. Despite their small size, stoats and weasels easily kill birds or animals much bigger than themselves, thus posing a particular threat to all ground-nesting birds. A stoat is capable of killing a young hare or fully grown rabbit many times larger than itself, which it does by biting the back of the neck to paralyse its victim.

Control is by shooting or trapping, usually with spring traps set in natural or man-made tunnels. Legislation passed in 2020 meant that stoats can now only be lawfully trapped in specific circumstances under licence.

▶ In the Outer Hebrides mink numbers on Lewis and Harris have been greatly reduced by trapping. No young mink have been caught there since 2015

HEDGEHOGS

Although beneficial to gardeners, hedgehogs can cause considerable damage to ground nesting birds by eating eggs and chicks. Legitimate means of control are strictly limited.

RABBITS

Rabbits were probably introduced to Britain by the Normans and have multiplied ever since. For hundreds of years they were commercially bred in closely guarded warrens, at first for their fur and later for their meat. They were a valuable commodity and penalties for poaching were extremely harsh. In the 1800s some large country estates still had large areas set aside as 'warrens' where rabbits were farmed. In the mid 18th century substantial wild populations became established in Britain and they soon became a pest. They were killed by every method available providing an additional income for estates as well as controlling numbers to protect crops from their prodigious appetites.

MYXOMATOSIS

In the 1950s rabbits were causing serious damage to much-needed food crops and myxomatosis, a horrific disease, was deliberately introduced to Britain in an effort to control the ever increasing numbers. This very nearly wiped out the entire population of rabbits. However, a few survived and, despite continuing sporadic outbreaks of the disease and persistent culling, by the late 1990s there were millions of them throughout the countryside in the UK. They certainly lived up to their reputation for multiplying.

Does (female rabbits) give birth to litters of three to eight, mate again within a few days and have several litters each year.

A new disease called Rabbit Haemorrhagic Disease Virus (RHDV) was discovered in tame rabbits in 1992 and first recorded in the wild in 1994. This does not seem to cause the dreadful suffering, or spread as rapidly as did myxomatosis. It is not as obvious because rabbits die quickly, often underground. Rabbit numbers have decreased by 60% in the last 20 years which has been attributed to RHDV. Rabbits are great survivors though, and it would be very surprising if they were to eventually become extinct in the UK.

Rabbits are mostly nocturnal and live in underground burrows. In addition to crop damage, rabbits' excavations can result in injury to livestock and damage to machinery. However, they are an important link in the food chain for predators and some eco-systems and are counted as a 'keystone species'.

Rabbits may be killed by almost any method except poisoning.

Shooting at night using a spotlight from a vehicle combines pest control with a popular sport and can account for a lot of rabbits in a comparatively short time. Ferreting is another country pursuit. There is no close season but ferreting is not carried out during the spring and summer because it is impractical.

Rabbits in large numbers can cause serious damage to crops and young trees

HARES

Although regarded as game, Brown hares on arable land can become a pest and in England and Wales they are not afforded the protection of a close season. However they may not be offered for sale between 1 March and 31 July. Legislation in Scotland introduced a closed season for the killing or taking of brown hares between 1 February to 30 September. They can only be killed during this period under licence.

Generally brown hare numbers are decreasing although their population levels tend to go through a ten-year cycle. In a few areas of Britain their high numbers can cause serious damage to crops and young tree plantings, so reducing the population to an acceptable level becomes a necessity. This is most frequently done by organised shoots that mainly take place in February.

Mountain (white) hares are found principally in Scotland and too large a population can harm the habitat. A new ruling by the Scottish parliament has banned the mass culling of mountain hares in Scotland. A licence is now required to kill them in Scotland at any time.

DEER

The population of all six species of deer throughout Britain is increasing, and is now larger than at any time in the last 1,000 years. At present there are thought to be around two million deer in total. Measures need to be taken to ensure they do not cause excessive damage to gardens, crops and newly planted woodland or that they become too populous where their food source is limited, such as in the Scottish Highlands, where they

◀ At certain times of the year, deer damage trees by rubbing the bark with their antlers to remove the velvet on them

can face starvation. Muntjac, an alien species, are multiplying at alarming rates and ravaging the undergrowth in woodland.

Deer are responsible for hundreds of road traffic accidents each year. Many are injured or killed in collisions with vehicles and innumerable human injuries and several fatalities are incurred.

Controlling numbers is restricted to shooting within designated seasons using specified high powered rifles and types of ammunition.

MOLES

As every gardener knows, moles can be a serious pest with regards to lawns, but likewise, they are to horse owners and farmers. The only real solution is to destroy the moles which is mainly done by trapping. The traps are set underground, are very humane and kill the mole immediately. In certain circumstances, professional pest controllers are permitted to use poisoned worms under specific licence.

AVIAN

CROWS

Carrion and Hooded Crows, the latter only found in the north of the UK, are probably the most serious avian threat to wildlife. Although in the main solitary, they sometimes form groups and also gather with rooks. A pair or crows can

▲ Carrion Crow stealing the eggs of a Great Crested Grebe

devastate the wild bird population within their territory by methodically searching for nests and taking eggs and chicks. They also attack weakly young animals such as newborn lambs, often removing the eyes even before the animal has died. Crows can often be seen feeding on road kills or other carrion.

Control is by shooting and trapping using cage traps such as the Larsen or Multi-catchers.

MAGPIES

▲ Magpies are known to plunder birds' nests for eggs and young chicks

These attractive but lethal birds are adept at systematically searching out nests in springtime to steal the eggs or young chicks and, being agile, scramble in and out of hedgerows looking for those of songbirds. Few songbirds survive if they nest within the territory of a pair of magpies. Like crows they are either shot or cage trapped, Larsen traps being particularly successful.

The extermination of a pair of crows or magpies in early spring will save the lives of hundreds of other birds.

There are many superstitions associated with magpies. They were considered evil crows for not wearing full mourning dress for the death of Christ and acquired the reputation for stealing jewellery and other shiny objects. Although usually seen in pairs, they sometimes group together giving rise to the saying 'one for sorrow, two for joy, three for a girl, four for a boy, five for treasure, six for gold, seven for a secret never told'.

JAYS

Jays are more elusive and not as commonly seen as crows or magpies. Although they too will steal eggs or chicks from nests, jays are usually more tolerated. Their population is sometimes swelled in autumn by migrants from northern Europe when they can be seen searching for acorns, many of which they bury. When they fail to find them, the acorns they buried germinate and grow into trees, so jays indirectly play a big part in establishing new trees.

Jays are most often shot although it is possible to catch them in cage traps.

JACKDAWS

They are opportunists and groups will gather to steal food from cattle, pigs or game birds as well as surviving in an urban environment. They too have a taste for eggs and chicks but do not search for them in the way of the other corvids. Jackdaws

▲ Jackdaws are small members of the crow family which will steal birds' eggs

nest in hollow trees and house chimneys. They frequently visit gardens and bird tables.

Surprisingly jackdaws can make good pets and school children used to adopt a fledgling should they find one. Control is by shooting or cage trapping.

ROOKS

▲ Rooks dig in the soil with their beaks in their search for grain and grubs

Although often mistaken for crows, rooks are in fact completely different in nature to our other native corvids because they are gregarious birds. Communal rookeries built high in the trees where they nest are a common sight both in urban and rural areas and their raucous calls are a familiar sound. They have certain woods where they traditionally choose to roost and at dusk they gather in huge, noisy groups on neighbouring fields prior to settling in the trees for the night. Over time their droppings build up to such a degree that the undergrowth beneath is killed off.

Rooks feed on invertebrates but they will also steal food put out for livestock and cause severe damage to grassland and arable crops by digging up newly sown seeds. They take eggs and young chicks so, at different times of year, they are the enemies of farmers, gamekeepers and conservationists alike. Occasionally, they will also eat carrion. In urban areas, rooks scavenge and have a particular liking for bread.

Shooting and cage trapping are methods used to control numbers, the multi-catch type trap being the most successful.

Country lore associates rooks with both bad luck and good fortune. A large group arriving in an area is bad luck but well-established rookeries are deemed to be a sign of good fortune and should they desert, then a calamity is imminent.

RAVENS

The largest of our native crows, Ravens inhabit upland areas of the UK although they are extending their range. They are fully protected by law. However, they are strong birds and can cause extensive suffering to young lambs by pecking at different parts of their bodies and starting to eat them before they have died. Any livestock which is sick and inactive is liable to attack. In cases such as this, farmers who are suffering serious livestock losses are able to apply for a licence to cull ravens.

▲ Ravens are large members of the crow family and are known to attack sick sheep and lambs

WOOD PIGEONS

In summer there are an estimated 5.2 million pairs of wood pigeons in Britain and increasingly they are spreading into urban environments. The population is swelled in winter not only with the young birds but also migrants from north and east Europe.

Wood pigeons are becoming less shy and are now common in towns as well as the countryside and they decimate cabbage, sprouts and other brassica plants in gardens. Their phenomenal appetites mean they cause severe damage to agricultural crops. They move about in large flocks which feed on any seed left lying on top of the ground when crops are sown. Peas prove very attractive to them, when they are first sown, when they are coming through and when they are swelled in the pods. In summer pigeons attack cereals when the grain is ripening, and find it particularly easy to feed in places where the weather has flattened standing corn. In autumn they feed under trees on fallen acorns and beech masts. Fields of rape attract huge numbers in winter when there is a shortage of other food; they find the green leaves very palatable.

Protecting crops from wood pigeons is an ongoing battle and they are dealt with in two ways – by culling or deterring them. Visually, bags/flags or streamers, which move in the wind, may be used dotted across fields. Gas guns and rope 'bangers', that go off with loud bangs at regular intervals, are also widely used to keep pigeons off of crops. The alternative is shooting which is the only efficient method of disposing of them. Usually this is carried out from a camouflaged hide, where the shooter waits hidden out of sight. Decoys are set out in a natural pattern in front of the hide to attract them and a large number can be accounted for in this way.

GEESE

They arrive in their thousands in late autumn to many coastal regions of Britain where they spend the winter. Here they feed on grassland and arable crops, causing a lot of damage through the amount they eat and from paddling up the wet ground with their large feet. Deterrents are used as for pigeons. Goose shooting is popular sport. This usually takes place around the coast at dusk when they are flying back to their coastal roosting grounds from wherever they have been feeding inland during the day. Greylags, Canadas and Pink-footed geese may legitimately be shot between 1st September and 31st January but cannot be offered for sale. Some greylag geese migrate to Britain in winter but the majority, along with Canada geese, are semi tame and resident on inland waters the year round. Their numbers are increasing and the livelihoods of farmers and crofters, particularly on many of the Scottish islands, are badly affected by the damage they cause to crops and grasslands.

Thousands of Pink-footed geese from Iceland descend on Norfolk every year and some farmers leave the tops of sugar beet, which remain on the ground after harvesting, for them to feed on. They prefer these to anything else and by doing so it prevents them moving onto their cereal crops.

Other species of geese have full protection throughout the year.

GULLS

Whilst gulls are usually associated with the coast there are many that live and nest on land.

They are more at home on farmland, moorland and reservoirs than beside the sea. Large flocks of Common and Black Headed gulls can be seen following a tractor ploughing a field and gobbling up the exposed worms as soon as the soil is turned over.

Gulls gather in their hundreds to scavenge for food on landfill sites. In the nesting season they steal eggs and chicks resulting in significant losses to species, many of which are endangered, that nest on moorland, coastal cliffs and the sea shore.

Greater Black Backed gulls, Lesser Black Backed gulls and Herring gulls are large birds and are recognised pests, but they require a special licence to cull them. Since the 1940s

Herring gulls and Lesser Black Backed have increasingly moved into towns and taken to nesting on the roofs of buildings. They are fearless and can be aggressive when defending their eggs or chicks as well as snatching food from people's hands.

STARLINGS

They are gregarious and the sight of huge flocks, known as **'murmurations'**, circling over their winter roosting sites is spectacular! The population is augmented in winter with migrants to Britain from the Continent. Huge flocks of starlings gather where food is freely available such as outdoor pig units where they are unwelcome guests because of the real risk of spreading disease.

INSECTS AND INVERTEBRATES

INSECTS

Those insects that specifically damage crops such as aphids, carrot flies, flea beetle and some insects in their larva and grub stages, have to be prevented or eradicated with the use of chemicals or natural substances applied as sprays, granules or a coating on the seed. Biological control, especially with the use of microscopic worm-like creatures known as nematodes, is the only method available to organic farmers. Beneficial nematodes as they are known are specific to the host pest which can then be selectively targeted.

FLIES

Horse flies, Blow flies and other smaller biting flies plague livestock during the summer months. Sheep are particularly at risk because the blowfly family – greenbottles, blackbottles and bluebottles – all lay their eggs on patches of dirty wool. These hatch into maggots which then burrow deep into the flesh of the sheep to feed, a slow and horrific death if not prevented by way of trimming, dipping or spraying with chemicals and shearing in early summer.

COMMON WASPS

Wasps are widespread and more prolific in some years than others. They nest on or in buildings or holes in the ground. If a wasp nest is accidentally disturbed they can be extremely angry and vicious. In the height of summer a nest may be home to up to 8,000 wasps! People with an allergy to wasps' stings can suffer from anaphylactic shock if stung which is life threatening.

Wasps are useful in some ways. They prey on other insect pests including small caterpillars, they pollinate plants and produce powerful antibiotics in their venom.

Common wasps building a nest inside bird box

TICKS

Ticks are potentially the most harmful insect of all and commonly live on sheep, deer and many other animals and birds. Ticks are mostly found on heather and rough grassland habitats, such as heaths and moors, but can be present almost anywhere. The minute spider-like insect attaches itself by its jaws to its victim and proceeds to suck out blood. Within a few days it becomes bloated and about the size of a blackcurrant before dropping off. If ticks are present in large numbers they can cause great distress to their host. Sheep are dipped to prevent this happening but it is impossible to treat wild birds and animals. Ticks get on humans and pets and need to be removed as soon as possible. A special tool is available but if they are pulled off it is extremely important to ensure that the head is not left buried in the skin. Ticks can carry a disease known as Lyme Disease which can be very debilitating to humans should they become infected.

SLUGS

An infestation of slugs in the ground can cause serious damage to freshly sown seeds and young plants. Chemical control includes ferric phosphate (suitable for organic systems). Metaldehyde slug pellets were banned for outdoor use from spring 2022. Biological control is most often used in horticulture which involves the use of specific nematodes.

FULLY PROTECTED BY LAW

HAWKS, HARRIERS, FALCONS, BUZZARDS

All birds of prey are fully protected by law and most species are increasing in numbers. They are all predators of other birds, animals or insects. Some species also feed on carrion.

Badger numbers are increasing; they like to dig deep holes and are linked to outbreaks of bovine TB in cattle

Sparrowhawks probably cause most harm to the general bird population. They are ruthless hunters as many a birdtable-owner has discovered and they take birds up to the size of a pigeon. On upland ground, the Hen-harrier can be a nuisance, taking any moorland birds as large as grouse and also the eggs of ground-nesting birds. Peregrines have a special appetite for racing pigeons. Although they can, in some instances, be quite destructive, birds of prey are not regarded as pest species.

OWLS

Most species of owl hunt at night and live primarily on small mammals such as voles, although tawny owls in particular sometimes take small birds, given the opportunity. Owls are not generally regarded as a pest, other than in very rare situations; in fact the ghost-like barn owl is a particularly welcome sight in the countryside and around farms, as it primarily catches rodents.

BADGERS

They now enjoy full protection and their numbers have increased accordingly with estimates of there now being up to 500,000, a tenfold increase since 1980. In the region of 50,000 are killed on the roads each year but this is not enough to prevent their numbers from multiplying.

Badgers live in social groups and are becoming established in areas where they have not previously been regularly seen. They have become widespread across the country and their excavations in fields, hedgerows and woodlands can be very damaging. They dig up the nests of bees and wasps and eat eggs or fledglings if they find them.

Badgers are the only animal in the UK which kills hedgehogs.

There is a strong suspicion that badgers are carriers of bovine tuberculosis, which can be transmitted via cows' milk to humans. This disease is highly damaging to the dairy and beef industry because cattle have to be regularly tested and any that prove TB positive are slaughtered. The rest of the herd is not permitted to be moved off the farm so cannot be sent for slaughter or moved elsewhere for grazing, which can result in welfare issues. Regular testing continues until the all-clear is given, which may take many months. Tests showed that in one area, 25% of badgers carried bovine tuberculosis.

Where there is a raised infection rate of TB amongst cattle that can be linked to a high local population of badgers, culling under licence has been permitted.

In September 2020 a government ruling extended the legal shooting of badgers in some counties in an attempt to control the spread of bovine tuberculosis. In some areas, the vaccination of badgers has been trialled but this means they have to be trapped first, causing stress and disruption to family groups.

Although it is possible to vaccinate cattle against TB, under EU rules this was not allowed for technical reasons. However, trials are underway to perfect a new vaccine. Whether there will be changes now that we have left the EU remains to be seen.

DOGS

So many dog owners are ignorant as to the harm their pets can cause in the countryside, particularly in the spring and summer when birds are nesting, mammals are breeding and sheep are lambing. Sheep worrying is a major problem for sheep farmers. Dogs can very quickly transform from being a pet to being a pest.

Both the owner and the person in charge of a dog that worries livestock (farm animals and poultry including game birds if they are inside a pen) on agricultural land are by law responsible for its actions and are committing an offence.

It is the natural instinct of many breeds of dog to hunt and chase and, if they can, to grab hold. Even those dogs kept on extendable leads are capable of frightening a bird off its nest so badly that it will not return and as a result its offspring perish.

A dog can legally be shot if it is caught in the act but usually the devastating outcome of an attack is only discovered afterwards.

GLOSSARY

DEFRA Department for Environment, Food, and Rural Affairs Issue licences for pest control.

NATURAL ENGLAND Sponsored by DEFRA Issue licences for pest control.

MAMMAL Animal that suckles its young.

AVIAN Birds in general.

CORVID Member of the crow family.

RODENT Gnawing animal such as a rat, a mouse or a squirrel.

FERAL Domestic animal that is living wild.

CLOSE SEASON Period when it is illegal to kill certain species of animals and birds.

LAMPING Involves the use of a powerful light shone after dark, most often from a vehicle, to detect a rabbit or a fox which are legitimate quarry.

NIGHT VISION Increasingly heat detecting thermal imaging is being used for pest control at night. Goggles and rifle-mounted scopes are available.

HIGH SEAT A seat, either free-standing or fixed to a tree, approximately 7-10 feet (2-3m) above ground level which allows for wide vision and a safe shot. High seats are used by deer stalkers and pest controllers.

TUNNEL Natural or man-made tunnel in which a spring trap is set.

SNARE A noose made of wire used to trap certain animals. Only free-running snares, wire loops that relax when the animal stops pulling, can be set lawfully.

CAGE/BOX TRAP There are many designs used to catch animals or birds without harming them.

SPRING TRAP There are numerous designs made to catch and kill specific species of animals. When tripped, they do so by springing shut and crushing the body. There is strict legislation regarding the type of trap, where and how it must be set (ie it must be covered) and specifying the species for which it may be used.

LARSEN Cage trap designed to catch one or two corvids at a time by using a live decoy.

LETTERBOX/MULTI Large cage trap designed to catch a number of corvids at one time using bait and/or live decoys.

POISON Toxic substance. Can only be used under licence for pests other than rodents.

GAS Chemical substance used underground which when exposed to air releases a poisonous gas.

BIOLOGICAL CONTROL Pest control using natural substances thus dispensing with the need to use harmful chemicals.

Rhododendron ponticum is a very invasive species which was a favourite of Victorian landscapers

ALIEN & INVASIVE SPECIES

When is an animal, insect or plant an alien species and when is it an invasive species? When it begins to prove to be a nuisance or a risk to our native wildlife, probably. Some 'foreign' alien species find a niche in our ecology without causing any harm, others turn into a plague, in which case they are categorised as being invasive.

Invasive species have cost the UK economy at least £5bn in the last 50 years.

There are now estimated to be between two and three thousand invasive species, in one form or another, in Britain a number of which are having a devastating impact on our native plants and wildlife. Others rapidly overpower and displace our indigenous flora and fauna which have taken hundreds, if not thousands of years, to evolve naturally and establish a place in our ecology. There is no place for these alien invaders in this complex mosaic but they force their way in, upsetting the natural balance in the process. It is estimated that invasive species in the UK now cost the economy £1.8 billion a year.

There are strict controls regarding bringing plants and animals into this country and for a very good reason. Global warming is hastening the success of invaders by enabling some of them to survive and encouraging them to move northwards and spread across the country.

In the case of invasive animals, controlling numbers means culling such as grey squirrels, mink and brown rats which invaded Britain early in the 18th century. The question though is how long is it before an alien species, already well established in our countryside and part of the landscape, is considered to have become indigenous? Theoretically, horse chestnut trees aren't native to Britain, they were introduced in the late 16th century from Turkey.

Rhododendrons introduced from Europe and Asia in the late 18th century have now become highly invasive. Brown hares were introduced by the Romans for sport. Rabbits were brought to our shores by the Normans for food. Red-legged (French) partridge were introduced from France in 1770. These have all become an accepted part of our countryside but none of them are indigenous to be precise.

There are three reasons why plants and animals have been deliberately introduced – for sport, for food or aesthetic value. The Victorians saw many plant species and a few animals on their travels which they thought would enhance their great estates and the surrounding countryside and brought them back as ornamentals. In the long term some have been welcome but many others have proved disastrous.

Various methods are being tried in an attempt to retain control of alien plant species. One biologically friendly way with insect pests is to introduce another parasitic insect which will prey on them; this is a treatment increasingly used. The Brown Marmorated Stink bug, native to Asia, was first identified in the wild in 2020. It is a serious agricultural pest. One proposal has been to introduce a parasitic wasp which lays its eggs in those of the Stink Bug to stop its spread but there is always a risk attached to introducing yet another non-native species.

Foreign invaders reach our shores in several ways. Many arrive on imported plants, some hitch a lift on the plastic littering our seas and a few make use of freak weather. Global travel also aids their distribution when travellers, either deliberately or inadvertently, bring something back with them from foreign lands. Other invaders were originally captive but have become established through being accidentally or deliberately released. Climate change is also allowing many more alien species to survive and spread.

Various species not covered in the *chapter Pest Species page 190* which are causing concern to conservationists trying to safeguard our indigenous wildlife are listed below.

ANIMALS

▲ Muntjac deer are very secretive by nature and cause serious damage to plants and shrubs growing in our native woodlands

MUNTJAC
One particular concern is the damage they are causing to our native bluebells which are relatively rare in the rest of the world.

COYPU
were originally introduced in 1929 to be farmed for their fur in East Anglia and some southern counties where they spread rapidly and caused great damage. A campaign in the 1980s successfully managed to eradicate them.

GLIS GLIS
also known as Edible Dormice, were introduced from Western Europe in 1902 by Baron Rothschild to his estate in Hertfordshire. Squirrel-like in appearance and habits, they are nocturnal and hibernate for six months through winter and early spring. They invade houses in their search for somewhere warm and dry to hibernate. Lofts and cupboards are favourite places. They chew through electrical cables. The

main population is in the Chilterns within a 25 miles (40km) radius of Tring and culling is carried out to limit their expansion.

RING-NECKED PARAKEETS

first became established in the wild in the 1970s and are gradually spreading across the country. Originating from Africa and southern Asia they were not expected to survive in our harsher climate – but they did. They live mainly in London suburbs and the south east but satellite populations have been reported in Birmingham, Glasgow, Oxford and Manchester. There are over 30,000 Ring-necked parakeets living wild in the UK and they gather at dusk to roost in large numbers. Parakeets damage crops and because they nest in holes in trees there is concern they are displacing our native woodpeckers, kestrels, owls and bats. They feed on seeds and nuts so are depriving some of our native bird and mammal species of winter food.

EGYPTIAN GEESE

Introduced to Britain in the 17th century from sub Saharan Africa, along with **Canada Geese** from North America at the same time, they are now at pest level in some places.

EUROPEAN BEE WOLVES

are solitary wasps that prey on honey bees. They are colonising Britain as a result of global warming. First recorded on the Isle of Wight in the 1980s, they have now reached Yorkshire. Honey bees are already under threat and a predator such as the bee wolf depletes colonies even further.

◄ Ring-necked parakeets first became established in the wild in 1970 and in some areas are posing a threat to our native wildlife

ASIAN HORNET

is an unwanted invader heading for the UK from France where it escaped in 2004. Since 2016 there have been 17 confirmed sightings in England and nine nests have been destroyed. Asian Hornets are large predators which feed on pollinating insects and pose a serious threat to our already at-risk bees. There can be up to 6,000 Asian Hornets in one colony. It is of grave concern that they may become established in Britain. When a sighting is confirmed, experts from the National Bee Unit (NBU) and the Animal and Plant Health Agency (APHA) work quickly to find and destroy any active nests in the area.

▲ Egyptian Geese have been resident in Britain since the 17th century but recently there has been a great increase in numbers

▲ Canada Geese originated in North America but are now so numerous they have become a pest

ORIENTAL CHESTNUT GALL WASP

is an invasive insect pest of sweet chestnut trees first found in England in 2015. The wasp causes galls on the buds and leaves of sweet chestnuts, disfiguring and weakening the trees, rendering them vulnerable to other pests and diseases. The release of a parasitic species of wasp which attacks gall wasps has been approved as a method of biological control. This wasp is already naturally present in England but only in small numbers.

HORSE CHESTNUT LEAF MINERS

bore into the leaves of their host tree making them shrivel and turn brown before dropping prematurely. Bearing candelabra-like pink and white flowers in spring, these iconic trees are a common sight in parks, gardens, streets, on village greens and along roadsides but rarely in woodland. In autumn, their fruits have kept generations of boys supplied with conkers. Horse chestnut trees are native to the Balkan Peninsula and were first introduced in the UK in the 16th century. This specific leaf miner is the larval stage of a micro-moth which arrived in the UK from Europe in 2002. The pupae overwinter in leaf litter and emerge as adult moths in spring to lay their eggs on the leaves. Year after year, the infestation of horse chestnut leaf miners gradually weaken the tree, making it vulnerable to disease. Horse chestnut trees are also susceptible to a recently introduced bacterium which attacks and kills the bark of infected trees. In severe cases the damaged bark peels away from the tree exposing the wood beneath which can result in the tree dying.

GREAT SPRUCE BARK BEETLE

was accidentally introduced into the UK in 1982 and is now present in western England, Wales and southern Scotland. It damages spruce trees by tunnelling into the bark. A predatory beetle which in turn preys on bark beetles is helping to control them. Spruce trees are very important to the UK economy.

HARLEQUIN LADYBIRDS

became established in the UK in 2004 and by 2017 had become widespread across Britain. Originating from Japan, Harlequin ladybirds were introduced around the world as a biological control for

Leaf miner beetles have been present since 2002 and attack horse chestnut trees turning their leaves prematurely brown

aphids. The unforeseen problem is that they also feed on other ladybird larva. They look very similar to our own native ladybirds.

OAK PROCESSIONARY MOTH

lives almost exclusively on oak trees. It arrived on imported trees in 2005 and was first identified in south-west London from where it has spread. It is subject to a government-led programme of survey and control to minimise its population, spread and impact. The caterpillars can soon defoliate the tree. As their name suggests, hundreds of them follow one another in a line. The caterpillars are deemed a health hazard to both humans and animals. They are covered with thousands of hairs which they fire off in defence. These hairs are toxic and can cause rashes and respiratory problems in humans.

DIAMONDBACK MOTH

is resistant to most insecticides so treatment is near impossible. It is migratory and in some years there are large influxes from Europe. Its caterpillars feed on brassicas (kale, sprouts, cabbage etc) and in 2016 it was recorded that they caused a 15-20% reduction in crop yields.

BROWN MARMORATED STINK BUG

is the newest unwanted invader to be identified in Britain. It poses a serious threat to fruit and vegetable crops and attempts to invade people's homes in winter. The stink bug originates from the Far East and emits a foul smell when threatened.

INVERTEBRATES

Molluscs that live in fresh water arrive in the UK from as far away as the Caribbean adhered to discarded plastic in the sea, stuck to ships' hulls or in the water ballast. They are spread on fishing equipment, by birds and flooding.

ZEBRA MUSSELS

first reached the UK from the Caspian Sea 200 years ago. They breed and spread rapidly and in large numbers block water treatment works. They also displace native species and have decimated our populations of native freshwater mussels.

QUAGGA MUSSELS

are equally destructive. Originating in the Ukraine they were first recorded in the UK in the River Thames near Heathrow Airport in 2014 and have recently been identified in the East Midlands.

ASIAN CLAMS

were first discovered in Britain in 2004. They out-compete our native freshwater mollusc species and also pose a threat to spawning grounds. Asian clams have become established in the Norfolk Broads and are spreading rapidly. Researchers recently found that 95% of the shells collected from the river Thames were from Zebra Mussels and Asian Clams.

PACIFIC OYSTERS

These were initially introduced to the UK from Japan to supplement our shellfish industry. Escapees have now become established in the wild and with the rise in sea temperatures due to global warming, numbers around the southern coasts are increasing at a worrying rate, posing a serious threat to our native oysters.

KILLER AND DEMON SHRIMPS

originate from the Caspian Sea and are substantially larger than our native freshwater shrimps. The Killer shrimp was first recorded in 2010 and the Demon in 2012. The former is known to prey on a wide range of native aquatic animals, fish eggs and even young fish. It often kills its prey but leaves it uneaten. The spread of these species will have a profound impact on aquatic ecosystems across the country.

AMERICAN SIGNAL CRAYFISH

were introduced from North America in 1975 by the British government for export to what was then a lucrative Scandinavian market. With hindsight it was a disastrous decision. They carry a disease which can prove fatal to our native crayfish but doesn't affect the American ones.

Our native white-clawed crayfish are nearing extinction due to the dominance of the larger signal crayfish.

They burrow into river and canal banks causing erosion and collapse. Efforts are being made to trap the American signal crayfish. Their huge claws litter many riverbanks throughout the UK.

CHINESE MITTEN CRABS

are the only crab in the UK to live in fresh water. They hatch in marine habitats and lower estuaries and move upstream as they develop into adults. They damage fishing gear and burrow into the muddy sides of streams and rivers. Chinese mitten crabs originate from eastern Asia and were first identified in the Thames Estuary in 1935. They are documented as being present at several sites throughout England and Wales including the Thames, Tyne, Humber, Ouse, Tamar and Dee.

SPANISH SLUGS

were first seen in Britain in 1954 and are susceptible to hard winters so their expansion has been erratic. However, under favourable conditions they can rapidly reproduce and the recent warmer winters are conducive to this. Spanish slugs cross breed with some of our native slugs. They are 4-6 inches (10-15cms) in length and usually a shade of brown. They eat excrement, carrion, garden plants and crops not normally susceptible to slug attack.

NEW ZEALAND AND AUSTRALIAN FLATWORMS

have been established in Britain for more than 40 years and are causing concern as they feed exclusively on our native earthworms which play such a vital role in maintaining soil quality. The Australian flatworm is most frequent in south-west England while the New Zealand flatworm is mainly found in Scotland, Northern Ireland and the north of England.

NORTH AMERICAN BULLFROGS

are not invertebrates but are voracious non-native predators originally introduced to Britain through the pet trade. Since the 1990s they have successfully bred in the wild in the UK, probably through owners irresponsibly disposing of their tadpoles in local ponds.

American bullfrogs are huge (up to 8 inches [20cm] in length) and eat amphibians and other small animals. Since the mid 1990s they have bred around Britain and populations are removed through an eradication programme.

TERRESTRIAL PLANTS

Seeds or particles of alien or invasive plants attach themselves to animals, clothing and equipment or get dispersed in floodwater. Controlling them is exceedingly difficult and eradicating them nigh impossible. Most die back in winter, disappearing out of sight only to reappear in spring with a flourish.

Some of the most problematic plants are the result of being imported as ornamentals, mostly by the Victorians to grace their landscaped gardens and parklands, which spread into the wild.

It is an offence to ignore the legislation regarding the following species growing in the wild in Britain.

JAPANESE OR ASIAN KNOTWEED

was introduced to Britain as an ornamental by the Victorians. It has become a scourge across Britain and because it spreads rapidly underground, it is extremely difficult to eradicate. This large-leafed, bamboo-like plant forms clumps, which can grow more than 3 inches (10cm) in a day and reach a height of 10 feet (3 metres). It bears creamy-white flower tassels in late summer. It is incredibly vigorous and new shoots can force their way through structures, concrete and tarmac.

Japanese Knotweed is one of the most destructive weeds in Britain, reproducing from tiny fragments of rhizome in the soil and appearing in a variety of habitats including along waterways.

Himalayan Balsam was introduced by Victorian plant hunters and has now become widespread along our rivers, streams and canals

Homeowners can be prosecuted if they fail to control Japanese knotweed on their property and heavy fines or even imprisonment can be imposed if plant material or contaminated soil is transferred into the wild. There are specialist contractors who deal with its elimination and disposal.

HIMALAYAN BALSAM

was brought to this country from the Himalayas by Victorian plant hunters in 1839 and was first grown at Kew Gardens. A deceptively attractive pink-flowered plant that can grow taller than a man, Himalayan balsam is an aggressive coloniser which has become widespread across England, Wales and Northern Ireland but not commonly in Scotland. Along our rivers, streams and canals its sheer volume displaces our native plants.

GIANT HOGWEED

is native to the Caucasus Mountains and was introduced as an ornamental to Britain in the early 19th century. It is truly a giant growing up to 16 feet (5 metres) tall and is now widely distributed across the UK, not only beside waterways but also in many other settings. The sap of giant hogweed is toxic and touching or even brushing against the plant releases a chemical which reacts with sunlight and can leave human victims with horrendous burns and blisters to the skin.

AMERICAN SKUNK CABBAGE

an import from North Western America, grows in wet areas and has spread across Britain most noticeably in the south and west. It was banned from sale here in 2016. American skunk cabbages grow up to 5 feet (1.5 metres) high and have bright yellow unpleasant-smelling flowers. The creeping roots spread rapidly causing extensive damage in the vicinity.

◀Skunk Cabbage is an alien species imported from north-west America and first identified as growing in the wild in 1947

SPANISH BLUEBELLS

were introduced by the Victorians from the Iberian Peninsula as a garden plant. They are similar in appearance to our native bluebell but slightly larger and paler. Pure native bluebells are on the decrease as the Spanish variety is spreading and readily crosses with them, resulting in hybrids.

RHODODENDRON PONTICUM

grow into dense thickets and make a colourful sight in spring. A favourite of Victorian landscapers, there are now few areas of Britain not affected by this hugely invasive plant. It is estimated that they now form about 3.3 per cent of Britain's total woodland. The large leaves are toxic and exclude the light, making it impossible for any other plants to grow beneath which diminishes the presence of wildlife. Rhododendrons are also carriers of diseases which are fatal to some of our native trees.

PIRRI PIRRI

is a plant species native to New Zealand and Australia first recorded in the UK in 1901. A dwarf shrubby plant, widespread in some dry coastal areas, it forms dense mats which crowd out native plants where it grows. During late summer its prickly burrs hook themselves to people's footwear, clothing, dogs, other animals and even birds, thus spreading them. It is proving very difficult to prevent this happening.

AQUATIC PLANTS

Some invasive freshwater aquatic plants are overrunning our waterways having been originally purchased as ornamental pond plants. These invasive plants grow prolifically and, after clearing out their ponds, owners have dumped them along waterways. The plants listed below grow at alarming rates in still or slow-moving waters and form large dense impenetrable mats on the surface which starve the water of oxygen. These aquatic plants are also causing very serious problems by blocking drainage networks and water-handling systems.

FLOATING PENNYWORT

is a native of North and South America and parts of Africa. It can grow up to 8 inches (20cm) a day! It first appeared in the south of England and is spreading northwards having now reached Wales and the Midlands.

NEW ZEALAND PYGMYWEED

is another similar noxious plant. Also known as Australian swamp stonecrop it was introduced in 1911 and was first recorded as growing in the wild in 1956. It is widespread across England and Wales. Small fragments, which can be accidentally carried on clothing, fishing equipment, boats or by animals, easily take root.

WATER FERN

is a floating fern with a red tinge to the leaves which can cover 100% of the water surface as a dense carpet up to a foot (30cm) thick. Originally native only to North and Central America, in the last 50 years water fern has spread rapidly across England, Wales and is extending northwards.

PARROT'S FEATHER

is behaving in a similar manner to water fern.

WATER PRIMROSE

was first identified as growing wild in 2009. Since then it has established itself in watercourses, ditches, ponds and lakes predominately in the south of England. The Environment Agency are co-ordinating attempts to eradicate it before it spreads further afield.

DISEASES

More and more imported diseases are being identified in the wild. Largely introduced to the UK through importations of timber, young trees and plants from abroad, the diseases come in bacterial, fungal, virus and insect forms. At least 20 are attacking our native trees, with six having reached epidemic levels.

New, stricter measures regarding the importation of trees and plants were introduced in April 2020 in an attempt to further safeguard the UK from the continuing range of threats not only to our native plants but also to the forestry and horticulture industries.

Dutch elm disease was the first to cause devastation and since then there have been numerous other diseases which have had serious repercussions.

◀ Invasive water weeds out-compete our native freshwater aquatic plants, deoxygenate the water, prevent amphibians and invertebrates from reaching the surface and even disrupt movement of animals on the water surface itself.

The saddest thing to see is some of our magnificent veteran trees, including possibly the iconic ancient Caledonian pines in Scotland, succumbing to diseases that have been introduced. There are few trees species that are not at risk.

Of particular concern is the bacterial disease of plants known as Xylella fastidiosa which originates in the Americas and has already been identified in several European countries. It is transmitted by insects to host plants and an outbreak in the UK could affect several species of widely growing native broadleaf trees in the UK, such as oak, elm and plane, as well as a wide range of other commercially grown plants. Infected plants can die and there is no known cure for the disease.

DUTCH ELM DISEASE

was accidentally imported into the UK from Canada in the late 1960s.

Dutch elm disease has killed over 60 million of our elm trees.

It is a fungus which is spread from tree to tree by elm bark beetles which bore through the bark. The movement of elm saplings, and products such as logs with the bark attached, mulching bark and crates made from elm, caused the disease to spread rapidly across the UK. Once a common sight, magnificent elm trees were often found growing in field hedgerows. Sadly a mature elm is now a very rare sight.

ASH DIEBACK

was first confirmed in the UK in 2012 and is predicted it will kill 95% of our ash trees in time. It is carried by another type of fungus which is spread by the spores being blown in the wind. Ash die back originated on saplings imported from Europe. Thousands of infected ash trees are being cut down to try to stem the spread of the disease.

PHYTOPHTHORA RAMORUM DISEASE

is now widespread and can affect 120 different species. It is a contagious fungus which is easily spread and is likely to have initially come from rhododendrons. It was first discovered on larch trees in 2009 and has led to thousands of hectares being felled around the UK. It can also affect sweet chestnut. Fortunately our native British oaks do not seem to be very susceptible.

PROBLEMATIC NATIVE PLANTS

Not all plants causing concern are alien to the UK; some of our native plants are not without their problems.

Under the Weed Control Act 1959, landowners are required to take action to prevent the spreading of Common ragwort, Spear thistle, Creeping thistle and two varieties of dock.

BRACKEN

is a very common noxious plant. With its underground root system it rapidly takes over areas and conservationists fight an ongoing battle to prevent it from engulfing other plant species. It is now known to be capable of causing cancer in its green state and harbours ticks when it has died off. There is an estimated two and a half million acres of bracken growing wild across Britain. For centuries it was cut and

used for animal bedding. Eradicating bracken is exceedingly difficult although it can be cut and composted. An environment-friendly use is to make it into bio-fuel; it is claimed to burn hotter than oak and to last longer. The bracken is harvested, dried, chopped and compressed together to create 'Brackettes'.

COMMON RAGWORT

with its yellow flowers, is toxic livestock in a dried state and causes death if it is consumed in hay.

RUSHES

Three native species of rush, possibly due to climate change, have spread rapidly in recent years and are invading uplands and swamping other vegetation. They are ruining pastures for grazing and rot nesting sites for some of our less common birds. Rushes spread through rhizomes and also through seeds which can lay dormant in the soil and germinate decades later.

Advice on invasive species is available from the following statutory nature conservation organisations:

Environment Agency

Natural England

Natural Resources Wales

Scottish Natural Heritage

Department for Agriculture, Environment and Rural Affairs (Northern Ireland)

Red Deer Stags are the largest mammal found in Britain

COUNTRY SPORTS & QUARRY

Thousands of years ago, the human race survived because they were 'hunter gatherers' living off of what they could find and catch. That urge is still strong in some people and they gain great satisfaction from enjoying what they have caught or shot as a Sunday roast or a mid-week stew. Everything that is shot or hunted has lived part, if not all, of its life completely wild in its natural state. Fieldsports were once perceived as being the prerogative of the wealthy but this is no longer the case and they have become accessible to a broad spectrum of people. The control of pests that threaten people's livelihoods or health is another aspect of country sports which has evolved.

Working dogs feature in every fieldsport with the exception of angling. Packs of fox and fell hounds hunted the fox; harriers and beagles the hare; shaggy otterhounds originally hunted otters; stag hounds red deer and bloodhounds hunted human scent. Fast-running greyhounds and lurchers were kept to course hares. In the shooting field, spaniels of several different breeds were used to flush game out of the cover, and retrievers were kept to find and retrieve shot game. On the grouse moors the mission of pointers and setters was to locate grouse tucked down in the heather and flush them on command to a waiting gun.

Countrysports offer the opportunity for people from all walks of life and who share the same interest to mix socially. Employment and income generated by country sports plays an important element in the rural economy. Numerous pubs, hotels and restaurants rely on out-of-season trade passed on to them indirectly through fieldsports.

Many landowners, farmers and anglers with sporting interests pursue conservation measures at their own expense which benefits a lot of other wildlife.

Improvements are frequently made to rivers, lakes, ponds, hedgerows, woodlands, field margins, moors and marsh land. A wide range of plants are grown in strips or odd corners to create game cover for pheasants and partridges. These provide both food and shelter through the winter not only for them but a host of other birds and animals as well.

One thing that all country sports have in common is that the outcome is never predictable, which is probably much of the attraction. When the sportsman ventured forth in the morning they would never know what the day held in store. Of course, there is always a minority in every sport who have no principles and disrespect rules and etiquette. It is these who make newspaper headlines and attract bad publicity for the vast majority who take pleasure from their countrysports which include tradition, respect and discipline.

HUNTING

Hunting wild animals with packs of hounds was a very popular centuries-old tradition that was brought to an end when the Hunting Act 2004 came into effect making the hunting of wild mammals with dogs illegal in England and Wales (the Scottish Parliament had already legislated against it in 2002). Hunting deer, hare or the fox with a pack of hounds, whether on horseback or foot, was banned, as was coursing the hare with greyhounds or hunting them with packs of harriers or beagles.

NATURAL PEST-CONTROL

Originally hunting was a sport exclusive to the landed gentry, as much as being a mark of social standing as anything. Increasingly over the last century people from all walks of life were able to participate. They enjoyed hunting for the pleasure they gained from watching dogs using their sharply honed sense of smell, a thousand times more sensitive than a human, to puzzle out the scent trail and maybe eventually come to terms with their quarry. But the result was never guaranteed because the fox and hare are skilled in the art of survival and use cunning tricks to avoid being caught.

Even though the environment in which the sport took place had greatly changed over time, hunting and coursing remained steeped in tradition and it was something that those who participated generally took great pride. There were unwritten guides to etiquette, dress and the manner in which things were done. The vast majority of participants held great respect for their quarry. It may seem difficult to believe but it was the sport they relished not the killing.

When hunting foxes was banned in 2005 it was replaced with trail hunting which proved a popular alternative for riders

▲ Packs of Bloodhounds are still permitted to hunt as they follow human scent

When the ban came into force in February 2005 there were more than 180 packs of foxhounds in Britain and all of them are still operational because they switched to hunting an artificial scent trail laid prior to the meet. The 19 harrier packs and 60 beagle packs have also adopted the same strategy to allow them to continue hunting. It's permissible for beagle packs to hunt rabbits although they do not generally provide good sport. Following an artificial scent line is known as **drag hunting**, something which packs of bloodhounds have always done but in their case it is human scent they follow. That packs of hounds are permitted to exist is a contentious issue and pressure is coming from several fronts to completely ban any form of hunting.

Mounted foxhound packs continue to hold their annual Point-to-Point race meetings. Some foxhound packs were hunted on foot and evolved over time to control the wily foxes living in mountainous areas and in particular the Cumbrian Fells. These packs provided an invaluable service to farmers in remote, mountainous areas, particularly at lambing time, when there were no alternative methods available of dealing with foxes that were killing lambs. Small hardy breeds of sheep live their whole lives out on the hillsides and are extremely vulnerable to fox predation.

Following on from what had previously been a voluntary otter-hunting ban, self-imposed by hunters when it became evident that numbers had suffered a dramatic decline, otters were given complete legal protection in 1978. Otterhound packs instead turned their attention to American mink, which were colonising our waterways in increasing numbers and decimating wildlife wherever they had taken up residence. Even though mink are ferocious killers and are an alien species which have no

HOUND TRAILING

Hound trailing with fell hounds remains a popular summertime sport in Cumbria. A scent trail is laid by dragging a sack soaked in a mixture of paraffin and aniseed oil for ten miles, cross country over the Fells and the natural obstacles such as becks and stone walls. Fell hounds for trailing have been bred for their speed and stamina. They line up, are all released at the same time and are avidly watched through binoculars by their owners. Once they are back in view they are encouraged to finish quicker with shouts, whistle blowing, and food bowl rattling. The first hound home is the winner.

place in our countryside, they are wild mammals and hunting them with a pack of hounds was also banned under the Hunting Act 2004.

The otterhound as a breed is now on the verge of becoming extinct.

COURSING

While packs of hounds survived the ban by changing the way they conducted their sport, it brought coursing to an abrupt end in Britain. It is the oldest of all fieldsports and dates back to 4,000BC. Nothing could be found to replace the official coursing meetings that would test the skills of the greyhound in the clever ways a hare did as it avoided being caught. Coursing meetings were held under strict rules designed to give the hare every opportunity to escape unharmed from two greyhounds, which hunt only by sight. Local and regional competitions were held during the autumn and winter culminating with the Waterloo Cup in mid-February which always took place at Great Altcar in Lancashire. The final one, held in 2005 was the 158th.

Illegal coursing however, which affords no such respect for the quarry or the countryside, continues. It is carried out by unscrupulous individuals, whose only interest is that of winning bets.

FERRETING

Domesticated ferrets were being used 2,000 years ago. Ferrets are descended from the wild polecat that can still be found in a few parts of Britain.

Ferrets are used primarily for hunting rabbits but are sometimes used to flush out rats. In recent years they have also become popular as domestic pets. By nature they are natural predators and can be quite vicious at times but when properly handled become very tame and even affectionate.

Ferreting is usually carried out in late autumn or winter when the vegetation has died back and there is less likelihood of very young rabbits being about. Working ferrets are transported in small specially designed boxes or ventilated bags. One or two are put into the holes of a rabbit warren where they work their way around underground.

Rabbits thump their hind legs on the ground when alarmed, a sound that ferreters listen for. Usually the rabbits try to escape by bolting out of the holes although occasionally a ferret will catch or corner one underground.

A collar with a small transmitter is put on the ferret; this emits a signal that is picked up by a locator enabling the ferreter to pinpoint its position. A good spade or graft, plus a billhook or saw are also often needed, as the ferret may be several feet down beneath stones and roots. A sharp pocket knife is another vital part of equipment as caught rabbits are usually paunched (intestines removed) soon after they are killed. To make carrying them easier, the thin skin above the hock on one hind leg is pierced and the other hind foot pushed through the hole. This enables several rabbits to be carried on a stick passed between the hind legs of each one.

Female ferret is a jill, the male a hob and their offspring kits

There are several ways of catching and killing a rabbit after it has been bolted by ferrets. Most commonly, nets are placed over every hole in the warren in which the rabbits become entangled when they try to escape. Grabbed by the back legs, the rabbits are quickly pulled out and killed by hand. Sometimes they are allowed to bolt and are shot as they run away.

Rabbits are classified as a pest species and as such, the hunting ban does not apply and dogs can be used to catch them.

Lurchers are often used to catch rabbits. Occasionally a long net is placed at a distance from the rabbit holes to prevent rabbits from escaping completely. A good dog will detect and **mark** (indicate) any holes that have rabbits in them while ignoring ones that are empty. This avoids putting ferrets in unoccupied holes.

Ferreting is a sport enjoyed by all ages but usually only involves two or three people. Like all field sports, the outcome is unpredictable and the bag for the day may be pleasing or disappointing. If a ferret decides to stay underground it may take a lot of time and effort to find it and dig it out, but the good days make up for the bad.

Within the heirarchy of falconry the Goshawk was flown by landed gentry and the clergy in the Middle Ages

FALCONRY

Falconry is described as the sport of taking live wild prey, such as game birds or rabbits, in their natural state and habitat by means of trained hawks. Approximately 25,000 people in the UK keep raptors (birds of prey), of which about 4,000 fly them at live prey. Strict legislation is in place to ensure that, in the UK, all the birds used are bred in captivity. They are required to have an identification ring on their leg or be microchipped and most species need to be registered with the authorities. None are taken from the wild.

The incredible eyesight, speed and agility of birds of prey make them impressive to watch, and falconry is a hobby that is becoming increasingly popular. A great deal of time needs to be spent with the bird to create a bond strong enough that it will voluntarily return to its handler when allowed to fly free.

A falconry licence needs to be obtained from Natural England. For those who wish to find out more it is possible to attend organised courses. Visit www.britishfalconersclub.co.uk for further details.

Falconry was being practised as long ago as 2,000 BC and at one time was the premier hunting sport in every European court. It was thought to have been introduced to England by French nobles in about 860 AD. In the Middle Ages anyone who took a wild falcon or interfered with one at the nest was condemned to death. A scale of values evolved whereby Gyr falcons could only be flown by royalty, peregrines were for noblemen and goshawks and sparrow-hawks for landed gentry and the clergy. In present times falconry is still a very popular sport in the Middle East.

Falcons, hawks and eagles have incredible eyesight and it is natural for them to chase a moving object. When one is flying free, in order to get it to return to its handler, a feather lure on a string, incorporating a small piece of meat, is swung round in the air to attract the bird's attention. As soon as it grabs hold of the lure, the bird lands on the ground and either rests or eats the meat. This allows the handler time to approach it, gently catch hold of it and place a hood over its head and eyes to quieten it. They will also fly straight onto the handler's leather-gloved fist when tempted with a piece of meat, usually a dead chick. They are held or tethered with a cord attached to leather straps on their legs known as '**jesses**'.

Falcons and hawks are flown at some airfields to scare away other birds because of the danger they may cause to aircraft on landing and take-off. They are also sometimes used in towns and cities to frighten away pigeons and seagulls where they have become a pest on buildings.

A falcon or hawk in flight is able to spot its prey from several hundred feet away. Peregrine falcons catch their prey in the air by plummeting downwards in a '**stoop**' to catch and kill their victim with their talons.

> *Peregrines are the fastest creatures on earth with the speed record being held by one recorded at 217mph in a stoop.*

Many peregrine falcons were destroyed during the last war as they killed carrier pigeons which were used to carry messages, particularly from ditched pilots whose planes had been shot down. It was common practice that pilots took a homing pigeon with them when in action. In an emergency this could be released and return to base carrying information of the whereabouts of the stricken pilot. Conversely, some peregrines along the south coast were spared to intercept pigeons possibly carrying messages from German Secret agents operating in Britain.

Numbers of peregrine falcons are now increasing with many having taken to nesting on large buildings and towers in towns and cities.

It is common practice to fit a small transmitter onto a bird that is flown so that it can be located should it disappear from sight.

▲ A falconer with a Golden Eagle

Those who use falcons, eagles or hawks for hunting usually work them in conjunction with a dog to mark or flush the quarry. Pointers and setters are a popular choice on open ground and spaniels where there is more cover.

FALCONRY GLOSSARY

AUSTRINGER A person who flies a short-winged hawk

BROAD-WING A bird that has large broad wings and soars in the sky. It is normally used to catch mammalian prey

LONG-WING A member of the falcon family which have long, narrow, pointed wings and primarily catch avian prey in flight

SHORT-WING A member of the hawk family which has short wings and a longer tail making it agile enough to hunt in woodland

CAST Launch the bird off of the glove

HOOD A covering made of leather put over the bird's head so it cannot see. It is used to quieten the bird when it is being handled or transported

ANKLETS Leather strips fitted around a bird's lower leg like a collar

JESSES Thin leather or cord straps attached to the anklets which allows the falconer to restrain the bird when it has settled on his gloved hand or is being handled

MANTLE The posture a birds of prey adopts with wings outspread shielding the prey it has caught.

RAPTOR Bird of prey

FISHING

Fishing is one of the most popular outdoor pastimes in Britain with an estimated 3.3 million people enjoying the sport which increased by a third of a million during the Covid pandemic in 2020/21 when people weren't permitted to socialise in great numbers. Many disabled people have found it is an outdoor recreation that is readily accessible to them and there are several organisations that represent disabled anglers. One such is the Wheelyboat Trust, a UK charity with over 200 specially-designed boats across the country.

Every angler over 13 is legally obliged to be in possession of a rod fishing licence, issued annually by the Environment Agency, which must be carried at all times. Since April 2017 children from the age 13 to 16 are entitled to a free UK fishing licence. There is a moral obligation for those who fish not to leave any discarded litter, fishing line or hooks behind. Animals and birds in particular can get tangled in the line or swallow hooks, often resulting in death.

Poaching can be a problem. In Scotland water bailiffs, appointed either by the Scottish Government or District Salmon Fishery Boards, have certain statutory powers of entry, search, seizure and arrest. Similarly, in England and Wales, water bailiffs are appointed by the Environment Agency. It is an offence to obstruct them.

COARSE OR GAME FISH?

There are 38 species of freshwater fish native to Great Britain and at least 12 introduced species. They are divided into two categories – coarse fish and game fish (the salmonidae family).

Otters, mink, herons and cormorants all prey on freshwater fish. Cormorants can be culled under licence and mink by legal methods. The invasive American Signal Crayfish feed on juvenile fish and eggs.

Ownership of land adjacent to a river extends to the centre of the water course and with it goes the right to fish by legal methods. It is the owner's responsibility to maintain and keep clear of obstacles the river bed and banks of the water course and to clear any debris.

Many lakes are owned by local fishing clubs and reservoirs are often owned by water companies; both are kept regularly stocked with various species of fish. Most canals in England and Wales are maintained by the Canal and River Trust.

Owners and tenants are obliged to control weed growth in their rivers and on the banks which would otherwise become congested and overgrown. That on the banks can be cut either by hand, by using a strimmer, or by tractor-operated machinery. Where they are grazed by livestock, trimming isn't usually necessary. Weed growth under water can be removed by using a rake and a bucket, an old fashioned scythe, a chain scythe, worked by two people one either side of the river, or by boat: some specially built ones incorporate a mechanised blade.

There are two kinds of river plants, rooted ones and floating mats of vegetation and algae. The latter need to be completely removed from the water. Non-native aquatic plant species are causing significant management problems in lakes and rivers, reducing oxygen levels, causing blockages that smell as they rot and release toxins into the water.

The banks may host three alien plants: Japanese Knotweed which grows to 10ft high (3 metres), Himalayan Balsam which can reach 8ft (2.5 metres) and Giant Hogweed 15ft (5 metres).

Disposal of a large mass of vegetation can be a problem and there are restrictions on the methods used if poisonous or alien plants are involved. Dry material can usually be burned but the wet needs either to be spread out thinly on the banks or piled in small heaps where it can be left to rot down. Where vegetation is cut in moving water, a boom can be put in place downstream to collect the debris, which can then be dragged out and either disposed of on the land or taken to a landfill site. River fisheries usually co-ordinate their weed-cutting activities so that debris floating downriver doesn't interfere with other anglers.

There are legislative controls and moral obligations for freshwater fisheries regarding the introduction of fish, possibility of night fishing and application of a close season.

Game fish (which does not include rainbow trout) are present in most of the rivers throughout Britain. They spawn in late autumn and early winter but Wales, England and Scotland do not share a common close season. Generally speaking game fishing takes place between early spring and the autumn. The principal Scottish rivers have their own individual open seasons for salmon.

Much conservation work is being done to control invasive species and make UK rivers more accessible for fish. Some species spawn in specific areas and require shallow gravel beds in which to lay their eggs. Attention is being paid to restoring or creating these to provide ideal conditions. Many rivers once blocked by weirs and dams have installed fish and eel passes, allowing them to travel much further upstream.

COARSE FISHING

Coarse fishing in lakes and rivers for our native freshwater fish, excluding trout, sea trout and salmon, is a very popular hobby. Although people in most other countries eat coarse fish, the British don't. In England and Wales the close season for coarse fish is from 16th March until 16th June, during the spawning period, but this doesn't apply to Scotland or still waters (ponds and lakes) and, more recently, to canals which can be fished throughout the year.

It is illegal to leave a rod unattended while fishing.

Various baits are used to lure coarse fish onto hooks. They are weighted to keep them submerged but the use of lead for weights is banned due to the risk of wildfowl and swans being poisoned through consuming them. A coloured float can be attached to the line which floats on the surface indicating the position of the hook.

Fishing for trout

The Environment Agency is closely involved with intensive stocking of still waters, the effects of predators on fish (eg cormorants), the theft of fish, discarded angling litter such as line and hooks, and the impact of releasing live bait and foreign exotic species.

Much of the coarse fishing on ponds, lakes, reservoirs and stretches of rivers is run by angling clubs who have either purchased, leased or negotiated rights to fish the water. The clubs' objectives are to promote and protect the angling interests of their members and to improve facilities for their benefit. Clubs maintain a good stock of fish, care for the ground they own or lease, and organise regular clean-up days to keep their areas attractive.

Fishing competitions are commonplace. Designated areas are marked out with numbered pegs every few yards and competitors draw their numbers at the beginning of the day. Prizes, sometimes substantial amounts of money, are awarded for the highest aggregate weight of the day's catch and for the heaviest individual fish.

There are grave concerns as to the detrimental effect fish farming is having on wild salmon

GAME FISHING: THE SALMONIDAE FAMILY (TROUT AND SALMON)

Brown trout are a highly prized catch. Some of the best fishing for wild trout is in England, the most sought-after probably the pristine chalkstreams of Hampshire and limestone rivers of Derbyshire. However, many rivers, once famed exclusively for their wild trout, are now being stocked with captive bred fish. These elite areas can be very expensive to fish but cheap or occasionally free game fishing can be found in less favoured upland areas.

The purists fish only with an imitation fly attached to the hook for wild brown trout. The end of May or early June is known as 'Duffers' Fortnight', when millions of mayflies hatch providing a bonanza of food for hungry trout and making them easier to tempt with an imitation fly on a hook. Later in the summer it is no easy task to attract a uninterested fish to take a fly and it can prove very frustrating. Some knowledge of which species of insect trout might be taking or where they are likely to be skulking can help.

Trout fishing is a very challenging sport. Some mature brown trout living in large Scottish lochs have turned to eating other fish (ferox) and may weigh up to 25lb (12kg) and grow to a length of nearly 3ft (90cm). But the majority of brown trout weigh under a pound.

Rainbow trout Some aspects of game fishing have succumbed to commercialism and rainbow trout, introduced from North America in the early 20th century, are bred in large numbers and released into lakes and reservoirs to supplement affordable game fishing opportunities. Sometimes artificial bait such as a spinner is used to attract their attention. Unlike brown trout, they do not breed in the wild (except in three rivers) so waters are regularly restocked. Stillwater rainbows can be caught all year and are the choice of commercial fisheries as they grow one and a half times quicker than brown trout and are easier to rear.

Rainbows are raised in hatcheries from breeding stock (known as cock and hen fish). These are kept to produce eggs that are hatched in special indoor tanks during the winter. The tiny fish (**fry**) are transferred to outdoor tanks (**stews**) in early summer where they are fed high-protein rations. They are taken out either for restocking or for the table usually when they weigh 1-1.5lb (500-700g). Fish hatcheries raise brown trout in the same way.

Brown and rainbow trout live in rivers or lakes. Riverkeepers or water bailiffs can be employed to care for the fish and their environment. Marginal weed growth is trimmed and predators such as mink and rats are controlled, also some predatory species of fish which would eat eggs or fry. Electro fishing is often carried out in spring and autumn on trout streams to take out unwanted or predator species such as pike.

Eels used to be trapped and sold for human consumption and many rivers have built-in

The river Ouse in Sussex is said to produce the largest average sea trout of any river in England or Wales

eel traps. However, due to the decline in eel numbers since 2010, they have now become a protected species.

Sea trout are a strain of brown trout that have adopted a lifecycle similar to that of a salmon by spending part of their lives at sea.

Known as **sewin** in Wales and **peal** in the West Country, some fishmongers confusingly call them Salmon Trout although they are not salmon at all. Small sea trout weighing a pound or less are called **finnock**, **herling** or **schoolies**. Sea trout are fished for at night and are unpredictable in their habits.

Grayling are an unusual member of the salmonidae family frequently found alongside trout but only in rivers. Unlike salmon and trout, which spawn in the autumn, grayling breed in the spring and share a close season (March 16th to June 16th) with coarse fish, meaning that they can be legally caught throughout the winter. The grayling is a sensitive fish and can be a good indicator to the health of a river.

Salmon Fly-fishing for salmon on select Scottish rivers was once the ultimate dream for many freshwater anglers but there has been an alarming 70% decline in the number of salmon in the last 25 years.

A mature salmon leaps a waterfall on its return to spawning grounds upstream

Atlantic Salmon prefer rivers whose head waters are relatively shallow and stony, where they can lay their eggs in gravel beds (**redds**), although they will spawn throughout the river including the lower reaches. The continuing decline in salmon numbers in the rivers throughout Britain is causing much concern, and scientists are working hard to pinpoint the problems so something can be done.

Fewer than 5% of salmon are now returning to their rivers when 50 years ago it was 20%.

Our native wild salmon are slow growing and have a complicated and hazardous lifecycle which involves spending part of their lives at sea before returning to breed in the upper reaches of the same rivers where they were hatched. Monitoring the period salmon spend at sea is extremely difficult. Fresh-run salmon and sea trout in a river can be easily identified by an infestation of sea lice that they acquire only at sea. These parasites can't live for long in fresh water so their presence indicates that the salmon caught has recently arrived from the sea rather than is returning to it. There is a close salmon season in England, Wales and Scotland, generally from mid-October to mid-March although there are regional variations.

Spawning occurs in November and December and the eggs, which are fertilised by the males after being laid on redds by the hen fish, hatch out in early spring and are called **alevins**. As they begin to develop, they are known as **fry**. After two to four years in the river as **parr** they depart in late spring or autumn, at which stage they are known as **smolts**. After spending a minimum of one year at sea they return to the river as **grilse**. After spawning, both the male and female fish are exhausted and are named **kelts**. Few have enough strength to survive the journey from the upper reaches of the rivers back to the sea and even fewer ever return to spawn again.

The commercial farming of Atlantic salmon takes place in sea lochs and around the west coast of Scotland.

Farmed salmon was the biggest UK food export in 2019 with 94,000 tonnes sold abroad, making a significant contribution to the Scottish economy and creating employment in many remote areas.

There are more than 200 fish farms and it is an expanding industry but they pose a serious threat to the wellbeing of our native wild salmon stocks.

Farmed salmon are fed on processed feed rations, the protein content of which is often fish-based, sourced from fish waste products. The salmon are closely confined in pens in coastal waters and sea lochs off Scotland's west coast, often on the migratory routes taken by wild salmon.

Farmed salmon are the same species as our indigenous salmon but a completely different strain. Numerous complications are encountered with rearing them. There is serious concern over the risk to wild salmon in the form of disease that come from salmon farms: water pollution, parasites, in particular sea lice; and escapees.

An unnaturally heavy burden of sea lice being passed on to wild salmon has a debilitating effect. Escaped fish interbreed with our native

There is a 'catch and release' policy in place to protect stocks of wild salmon

wild salmon, the progeny of which don't possess the natural instincts needed to follow their unique lifecycle and to return to rivers to spawn. Their young are not able to survive and the next generation is lost forever.

Salmon fishing contributes a valuable source of revenue to large estates as well as much needed jobs in rural communities. In recent years river habitat needed for successful breeding, controlling predators and in some cases releasing young fish bred from wild stock into tributaries of the main rivers, achieved optimistic results. The practice of netting salmon in river mouths and coastal areas, which was considered to be a serious threat to already reduced salmon stocks, has been limited through buy-out initiatives, although the threat from illegal netting remains. Conservation measures to help salmon reach their spawning grounds include installing fish passes so they can bypass the barriers and their migratory instinct is so strong that they readily use these. But even these measures have proved not enough to halt the worrying decline. A general salmon catch and release policy, with a few exceptions, was made mandatory in 2015 although it had already been adopted in many places.

Over 90% of salmon now caught are returned to the river in an effort to help conserve this iconic species.

It would take at least five years before any improvements through conservation measures became apparent. The decline in numbers may have been slowed down but it has not been halted.

It appears that climate change is affecting wild salmon. River levels rapidly rising or periods of drought seriously restrict the natural movement of fish. Researchers are surprised to find that more fish are being lost in rivers than at sea.

The decline of wild salmon stocks in UK rivers has had the knock-on effect of damaging local economy and employment. It affects ghillies, estate incomes and hospitality.

It is very much hoped that the combination of conservation and biosecurity measures, together with the voluntary co-operation of anglers reducing the number of fish they take, can ensure a future for wild salmon in the UK.

FISHING / ANGLING GLOSSARY

COARSE FISH All fish such as carp, perch, chub and pike found in fresh water rivers, canals, ponds and lakes that are not game fish. They are seldom eaten and generally returned to the water once caught

GAME FISH The trout and salmon family which include grayling and char. They are highly regarded for their sporting qualities and are also very good to eat

COCK A male fish

HEN A female fish

RUN Passage of salmon or sea trout up a river

SPAWN Breed. The female fish lays eggs that are then fertilised immediately by the male

REDDS The gravel beds where fish lay their eggs

FRY A freshly hatched fish developed enough to feed itself

GHILLIE Person employed to assist and advise salmon fishermen

BEAT A designated stretch of river

TACKLE Any or all of the equipment used by an angler to fish

ROD A person who fishes or an item of equipment he uses

FLOAT Device used to keep the bait at a certain depth and to indicate a bite

FLY An artificial lure incorporating a hook, usually made from fur, feather or man-made material and is designed to resemble an insect

SPINNER/LURE Artificial bait that wobbles, jerks or rotates to attract fish.

BARBLESS HOOK A type of hook which is not barbed and causes little physical damage to the fish when it is removed

BAIT Edible item attractive to fish such as bread or maggots

LIVE BAIT The use of live fish to catch predatory species such as pike. Now illegal

GROUND BAIT Food thrown into the water to attract fish

DISGORGER Small tool to aid the removal of a hook

PRIEST Small, heavy object used to kill a fish so called because it administers the fish's last rites

GAFF Hooked tool (now illegal) used to land a fish

LANDING NET Hand held net used to assist with landing a fish

KEEP NET Large net used to hold caught fish until weighed, released, etc

COMMERCIAL FISHERY Water (usually lakes) open to the general public

AQUACULTURE Fish farming

SHOOTING

Shooting is not only a sport but includes pest control for rabbits, foxes and pigeons, and deer control using a rifle. For those who prefer to be out in the worst of the weather, often sharing only the company of their dog, the choice will be wildfowling.

Others find their pleasure in firing at targets on ranges with a rifle or testing their skill with a shotgun shooting at clay pigeons.

There are over a million people in Britain who shoot with either a shotgun or a rifle. A valid certificate, issued by the police, is a legal requirement for both. Stringent regulations are in place regarding the safe storage of guns and ammunition.

SHOTGUN

Of all the fieldsports, shooting has probably changed the most in the last few decades although it was unaffected by the Hunting Act. The invention of modern shotguns and cartridges in the middle of the 1800s, which dispensed with the laborious task of preparing the gun for each shot fired, created a surge of interest in shooting. From then on a vast amount of money was spent by wealthy landowners on improving their estates and employing gamekeepers to rear and protect an ever-increasing number of pheasants and partridges. This huge investment in shooting resulted in a landscape that had been originally fashioned for agriculture and hunting being redesigned to suit shooting, which is why the layout of many big estates look the way they do today.

After the Second World War it took several years for shooting to become re-established for there was little spare grain to feed to game birds and most estates had been neglected because gamekeepers and farmworkers had been away fighting for king and country. Very few landowners were any longer in a position to bear the cost of running a shoot purely for invited guests. The answer was to form a **syndicate**, usually of eight or nine people, who would share the annual costs in return for an agreed number of days shooting each season.

This system proved popular and many shoot managers were able to expand their ground by leasing shooting from neighbouring farmers. The demand for shooting has steadily increased ever since and shoots began to let shooting by the day instead of the season.

Shoots actively manage 1,236,000 acres (500,000 ha) of woodland and 247,000 acres (100,000 ha) of smaller copses. Shooting may be organised by the owner on their privately owned land. Otherwise possibly by a tenant farmer on the ground he rents or, as commonly happens, the shooting rights are let off separately meaning land may be farmed or owned by one person and shot over by someone else.

Today, UK shoots play a part in conservation by maintaining 62,000 acres (25,000 ha) of cover crops which provide important sources of food and shelter for wild farmland birds, as well as game, particularly during the winter.

Driven shooting is the most formal type of shooting and involves a team of beaters, usually no fewer than 10 who are employed to walk across fields and moors or through woodland to drive gamebirds towards a team of guns, normally numbering 8 to 10, who are waiting at numbered positions. Before the day begins, the guns will have drawn their numbers to decide where they stand and by rotation they move to a different numbered peg for every drive. Normally between five and eight drives are done in a day – three to five in the morning and two or three in the afternoon. **Pickers–up** with dogs are also employed. They stand well back behind the line of guns to find and collect shot birds and any that may have been wounded. Shot game is tied by the head into **braces** (pairs) and hung on rails to be transported back to a **game larder** where it is cool and fly proof.

Although driven shoot days are formal they are also very social occasions with a lot of banter amongst the guns and the beaters. The guns, like the gamekeeper, are expected to be smartly dressed, often in tweeds. Sometimes when a large **bag** is anticipated, two guns may be used by each person shooting and a **loader** is employed to quickly load the gun that has been fired and pass it back. These are always people experienced in handling firearms, often other keepers, and they too will usually be wearing tweeds.

▶ Shooting at moving clay targets is a popular sport

However, there is no such protocol expected from people behind the scenes. **Beaters** and **pickers-up** can wear any type of clothing they like. Sturdy footwear is a must and when beating in woodland, thorn-proof leggings are needed protection against brambles. Each beater is also expected to equip themselves with a stick to stir game birds out of the cover and to make a tapping noise to encourage them to run forward. Beaters on the edges of partridge or grouse drives are known as **'flankers'** and usually carry a flag which they flap and wave to encourage the birds to fly in the required direction. On moors and in thick woodland, beating can be a strenuous job but it is one that both fit pre-teens and even some octogenarians seem able to cope with. Beating is good exercise but poorly paid. For the young it is a handy source of pocket money, for other keepers and working people it is an opportunity to go onto different shoots and to socialise. It offers pensioners an interesting lifeline that keeps them active and supplements their pensions. Mostly people go beating because they enjoy it, not for the money they receive.

At the end of the day guns will be given at least one **brace** of birds each. Surplus game is collected by, or taken to, game dealers some of whom process it and sell direct to the public.

The British do not eat a lot of game so most ends up being exported to the Continent. Oven-ready game bought directly from farmers' markets, butchers or game dealers is not overly expensive. Game meat is slowly becoming more popular and is now available in some larger supermarkets. Game will have spent most, if not all of its life, living free in the wild. It is full of flavour and contrary to popular belief will not have been hung until it smells.

The British Game Alliance is the official marketing board for the UK game industry, a not-for-profit organisation working to promote the value of all feathered game to the public whilst exploring new marketing ideas at home and overseas.

Full-time gamekeepers of which there are some 3,000 in Britain, are usually employed on

Wild Red Grouse test the skill of waiting guns

formal driven shoots and there may be several keepers on very large estates. Nearly as many are employed part-time on smaller shoots. Their main jobs are to legally control pests and predators, care for the game birds and prepare for, and organise, shoot days.

On lowland shoots it is common practice to grow several small areas of game cover for pheasants and partridges. Maize is a popular choice. Kale is also sometimes grown and occasionally left for a second year so that it goes to seed and becomes even more attractive. There are also many other crops such as artichokes, buckwheat, mustard, quinoa and sorghum as well as mixes of seed-bearing plants including sunflowers and phacelia. Strips of mixed game cover add greatly to the biodiversity of the countryside attracting many other species besides game birds.

Rough shooting Here the guns themselves do the work of the beaters by **flushing** game, usually with the help of dogs, and then waiting for the birds to attain a reasonable height and distance before shooting at them. Only a small number, if any, partridges or pheasants are released on rough shoots which are organised on a 'do-it-yourself' basis, sharing the chores of

Large sporting estates have tweed woven to a pattern exclusive to them

pest control if carried out, feeding, ride cutting, etc. At the bottom end of the scale are those who have access to a bit of ground and just like to have a potter round, maybe on their own, with a gun to see what they can get. They are quite happy with the odd rabbit, pheasant or duck without having had to do any of the work caring for them.

Field trials A spin-off from shooting are field trial competitions where specific breeds of gun dogs are tested for their ability under natural conditions in the shooting field.

QUARRY SPECIES AND THEIR MANAGEMENT

Wild pheasants and partridges Wild pheasants and partridges can thrive with good management. It is very important that estates preserve their wild strains because artificially reared birds do not breed and survive in the wild with as much success. Management is concentrated on predator and pest control and the provision of good habitat. Game cover crops not only provide winter food and protection but also attract insects which are vital for chick survival during the first few weeks.

High overheads (wages, rates, vehicle running costs etc) mean that it is rarely deemed

LEAD SHOT

There is environmental concern over the use of lead shot and plastic cases and wads in shotgun cartridges. The latter are not biodegradable and if not picked up after a shoot, litter the countryside. Lead shot has already been banned from use over wetland areas. Moves are underway to do away completely with the use of lead shot and single use plastic cartridge cases and wads. Alternatives available include steel, bismuth, tungsten-based and copper coated shot and paper cases and wads.

economically viable to employ a gamekeeper solely to produce wild birds. To ensure sufficient shooting, the answer on some estates is to supplement the number of wild birds by purchasing cock pheasant **poults** (young birds) for release. The policy is normally to shoot only cocks throughout the season.

Pheasants are found right across Britain apart from on the highest ground. There a number of strains many of which have been interbred and it is not unusual to see pure white or black pheasants in addition to the more normal colourations.

Pheasants are artificially reared and released each year for shooting. In preference to keeping laying stock and hatching the eggs, some estates now purchase chicks when they are a day old and many buy in young poults when they are seven to eight weeks old from specialist game farms.

A pheasant is fully grown when it is 18 to 20 weeks old. The pheasant shooting season opens on 1st October but serious shooting does not normally take place until much later in the month or the beginning of November.

The majority of pheasants for shooting are reared outside in temporary huts and pens in as natural conditions as is possible.

Pheasant poults are usually taken off the rearing field or arrive from the game farm at around eight weeks old when they are released into substantial pens sited in woodland. By this age they are hardy and fully feathered; in fact they are already beginning to moult their juvenile feathers which are replaced with adult plumage. Sometimes a small numbered metal or plastic wing tag is inserted into the thin skin of one wing for identification purposes.

Release pens are designed to be an intermediate step between the protected environment of the rearing unit and exposure to complete freedom in the wild. The large, open-topped pens, at least 6ft (2 metres) high, are constructed with wire netting and are usually in woodland enclosing a variety of natural vegetation, shrubs for shelter, even trees along with some open areas. Within the safety of these, pheasant poults gradually become acclimatised to their new surroundings, learn to go to roost at night, in low bushes to start with, and to recognise danger.

The pens are often protected by electric fencing from large animal predators and there are other avian deterrents against such as tawny owls and sparrowhawks. Inserted at intervals into the

A male (left) and female pheasant

release pen wire netting are small 're-entry' grids, narrow enough to exclude foxes while allowing access back into the pen for any young pheasants which have escaped. Short tunnels are built inside the pen over the grids to prevent those inside finding a way out.

Inside the pens, and outside later on, the birds are provided with fresh drinking water and food which is either put in food **hoppers** from which they help themselves or scattered by hand on tracks cut through the vegetation. For the first few weeks they continue to be fed on nutritious pelleted food but as they grow larger, wheat, sometimes mixed with kibbled maize, is introduced. They also find insects and invertebrates as well as feeding on plants such as stinging nettles. When they are not busy searching for food or resting, young pheasants delight in dust bathing when the soil is dry enough.

There is always the risk that a fox may manage to dig or climb into the pen. This nearly always results in carnage as foxes kill beyond hunger. Any young pheasants not killed outright will be seriously stressed. This is the main reason why fox control is so important to game rearers.

Stoats, mink, rats, feral cats, badgers, and birds of prey are all pheasant predators. While deaths are not likely to be on the same scale as from fox attacks, these predators will keep returning once they have found an easy source of food. The keeper, apart from setting traps and snares for those he can legitimately destroy, rigs up deterrents for those he can't.

After a few weeks in the release pen, most of the poults discover they can fly out and will have become familiar with their immediate surroundings. Young pheasants are by nature wanderers and straying too far from the release site is another problem the keeper has to contend with. He always hopes they will return for their evening feed. Eventually, well before the start of the shooting season, the pheasants are given their complete freedom. The release pen is opened up and the keeper begins to scatter grain, normally wheat and maize, in the outlying woods and strips of game cover to spread his birds out over the shoot while hopefully keeping them in areas where he wishes them to be. He may resort to using a dog to chase them away from shoot boundaries or roads etc.

Some keepers feed daily by hand but most put the grain in hoppers, placed at frequent intervals around the shoot. These hoppers may be plastic barrels or metal drums fitted with a slit or a coil from which the pheasants can peck out the grain. Another popular method is to use a quad bike fitted with a 'spinner' on the back which scatters food over the ground. The main control a keeper has over his birds' whereabouts is by feeding but when natural food is plentiful in hedgerows, game covers and cornfields then his birds become independent and show little inclination to feed on grain. Reared pheasants that remain when the season ends have a reasonable chance of surviving the spring and summer if they have not succumbed to predation.

French/red legged partridges have become extremely popular on driven shoots. They are not very successful breeding in the wild so are artificially reared, many hatched from eggs imported from France or Denmark.

Partridges are birds of open farmland and they also do well on marginal ground such as the edge of moorland, thus utilising ground on shoots to the maximum. They add variety to the day's shooting and as the partridge season begins a month earlier than that for pheasants, it also extends the shooting season.

French/Red Legged partridges are mostly reared on grass using a similar system to that for rearing pheasants, but they are easier to manage providing they remain healthy. The chicks may be kept indoors for the first two or three weeks before being transferred outside into rearing units.

Partridges are kept on the rearing field for longer than pheasants, often until they are ten weeks old. This is partly because they are released onto arable land and it is advisable to wait until the cereal harvest is well underway so they do not become lost in standing crops. Partridges sleep on the ground so there's also a real threat of them being cut up by machinery at night as combining and cultivations often continue until well after dark. They are also at risk from the same predators as pheasants.

Because French/Red Legged partridges are gregarious by nature, except in the breeding season, a different method of release is usually employed to that for pheasants. Small temporary pens covered with a net are erected, well apart, in game cover or corners of fields where they are not likely to be disturbed. Approximately 25 to 50 birds are put in each pen where they remain for only a few days before gradually being released a few at a time. Those that have been let out tend to stay in the vicinity of the pen where food and water are provided. Feeding further afield, to spread the birds out, is done by hand, hopper or quad bike and spinner. Partridges show a preference for pelleted food, so wheat is usually introduced into their diet later than it is for pheasants. Where a seed mixture is grown for game cover, or where there is an abundance of accessible weed seeds, partridges will also be tempted by this natural feed.

A French/Red Legged partridge is fully grown at about 14 weeks old. It is recommended that they are released several weeks before shooting is planned allowing them time to become wild and become well acquainted with the surrounding area.

English/grey partridges are indigenous to Britain having been recorded as far back as the Iron Age. They are rarely reared because captive strains do not remain in the area where they are released and are difficult to manage on

Pair of Red-legged Partridges

a shoot day. The chicks, when first hatched, are as small as bumblebees and are highly strung which makes them more difficult to rear. The best results are achieved using a broody bantam (small chicken) but these are no longer easy to acquire and their care is time-consuming. Released birds from captive-bred strains which survive the shooting season have difficulty rearing broods naturally. Where an estate has a truly wild resident population of English/ Grey partridges, they do not introduce reared birds because it is very important to preserve the wild strain.

A century ago English/Grey partridges were common in the wild on farmland. In Edwardian Britain there were one million pairs but various factors, most of which stem from changes in farming practices since the last war, have caused a very serious decline in numbers due to habitat loss and increased use of pesticides which destroy the insects that are vital for newly hatched chicks to feed on. They have declined 93% across the whole of Europe in the last 50 years.

There is now grave concern how much longer they can survive. Very few English/Grey partridge are shot these days; in fact most shoots have put a voluntary ban on shooting them unless there has been an unusually successful

▲ The Grey Partridge is struggling to survive in the wild because of the pressure of modern farming methods and loss of habitat

breeding year. Some estates are spending huge amounts of money safeguarding their remaining wild stock by creating the ideal habitat and conditions needed specifically for them to flourish. For all their investment, bad weather at hatching time in June can have disastrous results. A lot of research is also being conducted by the Game and Wildlife Conservation Trust whose principal funding comes from gamekeepers and shoot owners.

The iconic English/Grey partridge is probably the most cherished of all game birds and has always been a favourite of those who shoot. It has an independent character and it will not be for lack of effort by the shooting fraternity should it fail to survive.

Grouse Grouse inhabit heather moorland and are all truly wild birds: they are never reared artificially. Their survival basically depends on three factors ✦ how well predators have been controlled ✦ how well their habitat has been managed and ✦ how kind the weather has been while the hens were sitting on eggs and when the chicks first hatch.

It is estimated grouse shooting contributes £32 million to the local economy during a normal season.

In Scotland, which is famed for grouse, there are currently about 120 grouse shooting estates which, under new proposals brought about through concerns over raptor persecution, will, in future, need licenses to operate.

In a good year, when broods have done well and there is an abundance of grouse, moorland can yield a useful income to estates from shooting the surplus. The moor can only sustain a certain number of grouse; they will not thrive if too many are left at the end of the season. However in a poor year, shooting grouse is strictly curtailed or even cancelled completely in order that a viable population of breeding stock is left for the following year.

Grouse and heather

Grouse are moorland birds and heather is a major part of their diet, so heather preservation and management is of great importance. Heather growth is regulated by burning strips which is done on a rotation of approximately seven to ten years. This work is carried out, under licence, between the end of October and mid-April although there are very few days when weather conditions are benign enough for burning to be carried out. Grouse moor keepers are experienced in managing fire and have the necessary training and equipment to deal with any incidents. Their services are frequently called upon when wildfires break out on unmanaged moors.

As grouse are very territorial, only small areas of heather are burned. They need a mix of different stages of growth within each territory of approximately five acres (2.5 hectares) in size. This system provides them with young heather shoots for feeding on and old tall heather in which to shelter and nest. Besides heather management, bracken, which is very invasive, is also cleared. Grazing by cattle and sheep is regulated to provide optimum conditions for moorland plants to thrive and predator control is carried out. Another conservation measure in practice is reinstating areas of moors previously drained.

A mosaic of different stages of heather growth provides feeding and nesting opportunities for grouse and other birds

Heather forms the principal part of grouse diet and grouse are not given any supplementary food although small piles of grit are put out across the moor to help them digest the fibrous heather. Grouse usually have to share the moorland with sheep which, in moderation, can be an aid to management. Excessive numbers however, damage the habitat by overgrazing and also become a health risk.

Disease and grouse

Disease in grouse is more prevalent in some years than others, more so when numbers are high. Grouse can be badly affected by strongylosis, a debilitating intestinal roundworm. Grouse find their own food and water so the only way of administering treatment is by providing medicated grit which has been treated with a wormer. It is only available under licence and there is a statutory withdrawal period prior to the shooting season.

Another disease to strike grouse is one they share with sheep. Ticks are prevalent on the moors. They get on sheep and deer as well as grouse and carry a disease called 'Louping ill' which is easily transmitted. A heavy infestation of ticks can seriously weaken grouse which

▲ Red grouse are truly wild birds

need to be in good condition all year round to survive living and breeding on the open moors. Efficient tick control on sheep therefore plays an important part in grouse management.

In some areas serious damage may be caused by beetles that eat the heather, which reduces the amount of food available to grouse and can cause deterioration to their well-being. Heather burning can reduce infestations.

The grouse season

The grouse shooting season traditionally begins on 12th August but many estates do not start until later in the month. Grouse are usually driven over a line of guns who are concealed in '**butts**' which have been built out of stone or other materials. Sometimes they are sunken into the ground. Grouse fly forward, fast and fairly low, often following the contours of the ground. Early in the season they stay in family groups but later on join together in what are known as '**packs**'. Organised shooting finishes at the end of October. Where grouse numbers are low and insufficient to justify the cost of driven shooting, then '**walking up**' is an alternative. A

◀ How successful red grouse are rearing in their newly hatched chicks is very dependent on the weather

An experienced person can tell them apart by looking at their wing feathers and even sometimes their toenails.

Other duties carried out by a grouse moor keeper, besides predator control and heather burning, are the maintenance of tracks and butts and generally monitoring the condition and distribution of the birds. His or her beat may cover several thousand acres. They have to be familiar with every inch of it and be aware of what is happening on it throughout the year. Many estate owners are involved with conservation work by way of restoring moorland and peat bogs.

team of guns with their dogs line out across the moor and walk forward shooting at any grouse they happen to put up, always giving them a sporting chance.

Another option, on a lesser scale, is to shoot over pointers or setters. These dogs range widely and immediately they scent a bird they naturally indicate its position. They are trained to stop and mark where the grouse is crouching, long enough for the person shooting to get close before the handler gives them the command to flush. Grouse fly fast and are not easy to shoot.

At the end of a day's grouse shooting, the birds are separated into old and young.

Black Grouse or Blackcock are another member of the grouse family but are mainly in Scotland. Although, for the present, they remain on the quarry list (ie can be shot) they are no longer common and are very rarely shot as shoot owners wish to preserve them.

Thanks to conservation projects, their decline has been reversed. The area in which they congregate is known as a lek.

Controlled burning plays an important part in managing heather moorland to benefit grouse

▲ Although Black Grouse remain on the quarry list they are very rarely shot

Ptarmigan are small grouse that live on top of some of the highest mountains in the Highlands of Scotland. In winter they turn white. Although included on the quarry list, there are few of them and they are very seldom shot.

Ptarmigan are members of the grouse family which turn white in winter and live on the tops of Scotttish mountains

Woodcock are one of a family of birds known as 'waders' although in fact they have taken to living on the land while seeking out wet ground on which to feed. They are mainly nocturnal and spend the day hidden in thick cover. Rhododendron woods are a favourite haunt. They are quite common in some areas and resident throughout the year with numbers being swelled in winter with the arrival of migrants from Northern Europe. Usually only

solitary birds are encountered. When flushed they provide a challenging shot as they have a zig-zag pattern to their flight.

▲ The population of resident Woodcock increases in winter with migrants from Europe

Snipe are small wading birds similar in appearance to woodcock but inhabit boggy or marshy areas. They are prolific in some localities and also offer a challenging sporting shot.

Common Snipe flushed from marshy ground provide a challenging target

Flighting mallard

Golden plover are another small wading bird whose numbers are decreasing. They nest on open moorland where they often benefit from the protection afforded them by grouse moor keepers. In autumn and winter they leave the moors and form large flocks moving south to feed on farmland and river estuaries.

WILDFOWL

Mallard are the only breed of duck reared artificially in any quantity for sport. They are sometimes released onto inland ponds and lakes to create additional, varied shooting on an estate. When reared they do not normally venture far from where they were released so can usually be relied upon if an extra drive on a shoot day is needed. With the right breeding strain and correct management, reared mallard can provide some interesting sporting shooting to supplement a partridge or pheasant day. The mallard season opens on 1st September.

Other species of wild duck appear on inland and coastal waters particularly in winter. Shooting them can be challenging. Barley is a favourite food of ducks and inland ponds and lakes are often fed in winter to attract them in. Shooting takes place just before sunset, or occasionally at daybreak, when the wild ducks naturally fly in to feed. Numbers and species are unpredictable which makes it even more exciting for the guns patiently waiting, hidden out of sight, in hides. Wild mallard and teal are the most common but ability is needed to distinguish between the species of ducks that can be legally shot and those that are protected – a challenge at dusk. This form of shooting is known as '**flighting**'.

Geese Canada and greylag have become common on inland waters in recent years where they have become resident and now breed, sometimes in pest proportions. While they may offer a shot when ducks are being driven off a pond or lake, geese soon fly right away so numbers killed in this way are minimal. Some species of wild geese are fully protected by law but there are others that are legitimate quarry which frequent coastal regions in winter.

COASTAL WILDFOWLING

Wildfowl (ducks and geese) frequent many areas of coastal marshes and foreshores during winter. They are truly wild birds and most are migrants who arrive in October from their breeding grounds in Northern Europe or Iceland. Geese come in their thousands to spend winter in the warmer British climate. It's estimated that 200,000 Pink-footed geese now overwinter in the UK.

The foreshore is the area of coastline between high and low water marks where wildfowlers seek their sport. Wildfowling is a solitary sport and not for the faint hearted. It involves hours concealed in hides, drains or even boats waiting for the birds to flight from their coastal roosting sites to inland feeding areas at first light or ambushing them on their return at dusk. Accurate identification of legally protected species, which mustn't be shot, is essential.

Coastal wildfowlers mostly rely on mud-filled creeks that criss-cross the salt marshes, left empty by the receding tide, to conceal themselves. They often put a few decoy birds out before taking up position long before it gets light or dusk begins to fall. Then they wait patiently not really knowing what species, if any, of duck or goose may come over them or even whether they have chosen the right place to wait. Weather has a big influence. Warm, waterproof and camouflaged clothing is essential, as is a good knowledge of tide patterns to avoid being marooned by incoming tides that creep along the creeks and can easily cut a person off. Drowning and death through exposure are the dangers. A strong dog is needed to retrieve shot ducks or geese from inaccessible parts of the marsh.

There are many wildfowling clubs around Britain's coasts and they set themselves high standards. Newcomers must demonstrate a good understanding of the sport. They then spend a probationary period with an experienced wildfowler before being allowed out on their own. There are strict limits on the number of birds that can be taken at any one time. The clubs carry out a lot of conservation work on their marshes during the close season and often warden them so that breeding birds are not disturbed. They also work closely with local nature reserves and other conservation organisations as well as setting up displays at country shows and game fairs.

Unlike game birds, wildfowl can see reasonably well in the dark and may continue to flight all night if it is moonlight. Much depends on the weather conditions.

Generally speaking, the worse the weather, the better the chance of a wildflowling outing being successful.

When the wind is howling from the north and bringing with it flecks of snow, most people draw the curtains and turn up the central heating, not so the wildfowler for that is what he has been waiting for. However, in sub-zero temperatures when the ground and water is frozen and life is difficult for wildfowl and waders, shooting is suspended.

The species of wildfowl that may legally be shot in Britain during the open season are as follows:

DUCK Common Pochard, Gadwall, Golden Eye, Mallard, Pintail, Shoveler, Teal, Tufted Duck and Wigeon.

GOOSE Canada, Grey-lag and Pink-footed.

SHOOTING SEASONS
FOR ENGLAND, WALES AND SCOTLAND

GAME GROUSE August 12th to December 10th

BLACKGAME August 20th to December 10th

PTARMIGAN August 12th to December 10th

PARTRIDGE September 1st to February 1st

PHEASANT October 1st to February 1st

WADERS COMMON SNIPE August 12th to January 31st

WOODCOCK October 1st (Scotland Sept 1st) to January 31st

GOLDEN PLOVER September 1st to January 31st

COOT/MOORHEN September 1st to January 31st

WILDFOWL DUCK AND GOOSE September 1st to January 31st (Extended to February 20th below the coastal High Water Mark)

SHOOTING GLOSSARY

SHOTGUN A gun that fires cartridges containing small spherical pellets known as shot made from lead or other compounds. This may vary in size according to the intended quarry. Shot size is numbered, the lower number being the largest. A cartridge usually contains approximately an ounce (28 grams) of shot. Shotguns are used for shooting moving targets up to about 50 yards (50 metres) range. Shotguns have one or two barrels and are manufactured in several different sizes known as gauges or bores, the smallest being .410 and the largest is a 10 bore. The most commonly used is a 12 bore

SIDE BY SIDE Shotgun with two barrels side by side

OVER AND UNDER Shotgun with two barrels one above the other

RIFLE A gun that fires a single bullet a long distance with great accuracy. The barrel has spiral grooves inside. Rifles are used to kill animals when they are stationary

AIR RIFLE Type of gun which is not very powerful that fires a single pellet propelled by compressed air or gas

CALIBRE Barrel size of a rifle

MAGAZINE Device for holding and automatically dispensing rifle ammunition.

GUN SLIP A cover for a gun

GUN Person carrying a gun on a shoot

DOUBLE GUN Type of shooting where two guns are used alternately by one person

LOADER Person assisting someone shooting with two guns

BEATER Person not carrying a gun, employed to drive game towards standing shooters

PICKER UP Person with dogs employed to collect dead or wounded game

FLANKER Person on the edge of a beating line who usually carries a flag to encourage birds to fly in the right direction

STOP Person placed in a position to prevent game birds from escaping out of a drive

SEWELLING Strips of plastic tied onto lengths of string which is hung up to discourage pheasants running past

BEAT Designated area on a shoot

DRIVE Designated area brought in by the beaters

PEG Numbered marker indicating where a person shooting has to stand

GUN STAND Clearing cut in thick vegetation for a gun to stand in

BUTT / HIDE Place where people can conceal themselves

BAG Term used to describe the total amount of game shot on a day

GAME CART Vehicle used to transport dead game

BRACE Two birds tied together, if possible one of each sex. The bag is usually counted in braces

CLAY PIGEON Small disc that is launched into the air and used for practice or competitive shotgun shooting

TRAP Mechanical device for launching clay pigeons

HABITAT Environment in which a creature lives

RIDE Wide path cut through woodland or other dense cover

GAME COVER Block or strip of a crop grown especially for the benefit of game birds

CLUTCH Number of eggs a hen bird lays before her natural instinct makes her go broody and want to incubate them. If the eggs are removed from the nest soon after they are laid then this instinct is suppressed and the bird continues to lay. Embryos inside eggs do not start to develop until they are warmed to body temperature by the hen sitting on them almost continuously

BROOD Family of young birds

POULT Young game bird

ROOST Place where birds spend the night

JUG Applied to pheasants when they sleep on the ground at night instead of in a bush or tree

COVEY A small group of partridges

WILDFOWL Ducks and geese

FLIGHT Movement of birds to and from roosting and feeding areas

SKEIN A flock of geese in flight, very often in a V formation

FORE SHORE Area of coastline between high and low water marks

DECOY Imitation animal or bird used to entice others to come close

BGA British Game Alliance Assurance scheme marketing game that has been ethically reared and sustainably managed

GWCT Game and Wildlife Conservation Trust

BASC British Association for Shooting and Conservation

CA Countryside Alliance

NGO National Gamekeepers Organisation

CPSA Clay Pigeon Shooting Association

DEER

Of the six species of deer found in this country, only two are native to Britain. With the exception of Chinese Water Deer, all the males, known as stags or bucks, have antlers. Unlike the horns on cattle and sheep, a deer's antlers drop off each year and new ones immediately start to grow which are covered in skin known as **velvet**. As the antlers become fully developed and harden, this skin dies and is rubbed off. No females of deer species found in the UK have antlers. Red, Muntjac, Fallow and Sika all lose their antlers in the spring. Roe bucks are different and lose theirs in November and December.

Nearly all species of deer have a white rump which, when the hair is raised, acts as a danger signal to others when they are startled.

Apart from Muntjac, which breed all year round, female deer only come into season for a few weeks each year.

The mating season is known as the **'rut'**. Newborn deer have spotted coats that act as excellent camouflage and they are left hidden in cover for long periods. Their mother only comes back to feed them occasionally although she is unlikely to be very far away. Males take no interest in their offspring.

UK deer population is thought to be around two million, an estimated one million of which live in Scotland. This is the highest population for more than a thousand years.

None of the deer species in the UK have any natural predators except occasionally a very young roe or muntjac may be taken by a fox. Deer numbers across Britain continually increase and in some areas are at pest proportion. Where there is a concentration of deer there is always the risk of disease and, in the case of red deer in the Highlands of Scotland, starvation in a hard winter is a distinct possibility. Culling

Sika stags are interbreeding with native Red deer

is essential in order to keep numbers at a manageable level.

Approximately 80% of wild deer harvested in the UK go to restaurants or the hospitality trade.

The Covid pandemic in 2020/2021 greatly reduced demand and with only a limited market, culling was reduced which allowed deer numbers to expand, further aggravating the situation.

Human intervention is necessary, but not always condoned, to prevent numbers spiralling out of control. Large populations result in serious damage to agricultural crops, gardens, woodlands, forestry and the habitat in which they live. Sika, Fallow and Red deer strip bark from trees, which results in bacterial and fungal damage, rendering the timber unsaleable.

There are strict legal regulations in the UK with regards to shooting deer. Only a rifle can be used and night shooting one hour before sunrise and one hour after sunset is prohibited.

Deer are responsible for an estimated average of 74,000 road accidents annually some of which result in human injuries and fatalities. Deer appear suddenly out of woodland, frequently after dark, onto roads and are often followed by others. Road signs, erected where there are accident black spots, warn that there are deer in the vicinity. Light reflectors on the verges are used in some places to deter deer from venturing onto roads.

The deer population can increase by around 25% to 30% each year so control becomes a necessity. There are also welfare issues and the culling of sick and injured deer is always a priority.

DEER AND THE LAW

There was no ruling on the methods by which deer could be killed until the Deer Act 1963 was introduced. This Act brought in legislation to

ensure that culling was as humane as possible by introducing close seasons, regulating the methods used and banning the use of unsuitable guns and ammunition. Using legal rifles is the only legitimate method for killing deer and there are precise specifications as to which calibre and ammunition sizes may be used for the different species. Generally speaking it is illegal to shoot deer from a moving vehicle or to use a vehicle to drive deer.

Legislation in Scotland and Northern Ireland differs from that governing England and Wales. Moral codes have been introduced to improve the

Red, Sika, Roe and Fallow deer begin to grow a new set of antlers each year as soon as the old ones have dropped off

general welfare and methods have been developed to allow selective culling. The vast majority of deer are culled by professional or amateur stalkers who control deer within a certain area. Stalking is often let and is a popular sport.

Male deer lose their antlers each year and grow new ones; the older they get, the bigger the antlers although the quality may ultimately deteriorate when the animal is old. A guest stalker usually pays according to the quality of the stag's or buck's antlers and a lesser amount for females and inferior males which are taken out to improve the breeding quality. Trophy heads are much sought after by sportsmen and women and there is an international scale using weight and length criteria to ascertain whether they fall into bronze, silver or gold categories. The revenue creates a useful income for the landowner, who retains the carcase. It is also a way of reducing the numbers of deer, although sporting estates that offer trophy stalking often retain a high density of deer in the first place. Less experienced stalkers are usually supervised and assisted by a knowledgeable person. They will have had to prove themselves to be competent using a rifle, equipped with a telescopic sight, and accurate on a target, before being permitted to embark on a foray to shoot deer.

It is very important that a shot should only be taken when the quarry is stationary and within killing range; safety and the animal's welfare is a priority at all times. It is quite possible for a deer that has been shot accurately through the heart, and is effectively dead, to run a hundred yards before actually keeling over. In thick undergrowth even this is far enough to make it difficult to locate the animal. It is therefore recommended that those stalking in dense cover should have a dog with them, trained to follow a blood scent, so that should a deer move away from the place it was shot it can be tracked.

Red stag with antlers in velvet

Deer control throughout Britain is an important element of the countryside, not only for humane and ecological reasons but because it generates over £100 million annually, providing a lifeline to rural businesses.

A significant proportion of this comes from wild Red deer that roam the Scottish Highlands. Males are culled to control quality and females to control quantity. While venison from these animals cannot claim to be entirely organic it must be as near as is possible, for they are completely free range. There is only a slight possibility of them having had indirect contact with chemicals and they receive no medication, a fact that has not gone unnoticed as consumption of wild venison is increasing. Even so, most of the carcases of deer culled in Britain are exported to the Continent.

STALKING METHODS

There are several methods of stalking deer which is determined by the species and the terrain.

One method, where the cover is dense with open areas, is to erect a high seat about 8 to 10ft (3-4 m) above the ground on the edge of woodland where a person can sit and wait undetected; deer have keen hearing and scenting abilities. This also means that when a shot is fired it is angled towards the ground, which is very important from a safety aspect. Early morning and evenings are the best times to see deer and they can sometimes be attracted by calls.

The other popular method is to carefully approach a suitable beast. This needs a great deal of stealth and cunning especially on an open hillside when it may take several hours to get within range of the selected animal and be in position to take a safe shot.

Both methods require an infinite amount of patience for all deer are wary creatures.

Muntjac are particularly difficult to stalk because they like living in dense undergrowth.

Deer are always bled and **gralloched** (gutted) immediately after they have been shot so this is also part of the exercise.

There are several thousand professional deer stalkers in Britain most of whom are employed in the Highlands of Scotland, providing work in remote areas.

BRINGING DEER OFF THE MOUNTAIN

It is a necessity to remove the old and the sick and to control Red deer numbers for they would starve in winter on the hills and otherwise die a slow death. One of the difficulties associated with culling Red deer, besides the need to have the right weather conditions, accessibility, no

Male Muntjac deer with a juvenile

disturbance from hill walkers and being able to locate the beasts in the first place, is one of getting them off the hill after they have been shot. Sometimes, where the terrain is very steep or rocky, they have to be manually dragged through the heather to the nearest track. Occasionally a special breed of pony (**garron**) is used and sometimes they can be reached by an ATV (all terrain vehicle).

While some people look on deer stalking as a sport, keeping control of numbers is an absolute necessity and involves killing females to reduce numbers. It is sometimes the policy in Scotland when shooting a Red hind to take her calf as well. If it is a late, undersized calf, maybe not having been born until July, it might still be dependent on her. Without its mother's milk it would be unlikely to survive the harsh winter.

DEER SPECIES

Red deer are Britain's largest animals standing up to 4ft (120cm) at the shoulder and mature males have large, impressive antlers. Neolithic men in Britain used their antlers as picks for digging. Red deer have been kept in parks for centuries both to enhance the landscape and as a way of providing food; they were also used for hunting. An individual would be caught and 'carted' to a suitable area where it was released to be hunted with hounds by followers on horseback. Often when the hounds held the stag at bay it would be unharmed and could be caught up again and taken home to provide sport for another day. This practice only ceased in the 1960s.

Much of the British stock of Red deer has been 'improved' in the past by interbreeding with their larger Continental or North American relatives, producing bigger stags with huge antlers. In medieval times there were over 2,000 deer parks. Today descendants of these deer are sometimes kept in parks such as Richmond Park where there

are some magnificent specimens. Since the 1970s some domesticated Red deer have been kept in large paddocks and farmed for venison.

In the wild, Red deer are the species common in the Highlands of Scotland and depicted in art as the Monarch of the Glen. Over centuries they have been forced to adapt to living and surviving on the open heather-clad hills although this is not their natural habitat. They were originally animals of the forest. Highland Reds are smaller than the Red deer. The Reds thrive better in forests and farmland and can be found in south-west England, Wales, Yorkshire, the Lake District, Dumfries, Galloway, the New Forest, parts of Sussex and in some areas of Norfolk and Suffolk.

In summer their coats are reddish brown with a pale colour rump and a short tail: in winter they are a drabber colour. Although gregarious by nature, the sexes spend much of the year living apart in separate herds. Only the stags have antlers which they lose in April or May, the rut is around October/November time and the young, known as calves, are born in June. Mature stags grow impressive branching antlers which are much prized by sportsmen as trophies. As they grow older, each year more points appear on the antlers.

When there are six points on each antler (twelve in total) the stag is known as a 'Royal' and one with sixteen is a 'Monarch'.

Red deer living in nutritious arable areas and those kept in parks can reach in excess of twenty points.

The stalking of stags is often let and involves stealth and patience. Clients are accompanied by a stalker or knowledgeable ghillie. Traditionally the carcase was brought off the hill on a pony. Poorer quality stags and hinds are generally culled by professional stalkers. The income received from sportsmen and the sale of carcases is a welcome contribution particularly to Highland estate owners whose land is of limited use for agriculture. Red deer are very prolific and numbers have to be rigorously controlled to prevent damage to crops and trees as well as the threat to them of starvation through over-grazing on the hills.

Roe deer are Britain's other native species of deer and are much smaller than the Red, standing just over 2ft (65cm) at the shoulders. Records of them date back to before the Mesolithic period (6,000 to 10,000 years BC). Roe were treated as a pest and, by the 19th century, the population was confined to Scotland with only isolated pockets elsewhere. In 1962 they were given legal protection with a designated close season when they could not be killed.

Roe are now widespread throughout the British Isles and their numbers are fast increasing, although they are not found in Northern Ireland. They are secretive by nature, preferring to spend most of the day hidden in cover and are most likely to be seen in the evenings when they come out to feed on the edge of woodland. In summer their coat is short and a rich red colour, while growing thicker and turning a mousy grey/brown in winter. They appear to have no tails but have distinctive white rumps on which the raised hair, accompanied by a dog-like bark, acts as a conspicuous warning to other deer. Roe often live in small family groups of about five to eight with the young bucks ejected when they are about a year old. Once mature, bucks become territorial. Roe are rarely kept successfully in captive situations.

Mature Roe deer does very often give birth to twin fawns

▲ Fallow Buck

Only the bucks have antlers which are **cast** (shed) in November or December. The rut is in late July or August and roe are unique among deer in that, after conception, there is a delay and the embryo does not become implanted into the uterus until early January, when it continues its normal development. After this extended pregnancy the young (kids), usually twins, are born in May.

Roe can cause extensive damage to young trees as they eat the new growth on the top and side shoots. The bucks thrash and rub young saplings with their antlers when attempting to remove the velvet or mark their territories. A good **head** (set of antlers) is a much-prized trophy although it normally has only six points in total. Roe stalking is often let on private estates. There are not many trophy-standard bucks so some young bucks and those with poor quality antlers as well as surplus does need to be culled to control numbers and improve the quality. Roe venison is excellent meat.

Fallow deer were probably introduced to Britain by the Normans. They are medium sized standing about 3ft (90cm) high. Gregarious by nature, herds are widespread across the UK, although not in huge numbers. For centuries, large herds of Fallow deer have been, and still are, popular adornments in parkland surrounding stately homes but, as they are kept in an enclosed area, their numbers still have to be rigidly controlled. They are also sometimes farmed for venison.

Fallow vary greatly in colour: some of those kept in parks are pure white while others are almost black (**melanistic**). The most common colour is a sandy brown with white spots in summer that disappear as the winter coat grows. There is a colouration known as '**menil**' where the deer are a lighter shade and retain their white spots throughout the year. All fallow have a characteristic white rump and a fairly long tail which is constantly being flicked. Only bucks have antlers which grow fairly large and are of a flattened shape – these are shed in March. The rut is in October or November and the single fawn is born in June. Like Red deer, fallow antlers grow more points as the animal matures and can make an impressive trophy.

Fallow deer, like Red deer, were once hunted with packs of buckhounds and the familiar 'White Hart' pub sign often depicts a white fallow buck.

Sika deer were first introduced to Britain from Japan in the mid 1800s. They are similar in size to a fallow and like them have spotted coats in summer and a white rump. There are scattered groups around Britain, particularly in Dorset and Lancashire, and there is great concern in Scotland because they are inter-breeding with the native Red deer. Only the stags have antlers, which are similar in appearance to a Red deer but smaller and narrower, usually having a total of only six points. Sika are solitary for much of the time but form small groups in winter. The sexes stay segregated and only come together for the rut. Stags lose their antlers in April; the rut is from September to November and hinds give birth to a single calf in May or June.

Muntjac or Barking Deer originate from China, and in 1838 were first brought to Woburn Park in Bedfordshire. Since then a wild population has become established, partly through escapes and deliberate releases. One major escape occurred from Woburn Park during the last war, when a plane crashed through the perimeter wall. Since then, despite suggestions they wouldn't survive our harsher climate, they have spread and become established in pest proportions in many areas.

Muntjac stand only about 18in (50cm) high and are often mistaken for a fox as their coat is similar in colour and they have a relatively long tail which is raised when they are alarmed. They sometimes appear to be hump-backed and they also bark which is how they got their alternative name. Muntjac are territorial and very secretive by nature, living either singly or as a little family unit. The bucks have small razor-sharp canine tusks and short antlers with only a single point (occasionally two when older), which they usually lose in late spring.

Muntjac eat almost anything including yew and brambles, they rarely leave dense cover and it is extremely difficult to estimate the population and even more so to efficiently keep control of their numbers. They are responsible for a significant amount of damage to undergrowth and plants in woodland which completely alters the ecosystem and in turn affects wildlife living there. They breed all year round and females mate again soon after giving birth so reproduce very quickly.

Efforts are being made to prevent muntjac becoming established in Scotland.

Muntjac can be culled throughout the year but the British Deer Society recommends that juvenile females and heavily pregnant females, if identifiable, should be selected if at all possible. Adult females in close company with a male should not be culled as they may well have recently given birth to a fawn. If these guidelines are followed, the risk of orphaning dependant young is significantly reduced. Over the past 40 years, muntjac deer have spread rapidly across England and Wales and have found their way into towns and cities along railway embankments and canals. They have taken up residence in suburban gardens and parks, but being so secretive, are rarely seen. In fact they'd hardly be noticed if it wasn't for the damage they cause through eating the plants. They also pose a risk for road users.

Chinese water deer originate from China and Korea and are the least common deer in Britain. They were first kept at London Zoo in 1873 but escaped from Whipsnade Zoo in 1929. They have only become established in the wild locally in parts of south-east England. As their name implies, Chinese Water Deer prefer reed beds and a marshy environment; their main strongholds are in west Bedfordshire, the Cambridgeshire fens and the Norfolk Broads although there have been sightings in other areas.

Chinese Water Deer are slightly larger than muntjac and lighter in colour. In winter their grey coats tend to look woolly. Neither sexes have antlers although the males have tusks. The rut occurs in November or December and females can produce up to six fawns, but one to three is much more usual, between May and July.

It is estimated that up to 40% of Chinese water deer fawns die within the first four weeks of life.

Because Chinese Water Deer numbers are still at a low density, have restricted national distribution and are solitary by nature they have not, so far, caused any problems.

Chinese Water Deer

DEER SHOOTING SEASONS

ENGLAND AND WALES

RED STAG, SIKA STAG, FALLOW BUCK:
August 1 – April 30

ROE BUCK: April 1 – October 31

CHINESE WATER DEER BUCK:
November 1 – March 31

RED HIND, SIKA HIND, FALLOW DOE, ROE DOE, CHINESE WATER DEER DOE:
November 1 – March 31

MUNTJAC: no statutory close season (see notes on species)

SCOTLAND

RED STAG, SIKA STAG AND RED/SIKA HYBRID STAGS: July 1 – October 20

FALLOW BUCK: August 1 – April 30

ROE BUCK: April 1 – October 20

RED HIND, SIKA HIND, RED/SIKA HYBRID HIND, FALLOW DOE:
October 21 – February 15

ROE DOE: October 21 – March 31

NB Recommendations were made in February 2020 that the Deer Close Seasons for Scotland should be replaced with a new Order in which the close season for females of each species is set to start on a date in the period 1st to 15th April (inclusive) and end on a date in the period 31st August to 15th September (inclusive), and in which no close seasons are set for males of each species.

NORTHERN IRELAND

RED STAG, FALLOW BUCK, SIKA STAG:
August 1 – April 30

RED HIND, FALLOW DOE, SIKA HIND:
November 1 – March 31

DEER GLOSSARY

STAG Male Red or Sika deer

HIND Female Red or Sika deer

BUCK Male Roe, Fallow, Muntjac or Chinese Water deer

DOE Female Roe, Fallow, Muntjac or Chinese Water deer

CALF Young of Red or Sika deer

FAWN Young of Fallow, Muntjac or Chinese Water deer

KID Young of roe deer

PRICKET A yearling fallow buck or red stag. In Scotland they are called 'Staggies'

ANTLERS A bracket structure that is composed of bone which grows from pedicles on the heads of male deer except Chinese Water deer. Antlers are shed and regrown each year

HUMMEL A Red stag with no antlers

POINTS The number of spikes on an antler

CAST When the antlers drop off

HEAD Antlers on a deer

TROPHY An extra-fine quality head. An official assessment taking into account the length and weight can be made as to whether it is of gold, silver or bronze standard

ROYAL Any red stag with a total of 12 points, six on each antler, is referred to as being a 'royal'

IMPERIAL Red stag with 14 points

MONARCH Red stag with 16 points

VELVET Skin that covers and nourishes the growing antlers, it is shed when the new antlers are fully developed which causes great irritation to the animal

RUT The mating season. Males are usually very vocal at this time.

VENISON The meat of deer

CULL Kill a selected animal

GRALLOCH Remove intestines and stomach.

STALKER Professional person who shoots deer or takes a client out to shoot deer

GHILLIE (Scotland) Person who assists a stalker (or fisherman)

GARRON Pony used to carry shot deer off the hill in Scotland

ATV All terrain vehicle

BDS British Deer Society. A registered charity founded in 1963 devoted to the welfare of deer. Provides education and training on deer and their management

Sheepdogs are indispensable assistants when gathering sheep on open ground and moving a flock

WORKING DOGS

Dogs have a sense of smell that is somewhere between 10,000 and 100,000 times more acute than ours depending on the breed. Some breeds, such as spaniels and retrievers excel with their scenting abilities.

'Sniffer dogs' are often trained to locate or indicate one particular scent.

Canines also possess a range of hearing that is far superior to that of humans. They are able to hear nearly twice as many frequencies and sounds, four times further away. Dogs can clearly hear the high-frequency sounds which humans cannot. A sheepdog is capable of responding to a whistle up to a mile away.

Over the years, breeders have selectively bred dogs with one of two things in mind; either to breed the best looking or ones which excel in their work. It is not often that a specimen can combine the two.

Tail docking is a contentious issue but for working dogs is purely functional, not done for cosmetic reasons. For example, a spaniel's natural lively tail action when it is working in thick cover can soon result in the tip becoming severely damaged causing great discomfort and a serious risk of infection. Although docking was banned in Britain in 2007, exemptions have been made for spaniels, HPRs and terriers bred specifically for work. Docking must be carried out by a vet when the puppies are five days old or less and some form of evidence will be required as confirmation that they will be sold to working homes. Commonly their tails will be docked by about a third which is sufficient to greatly reduce the risk of injury.

In the countryside, working dogs and their handlers' work together as a team. Dogs are invaluable, particularly to shepherds, and often are their sole companions for most of the day.

TYPES OF DOGS

Terriers will work underground. Generally speaking they have a strong desire to kill and to please themselves; they show no fear and do not hesitate to defend themselves. In particular they play an important role in fox and rat control.

Beagles And Harriers/ Fox, Stag And Otter Hounds all have excellent scenting powers and stamina and will follow a scent trail for long distances. They are capable of quickly dispatching a fox, hare or otter. For centuries hounds were kept in packs. Since hunting live

▲ Terriers are used for controlling pests such as rats

quarry was banned in 2005, the packs have been following an artificially laid trail. The breeds are being preserved but the working bloodlines, which were selectively bred for centuries, are being lost. Otterhounds are in grave danger of becoming extinct.

Bloodhounds have long been used to hunt humans and were once relied upon by the police to track down villains. There are about 20 packs of bloodhounds in the UK who hunt a human scent laid by a runner, known as the 'clean boot'. The bloodhounds are followed on horseback in the way foxhounds once were.

Greyhounds/Whippets/Salukis are known as sight or gaze hounds that hunt entirely by sight, not sound or scent, relying solely on speed to catch their quarry. Once used to course hares, this sport was also banned in 2005.

Lurchers are an intelligent mix of fast running breeds that combine hunting by sight with the use of scent. Lurchers or greyhounds are sometimes used by pest controllers to play a part in catching rabbits.

Collies are a very active breed with strong natural instincts to gather together animals or birds that can be driven, such as sheep, cattle, ducks, geese etc. They're trained to obey orders,

Foxhound packs are now only permitted to hunt artificial trails that have been laid

© S Whitehead

▲ Lurchers are used to catch rabbits

conveyed by either voice or whistle, and to run wide to fetch sheep from a distance. When driving them, they respond to commands to turn them to the right or left.

> *'Come by' is the instruction for the dog to move around the sheep in a clockwise direction and 'Away to me' to go anti-clockwise.*

Once the flock is gathered, the sheepdog will stealthily creep or lie down when instructed. Collies are also often used for search and rescue work such as mountain rescue.

GUNDOGS

The scent working dogs rely on can be very inconsistent depending on weather conditions. One day it may be very good and the dogs can work with speed and another day it will be poor which makes tracking very difficult. Scent has often been likened to a light plume of smoke coming

▶ Working Springer spaniels are never happier than when they are working

from a slowly smouldering fire. It can linger on the ground and surrounding vegetation, it can hang in the air or be swept away. It is generally best on days when there is dampness and a gentle breeze or when the ground is warmer than the air temperature which often happens later in the day. It is extremely interesting to watch dogs working a scent line – for their noses are as effective for them as sight is for humans. Most people find it fascinating to watch a dog puzzling out a situation and it is one of the reasons why so many take an interest in field sports.

Spaniels are very active dogs with a natural instinct to work the cover with a zig-zagging action known as **quartering**. Cockers and English Springers are the most popular. In the shooting field they are used to hunt for pheasants, grouse, rabbits etc which they locate by scent. They then **flush** (make run or fly) their quarry and are trained to retrieve it to their handler when it has been shot. They are good

Working cocker spaniels are very energetic

▼ Labradors are popular as shooting companions

all-rounders but some can be headstrong and difficult to control. Spaniels are also frequently used as 'sniffer' dogs.

Labradors and Retrievers have superior scenting abilities and a strong desire to carry objects. In the shooting field they are mostly used to find and fetch shot animals or birds and are invaluable for retrieving wounded game. Some are also trained to hunt for and flush game or rabbits. Labradors and retrievers are very intelligent and biddable. For this reason they are also often trained as guide dogs, assistance dogs and for investigative work as 'sniffer' dogs.

Pointers are dogs that range widely in search of game which they locate by scent, marking its location and then standing absolutely still while staring in its direction. They will hold this stance

until given the order to move forward and flush whatever they have located. With the exception of English Pointers, they are also trained to retrieve after the quarry has been shot.

Setters comprise four breeds which are all native to the UK. They work in a similar fashion to pointers but are not trained to retrieve. They were once commonly used in the shooting field but are not nearly so popular today.

DOGS AT WORK

Training working dogs involves developing their natural skills while suppressing undesirable traits and instilling obedience, all of which takes kindness, time, understanding and patience.

Sheepdogs are invaluable to shepherds particularly those who keep their sheep on open hillsides and moors. It takes between 18 months and 2 years to fully train a sheepdog. Border collies, which are generally black and white, are the most popular.

For every mile the shepherd walks his dog will cover roughly 15.

Their usefulness becomes very apparent when gathering sheep in the wild uplands of Britain. In winter they are able to locate sheep which have become buried under deep snow.

Quadbikes are all terrain vehicles (ATVs) which can be driven cross-country over rough ground. Before the era of the quadbike the only places a shepherd could get to with a vehicle were those that could be reached by a track; otherwise is was on foot, and likewise for his dogs. Sheepdogs very soon latched on to the fact if they hitched a lift on a quadbike to ride pillion, it saved them a lot of running!

Police Dogs

2,500 are employed by the police service in various capacities. Crowd control and the tracking and apprehension of criminals are aspects of police dog work that most people are familiar with. Once German Shepherds (Alsatians) were the most popular breed for police work but the Belgian Malinois has now taken over that position. Police dogs play a large part in security measures protecting many Ministry of Defence sites across the UK. Other sections of the Police Force specialise in using dogs with amazing scenting abilities to sniff out such things as drugs, money, contraband and firearms. Labradors play a part but often the more active breeds such as springer and cocker spaniels are preferred.

KENNELS

Many working dogs are kennelled outside. They are kept, either singly or sharing with one or two other dogs, in a small draught-proof shed with access to an attached run. Bedding inside is very often straw or shredded paper on a raised bench which makes it cosy. Keeping dogs in kennels is not unkind providing their living quarters are dry and free from draughts. They have their own 'house' and 'yard' and are not subjected to the continual disturbance that living in a busy household can bring.

Packs of dogs, such as hounds, are kept in communal kennels with maybe 20 or 30 sharing a bedded area, lounging area and large outside run. Sexes are usually segregated.

Working sheepdogs, especially in the north, are sometimes kept tied to their kennels with a few feet of chain. They are used for work every day so get plenty of exercise. It is more practical to keep a long-coated dog outdoors because they can get very wet and dirty when they are working and they also act as guard dogs.

Most people who work dogs have huge respect and appreciation for their incredible abilities. Man has utilised and cultivated the skills of different breeds for centuries and probably owes much to them for his own survival.

GLOSSARY

GUNDOGS

ESS English Springer Spaniel.

HPR Hunter, Pointer, Retriever.

GSP German Shorthaired Pointer.

GWP German Wirehaired Pointer.

FTCh Field Trial Champion.

FTW Field Trial Winner.

FIELD TRIAL A trial held under simulated shooting conditions using non captive live game or rabbits to test a gun dog's obedience and working ability.

COLD GAME TEST Similar to a field trial but using cold dead game instead of live.

WORKING TEST A test held under artificial conditions using dummies to assess a gun dog's obedience and working ability.

DUMMY An artificial object used to teach a dog to retrieve.

CHOKE LEAD A slip lead, a running noose used to restrain a dog.

STEADY Under control at all times when off the lead.

RUN IN Chase after something without having been given the command to.

MARK Indicate where the quarry is.

PEG Catch unshot game, often when it is sitting tight.

FLUSH Make an animal or bird run or fly.

RUNNER Wounded bird that is unable to fly.

SOFT MOUTH Capable of retrieving live game etc without harming it.

HARD MOUTH Used to describe a dog that kills or bites game.

NOSE Used to describe a dog's scenting abilities.

LINE Scent trail left by an animal or bird.

DRIVING IN / DOGGING IN Term for when a dog is used under control to chase pheasants or partridges away from boundaries, roads or other undesirable areas.

PICK UP Collect shot game with dogs.

PICKER UP Person who picks up shot game using dogs.

COURSE Hunt by sight

SHEEPDOGS

EYE The power a sheepdog has in controlling sheep by looking at them.

GATHER Round up the flock

SHED Separate sheep from the main flock

PEN Drive the sheep into an enclosure

BRACE Two sheepdogs working at the same time

GRIP Grab hold of a sheep

Spiders' webs in autumn woodland

CONSERVATION

About a quarter of land in England receives some form of protection, primarily to its wildlife, its habitat and the environment. The skills of people who live and make a living in the countryside also need conserving. There is still a demand for their expertise but not enough youngsters learning the trades to take over in the future. They and the tools they work with are part of our heritage.

The latest national State of Nature report showed that 41% of UK species studied have declined, with many at risk of becoming extinct in the not too distant future. There are many causes. Massive changes have been brought about by development, the construction of transport links, intensive agriculture, habitat destruction, increasing number of predators, displacement by invasive species and climate change. Nitrates and phosphates leeching from the soil in the form of agricultural fertilizers, and domestic and industrial sewage, are polluting our rivers, lakes and estuaries. This encourages the excessive growth of green algae which smothers and damages rare habitats and wildlife while also affecting people's leisure activities.

In September 2020 the Environment Agency reported that no English river had passed tests for chemical pollution, and just 16% were rated as being in good health.

Environmentalists, conservationists and scientists have to decide: should one species be culled in order to save another? General Licences are issued to control pest bird species in order to protect the nests of other bird species, farmers' crops or livestock.

Conservation often calls for the elimination or reduction of invasive flora and fauna. In the case of animals this may mean culling such as grey squirrels, mink and red deer.

Lundy Island, in the Bristol Channel, became overrun with rats that killed nearly all the nesting sea birds. Once a prolific puffin colony, it was reduced to only 20 in the year 2000. Eliminating the rats has meant that numbers have now recovered to about 400.

LESS CARRION

Striking a balance is the challenge. Birds of prey populations are escalating, as are relatively common species such as magpies, crows and gulls which take their toll at nesting time.

Many species would feed on carrion were it available, but there is now legislation in place that livestock carcasses must be disposed of in an approved way and not left where they died. Sheep roam thousands of acres of the UK's wild moorland, the haunt of many large birds of prey, and the carcasses of those that died once provided an abundant food source. Deprived of this, it becomes necessary for them to hunt live prey thus imposing further pressure on our wildlife.

In recent years there has been a trend for preserving predatory species, many of them large birds or animals. But what are the long-term effects they are having on populations of their prey? Predators need to find food every day and do not discriminate which species they catch to satisfy their appetites.

Capercaillie are an endangered species of bird but their survival is in jeopardy in part because of increasing numbers of predators. Ironically, while the successful efforts of conservationists have led to growing numbers of rare pine marten, they share the same habitat and prey on capercaillie as well as endangered red squirrels.

EXCESS DEER NUMBERS

The exploding population of deer has got out of hand. Red, roe and fallow are even becoming urbanised, with populations living in city centres, in parks, gardens and old cemeteries where they are even eating floral tributes. Deer in excess numbers cause serious damage to forestry, moorland, crops and set back conservation efforts. Fencing deer out of protected places only puts more pressure on the surrounding areas. Realistically the only way to preserve the habitat is to reduce deer numbers.

▼ Capercaillie are large members of the grouse family which live in Scottish forests and are now very rare

ONE GAIN IS ANOTHER'S LOSS

Conservation is a complex subject as it encompasses so many diverse aspects of our countryside nearly all of which interact with each other. Wind turbines produce green energy but at the same time blight the landscape and already cover thousands of acres of our countryside. Seven commercial space ports are planned to be developed in 2022 – some of them to be built in precious habitats. Providing access to remote sites results in further irreparable damage.

Studies have shown that tree planting over wide areas can reduce biodiversity with little impact on carbon emissions. A separate project throws doubt on the amount of carbon that new forests can absorb and suggest it might have been overestimated.

Large-scale planting of trees in a bid to reverse climate change will destroy existing habitats and lead to the loss of many species within that area. Dead or dying trees are removed to be replaced with new plantings. These old trees are hugely important to many species of insects and birds which, without them, wouldn't survive. They are miniature nature reserves in their own right which should be conserved not destroyed. Blanketing what is now open land with forests would completely change the environment and obliterate ecosystems which support large communities of plants, animals, insects and microbes, many of which can only survive in specific conditions.

Insects are bottom of the food chain and play a vital role. Life on earth is dependent on them. Not only are they a source of food for wildlife, some species pollinate plants and others prey on those that are pests.

THE BENEFITS OF COWS

The number of insects in the UK has dropped by 25% in the last 30 years. Modern arable farming practices are much to blame; large fields and monoculture are sterile places. Insects are

▲ Dead and dying trees are home to many species

far more prolific where there is livestock and in particular cattle. There used to be many more small farms which kept them. In summer swallows could be seen swooping low amongst the herd catching flies which were attracted to them. There would be beetles and invertebrates rummaging through cowpats.

A field with cows in is an ecosystem in itself and their contribution to global warming is offset by the biodiversity associated with their presence.

The removal of hedgerows hasn't helped as it is where many insects live.

MAN'S DUTY TO KEEP THE BALANCE

Our environment is like an enormous jigsaw where everything needs to fit into place to be complete. It's only able to support a certain number of any one species; the balance is very easily upset by preserving some of the more iconic species and ignoring the mundane.

Open minds are needed to achieve a realistic perspective of what is actually happening in our countryside and what are the best ways of preserving it. Our primitive ancestors began to interfere when they started to farm, upsetting the balance of nature.

Chough are an endangered species which benefit from the presence of cattle to ensure their survival

Conservationists and bureaucrats need to have honest conversations with those who live and work in rural areas, and more to the point, they need to listen to them. It is the locals and farmers who experience on a daily basis the pressures there are on many species of wildlife, farm livestock and livelihoods. 'Aim to Sustain' is a recently formed formal partnership between a number of rural organisations whose intention is to promote the wide-ranging conservation, biodiversity and community benefits that are such a big part in our countryside. Hopefully they will be listened to.

Culling is a form of management. It does not mean wiping out a species, merely keeping its numbers under control as an aid to restoring the balance. It is a task that needs carrying out in an unbiased, realistic way.

Leaving the EU has meant that the UK will no longer be obliged to conform to Europe's Common Agricultural Policy (CAP). A new Environmental Land Management Scheme (ELMS) is being rolled out which will see farmers paid for the work they do that enhances the environment, thus benefiting the public, rather than paying farmers for the land they farm.

It is estimated that 12% of land needs to be actively managed to conserve nature as compensation for modern farming practices. Organic farms are estimated to be 50% richer in flora and fauna. By using parts of the farm that are unproductive, due to location or soil quality, and unmanageable corners in fields, new environmental payments can compare favourably with the decreased financial returns from cultivating these difficult areas.

LOW CARBON FOOTPRINT OF UPLAND GRAZERS

Over 80% of wet and hilly UK upland areas are permanent natural grasslands, which are virtually unspoilt and undisturbed, supporting a sustainable habitat on which cattle and sheep graze. Because of the way they are farmed the carbon footprint of these animals is amongst the lowest in the world for meat production.

GREEN RECOVERY CHALLENGE FUND

In September 2020, as part of the government's 10 point environmental plan, the Green Recovery Challenge Fund was launched. It is a key part and will enable environmental charities and their partners to restore nature and tackle climate change. The fund will not only safeguard 2,000 existing jobs but help create up to 3,000 new jobs for ecologists, surveyors, nature reserve staff and education. In the meantime England's largest nationwide initiative to restore nature has

UK GOVERNMENT CONSERVATION AND ENVIRONMENT BODIES

- **Natural Resources Wales, Scottish Natural Heritage** and in Northern Ireland, **the Department of Agriculture, Environment and Rural Affairs** fulfil similar roles to **Natural England (NE)** *see page 174.*
- There are several categories of nationally protected areas in the UK, many of which overlap each other. There are **National Parks, National Nature Reserves (NNRs)** and **Sites of Special Scientific Interest (SSSIs).**
- **Wildlife Trusts, RSPB and Woodland Trust**
- Other nationally protected areas are designated as:
  Area of Outstanding Natural Beauty (AONB), classified as **National Scenic Areas** in Scotland, which are areas given protection to conserve and enhance the natural beauty of the designated landscape. In England changes are being made to bring together AONBs and National Parks and rebrand them as 'one family of national landscapes'. In autumn 2020 it was announced tha the UK is set to get a number of new National Parks and Areas of Outstanding Natural Beauty (ANOBs) classified as National Scenic Areas.
- **Heritage Coast** is a length of coastline designated by the Countryside Agency in England and the Countryside Council for Wales in Wales, as having notable natural beauty or scientific significance. This includes parts of coastal areas of the South Downs, West Dorset, Flamborough Head, and Bempton Cliffs. Work in achieving the aims of Heritage Coasts is undertaken by the relevant local authorities with help from national and local stakeholders and local communities.
- **Unesco World Heritage Sites** These are defined as 'a natural or man-made site, area, or structure recognised as being of outstanding international importance'. There are 32 in the UK including the Jurassic Coast in the south of England and the Lake District which was designated in 2017.
- **Environmentally Sensitive Areas (ESAs)** – There are 22 ESAs in England, covering approximately 10% of agricultural land, which offer incentives to farmers to adopt agricultural practices which safeguard and enhance parts of the country particularly with regards to high landscape, wildlife and historic value. In 2005 the original ESAs were brought under the new Environmental Stewardship Scheme
- **Special Areas of Conservation (SACs)** are protected areas in the UK.
- **Special Protection Areas for Birds (SPAs)** are protected areas for birds in the UK.

been launched. Farmers and landowners are set to play a key part through the Nature Recovery Network (NRN) Delivery Partnership led by Natural England. A further source of funding for conservation comes from the National Lottery Heritage Fund.

THE COMPOSITION OF OUR COUNTRYSIDE

Nearly 3,000sq miles of Britain's meadows and grassland have been lost this century. On the other hand, global warming has instigated a surge in tree planting to combat carbon emissions.

In February 2020 the Woodland Trust called for one fifth of the UK to be planted with trees.

Over the last 75 years, the UK has lost 97 % of flower-rich meadows and 50% of hedgerows. A total of 60% of flowering plant species are in decline. Efforts are now being made to join conservation areas with 'corridors' to link them together so that wildlife can move freely from one to another instead of living in isolated pockets.

ANCIENT WOODLAND

Rothiemurchus, in the Cairngorms, is one of the largest surviving areas of ancient woodland in Europe.

Ancient woods are not just about trees but also the plants growing within them which in turn support numerous species of wildlife and insects. It is a fragile habitat. Half of the world's bluebells grow wild in old woodland in the UK but they are under threat from the expanding population of muntjac deer and through cross pollination with non-native Spanish bluebells.

The Caledonian Forest was formed at the end of the last Ice Age and covered much of Scotland. Now only a few fragments remain amounting to only about 1% of its original 1.5million hectares. It is a truly ancient woodland with a mix of naturally growing, self-seeded Scots pine, juniper, birch, willow, rowan and aspen. Imposing old Scots pine trees may be up to 700 years old. Some are bent and were not ideal to harvest; it's thought this characteristic was what spared them from the woodman's axe for so long.

There is a growing conflict of interests when conserving ancient woodland in Scotland. There is a burgeoning population of deer, now estimated to number about one million, a figure that is unsustainable. They naturally feed on new growth and in some places like the Caledonian Forest, the next generation of trees have been eaten by deer. To maintain the status of ancient woodlands it is essential that there is a continuing succession of young, self-seeded trees at different stages of growth. Protecting large areas of trees with fences excludes deer which deprives them of food increasing the very real risk of starvation.

Conservationists face a dilemma as some want to see woodland restored and planted to combat global warming but don't want to sanction the culling of deer. With no natural enemies it is man who has to decide on welfare issues which concern deer in Scotland. So great is the problem it is possible that legally enforceable deer culls may need to be introduced with landowners being allocated a set annual quota to cull.

▼ Bluebells are native to Western Europe with the UK their stronghold where they can be found growing in ancient woodlands

▲ Wild flowers growing naturally in the Western Isles of Scotland

Woodland provided almost everything our ancestors needed – food, medicines and fuel to keep warm or cook by, wood to make or build things. Wood was also burned to make charcoal which was used as a medicine, for smelting iron and in making gunpowder. Over the centuries many hillsides which were once wooded have become devoid of trees and shrubs because of the introduction of livestock. With today's new environmental payments for nature and fewer for agricultural production, work has already begun in restoring what was once the natural habitat. The Howgill Fells in Cumbria are a prime example. Large areas are being fenced to exclude deer and livestock and planted with native trees including hawthorn, rowan, willow and birch. This has already happened on Ravenstonedale Common where 462 acres (187ha) has been enclosed and scrub, hawthorn and tussocky grass is already appearing creating an attractive area of foraging and shelter for birds and small mammals.

Originally, the term 'forest' referred to a large area that included several different types of land forming the exclusive hunting preserve of the monarch, or noble. The New Forest in Hampshire is a prime example. Ancient woodland within these so-called 'forests' were frequently Royal Parks.

WILDFLOWER AND OLD MEADOWS

97% of our wildflower meadows have been lost since the 1930s, a loss of over 7 million acres (3 million hectares). Only 2,500 acres (1,000ha) remain in Britain.

In 2021 the government's Green Recovery Fund set out to create a further 1,250 acres (500 hectares) of meadows.

Old established meadows which have been grazed and left untouched for decades are of ecological importance. Besides locking in carbon, they host a plethora of plants, invertebrates and various organisms in the undisturbed soil.

Since the food shortages of WWII, six million acres of meadows were ploughed up to grow cereals. These species-rich grasslands are a source of medicinal plants and store carbon on a par with trees. Wildflower meadows can support up to 150 separate species and up to 40 plant species may be found in a square metre of chalk downland meadow. These plants can sustain 1,400 invertebrate species which provide food for birds.

Save Our Magnificent Meadows is the UK's largest conservation partnership project and across the country many of the wildflower meadows which have been restored can be visited. A National Meadow Day is held each year in July to highlight the work being carried out. Grazing with cattle plays an important part in wildflower meadow management although they are excluded from the meadows in spring and early summer. The grasses and flowers are left to grow until August allowing the seed to set before being mowed. The cut grass is turned and left to dry before being made into hay. This action causes the seeds to be shaken out and fall to the ground. Once there is enough regrowth, cattle are returned to graze in the meadow, trampling seeds into the ground which helps them to germinate. New wildflower meadows can be established by spreading hay from existing ones, which includes seeds, onto bare ground where the top sward has been removed.

On a much smaller scale, the gardening public are being encouraged to plant patches of wild flowers, and seed mixes can be readily purchased. Highways England is also looking to encourage species of some plants to grow by managing road verges in certain areas in a different way.

DOWNLAND

Chalk grassland is known as downland which consists of a thin layer of poor soil on top of chalk allowing many species of small flowers and plants to grow that are unique to this habitat and which, in turn, are host to several different species of butterfly. The UK has the largest area of downland in Europe, which is predominately found in southern England.

About 99% of natural downland has been destroyed in the last 100 years. Some areas managed to survive because of the poor soil fertility. Water is a sparse commodity on the downs and dew ponds were built which mysteriously retain a level of water naturally throughout the year.

If downland is left uncultivated, and not regularly grazed, it quickly reverts to scrub.

Traditionally flocks of hardy sheep close grazed the sward, such as Southdown,

Native flowers bloom where woodland has been freshly coppiced

Hampshire Down, Wiltshire and Dorset Down which were able to thrive in the habitat. Every day individual flocks were turned out onto the open, unfenced grassland under the watchful eyes of the shepherds employed by their owners. They would be brought down onto lower land at night.

Sheep nibble the sward very close to the ground and with careful management the remaining unique habitat is being preserved. Flocks of small, native Southdown sheep can once again be seen grazing on the South Downs but today electric fencing confines them to certain areas, instead of shepherds. The South Downs, extending from Eastbourne in East Sussex to Winchester in Hampshire, was designated as our latest a National Park in 2011.

The Wolds in Lincolnshire and Yorkshire are rolling chalk hills and valleys, similar to downland.

HEDGEROWS

Restoring hedges is very much part of 21st century conservation measures. A mix of species is planted including some that bear fruits which support wildlife in winter. Hawthorn is a popular choice as birds and small rodents feed on the haws as well as it being stockproof. Several different species of birds feed on berries found in hedgerows, the seeds and pips of which pass through them. These are widely distributed through their droppings.

Historians have a formula for calculating the age of a hedge. They count the number of tree and shrub species in a 30 metre length.

A single species hedge is likely to be less than a hundred years old while one containing ten to twelve may be up to 1,000 years old.

The greatest planting of hedges was during the land Enclosures of the 17th and 18th centuries when they were planted to keep people out and animals in. In upland areas dry stone walls were built for the same purpose.

Hedgelaying Although hedges are now cut by machinery, they were once all cut by hand. They were often '**laid**' to control their growth and make them stockproof and hedgelaying is a country skill still practised today. This is done in autumn or winter by partially cutting (**pleaching**) close to the base of each hedge plant, then bending the stems over without breaking them so they lay horizontally. Because the stem isn't completely severed, the plants will live and its the new growth next spring creates a thick, refreshed hedge. There are many different regional styles of hedgelaying.

Ancient hedges comprising of mixed species dotted with trees provide excellent wildlife habitat and create corridors along which species can move freely between different areas. As many as 600 species of plants, 1,500 insects, 65 birds and 20 mammals have been recorded in hedgerows.

WALLS

Where stone is plentiful especially in upland areas walls take the place of hedges. Some of them are hundreds of years old and there are an estimated 125,000 miles remaining, a feature notably in the Lake District and Yorkshire Dales. Walls afford shelter to animals that live out on the moors and fells and provide a unique habitat in which reptiles, birds, small mammals and toads find food, shelter and nest sites. In some circumstances walls can act as a firebreak.

WATER COURSES

A worrying amount of agricultural pollution leeches into our water courses. It comes from fertilisers, pesticides and effluent from various sources including the vegetable and salad processing industry. This waste water might be contaminated with traces of pesticides.

Other contaminants come from rubbish, industrial chemicals, sewage discharge, run-off from roads, and microplastics. In times of excessive rainfall, it is occasionally necessary for untreated sewage to be discharged into our rivers when sewage plants are unable to cope with the volume of water passing through them. Only one in seven English rivers meets a good ecological standard. Few rivers in the UK are 100% safe to swim in.

Pollutants can cause algae to bloom which deprives the water of life-giving oxygen and

THE RIVER THAMES

The river Thames is a prime conservation example. 70 years ago is was so polluted in its lower reaches it was declared biologically dead. Major improvements to sewage treatment works over time have worked wonders although it is still inadvisable to drink its water or swim in it. Nevertheless, 115 species of fish, including salmon and 350 types of invertebrates now thrive in its tidal waters stretching from its estuary mouth as far as Teddington Lock. Sadly though, some of the highest levels of microplastics for any river in the world are now being recorded in the Thames, undermining the hard work that has gone into reinstating water quality.

results in the deaths of many freshwater fish inhabiting our streams and rivers. All UK rivers, lakes and streams ('becks' in the north of England and 'burns' in Scotland) suffer from some degree of pollution. Good work has been done in improving some of our rivers.

Canals in the late 1700s and early 1800s were the transport arteries of Britain but in the 19th century railways ousted their popularity and for a century canals were neglected. Now, because of restoration work, they are becoming

increasingly popular as holiday destinations; and tranquil places where nature can find refuge.

 Since 2012, canals in England and Wales have been managed by the Canal and River Trust, a charitable organisation which looks after 2,000 miles of waterways, nearly 3,000 bridges, more than 1,500 locks and 335 aqueducts. The government-owned Scottish Canals are responsible for those in Scotland.

CHALKSTREAMS

There are only 200 chalkstreams globally, 85% of which are in England. The remainder are in northern France. As their name implies they are confined to areas of chalk extending southwards from the Yorkshire Wolds.

The word 'chalkstream' also applies to winterbournes, small waterways which are normally dry throughout the summer months. Chalk is a highly porous, permeable rock and rain falling onto ground where there is chalk percolates directly through, where it acts as an aquifer. The groundwater takes months to flow through the chalk bedrock, before re-emerging lower down the slope as springs. Chalkstreams are usually wide and shallow with crystal clear water of a consistent temperature flowing over a gravel bed, the clarity and purity due to the chalk's filtering effect. Chalkstreams are full of freshwater invertebrates, are noted for flyfishing and Hampshire's chalkstreams also afford the perfect conditions in which to grow watercress on a commercial scale.

HEATHER MOORLAND

Moorland landscape was ratified as globally important at the 1992 Rio Convention on Biodiversity. However, the best way of managing it is an extremely contentious issue.

About 70% of the world's upland heather moorland is in the UK.

Heather moorland is one of the most rare habitats in the world, even more rare than rainforests.

> *Heather moorland soil is predominately peat which locks up vast quantities of carbon.*

There are also areas of lowland heather moorland which are found on light, sandy soils. The management by landowners for driven grouse shooting is probably the reason the UK has retained so much of its ling heather moorland. Managed grouse moors support 33 different species of birds, some of them endangered, compared with only 15 species on unmanaged moors. The breeding success of hen harriers is very dependent on them finding sufficient prey on which to feed their chicks, and grouse feature as part of their diet.

Forty per cent of heather habitat has been lost since the Second World War. Many moorlands are close to industrial areas or where coal was once mined and fumes from factories nearby slowly killed the vegetation. Big improvements have been made regarding air pollution and one of the biggest threats now comes from extended periods of drought. Not only is the fire risk greater but the heather suffers when moors become parched.

Damage from the heather beetle is also blamed for the decline. When heather is seriously stressed it is unlikely to flower and therefore not reproduce by setting seed. In recent decades thousands of acres of heather moorland have been planted with trees. The trees dry out the peat beneath which can release more greenhouse gases than the trees absorb.

Grouse and heather moors

Red grouse diet consists predominantly of the shoots, seeds and flowers of heather. Many estates in Scotland and Northern England have a world-wide reputation for the high quality traditional grouse shooting they offer. Gamekeepers are employed to manage the moorland which they do to benefit the grouse. Several other species of birds in rapid decline which nest on heather

The River Test ia a pristine chalkstream renowned for its trout fishing

moorlands, including curlew, oyster catchers, golden plover, lapwing, hen harriers, merlin and short-eared owls, also benefit from the way in which gamekeepers manage the heather.

In north-east Scotland, mountain hare numbers are 35 times higher on driven grouse moors compared to unmanaged areas and this obvious trend is reflected elsewhere.

The mix of heather habitat created by managed burning not only provides birds with nutritious food through new growth, and abundant insect life for freshly hatched chicks to feed on, but also protective cover for ground-nesting birds to safely nest in. Managed moors have only limited public access, unlike unmanaged moors where disturbance is much greater. If ground nesting birds are put off their nest when they are sitting on eggs by either a dog or human intervention, they are very unlikely to return to it. Because of loss of habitat, red grouse are on the amber list of British birds, meaning the population is classified as vulnerable. Where they are thriving most is on moors managed by gamekeepers. If it

▲ Heather moorland is one of the world's rarest habitats 70% of which is found in the UK's uplands

wasn't for this, they may well have been put on the endangered red list!

In the 1960s and 1970s it was government policy to drain moorland in order to improve sheep grazing. Grouse moor managers and other moorland landowners are now attempting to right this wrong. They are re-creating areas of wet moorland by blocking the drains which were put in. It is estimated that around 45,000 acres (18,000ha) of moorland habitat on grouse moors has already been restored in this way across northern England. This work is also helping in some small way to combat flooding at lower levels.

Heather burning

The way in which heather moorland should be managed is a contentious issue, as it involves burning. There are four key requirements that are essential for any ground-nesting birds to be successful – habitat, food, being undisturbed and predator control. Grouse moors are managed to provide all these. This includes controlled, rotational burning (known as **muirburn** in

Scotland) which has been practised continuously for nearly 200 years. This involves a quick burn over small areas to clear the surface vegetation. Only small patches of heather are burned in a ten-year rotation to create a mosaic of heather in different stages of growth which, in turn, creates nutritious food and nesting cover. It provides fresh growth for sheep grazed in the uplands to feed on and acts as a firebreak reducing the amount of combustible material on the moors. Heather left to its own devices becomes old, coarse, woody and unpalatable to both grouse and sheep.

However, many conservation bodies strongly disagree with heather moorlands being burned, although without this form of management, in time, the heather grows thick obliterating all other plant life and eventually dies.

Scientists at the University of Leeds are of the opinion that burning grouse moors degrades peatland habitat, releases climate-altering gases, reduces biodiversity and increases flood risk. But without controlled burning, moors are subject to large wildfires, and following an outbreak of heather beetle, burning the affected heather, helps in the restoration of damaged moorland. Blood-sucking ticks are another problem on moorland which regular burning helps to control.

For 5,000 years fire has played a part in land management in the UK. Our ancestors knew that edible regrowth would quickly follow the burning of old rank heather and grasses and

Curlew are an endangered species which nest on moorland

used it as a tool to improve grazing for their animals. Moorland burning can be traced back many centuries. It originated in heathland areas of southern Britain and was later used in the eighteenth century when land in Scotland began to be managed for farming sheep on a large scale.

Controlled burning in upland areas today can only be carried out under licence between 1 October and 15 April by qualified operators. Burning is completed before any birds begin nesting and the fire passes over the ground quickly so the peat beneath never becomes hot. New heather shoots soon emerge. In January 2021 the government announced a ban on burning habitats where peat is more than 40 centimetres deep on specific sites unless a special licence has been granted. Several large land owners have completely banned their tenants from burning heather for any reason.

In the West Country, grazing is part of the way the moors are managed. There needs to be a balance between sufficient grazing and overgrazing to maintain the natural habitat.

On Exmoor, Dartmoor and Bodmin Moor, farmers carry out '**swaling**', the local name for controlled burning. In areas where this has not been done, gorse, bracken and scrub has become rampant, dominating the natural grasses and

◀ **Golden Plover are one of the species that benefit greatly from grouse moor management**

Wildfires as opposed to controlled burning on heather moorland cause irreparable damage

heather which provide food for cattle, sheep or ponies. As the gorse, bracken and scrub encroach further onto the moor so grazing is reduced creating an overstocking situation. But reducing the number of animals grazing on the moor allows the growth of gorse, bracken and scrub to spread, further reducing the area of grasses and heather.

WILDFIRES

Extreme weather is increasing the risk of out-of-control wildfires which in the UK destroy vast expanses of moorland at the expense of the flora and fauna.

Vast areas of old rank heather or grass without firebreaks, which become parched in hot weather, are always going to be at high risk. Wildfire consumes not only the surface vegetation but can also infiltrate the peat beneath, whereupon it is nearly impossible to extinguish and can smoulder for days. Once this happens, carbon dioxide is released back into the atmosphere and the peat is completely destroyed. Recent wild fires have decimated large expanses of protected areas which are of very significant ecological importance. The heather does not regenerate, the peaty ground beneath is permanently damaged and being exposed makes it liable to erosion and the further release of carbon dioxide.

DESTRUCTION ON MOORLAND WITHOUT CONTROLLED BURNING

Hot weather in the summers of 2018, 2019 and spring 2020 led to numerous wild fires decimating hundreds of square miles of moorland. 137 large wild fires were recorded in 2020 alone. A severe fire on Saddleworth Moor in 2018 spread over seven square miles (18sq km) and raged for three weeks and again in spring 2019. Whole populations of rare animals were wiped out when 1,730 acres (700 ha) of peatland habitat on Marsden Moor in West Yorkshire burned. Another blaze in April 2019 took fire crews four days to put out and a further one in April 2021 decimated another part of the moor. April and May 2020 were unseasonably warm and very dry with disastrous fires which came at a time when many moorland birds were nesting. A large area in Derbyshire's Peak District measuring about four square miles burned for five days.

This rate of destruction cannot be allowed to continue. As a defence against wild fires, rangers and volunteers have planted tens of thousands of sphagnum moss plugs, built leaky dams to retain water on the moor, and cut vegetation breaks near car parks and alongside roads in an attempt to prevent fires from spreading. Burning small areas in rotation, as is practised as part of responsible grouse moor management, also creates firebreaks limiting the extent to which a fire can travel. Walls too, help stop the progress of a wildfire.

LOWLAND HEATHLAND is one of the UK's rarest habitats and less than 20% remains of that in existence 200 years ago. Lowland heathland is found in areas of sandy, impoverished soils below 300m. It once covered much of the southern half of England but has now become fragmented and, without traditional management methods, the natural grasses and heather have been invaded by scrub and trees.

Lowland heath is home to many rare plants and declining animal species such as adders and lizards.

Breckland is a large and unique area of sandy soil extending from parts of Norfolk into north Suffolk. It was once all lowland heath but much of it was planted with conifers after the First World War and other parts later ploughed to grow crops. Sections remain however, which have been maintained as nature reserves and are carefully managed. A survey carried out in 2010 in Breckland's diverse mix of forest, heath and farmland recorded 12,843 species, many of which are found nowhere else in the UK.

PEATLANDS
Peat is an accumulation of partially decayed vegetation, the majority of which is sphagnum moss, which took thousands of years to form.

There are three types of peatlands in the UK
- blanket bog in the uplands
- raised bog in lowland areas
- Fens in wetland localities. Combined, they cover around 7.5 million acres (3million ha) and 22% of the total area remains in a near-natural condition. Peatland has become one of the UK's most threatened habitats. During and after the Second World War, drainage ditches were cut in areas of peatland to create additional grazing land. Funding has now been made available to repair and restore this unique habitat although for many years numerous estates were already

Digging peat has become a contentious subject but it is still dug for fuel by some residents on the Western Isles of Scotland

reinstating thousands of acres of blanket bogs. Launched in spring 2021 the Nature for Climate Peatland Grant Scheme (NCPGS) is a new competitive government grant scheme. It will pay 75-85% of the total costs of peatland restoration projects in both lowland and upland England and will run until 2025.

The Moorland Association look after around 500,000 acres (200,000 hectares) of deep peat and a recent survey of members suggests they have already restored 7,800 acres (3,157 hectares) of bare peat on their land in the last 10 years.

Peat can reach up to 10 metres deep and has developed slowly over hundreds of years. A peat bed of this depth has probably taken 1,000 years to form. It takes 10 years for 1cm of peat to form.

70% of our water comes from upland areas. Where peat is half a metre or more in depth, it is classified as a **blanket bog**, also known as **blanket mires** or **featherbed bogs**. They have poor drainage and water forms in many pools on the surface. They act like giant sponges slowly soaking up rainwater which then trickles through the peat soils and is gradually released into streams and rivers. In the UK, blanket peat bogs can be found extensively in the wettest parts of the north and west. They are recognised as

▲ Peat bogs play a huge part in combatting climate change

being the largest and most efficient carbon store on earth, locking away ten times more carbon per hectare than any other type of ecosystem.

The UK has 13% of the world's blanket bogs.

Restoring and maintaining blanket bogs will help reach targets for reducing carbon emissions as well as protecting habitat and biodiversity. The largest blanket bog area in the world is in the Flow Country in the north of Scotland which stretches across Caithness and Sutherland and covers about 1,500sq miles (4,000sq km).

Researchers have found that one of the best ways to increase sphagnum moss, from which peat is formed and which increases the bogs' resistance to drought, is through occasional burning. Ecological research has shown the density of mosses were found to be up to five times higher on areas burnt between three and 10 years earlier, but very low in areas left unburnt or unmanaged for 17 years or more. Protection is given to blanket bog habitats. Regulations prevent the burning of specified vegetation on areas of peat more than 16 inches (40cm) in depth, on a site of special scientific interest that is also a special area of conservation or a special protection area. Controlled burning of surface vegetation by experienced people does not harm underlying peat as it only removes the top growth.

Peat bogs, which are undulating areas of spongy hummocks built up from sphagnum mosses, play a hugely important part in the fight against global warming. They cover only 3% of the earth's surface but store 20% of soil carbon and act as water filters.

Peat, if disturbed in any way, whether by peat digging, tree planting, road building or wind turbine construction releases locked-in carbon into the atmosphere. In the middle of the twentieth century, Scotland decided, somewhat unsuccessfully, to transform peat bogs into forests. Strict UK Forestry Standards now prohibit tree planting on deep peat.

Uses of Peat

Peat was once cut mainly by crofters in remote areas as fuel for their fires, and many crofters still have rights to cut peat attached to their property. For decades peat has been used as partial fuel in some Irish power stations although this is now being phased out and the sites reinstated as bogs.

Whisky distilleries, of which there are 130 in Scotland, will continue to need to use peat fires in the process of malting barley, which is what gives whisky its flavour.

Peat was once only cut on a small scale by hand but huge machines are now used to cut and package it. These machines are able to slice away in minutes what has taken centuries to form and completely destroy the site in the process, which is of great concern to conservationists.

Peat-based garden compost is still sold but a wide variety of peat-free composts are available

▶ Centuries ago large areas of agricultural land were reclaimed from low-lying fenland of which only small pockets remain

today made from recycled green waste, wood fibre and even a mix of wool and bracken. Wood chips, which would be suitable substitutes, are in high demand as fuel for biomass power stations. Coir is a peat-like substance which is a by-product of the coconut industry. It is sometimes used as a substitute but has a high carbon footprint.

WETLANDS

The Fens are an area of low-lying land in eastern England which were drained in the 17th century by engineer Cornelius Vermuyden to become fertile agricultural land. 'Washes' are tidal mud flats or water meadows which serve as temporary storage for excess fresh water, and can alleviate flooding.

Established wetlands are safeguarded and new ones created to provide a habitat for marsh-loving plants and birds. National Nature Reserve Wicken Fen in Cambridgeshire is the oldest wetland reserve in England and one of Europe's most important wetland sites. It extends to 630 acres (255 hectares) and supports over 8,500 species including an impressive collection of plants, birds and dragonflies. Wicken Fen comprises an area of original fenland that has never been drained. Reed beds, besides being important habitats, also naturally filter water.

Around the coast, salt marshes are being lost to rising sea levels and development. To compensate, farmland is being relinquished to the creation of new salt marsh habitats, allowing the sea to encroach in a controlled way, which may also reduce flooding risks elsewhere.

Grazing by cattle in summer plays an important part in conservation management of wetlands. Their grazing improves the habitat, their droppings attract insects and the divots their feet make in the soft ground harbour invertebrates.

LAKES AND PONDS

A lake is a static or very slow moving body of fresh water more than 5 acres (2 ha) surrounded by land, apart from where rivers enter or exit it. It becomes a pond if it is smaller in size, does not have moving water and is seldom more than 6ft (1.8m) deep. Some naturally-formed ponds are filled by underwater springs or rainwater; some of these are known as 'dewponds'.

There are about 10,000 lakes in Britain. The biggest natural lakes are found in the Lake District and the Scottish Highlands.

It is estimated that one million ponds have been lost in the countryside since 1940. There was once a pond on every farm and in nearly every village. There are said to be in the region of 22,000 in Suffolk alone, more than anywhere else in Britain. Ponds play an important role in the ecosystem and are home to many creatures – sticklebacks, toads, frogs, newts and dragonfly larvae to name but a few.

In the English Lake District there are 16 large lakes although only Bassenthwaite is named as a lake. The others are known as 'meres' or 'waters'. Technically, meres are relatively shallow in relation to their size, waters are deeper. In the Lake District, Windermere is the largest lake in England; and Wastwater at a depth of 259 feet (79 m) the deepest. There are also 'tarns' in the Lake District, created during the Ice Age where crevices in the tops of the fells later filled with water. In total there are about 200 tarns, and one of the most visited is Tarn Hows owned by the National Trust.

Wasdale, Cumbria is the deepest lake in England

Rewilding underway with the help of Tamworth pigs and Bagot goats

Meres are also found in the Breckland region in the east of England but they are much smaller bodies of water, and are curious features because they lie in depressions formed in the Ice Age topsoil and are fed by water from the underlying chalk aquifer, which has natural fluctuations in groundwater levels. Breckland Meres are often dry in winter, not summer, because rainfall from the previous winter takes months to permeate. There are also '**Broads**' in east Norfolk and north Suffolk, which are a network of mostly navigable rivers and lakes formed by the flooding of centuries-old peat workings. A very popular holiday destination, they are also a conservation area with a level of protection similar to a national park.

In Scotland lakes are called lochs. This also applies to sea lochs which are connected to the sea and are tidal, similar to fjords in Norway. Of the freshwater lochs, Loch Lomond is the biggest, Loch Awe the longest at more than 25 miles (41km) and Loch Ness the deepest with a depth of 788 feet (240 metres). Loch Ness has the largest volume of fresh water in Great Britain.

Many smaller lochs, known as lochans, have formed in peaty areas and are found mainly in the western and northern Highlands.

In Northern Ireland lochs are spelled loughs but pronounced the same. Lough Neagh in Northern Ireland is the UK's largest lake. In Wales a lake is called Llyn.

RESERVOIRS

Some lakes have been artificially created as reservoirs by damming rivers or raising the level of existing lakes, in order to supply water to large towns and cities many miles away.

Rutland Water in Rutland is the largest reservoir by surface area in England, although Kielder Water is the largest by capacity. In Powys the river Vyrnwy was dammed c1888 to create Lake Vyrnwy (Llyn Efyrnwy) reservoir and was the first large masonry dam to be built in the UK. Many reservoirs are also a source of green energy using hydro power and are surrounded by conservation areas.

REWILDING

Rewilding is the large-scale restoration of ecosystems in which nature can take care of itself. As part of some rewilding policies, grazing animals such as cattle and pigs are allowed to roam the site with a 'hands-off' approach, allowing them to live naturally. Where appropriate, missing species might be re-introduced and allowed to naturally shape the landscape and the habitats within, but this is hugely controversial.

The rewilding dilemma Abandoning or restoring land to its once-natural state will change what exists today. The UK has magnificent countryside and spectacular landscapes, some little changed since the 1700s. Farming and forestry is now carried out on an industrial scale. There are no longer sufficient wild expanses to reintroduce animals such as lynx and wolves. The reason they died out in the first place was because they came into conflict with the human population. Then it was only 5.5 million but now the population of Britain is approaching 68 million. The pressure placed on the countryside is huge.

How much impact rewilding will have on existing wildlife depends on how far the land has become distanced from being natural.

Rewilding will upset the existing equilibrium which has evolved over the centuries. What happens when it gets out of control? Beavers are already proving a problem in some places. Many species of plants and wildlife which thrive only in specific environments will be displaced. Some benefit from the cultivation of land or when it is heavily grazed. Uncontrolled dense cover will reduce the sunlight which many plants require. While rewilding will be of benefit to some species, it will deprive many plants, animals, birds and insects of the ecosystem that they have made their home and which they need to survive.

NATIVE WILDLIFE AT RISK

Indigenous species are those which have evolved through natural processes to become part of an ecosystem.

Native birds Many of our bird species are in serious decline, especially during the last 50 years. Conservation measures are in place to remedy some of the causes, but many species are migratory birds visiting the UK either in summer or winter. What happens to the birds when they are elsewhere? While 'abroad' they may perish in adverse weather conditions, their habitat may have been destroyed, and many species have to run the gauntlet of hunters in countries where they are not protected. Satellite tagging of some species of the larger migratory birds, such as woodcock and cuckoos, provides scientists with regular information but it is not possible to fit them on very small birds.

Many species of our farmland birds are decreasing, probably through a lack of food. Modern efficient but sterile farming methods destroy insects and invertebrates and leave fewer weeds and seeds which formerly sustained farmland birds. Woodland birds also suffer from the trend for tidiness when dying and fallen trees are removed, depriving many species of a valuable source of food as well as nesting sites for some. Many insect species including beetles and their larvae live in dead wood, providing food for several species of birds.

Native mammals According to scientists, a quarter of Britain's native mammals are at imminent risk of extinction. Birds of prey however are on the increase; part of the diet of buzzards and red kites includes carrion but this is scarce in upland areas, as recent laws now require dead livestock to be removed and disposed of. All birds of prey catch live prey which may impact on some mammal and bird species already in decline such as brown hares. Hungry raptors do not discriminate between common or rare species.

Nature conservation requires a very delicate balance and some organisations have been focusing on raptors, predator protection and rewilding rather than taking into account the long-term effect their policies might have.

BIRDS

Black Grouse

Grey Partridge – *see page 234*

Black Grouse – *see page 238*

Capercaillie are large, turkey-sized members of the grouse family which live only in mature pine woodlands in Scotland. They became extinct in the 18th century and were re-introduced in 1837 from Sweden. It is thought there may only be 1,000 remaining, 80% of them in the Cairngorms National Park. In 2001 capercaillie were placed under special protection. Loss of habitat, deaths as a result of flying into high, deer-proof fences erected around forestry plantations, wet weather in summer when the chicks are hatching, increased human disturbance and a growing number of predators both in the air and on the ground are all contributing factors. The resurgence of pine martens poses a particular threat.

Barn owls are the white ghosts of the countryside, mostly seen at dawn and dusk, also during daylight hours as they hunt for mice and voles in grassy places. Their numbers naturally fluctuate but in the last few decades, farming practices, removal of hedges and permanent grassland as well as lack of nesting sites have resulted in dwindling numbers. Conservationists have been making special nesting boxes, often triangular in shape, to compensate for the loss of old buildings and trees. Around 75% now nest in boxes and the population has trebled in the last 30 years.

Barn Owl

Hen Harriers, large predatory birds, have come into conflict with farmers and gamekeepers in the past but are now fully protected and conservationists have been working to get them re-established in the open areas they once inhabited. 2020 saw the best results for breeding success in England for the last 100 years with 60 chicks fledged, the majority of which were on managed grouse moors in the north of England. Hen harriers are particularly vulnerable as they nest on the ground and it is on grouse moors where they benefit from habitat management, predator control and availability of food.

Red Kites were once very common but became extinct in England and Scotland during the 19th century; only a very small number survived in central Wales. By the early 1930s there were only two breeding pairs remaining. Legal protection and careful conservation measures gradually brought red kite numbers to 50 in 1988, all still in mid-Wales. As part of a reintroduction programme, in July 1990 13 young birds were brought over from Spain and released in the Chiltern Hills. These measures proved to be an outstanding success and there are now about 1,800 breeding pairs of Red Kites and rising.

Red Kite

Ospreys are migratory birds of prey which winter 3,000 miles away in sub Saharan Africa. As breeding birds they became extinct in England in 1840 and in Scotland in 1916. In 1954 ospreys naturally recolonised in Scotland and since then, numbers have slowly increased. In 2001 a pair nested successfully in Cumbria and others have spread into Kielder Forest and Wales. Ospreys were trans-located to Rutland Water in the east of England in 1996 and since 2001 have regularly returned to breed there.

Osprey

Nightingales arrive in the UK in late spring from Senegal and Gambia. The UK population has fallen by more than 90% over the last 50 years. Changes in the countries where they over-winter

may be a factor but it is changes here in England that are probably affecting them most. Loss of breeding habitat is thought to be the principal cause. Nightingales set up breeding territories in the southern half of England in dense areas of shrubs which are becoming much harder to find. The encroachment of housing developments and a passion for tidiness reduces these often untidy-looking areas. Farming and woodland management play a part but some conservation measures have involved removing thickets in which nightingales might have nested. Another major cause is the explosion in the population of deer, in particular muntjac, whose browsing is devastating the woodland undergrowth.

Nightingale

Willow Tits

Willow tits feed mainly on insects and inhabit young woodland and damp areas of scrub, and are the most endangered species of our resident birds. Their numbers have dropped by 94% since the 1970s and they have become extinct in many parts of southern England, mostly due to loss of habitat. Their requirements are quite specific.

Willow Tits inhabit neglected areas and need standing decaying trees in which to nest.

Remedial conservation programmes in many places have 'accidentally' done away with these.

Turtle Doves come to breed in the UK from sub Saharan Africa. Their numbers have declined by 93% since the 1970s due to excessive hunting in Europe, disease and habitat loss on wintering and breeding grounds. In 2021 the Italian government approved a quota of 15 turtle doves per licensed hunter between 1-21 September. With half a million licensed hunters in Italy this could equate to the killing of 7.5 million birds.

Turtle doves thrive only on seeds not cereal grains so are ill suited to surviving modern UK farming practices. The new ELM Scheme is already funding conservation projects for land owners in East Anglia to provide feeding plots and other habitat improvements specifically for the benefit of turtle doves, which are in danger of global extinction.

Lapwing numbers have decreased by 80% since 1960 because of habitat loss through land drainage, predation, human disturbance, and the use of large, fast machinery which renders the operator oblivious to nests.

Lapwing

Curlew Numbers have been declining for the last 50 years, have halved in the past 20 and they have disappeared from many sites. Farming practices, predators and loss of habitat are to blame. It would be truly lamentable if the evocative, liquid call of the curlew as it flies over its territory, particularly familiar to those who live, work and walk in the hills, could no longer be heard.

MAMMALS

Red Squirrels were once widespread across Britain but have disappeared from most areas. The introduction of grey squirrels from America, which are larger, more dominant and carry squirrel pox which doesn't affect them but which kills our native red squirrels, has caused a decline. There are an estimated 250,000 red squirrels in Britain, compared to 2.7 million greys. The increasing number of pine martens might prove detrimental to red squirrel conservation.

Red Squirrel

Hedgehogs numbers have fallen dramatically in the last 60 years, from 30 million to one and a half million. They face becoming an endangered species in the UK. Most of their diet consists of invertebrates such as beetles, worms and slugs although they will take eggs and chicks during the nesting season.

The large-scale use of pesticides has greatly reduced the food available to them and the destruction of hedgerows is also a contributory factor although in the last decade many hedges have been reinstated and new ones planted. Luckily hedgehogs have taken quite happily to living in people's gardens. While rural populations may be falling, urban populations are probably rising.

At least 100,000 hedgehogs are killed every year on roads. Badgers, whose numbers have surged in recent years, are the only hedgehog predators and they are having an impact on their population.

Water Voles are another native species under serious threat of extinction, disappearing from nearly 95% of their former sites. Probably the most damaging to them has been predation by American mink which have invaded the rivers, streams and lakes that water voles call home. Re-introductions are being made through captive breeding programmes where the habitat is suitable and efforts are being made to remove the mink.

Dormice are endearing little animals found in the UK which are under threat. They live in the shrubby understorey of woodland and hedgerows and loss of habitat has resulted in the sharp decline in numbers.

Dormouse

More than a thousand captive-bred dormice have now been released into the wild in an effort to boost the population.

Mountain Hares, also known as Blue hares, are native to the uplands of Scotland, thriving best on moors managed for driven grouse shooting where conditions suit them best. Following concern over their falling numbers elsewhere, the Scottish government introduced new legislation in March 2021 banning the unlicensed killing of mountain hares. There are plans to re-introduce them to some areas where they have been lost.

Mountain hares only thrive in cold conditions and died out 6,000 years ago in England and Wales when the climate got warmer. In 1870 some were reintroduced but the only ones to survive were in the Peak District of Derbyshire, where there is now estimated to be a population of about 2,500. Global warming might result in them once again becoming extinct in England.

Scottish Wildcat Once widespread across the Highlands of Scotland, their last stronghold is in the Cairngorms, where it is thought that only 300 remain. Very few wild cats are genetically pure, as feral domestic cats have interbred with them. There are plans to create a conservation breeding centre at the Highland Wildlife Park

Scottish Wildcat

near Aviemore to ensure that the true Scottish Wildcat is preserved as a species and a release programme embarked upon.

Pine Marten are creatures of the forests and were once widespread throughout Britain.

Predators the size of a domestic cat, they were widely persecuted. Deforestation destroyed their habitat until they became one of the rarest mammals in Britain and almost extinct in England and Wales. Conservationists in Scotland are monitoring and working to encourage the re-colonisation of pine marten through enhancing suitable habitat by installing artificial den boxes as resting and breeding sites.

Pine Marten

51 were moved from Scotland to mid-Wales in 2015: and in 2019, a further 18 were moved to the Forest of Dean. The result of these relocations is proving successful and the Scottish population is spreading. To avoid extinction, reintroductions are being made elsewhere in Wales and England.

Pine marten are omnivorous and take eggs as well as small mammals and birds. There is concern that introducing pine martens may have an impact on populations of other species of animals and birds, such as capercaillie, which are themselves seriously under threat.

Long-eared bat

Bats Eighteen species live in the UK, seventeen of which breed here but in many areas, certain species of bats have all but disappeared. Remarkably 13 different species can be found on Ebernoe Common National Nature Reserve in West Sussex. Daubenton's Bat hunts over water.

All 18 species of bats are protected by UK law.

They need to live in sites where they can feed, roost and breed. The decrease in insect numbers has made it harder for them to find sufficient food and as old buildings are demolished or converted into houses and ancient trees are felled, there are fewer places for them to roost and rear their young. Colonies are becoming isolated although efforts are being made to link them up.

Bats are afforded special protection. As they occupy old buildings such as barns, churches and the roofs of old houses, it is an offence to disturb a colony. The relevant government agency needs to be contacted before any work or other form of disturbance commences.

Otters In 1978 otters in Britain became protected as they were on the verge of extinction. The drastic decline was caused by pesticides polluting rivers and streams and contaminating the fish and in particular the eels they ate. However, breeding programmes, subsequent releases into the wild plus conservation measures including reducing pollution were so successful that otters have made a comeback and are now a serious threat to fish stocks in certain areas.

Otter

INSECTS

Butterflies There are 57 resident species of butterfly in the Britain plus two who are regular visitors here from Africa – the Clouded Yellow and the Painted Lady. Every ten years or so vast numbers of the latter appear across the length and breadth of Britain, most recently in 2019. Painted Ladies fly 4,000km from Africa using the sun to navigate normally arriving in May or June, but are very much at the mercy of prevailing weather conditions.

Butterfly Conservation is a British charity devoted to saving butterflies, moths and their habitats throughout the UK. It currently has 30 nature reserves scattered across the UK where it monitors and records species as well as running an education programme.

Butterflies also benefit from agri-environmental schemes, increases in woodland cover and grazing levels, and a slowing in the rate of agricultural intensification. The caterpillars of most species only feed on very specific plants so the butterflies need to seek these out to lay their eggs on.

Most species of more common butterflies hibernate in our gardens or the countryside, some spending the winter as eggs, others as small caterpillars among long grass and leaves, and others as chrysalises. Five species hibernate as adult butterflies: the brimstone, comma, peacock, small tortoiseshell and red admiral, tucked away in dark, cool buildings in ivy or even in our houses. Habitat management can have an impact on the survival rate of many of the species.

Painted Lady butterfly

Moths Britain is home to 2,500 species of moths. The majority fly at night although there are a number that are active during the daytime. They play an important part in pollinating plants and are prey for bats and little owls. The larvae of five of the species eat fabric made from natural fibres.

Honey bees laden with pollen

Bees There are 270 species of bees in the UK, including 24 species of bumblebees but only one honey bee. The vast majority are solitary bees which do not live in a colony. Bees play a very important role as crop pollinators but a third of the population has been lost in the last ten years.

There are about 20,000 amateur beekeepers around the country.

Urban bee keeping has become so popular recently that these honey bees are threatening bumblebees, mining and mason bees, in towns and cities because there is insufficient nectar and pollen to support them all.

Honey bees living in colonies are susceptible to disease, one of which is the virus Chronic Bee Paralysis which prevents the bees from flying. It has spread across the country. However, most bee losses occur due to predation from marauding mites, beetles and spiders. Varroa mites infest hives and suck the bodily fluids from bees. Animals and birds also raid colonies, notably mice and greater spotted woodpeckers. Asian Hornets, a relative newcomer, and Bee Wolves, a kind of wasp, can devastate colonies.

The Asian Hornet is now considered to be the biggest imminent threat facing beekeepers in the UK today.

Bees try to fight them off but the wasps and hornets are bigger and more powerful. They steal honey and kill and eat or carry off the bees themselves and their larvae.

AQUATIC CREATURES
Stocks of naturally occurring freshwater fish in lakes and rivers are causing concern, particularly wild Atlantic salmon. Conservationists are working to counteract issues caused by water levels, pollution, and other contributing factors. Some species of fish need underwater vegetation in which to spawn while others need gravel beds and conservation measures include re-instating these. Fish and eels also need easy access to the spawning grounds and in many places fish passes and ladders have been installed so they are able to move freely up rivers.

Non-native salmon which have escaped from fish farms are worrying conservationists as they have been recorded in some rivers in which our native salmon, already at risk, live. The fear is they will interbreed.

Fish Ladder and eel pass

Crayfish There are seven species of wild crayfish in our rivers and streams but only one, the endangered White-clawed crayfish, is native to Britain. Of the six alien species, the one causing most concern is the American Signal Crayfish which escaped into UK waters in the 1970s – *see page 211.* There has been a decline of 70% in the last 50 years of our White-clawed crayfish and conservationists are attempting to preserve the existing population and to restock rivers and streams by moving some to locations where they will not be at risk.

Mussels The UK is home to six native freshwater species of mussels. One of these is the critically endangered **freshwater pearl mussel**. Ongoing neglect of our rivers and pollution have resulted in poor water quality and increased sediment in which the young mussels aren't able to survive. Given ideal conditions can live for over a hundred years.

Although freshwater pearl mussels can be found on a few rivers throughout the UK, the only viable populations are in Cumbria and Scotland and these are also under threat.

A dark, moonless night in autumn, coinciding with a period of heavy rain and high river levels, is often the trigger for eel migration.

Eels are the most mysterious of all our British wildlife and, although once common, numbers are in such sharp decline that they are now on the critically endangered list. Even though eels spend most of their lives in freshwater, adults migrate to the Sargasso Sea, 3,000 miles (5,000km) away, in order to spawn. The resultant larvae slowly drift back towards the UK during which time they metamorphose into tiny, transparent **'glass eels'**. On entering brackish or freshwater they develop into **'elvers'** which have the appearance of miniature eels, before making their way upstream

where they will spend the next 5-20 years. After this time as adults they return to the Sargasso Sea to spawn and then they die.

There are several reasons for the steep decline in numbers which conservationists are endeavoring to minimise. Man-made weirs, dams and hydro-electric schemes form barriers obstructing their free passage up rivers and streams. Where possible, eel ladders or passes are being put in place. It's proved impossible to breed eels successfully in captivity so they need all the help they can get to survive in the wild.

REPTILES
There are three species of snakes native to Britain but none in Northern Ireland.

All reptiles found in the UK hibernate in winter.

Grass Snake is our largest reptile and can grow to 4ft (1.3m) in length. It is not venomous and doesn't bite although it will defend itself by emitting a nasty smelling liquid. It chooses to inhabit damp areas and can often be seen swimming. Grass snakes reproduce by laying eggs in a pile of rotting vegetation, frequently a compost heap, where conditions are warm enough for them to incubate and hatch.

Adder, being venomous, has a fearsome reputation but, although a bite can be painful, its poison is generally of little danger to humans; fatalities are exceptionally rare. Dogs, however, are more at risk.

If given the opportunity when it is disturbed, an adder will always choose to slither away quietly rather than attack.

They are widely, but patchily, distributed across Britain and prefer heathland or dry woodland. Adders give birth to live young in late summer.

Golden Eagle

Smooth Snake is slightly smaller than an adder and is non venomous. It is very rare, being found only on heathlands in Dorset, Surrey and Hampshire. It also gives birth to live young.

Slow-worm is often mistaken for a snake but is in fact a legless lizard and prefers humid conditions and shaded areas in a variety of habitats, even in mature gardens. They can som etimes be spotted sunning themselves.

White Tailed Sea Eagle, often known just as the sea eagle, was once a common sight in Britain but became extinct in the early 1900s. A successful re-introduction programme on the west coast of Scotland was undertaken in the 1970s; there are now 150 pairs nesting in

Slow-worm

Sea Eagle

NORFOLK SEA EAGLES PLAN ABANDONED

Common Lizards can be found in a wide range of habitats across Britain and are the only reptiles native to Ireland. Like the slow-worm and adder, they give birth to live young.

Sand Lizards are very rare and specifically live in heathland habitats and sand dunes, where they lay eggs.

REINTRODUCTIONS
The British countryside has changed beyond recognition since many species became extinct.

Golden Eagle There are plans to relocate some young golden eagle chicks from the Highlands to southern Scotland where it is hoped they will eventually recolonise Cumbria. There are also plans to relocate golden eagles to Snowdonia in Wales.

In 2021 plans were approved to introduce a number of juvenile sea eagles, sourced from Poland, to the North Norfolk coast. However, the site in question is adjacent to The Wash, a very large bay and estuary stretching between Norfolk and Lincolnshire, in which there are already 142 offshore wind turbines and a proposal to more than double that number. The presence of these would have proved a hazard to them. Half of the pigs and poultry reared outdoors in the UK are raised in Norfolk and there were genuine worries that taking young poultry and piglets would prove a far easier option than fishing. The project to introduce the sea eagles to this site was later abandoned.

Scotland. It is the largest bird in Britain with an 8ft (2.5m) wingspan and an appetite to match. Sea eagles prey on fish, which they snatch from the water with their feet. They also hunt over huge inland areas causing concern amongst livestock owners as they find lambs and poultry easy to catch.

Attempts have taken place to re-establish a population of sea eagles in England, after 250 years, with the release of six birds on the Isle of Wight in the summer of 2019, seven in 2020 and a further twelve in 2021.

Great Bustard

Great Bustards are being reintroduced to Britain having become extinct in the 1830s. They are large turkey-sized birds whose natural habitat is open grassland. Salisbury Plain was selected as the ideal location. Since 2004 some have been hatched from eggs, reared and released each year and a population of approximately 100 has now become established in the wild.

Cranes are large graceful birds but, due to hunting and widespread drainage of wetlands, stopped breeding in Britain 400 years ago. They have been occasional visitors since but thanks to reintroductions and habitat restorations, they have once again begun nesting here. An estimated 200 cranes are now dispersed across Wales, Scotland, the Fens, Suffolk and Gloucestershire.

Beavers were last seen living wild in Britain in the 16th century and became extinct through being hunted for their fur and meat. In the spring of 2009 they were first reintroduced into the wild in Scotland and 10 years later, they became a protected species. Since then further reintroductions have been made in Scotland, Wales and increasingly in England. There are now populations around Britain, mostly in enclosures. At present it is illegal to release beavers without a licence although some have either been deliberately released or escaped and are living and breeding in the wild. In March 2021 some were introduced to the South Downs and more releases are being planned in Dorset, Derbyshire, the Isle of Wight, Nottinghamshire and Montgomeryshire. A colony of up to 15 family groups has now become established in the wild on the river Otter in Devon. In some areas problems are already emerging associated with the beaver colonies.

There are now an estimated 1,000 beavers living in Scotland and the population is rapidly expanding.

There is concern about the damage they can do. In one case a family unit built a dam in a culvert beneath a railway embankment in Perthshire. The ensuing flooding on either side threatened to undermine its foundations.

Beaver

Beavers were given protected status in May 2019 but a limited number of licences to cull beavers have already been issued in Scotland. There is concern that their dams may restrict the free movement of salmon, sea trout and brown trout making it difficult to reach their spawning grounds and the migration downstream of the young fish. By 2021 approximately 200 beavers were living on the river Tay. Those campaigning for their reintroduction believe their presence will help with flood management and improve biodiversity by enhancing and restoring natural environments. Many factors need to be taken into consideration when choosing release sites and the beaver introduction programme will be the subject of in-depth studies in coming years.

Wild Boar became extinct in Britain some 400 years ago due to conflict with those trying to grow crops. In the 1980s farmers re-introduced these big forest animals to rear in captivity to supply a niche market those wishing to experience a new exotic meat. Some escaped in the hurricane of October 1987, followed by deliberate releases into the wild, and they have since become established in several places around the country.

One of the largest wild boar colonies is in the Forest of Dean, currently estimated to be about 1,500.

Wild boar live in large family groups and sows regularly produce two litters of between 4-10 young a year. Wild boar are very destructive. They root amongst the leaf litter and damp soil in open woodlands as well as digging up grassland and road verges, destroying the habitat of other wildlife and plants. In France and Germany wild boar populations are spiralling out of control despite hundreds of thousands being culled annually. There is increasing concern in Britain not only about damage to agricultural crops and private property but also to the risk of boars transmitting disease to our extensive outdoor pig-rearing industry. They can be a danger to humans if provoked. A boar can weigh up to 150 kg and has sharp tusks. Sows are about one third lighter and are very protective of their piglets. Conflict in the future is inevitable.

European Bison became extinct in the UK more than 6,000 years ago. There are plans to release a small herd of the endangered wild European bison in Kent in the spring 2022.

European Lynx became extinct in northern Britain more than 500 years ago due to habitat loss, hunting and persecution. There are suggestions being mooted to release them as part of rewilding schemes in Scotland to help restore a natural balance in nature. Lynx are large, predatory cats the size of a border collie and the thinking is that they will help reduce the burgeoning number of deer which are damaging the natural habitat across Scotland. But it is not possible to programme a predator to only hunt one species, and sheep would provide a far easier source of food, and endangered species such as the wild cat, pine marten and capercaillie would also be at high risk of predation.

There are also aspirations to reintroduce wolves to the Scottish Highlands.

▼ Some conservationists would like to see the introduction of Lynx as part of rewilding schemes in Scotland

LIST OF PRINCIPAL CONSERVATIONISTS

 The National Trust is an independent charity and membership organisation founded in 1895 for the environmental and heritage conservation in England, Wales and Northern Ireland. It spends millions of pounds on projects each year to preserve and restore not only historic properties but areas of our countryside as well.

 The National Trust for Scotland Similar but separate to the National Trust.

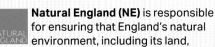 **Natural England (NE)** is responsible for ensuring that England's natural environment, including its land, flora and fauna, freshwater and marine environments, geology and soils, are protected and improved. It is sponsored by the Department for Environment, Food & Rural Affairs. (DEFRA)

 Wildlife Trust is a charitable organisation made up of 46 local Wildlife Trusts in the United Kingdom, the Isle of Man and Alderney. The Wildlife Trusts, between them, look after around 2,300 nature reserves covering nearly a quarter of a million acres (98,000ha)

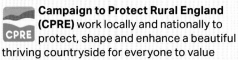 **Campaign to Protect Rural England (CPRE)** work locally and nationally to protect, shape and enhance a beautiful thriving countryside for everyone to value and enjoy.

 The Royal Society for the Protection of Birds (RSPB) is a charitable organisation registered in England, Wales and Scotland which was founded in 1889.Their work includes monitoring, protection and conservation projects for the preservation of birds. Across the UK the RSPB own 200 bird reserves totalling around 320,000 acres (130,000ha).

 The British Trust for Ornithology (BTO) was founded in 1932 for the study of birds in the British Isles. It is a UK charity that focuses on collecting data contributing to a greater understanding of birds and, in particular, how and why bird populations are changing. Their scientific research now extends to cover mammals, dragonflies, amphibians and bees.

 The Woodland Trust is the largest woodland conservation charity in the United Kingdom concerned with the creation, protection, and restoration of native woodland heritage.

 The Moorland Association members are responsible for over a million acres of the moorlands of England and Wales including preserving and protecting 860,000 acres of upland heather.

 The Rare Breeds Survival Trust (RBST) is a conservation charity set up in 1973. Its purpose is to preserve and promote native UK livestock breeds, some of which were in grave danger of becoming extinct.

 The Game and Wildlife Conservation Trust (GWCT) is generally thought to be a shooting organisation but, over the years, their research and conservation measures have extended far beyond game birds.

 Wildfowl and Wetlands Trust (WWT) is a wildfowl (ducks and geese) and wetland conservation charity originally founded by the ornithologist and artist Sir Peter Scott in 1946. It has 10 reserves around the country.

A large wind farm constructed on open moorland

RENEWABLE ENERGY

The UK, at present, is experiencing a period of climate change. The country, over time, has always gone through variable wet, dry, cold and hot episodes, often accompanied by extreme weather. The current situation may be different. Our weather is influenced by the jet stream 7-10 miles (11-17kms) above the earth. Global warming raises sea levels and affects plants and animals. It also raises water temperatures in lakes and rivers which in turn affects the fish, plants and microbes living in them. Many species have very specific conditions which they need to flourish while others are moving northwards as winter conditions become milder. Natural freshwater ecosystems, surprisingly, even if they have not been polluted by human actions, consist of a high proportion of carbon dioxide and methane. In shallow lakes this is released from decaying vegetation and forms sediment. Global warming is likely to aggravate this.

All these occurrences will have as yet unknown knock-on effects. It is not happening overnight but is insidiously creeping up on us. For COP26 in November 2021 the United Nations brought together 197 countries from across the world for talks in a bid to agree policies to reduce carbon emissions and combat climate change. However, unless they are all willing to work together, progress will be slow and targets will not be met.

China and India are continuing to build hundreds of polluting coal-fuelled power stations.

The UK currently accounts for less than 1% of global carbon emissions and the government has committed to reducing UK carbon emissions by 78% by 2035 (in comparison to 1990 levels) and attaining net zero by 2050. Net zero is defined as achieving a balance between the amount of greenhouse gas emissions released and the amount removed from the atmosphere.

The plan of action in the UK is complex and has seen the introduction of carbon credits for land usage which will influence the way forward nationally for farmers. It has been agreed though that carbon used to create imported food is not included in total carbon usage by the UK. More than 40% of food consumed in the country is imported so the UK is not directly accountable even though we are responsible for it.

Environmentalists see one of the answers to reversing climate change as being to plant more and more trees. It will take many years before a tree is mature enough to act as a viable carbon store, and caution must be exercised as to which sites are selected, as they might already be playing an even more important part in reducing carbon in the atmosphere than trees would.

Another way forward in reducing global warming is through the use of Renewable Energy, often referred to as 'Clean Energy'. The UK is excelling itself in the speed at which it is switching to creating green energy and reducing carbon emissions. Every year more wind turbines, solar panels and biomass plants are being built. Thousands of acres of land and the seabed are already dedicated to producing renewable energy and numerous projects are in the planning. Many landowners are leasing land for their installation as a lucrative

means of diversification, because the income is generous and guaranteed and not at the mercy of the weather.

The basic technology to produce renewable energy is simply about finding a way to spin the blades of a turbine to generate power.

Green electricity is generated from natural resources, such as sun, wind and water, although supply can't always be guaranteed. For this reason, back-up sources of energy need to be in place to keep the country supplied with power when the sun isn't shining enough and the wind isn't blowing or is blowing too strongly. In 2019 wind provided 20% of our energy requirements and solar power 4.1%. These percentages are rising as the number of turbines and solar panels increases. A large group of wind turbines or solar panels is known as an '**array**'.

BRITISH SUGAR COMPANY

The British Sugar company is a prime example of what can be achieved. Their four factories handle around 8 million tonnes of sugar beet a year and produce approximately 1.4 million tonnes of sugar. For every tonne of sugar manufactured, their processes result in less than 200 grams of waste – virtually zero! British Sugar's focus on driving-up efficiency while lowering its carbon footprint has huge environmental benefits.

Processes that are constantly replenished from sustainable sources such as waste and unwanted by-products, known as biomass, are also used to create power or fuel. More and more production plants are being built.

Nuclear power is also categorised as renewable energy and provides about 20% of the UK's energy requirements.

In 2008 coal was used to produce 40% of our power and since 2010 the country's reliance on coal has been cut from a third to almost zero. By 2020 only four coal-fired power stations remained, providing just 2% of UK power requirements. It is planned that the use of coal will be phased out in 2024 and the mining industry, which post-World War II employed 700,000 men, will be committed to history.

Several power stations have been demolished and some converted to natural gas which supplies about 40% of our energy. Others, such as Drax in Yorkshire, the largest in the UK, have converted to using compressed wood pellets for fuel, but a large proportion of wood pellets are imported from North America and Canada and carbon dioxide is emitted when it is burnt.

In 2020 biomass accounted for 12% of our energy requirements.

Coal will always be needed by some manufacturing industries, in particular steel and for those steam engines still running on Britain's hundred or so heritage railways. Even though there are potential sites which remain untapped in the UK, if sufficient isn't mined to satisfy demand it will need to be imported, most likely from halfway around the world, increasing the carbon footprint. Better to obtain these smaller amounts from the UK where everything is closely regulated. In May 2021 a ban was imposed on the sale of coal and wet wood for household burning in England. As more and more people have wood or multi-fuel burners, there is concern about increased carbon emissions.

WIND ENERGY

WIND TURBINES

A wind turbine converts kinetic energy from the wind into electricity. From the beginning of the 21st century they have appeared across the UK, on land and at sea, and there are plans to build thousands more. Harnessing power from the wind is one of the cleanest and most sustainable ways to generate electricity. Wind farms, though, are the subject of much controversy. There are currently no major UK-based wind turbine manufacturers so they all have to be imported although some of the rotor blades and cables are now made in Britain. The structures are enormous. The average height to the hub is 282ft (86m) and each blade might be more than 165ft (50m) long.

Wind turbines may be the greenest source of energy but their efficiency is entirely dependent on the weather. Turbines have to be shut down

Although the use of fossil fuels is being phased out, heritage railways such as the North Norfolk Railway need coal to keep them running

when wind speeds reach 55mph or over. Calm weather, usually spanning only a few days, means there is insufficient wind for the turbines to turn quickly enough to generate power.

The optimum wind speed for efficiency is 30mph.

ONSHORE There are over 7,000 onshore wind turbines, many of them in areas of natural beauty. To some they are a blot on the landscape. Some have been built on peaty heather moorland, a rare habitat. Conservationists are challenging them due to the huge disturbance caused when turbines are built.

Each turbine is assembled on a large reinforced concrete foundation, with service roads and a substation constructed to connect with the distribution network. The land is leased and ground rent is paid by the companies that own the turbines, which provides a welcome additional five figure sum to landowners for each turbine installed on their land.

The largest onshore wind farm is Whitelee at Eaglesham Moor in Scotland and consists of 215 turbines. Windfarms are normally owned by power companies but in some isolated places in Scotland, and on a few of the islands, a turbine will be in the ownership of the local community.

OFFSHORE With about 2,000 offshore wind turbines, and many more are being added each year, the UK is the world leader in offshore wind power and has more installed capacity than any other country.

There are massive wind farms, half of which are off the east coast of England. The majority are in the North Sea, others in the Irish Sea and one even in the already-congested English Channel. There are seven off the east coast of Scotland, one of which was the world's first floating wind farm.

The largest offshore wind farm in the world is Hornsea, 56 miles (90km) off the Yorkshire coast. This was constructed in four phases and covers 157 square miles (407sq km). It has 174 turbines.

The East Anglia Array is a proposed series of offshore windfarms comprising up to 1,200 turbines located around 30 miles (46km) off the east coast of East Anglia, in the North Sea. The first phase, East Anglia One, comprises 102 turbines and became operational in 2020. The London Array, 12 miles (19km) offshore in the outer Thames estuary, is also a contender with 175 turbines covering an area of nearly 40 square miles (100sq km). Maintenance of turbines in the sea is more costly than for those on land.

There are thousands of wind turbines sited offshore

Every windfarm has to be connected up to the National Grid. Sub stations are sometimes built to serve the more remote windfarms which are a long distance offshore but the power generated from many of them is carried through large sea cables to the mainland. There is concern about where substations are being built, on agricultural land.

Cables from proposed offshore windfarms Vanguard and Boreas will make landfall on the Norfolk coast. From there two trenches 50 yards (45m) wide will be dug to take them 37 miles underground to an inland substation previously built to connect the existing Dudgeon array to the National Grid. This substation will need to be extended by 18 acres (7ha) to service Vanguard and Boreas. This will cause the loss of a large chunk of agricultural land.

On the plus side the offshore wind farm industry has created work and breathed new life into several ports such as Grimsby and Great Yarmouth, which were suffering deprivation following the collapse of the fishing industry. Hull is also becoming a major manufacturing centre for turbine blades.

It is not possible to store electricity. In Scotland turbines have sometimes had to be powered down as they produce more than can be used. Some are so remote it is impossible to convey the surplus to England or Wales. Once installed, wind turbines are probably the greenest source of energy. Whether on land or sea, conservationists have expressed concerns about the threat they pose to birds. Offshore windfarms are frequently built in areas of the sea where the water is relatively shallow, often on sandbanks, and these are also the feeding grounds for many coastal species of birds, where fish are most plentiful. Birds on migration are at risk of contact with the turning blades because

many species fly at night. Turbines may also pose a risk to bats. Once a windfarm is established at sea though, and everything has settled, many species of fish and crustaceans adapt to living among the turbines. Some sea birds are taking to nesting on the infrastructure.

HYDROPOWER

Most old watermills were sited on rivers and used the flow of water to turn a big wheel which then, by a series of cogs and belts, drove horizontally-placed millstones to grind the corn. A few were known as **tide mills** and used the strength of the tides to produce tidal power. Today, similar principles are used in creating power from water although modern technology uses turbines to generate the power.

Most hydro schemes (energy from water) today rely on retaining water behind a dam, some of them built in Victorian times to supply water to big cities. Reservoirs are built high above the production plant and gravity causes the channelled water to flow at high speed through the turbines near the base. In a few cases it is collected in a lower reservoir and pumped back up to the top one. The Cruachan Power station on the edge of Loch Awe in Argyll and Bute is one such station that works on this principle. It temporarily stores energy at times of low demand, but when demand is high can reach full generating capacity in under 30 seconds. Construction began in 1959 and remarkably the power station was built a kilometre inside the solid rock of Ben Cruachan. Guided tours are normally available and it is like being transported into a James Bond film set. This is recycling in every sense of the word. A few hydro power stations make use of the natural flow of rivers but, being dependent on local rainfall, these levels vary. With its combination of high mountains, large inland lochs and plentiful rainfall, Scotland is ideally suited and began harvesting hydro

There are many hydro power stations in Scotland which make use of fast flowing rivers

power a century ago and now has 85% of the UK's hydroelectric energy resources. Hydro power, though, only supplies about 2% of the UK power needs.

On a very much smaller scale, the Archi–medean screw hydro turbine works on the same principle and looks like a giant corkscrew. Installed in a river at a place where there is a drop in levels, the water is channelled from the top to pass down through it. The pressure of the descending water passing through the 'screw' causes it to rotate which in turn creates energy which can be extracted by an electrical generator connected to the main shaft of the screw.

TIDAL POWER

Energy captured by harnessing the natural motion of the sea is sometimes called Blue power and is a more or less untapped source of green energy. Tides are far more predictable than wind and sun and technology to harness tidal power is rapidly being developed. Tidal power installation and maintenance is very expensive and more needs to be known about how it affects the environment. It can be used in two different ways: either by using barrages across estuaries or placing turbines underwater in narrow, fast-flowing channels of seawater. Submerged underwater turbines

and generators, working on much the same principle as wind turbines, convert the movement of water coming from the changing tides into electricity. In 2007 at Strangford Lough, in Northern Ireland the world's first-ever commercial-scale tidal power station (SeaGen) was developed, consisting of two 600kW turbines.

In July 2021 the Orbital O2, with the capacity to meet the annual demand for 2,000 homes began production off Orkney. The Severn, Dee, Solway and Humber estuaries are all possible sites for tidal energy-generating barrages in the UK. Commercial tidal turbine projects are planned for the Pentland Firth and the Sound of Islay between the islands of Islay and Jura in the Inner Hebrides. These prospective sites are where there are very strong tidal flows within narrow channels and relatively sheltered from storms.

WAVE POWER

With the length of the coastline around mainland Great Britain in excess of 11,000 miles (17,700 km) there is plenty of potential to harness the power of waves. Numerous devices have been developed, both floating and submerged, which either rotate or oscillate to produce electricity. A lot of development work has been done but no wave power schemes, as yet, have been adopted on a large commercial scale, due to the initial cost of building such structures, the possibility of damage from storms, the difficulties entailed in maintaining them and the potential harm they might cause to marine environments.

BIOMASS: CREATING GREEN ELECTRICITY

Biomass power is electricity generated using plant-based fuels. These include wood pellets, wood chips and bio-energy crops cultivated solely for energy generation. In addition domestic and food waste and by-products of the agricultural industry, such as straw and poultry litter, are used. These are either burned directly or converted to liquid biofuels or biogas. Power can also be generated from gas emitted from sewage sludge. Biomass power produces renewable energy from natural sources that won't run out or are sustainable.

Many power stations now burn biomass to produce this form of renewable energy. Burning waste at a high temperature is an alternative to sending it to landfill sites. Putting it simply, the heat released produces steam which drives a turbine to generate electricity.

Burning biomass produces the largest form of renewable energy in the UK but still leaves a sizeable carbon footprint.

In theory disposing of useable, unwanted waste products by these processes is a way of tackling global warming, but there are several negatives to the processes, not least emissions. The release of a certain amount of greenhouse gases is inevitable when waste is burned. The transportation involved is another issue. On the plus side, the solid and liquid residue left from the anaerobic digestion process, the volume of which is around 90-95% of what was fed into the digester, has a use. This by-product is known as 'digestate' which can be effectively used as fertiliser on agricultural land.

BIOGAS

Biogas can be captured from landfill sites. Power for greenhouses on a 30 acre site near Bury St

An Archimedes screw is a hydro-electric turbine powered by the flow of a river; this one at Philiphaugh estate, Scotland produces enough electricity to power 200 homes

Anaerobic Digesters work in a similar way as a cow's stomach to produce methane gas

Edmunds, Suffolk, comes from the local sewage works. Production of tomatoes, cucumbers and peppers has increased by utilising heat from the heat pumps used to treat the waste water and has reduced carbon emissions by 75%.

Most biogas comes from **anaerobic digesters** which use a fermentation process instead of burning. They are a very popular way of converting biomass into biogas. There are now hundreds in use and many more under development. The biomass used in anaerobic digester plants can be vegetable residues, food waste, straw, slurry and manure or specifically cultivated perennial energy crops such as miscanthus (elephant grass) or short rotation coppice such as fast-growing willow or poplar. Annual crops are also grown which are cut whole. Rye is cut before it fully ripens and maize is cut in September or October while it is still green.

Plant waste or matter is put in sealed composting tanks and then goes through a natural process which produces gas, the procedure similar to the way in which a cow's digestive system works. The biogas produced is used to make electrical power or heat. In 2019 the large RAF base at Marham in Norfolk linked up with an anaerobic digester plant close by at Swaffham which uses locally grown crops to generate green electricity. This partnership made RAF Marham the first British military base to run almost entirely on green electricity.

At the British Sugar factory at Bury St Edmunds in Suffolk, where sugar is extracted and refined from locally grown sugar beet, an anaerobic digestion plant was installed in 2016. It uses the pressed sugar beet pulp, a by-product of the sugar-making process, to produce biogas. Methane generated from the biogas is fed

Maize is sometimes grown specifically for use in anaerobic digester plants to produce energy and biogas

into a combined heat and power (CHP) plant generating green electricity.

Alternatively, biogas can be further processed into biomethane, which is barely distinguishable from natural gas and can be fed into the national gas transmission network.

BIOFUEL
Biofuels are manufactured from oilseed rape, sugar beet and wheat. Alcohol fuels (like ethanol or biodiesel) are often by-products from other manufacturing processes.

It's estimated that bioethanol in petrol reduces carbon emissions by the equivalent of taking 700,000 cars off the road.

Another British Sugar factory, this time at Wissington in Norfolk, produces bioethanol which is added to petrol. A blend of up to 5% bioethanol can be used in any unleaded petrol car on the road in the UK and was raised to 10% in 2021.

SOLAR ENERGY
Solar panels have been springing up everywhere, from the roofs of buildings in towns and cities to covering large expanses of our countryside. The size of some scheduled solar farms is mind-boggling, and many more are being planned. They can be used to generate electricity in any location that has access to sunlight, and solar power is ideal where power is needed and there is no access to the national grid.

Solar panels convert light from the sun into electricity, through photovoltaic (PV) cells. These PV cells are incorporated into each panel, which is covered in glass and contained within a metal frame. The panels are tilted towards the south and mounted between 1m and 2.65m above the ground. Typically about 250kw of power is produced per acre (0.4ha) of land used. On average a solar farm covering 25 acres (10ha)

Atomic power counts as being green energy - Sizewell, Suffolk

will annually generate enough power for 1,500 homes. Solar farms are expensive to install but apart from cleaning the panels twice a year and the occasional replacing of parts, they require minimal maintenance. Panels are expected to last 20-30 years before they need replacing.

Larger and larger solar farms are being built and there is concern at the huge amount of productive agricultural land which has been, and will be, lost to these projects.

SOLAR FARMS
Land-based solar farms, also known as 'solar parks' or 'solar fields', are large areas of interconnected solar panels positioned to harvest as much energy as they can from the sun. Because of the huge space they take up, they are located in agricultural or rural areas. Some may be as small as an acre while a few cover hundreds of acres. In 2020 the go-ahead was given to build Cleve Hill Solar Park, the UK's biggest solar farm, stretching over 950 acres (385ha) of grazing marshes on the north Kent coast. Solar panels are usually installed facing south but in a first for the UK, it will use an "east-west panel orientation", which should be able to generate 40 per cent more electricity. However, there are also

▲ Hundreds of acres of agricultural land are now covered with solar panels

proposals in the pipeline to create the even larger Sunnica solar farm complex on the Suffolk-Cambridgeshire border extending to 2,600 acres (1,000ha). Another near Chelmsford, the Longfield Scheme, is planned to be located on a further 1,400 acres (566ha).

Although solar farms are not built on high grade land, it is still land capable of producing reasonable yields of cereals as well as good quality grass, and in some areas root crops. As the panels are close to the ground and close to each other, realistically, the only agricultural use the land could have would be for grazing sheep. However, they do have the great advantage of being silent, producing no waste, and only a minimal amount of damage is caused to the land so there would be little problem in reinstating it later for agricultural use. There is serious concern though, that once agricultural land is used for solar farms, it converts to industrial status which opens up the opportunity for further development thus increasing its value.

RESERVOIR SOLAR FARMS

Solar farms also exist on reservoirs belonging to water companies. They provide an onsite power source for local water treatment works, without impacting on the land. Covering the surface area of reservoirs with solar panels also reduces water evaporation, and the cooling effect of the water can improve the efficiency of solar cells.

The largest floating solar farm in the UK (so far) is the one built on the QE2 reservoir, near London's Heathrow Airport which consists of more than 23,000 individual solar panels, covering 14 acres (5.7ha) which equals in size to eight football pitches.

The principal disadvantage of solar farms is their efficiency cannot be relied on. Although they can still function to a lesser degree on overcast or rainy days, when the sun sets they cease to function at all. The land they are installed on is mostly leased from landowners for a guaranteed return over a lengthy term, typically 25 years. Energy companies own most of the sites although a few are owned by local councils who have sometimes made use of old landfill sites.

Walking has become very popular with all ages and costs nothing except maybe car park charges. Long distances walkers need to be well equipped.

COUNTRYSIDE LEISURE

In the UK there are 160,000 miles (257,000km) of footpaths and bridleways, overseen by the Highways Authority, as well as many that have not been registered. In addition there is a 16,000 mile (26,000km) National Cycle Network. There is also land which has 'Open Access' on foot where it is expected that people will behave in a and responsible way. The Countryside and Rights of Way Act 2000 (the CRoW Act) gave people the right to walk on most areas of open country in England and Wales – which is defined as mountain (land over 2,000ft or 600 metres), moor, heath, down and registered common land. Forests and woodlands are excluded, other than publicly owned forests. 'Countryside Access' is the government website for online public maps of access land and further information about rights of access. There is greater freedom to roam in Scotland and no definitive list of rights of way. Landowners and the Highways Authority share the responsibility for maintaining footpaths, bridleways and byways. Parish and town councils also have certain discretionary powers.

Walking is now the most popular countryside pastime and accompanying dogs need to be kept under close control. Attacks on livestock cost farmers £1.5million in 2021.

WALKING AND HIKING

There are more than 80 **bothies** scattered across the wilder parts of the Scottish Highlands and a few others in very remote areas of northern England and Wales. Bothies are small shelters and were originally built so that shepherds would have safe places to find refuge. They are very basic, very often little more than a shell of a building, with no gas,

▲ One of 16 National Trails, the 100 mile (160km) Southdowns Way crosses the Southdowns National Park from Winchester in the west to Eastbourne in the east

electricity, running water or facilities. However, inside there is always somewhere a fire can be lit, a table and chairs. There are usually rudimentary beds, but not always. Bothies are rarely locked and are free to use, providing life-saving shelter in adverse weather or those caught out overnight.

Cattle and footpaths

There are often footpaths crossing fields with cattle in, which data shows to be the most dangerous animals in the UK. They should not be approached closer than ten metres but give them a wide berth if possible. Walkers are at particular risk; three were killed by cattle in the autumn of 2020. The majority of walkers have a dog with them which cows with calves instinctively regard as a threat and react defensively.

Because of the recognised risk, there are seven breeds of dairy bulls which are prohibited from being kept in fields which footpaths cross. It is permitted for bulls of other breeds to be allowed in fields with footpaths but only if accompanied by cows and/or heifers. When crossing a field occupied by cattle, first evaluate their mood; they may be relaxed, they may be inquisitive or they may show signs of aggression. Several injuries and deaths are caused each year to ramblers, often accompanied by a dog, through being trampled by cattle. The very sight of a dog can trigger a primeval reaction in cows of the need to defend

their calves. Dogs should be kept close and under effective control on a lead when around cattle, but if a cow turns aggressive let it off its lead. It can look after itself better than you can.

Young cattle are inquisitive and often run towards a person, especially if they have a dog with them. Holding the arms outstretched and shouting should be sufficient to slow them down.

Bulls and cows need treating with more caution. Because they are regularly handled, milking cows are normally placid and, unless one has just given birth out in the field, they rarely have calves running with them, nor a bull. However, beef breed cattle are a different matter and the large, chestnut-coloured Limousins, in particular, shouldn't be trusted. Beef cattle turned out to grass are pretty much left to their own devices and are therefore not so used to having people around them as are dairy cows. It is never a good idea to get between a cow and its calf. A bull is very often run with beef cows and their calves.

With a few exceptions a farmer is legally allowed to keep cattle, including bulls, in fields where there are rights of way, although he has a moral obligation not to if he is aware that an animal might be dangerous. There is no legal obligation for notices to be posted.

Another hazard which might be encountered by walkers and riders, particularly in arable areas, are bird-scaring devices. These are frequently used in winter and spring to protect crops and newly sown seeds from the attentions of birds, notably pigeons. Gas guns are programmed to emit extremely loud bangs at regular intervals, unnerving for humans as well as dogs and it can panic horses too.

Mountain biking is the sport of riding strongly built bicycles off-road, usually over rough terrain, and calls for technical skills, endurance and daring. Although cycling on

▶ Foragers need to have knowledge of the plants they are searching for - these Fly Agaric mushrooms are poisonous

designated footpaths is a grey area as far as the law is concerned, there are thousands of miles of bridleways through open countryside and along canal towpaths, riverside trails and disused railway lines that are accessible. In addition to these there are 67 specialist Mountain Biking Trail centres across the UK offering challenging man-made cross-country courses.

Foraging for food in the wild is becoming even more popular but it's all about sustainability.

Plants are protected by the 1968 Theft Act and it is illegal to dig up the roots to take a plant.

It is against the law to take anything on the Protected Species list or growing on an SSSI site. A list of these can be found on Schedule 8 of the Wildlife and Countryside Act (1981). Foraging should only take place in an area where there is a high density to gather, and plenty should be left. Taking plants for financial gain or profit is against the law.

Metal detecting has become a popular hobby. A licence is not needed but permission must be obtained from the landowner. Every

square metre of Britain is owned by someone. Parks and commons normally belong to local councils but many sites are, for various reasons, protected or have restricted access.

It is a legal requirement to report finds of gold or silver, items over 300 years old and groups of coins.

The discovery of human remains, ammunition and ordnance must be left untouched and reported to the police immediately.

Birdwatching is a very popular hobby. Twitchers (whose main aim is the sighting of rare birds) will travel across the UK to see them.

ON THE WATER

A licence is required to use a canoe, kayak or paddle board on British inland waterways. One is also needed for rowing boats, dinghies and even light inflatable craft. Buying a British Canoeing 'waterways licence' allows access to 5,000 of inland waterways, including those managed by the Environment Agency and the Broads Authority.

Licences issued by the Environment Agency are required to fish and sail on inland waters

In order that crops could be grown where there was little soil on rocky ground in Scotland it was dug and piled into ridges called Lazy Beds

OUR HERITAGE

Hidden signs of our history surrounds us in the countryside. Certain aspects of our countryside have changed only superficially in hundreds of years, and the mountains and fells, natural lakes and rivers, heather moorlands and Dartmoor tors still look much the same as they ever have done.

Signs of early farming methods are still obvious in some places.

A pattern of ridges and furrows, creating a corrugated effect, indicate where a communal method of strip farming was once adopted in large open fields close to villages.

The ridge (rig) and furrow system originated in early medieval times and in some areas continued into the 18th century. Similarly, small lazy beds can still be found in the more remote areas of Scotland. These are similar to ridge and furrow but instead of a plough being used, they were dug with spades to form banks up to 8ft (2.5m) in width, with narrow drainage channels between them, on which to grow crops.

History has left its mark everywhere. Ancient standing stones, known as megaliths, from Stonehenge to the Callanish Stones on the Isle of Lewis, can be seen. There are 57 hill figures cut into the slopes of chalk downlands. Most date back to the Bronze Age. Also to be seen are prehistoric burial mounds knows as tumuli or barrows. We have 3,300 Hill Forts, mostly Iron Age, 2,000 miles of Roman Roads. Then there are our ancient monasteries, churches and many rural villages can trace their roots back to the Domesday Book and some even further back to Saxon times. Within their names are words that Saxons used and which are still familiar today. Ford is a shallow crossing, Ham is a village, Hurst a wooded hill, Bury a fortified place, Mer once meant a lake, Ton or Tun an enclosed village or manor. Wick or wich was the produce from a farm, so for example sheep were kept at

Woolwich. Hundreds of years ago numerous old country towns were granted Royal Charters to hold markets and fairs which traditionally are still celebrated today. Many country pubs owe their existence to having once been coaching inns. Originally stage coaches would have had to stop every ten to fifteen miles to change horses and allow passengers the opportunity to alight for rest and refreshments. These inns were busy places, often in rural locations, on main routes between the larger towns. They would have employed many local people and had extensive stabling for the horses. These have now very often been turned into B&B or holiday accommodation. Other inns were on drovers routes in the days when cattle, sheep and even geese and turkeys were walked long distances to market. Here the drovers and their dogs would be provided with food and drink and a field nearby for the animals to rest overnight. Cattle from across the Scottish Highlands gathered in Perthshire at Crieff before embarking on the long journey south as far as Norwich. In turn turkeys from Norfolk were driven on foot to London's Smithfield Market.

Scattered across Scotland's Highlands and Islands are the ruins of isolated crofts abandoned during the Clearances. Between the mid 18th and 19th centuries crofters were evicted because landowners could make more money out of keeping sheep than people.

HERITAGE CRAFTS

Our heritage is also our people, animals, birds and plants. Trades, which once provided work in every village, have all but disappeared. Professions were handed down through generations of families. Amongst village residents there would have been horsemen, a carpenter, blacksmith, wheelwright, harness maker, boot mender, miller, baker, basket and rake makers, stone mason and in different areas brickmakers, flint knappers, miners and quarry men. Women worked in cottage industries finding employment as dress

▲ The Forge - Blacksmiths now need to be qualified to shoe horses

makers, seamstresses, dairy maids, laundresses, spinners and weavers.

The National Trust and other conservation bodies involved with restoration work continue to need people with these traditional skills. There are no machines that can replace them.

THATCHERS

Probably the biggest demand today for heritage craftsmen is for thatchers. Thatching is still done in very much the same way as it was a thousand years ago. Wheat straw or water reeds, such as Norfolk reed, are most commonly used; the latter will last for up to 60 years but straw for only half that time. Regular maintenance work is also required. Sedge is sometimes used to seal the ridge. Thatch is aesthetically pleasing and the most environmentally friendly of all roofing materials. Thatching a roof is labour intensive and requires great expertise and with more than 60,000 thatched buildings in Britain it is a trade that will always be in demand.

There are about 800 master thatchers in the UK and it takes at least five years to train to become one.

▲ The skills of the thatcher are still in great demand

Many thatchers place a signature straw finial on the ridge when they've completed their work which is often in the form of a fox, hare, pheasant, cat or dog. This tradition is said to stem from the days when finials were added to ward off evil spirits. In pre-war days farm labourers had the basic knowledge to thatch a hay or straw stack sufficiently well to keep the rain out.

Little has changed in the way thatching is carried out. The same tools are used although metal spars to hold the bundles of thatch in place have mostly replaced those that were cut and twisted from young coppiced hazel or willow. In the eastern counties of England these were known as **broachers**. Wheat for thatching is cut with a binder to avoid damaging the straw. The reed cutter scything his way across a marsh now uses a mowing machine which saves work by tying the reed into bundles at the same time as it cuts.

DRY STONE WALLING

Dry stone walling is a skill that was traditionally passed from father to son on family farms. Although principally in Wales, Scotland and the north of England, there are many other areas where stone walls have been built and styles vary in different parts of the country.

In Cornwall traditional dry stone walls are built with an earth core topped with grass. The height is sometimes increased with the addition of hedging plants or even small trees on top. After a few years they appear to be grassy banks.

Even though there are fewer youngsters today following in their father's footsteps, walls still fall down and need to be repaired and maintained and there are professionals who earn their living walling.

BLACKSMITHS

They shod horses, mended farm machinery and made tools, door fastenings and vermin traps, as well as the rims for wagon wheels. Conservation bodies still need people with traditional skills for restoration work.

▲ Stone walling is a heritage craft for which there will always be a need

◀ Hurdle making is an ancient craft using coppiced hazel

Each year a National Hedgelaying Contest is held to test the skills of hedgelayers in eight of the most popular styles.

WOODLAND SKILLS

Woodland once provided regular employment for many people. There were chestnut cutters who made paling fences, charcoal burners, broom makers, hazel cutters who made hurdles from coppiced wood and bodgers who turned chair legs and spindles for chair backs from green wood using a simple pole lathe which they would also have made themselves. Large timber was hauled using horses.

Very few people today earn their living from woodland by these means. There were also miners who extracted iron, lead, tin and copper, very often from remote sites in the countryside.

TRADITIONAL FARMING

There are only a few small working lowland farms left but there are still hill farming families who have been keeping sheep on the fells and uplands of Britain for generations. Their little

HEDGELAYING

Hedgelaying was once carried out as routine winter work on farms but today there are only a few specialists who practise the craft and earn a living from doing so. The stems of overgrown hedges are partially cut through at the base and then bent right over to lay in one direction. They are kept in place with stakes driven into the ground at intervals and then trimmed. In spring the horizontally-laid stems sprout new growth which grows vertically creating a neat and tidy stock-proof hedge. There are more than thirty different regional styles in the UK the newest of which must be the 'motorway' style.

Hedge laying is a heritage skill still much in demand

Ancient Chillingham Cattle have roamed wild for 800 years

farms are often isolated, tucked away out of sight in the hills, and have only a very small acreage of good grassland. Their sheep still live a semi wild existence out on the hills as they have for hundreds of years and the traditional way in which they are managed has changed very little in that time. These small farms, the shepherds and their sheep remain as part of our rural heritage.

Across the country, regional dialects are becoming a thing of the past and in danger of becoming obsolete as more and more of the population disperse and relocate. They are part of our heritage too. Farmers have their own distinctive vocabulary relating to agriculture, often regional, but as old traditional farming ways fade away, so too will the local vernacular. It would be a shame if these farming words were completely lost for they are very much part of our agricultural heritage. This is where oral history can play a big part in preserving the pronunciation of such words freely used in the past, as the way in which they are spelled when put on paper is purely guesswork.

RARE AND HERITAGE BREEDS
It would be a great loss too if more breeds of animals and birds, which once played such important parts in our country's agricultural evolution, were to disappear.

Between 1900 and 1973, twenty-six native breeds of livestock became extinct in Britain as well as many varieties of poultry.

Fortunately, some fifty years ago, a few far-sighted farmers realised what was happening to our traditional farm animals and set about preserving the breeds and ensuring there was a gene pool in place so they would never be lost. One of these was Joe Henson who set up the Cotswold Farm Park in 1971. He also founded the Rare Breeds Survival Trust in 1973 to preserve endangered native breeds.

There has been a resurgence of interest in our native breeds, including from conservationists.

Heritage breeds are slow growing and, as a consequence, meat from them has more flavour.

Whilst not commercially viable on a large scale it has meant that discerning consumers have created a market for them through being willing to pay premium prices. Breeders and producers have begun to recognise they are able to make a profit from native breeds of cattle, sheep and pigs and demand for their meat is helping to preserve them.

CATTLE

There are 34 breeds of cattle native to Britain, many of them now rare and a few on the critical list meaning there are fewer than 150 recorded.

Prior to the 1800s, when horse power superseded them, oxen or bullocks had for centuries been used for ploughing and as draught animals. There are many old illustrations of English Longhorns and, in the south of England, Sussex cattle pulling ploughs and wagons. These cattle would often have been fitted with iron shoes made in two half-moon shapes to fit each of their cloven hooves.

Horses proved to be stronger and more active than oxen, not so many were needed although they required more care. When horses took over the ploughing and pulling, different breeds of cattle were developed for more defined purposes. Red Polls and Shorthorns were bred for both their meat and their milk. Some breeds gained weight quicker than others. Lincoln Reds, Sussex, Red Polls and Devons (also known as Red Rubies) are old breeds, all dark red, and have long been recognised for their beef qualities and,

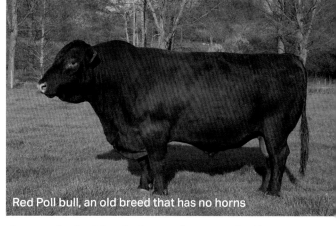
Red Poll bull, an old breed that has no horns

along with the Hereford, were kept specifically for meat. Others such as the Ayrshires, Jerseys and Guernseys were kept exclusively for milk.

English Longhorns and Shorthorns are two dual purpose breeds that were in danger of being lost. Several other traditional breeds were also facing extinction until the Rare Breeds Survival Trust began a breeding programme in 1980 to save them. Numbers of the now popular Aberdeen Angus were also very low at one time. Few Shorthorns are now kept for milk but the Beef Shorthorn like the Longhorn, has seen a revival as a beef-producing animal and are eagerly sought after by customers seeking to buy meat produced from traditional breeds. In Scotland, White Shorthorn bulls have become popular for crossing with other hardy native beef breeds such as the iconic Highland cattle which are so well equipped to survive the harsh Scottish weather. They can be kept outside all year and have recently been making a comeback.

Highland cattle date back to the mid 14th century and were originally black but the Victorians preferred the look of ginger coloured ones, which appeared from time to time, and so purposely bred them. These days the majority of Highland cattle are shades of brown.

Environmentalists too have been playing a part by using heritage breeds for grazing as part of their conservation plans, sometimes using

◀ Belted Galloways are a hardy breed often used in conservation projects

Loghorn cattle were a multi purpose breed used as draught animals before horses

breeds local to the area. Belted Galloway cattle are particularly popular as they are very hardy and visually attractive.

Other breeds still under threat are the Gloucester, Irish Moiled and White Park, British White, Shetland and Albion.

BRITAIN'S LAST WILD CATTLE

One of the most rare and remarkable herds is that of Chillingham cattle which have roamed wild at Chillingham Castle in Northumberland for 800 years. Their numbers naturally fluctuate. During the very harsh winter of 1946/47 this unique herd was reduced to five bulls and eight cows but over the subsequent decades numbers have gradually increased and now stand at approximately 100 in total. Since 2009 they have been confined to 330 acres (130ha) of the enclosed park. The herd is left entirely to its own devices with virtually no intervention from humans apart from the provision of hay in winter if needed. Following the devastating outbreak of Foot and Mouth disease in 2001, which threatened their very survival, a small number of animals were taken to a secret location in Scotland as a safeguard should disaster strike. This was the only time in centuries that human intervention on this scale had been considered necessary but it would have been a catastrophe if this special herd should, for any reason, become wiped out. Because they live a truly wild existence and there has been no direct human contact, the formation of this small isolated herd of Chillingham cattle has enabled researchers to experiment and collect fascinating and unique data.

SHEEP

The UK has 56 native breeds of sheep of which half are in decline or considered rare. Over the centuries they evolved to suit the districts in which they were kept. The breeds were usually named either after the areas they originated or according to their description. The size and appearance of our native sheep varies a lot and many of the northern breeds have horns.

A number of primitive breeds which are small and extremely hardy are found on several of the islands around the west and north of Scotland. Soay sheep, from the island of Soay in the Outer Hebrides, are the most primitive of all UK breeds and are thought to have

Soay sheep still live wild on St Kilda, a remote group of islands off the Outer Hebrides, nearly a century after the last inhabitants left

become established in the first century. Boreray sheep are descended from sheep domesticated by inhabitants of the islands of St Kilda, and evolved into a distinct breed in the 19th century. People ceased living on St Kilda in 1930 and a small flock were left to live wild on the tiny island of Boreray. They were later rescued and registered with the Rare Breed Survival Trust as 'critically endangered'. Hebridean sheep have very dense, course black wool and can be found in the Western Isles.

> *Since 1832 North Ronaldsay*
> *sheep from the Orkney Islands*
> *have been confined to living on the*
> *shore as a feral flock and have evolved*
> *to eat only seaweed.*

Shetlands are a breed of small, fine-boned sheep which have adapted well to living on their island.

Manx Loaghtan sheep have grazed the uplands of the Isle of Man for centuries.

In England, the Norfolk Horn is thought to be descended from Saxon black-faced sheep and their breed society was established in the 13th century. Renowned for the quality of their wool, at one time they were the most prevalent breed in East Anglia but by the 1960s were on the brink of extinction.

▶ The Badger Faced sheep is an ancient Welsh breed which has been part of the landscape for centuries

◀ The Portland Horn ram is an endangered breed

Our downland breeds of sheep are also very much part of our heritage. Many farmers became rich from the wool off their backs and financed the building of magnificent churches in the parishes where they lived. In 1813 it was noted that an estimated 200,000 ewes were being kept on the eastern South Downs in Sussex. Tended by shepherds, they grazed the downs from dawn until dusk when they were brought down to lower arable land often where a fodder crop had been grown for them. This was known as **folding**. Their droppings fertilised the soil making it possible to continue growing arable crops.

Cumbria is home to 99% of Herdwicks whose name derived from the Old Norse 'herdvyck' meaning sheep pasture. They can survive out on the open fells all year round where few other breeds could. Their lambs are black when they are born but their wool fades to nearly white as they age.

There are many other breeds that are at risk although some still a play a small part in modern sheep breeding. Thanks to the work of the Rare Breeds Survival Trust it is hoped they will all be able to survive as a living part of our heritage.

PIGS

There are 11 native pig breeds in the UK, all of which are considered rare and at risk of becoming extinct.

Native Large Black pigs have become a rare breed

The Berkshire is black with a white snout, white socks and a white tip to its tail. Gloucester Old Spots are white with distinctive black spots. In early autumn they used to be turned out in local orchards to graze and clear up the fallen apples.

The Large Black is Britain's only all-black breed of pig. The Tamworth is ginger in colour and originated in the Midlands. The British Saddleback is black with white front legs extending to a distinctive white band round its body and over its shoulders. The Oxford Sandy and Black is pale sandy to rust in colour with black patches.

The British Lop is a large white pig originally from the West Country and is noted for its very large ears which hang down over its face. Other all-white pigs native to Britain are British Landrace, Welsh, Large White and the Middle White with its characteristic snub nose and prick ears.

GOATS

Goats were brought to Britain in about 5000BC as domestic stock and originated in the Middle East. They first appeared in Scotland with Neolithic farmers keeping them some 4,500 years ago. Historically, feral goats of various colours have long been established in scattered populations over the wilder hills of the UK. Scotland still has a large population, most of them to be found deep in the Highlands. It is thought these were likely to have been abandoned in the late 1700s due to the Highland Clearances when landowners set about evicting their tenants. Today, herds also exist in Northumberland, Snowdonia, the Llyn peninsula and the Black Mountains, as well as on Lundy Island, in Cheddar Gorge in Somerset, and in the Valley of the Rocks on the edge of Exmoor.

The only other ancient breed of goat native to Britain is the Bagot goat which roams wild in Bagots Park, Staffordshire and is known to have existed continuously since the 1380s. These are easily identified as they have long hair, horns and are black on their heads, necks and shoulders with white bodies.

CHICKEN

All chicken have evolved from wild Red Jungle Fowl from south-east Asia. Because they are small and easily transported, over the centuries, chicken have been introduced to Britain from all over the world.

Chicken have become divided over time into three different types – those that are kept for laying, those that are bred for meat and others as dual-purpose poultry.

The popular white and black Light Sussex is a dual-purpose hen whose origins date back to Roman times.

There are 18 breeds that originate from the UK, some of which are on the Rare Breeds Society's watch list. In total there are 93 recognised breeds of chickens. Poultry fanciers are dedicated to preserving the indigenous breeds once common across Britain before intensive rearing and mass production took over, post Second World War. Bantams are miniature versions of the same breeds of chickens.

Cock fighting had been a traditional sport for hundreds of years in Britain until it was banned in 1835 and 60 years later in Scotland. It took place in a small ring known as a cockpit and large bets were placed. The most popular fighting breed was the Old English Game.

GEESE
Nearly all domestic geese are descended from the wild greylag goose. Two breeds evolved in Britain – Brecon Buffs and the Shetland. The latter was recorded on the Shetland Isles in the 17th century. Two others, the West of England and the Pilgrim, are also old breeds but UK standards were not set until comparatively recently: the West of England in 1999 and the Pilgrim in 1982.

Geese do not lay many eggs and then only in the spring but make good table birds and were often the choice for Christmas dinner or other celebrations. Nowadays, geese are most often kept for pets as lawn mowers or watch dogs.

They can become very tame although ganders are often quite aggressive. Large commercial flocks of hybrid white geese are reared outdoors for the table.

DUCKS
There are four breeds of ducks which have evolved in the UK, the oldest being the Aylesbury, a white duck bred for meat, which dates back to the early 18th century. Prior to 1815 it was known as the White English. Three other breeds have been developed as utility breeds which are prolific egg layers and which also fatten well. The Khaki Campbell has been a favourite with smallholders since 1901 as they are particularly productive. The Buff Orpington was developed at about the same time and more recently the Welsh Harlequin in the 1950s.

TURKEYS
Domesticated turkeys owe their existence to the wild black turkey from North America. Some were brought to Europe by the Spanish Conquistadors and first arrived in England in the 1520s. They were developed as a meat breed in East Anglia and became known as Norfolk Blacks, a breed still popular today. Besides the

▲ Narragansett turkeys originated in New England, USA and have now become a rare breed

Corn crops were cut using a binder, seen here drawn by two Suffolk horses, before combine harvesters were invented

Norfolk Black, varieties of Bronze turkeys evolved but the original types are becoming rare, having been replaced by the development of the more commercially viable Broad Breasted Bronze. The majority of turkeys produced commercially are now white hybrids.

HORSES AND PONIES

There are 16 breeds of horses and ponies native to Britain. Many are comparatively rare but the best known and widespread across the world is the Thoroughbred.

The heavy horses – Clydesdales, Shires and Suffolk Punches, were the tractors of yesteryear and are becoming rare. The Suffolk Punch, once the stalwart of East Anglian farming, is now an endangered species with fewer than 72 females remaining in the UK and less than 300 in the world. These breeds of heavy working horses owe their continuing existence to the devotion of a handful of enthusiasts who have preserved the breeds. Such large animals are expensive to keep

and not commercially viable. The smaller horses and ponies were the cars and vans of yesteryear.

Hackney horses and ponies were elegant carriage horses which have a natural but unusual high stepping action at the trot, and they have developed since the 14th century. The Cleveland Bay originated during the 17th century in England as pack horses, later became popular for riding and driving. For many years the Duke of Edinburgh very successfully used a team of Cleveland Bays in carriage driving competitions.

Ponies are smaller than horses and most breeds, such as Dartmoor, Exmoor, New Forest, Highland and Shetland, are named after the areas where they evolved and today remain living and breeding in a semi-wild state. Ponies are known to have roamed Dartmoor for more than 3,000 years and today there are about 1,200 Dartmoor ponies on the moor. Exmoors are a very popular breed amongst conservationists and frequently used for helping to restore habitat on nature reserves.

▲ Eriskay ponies, used by crofters on the tiny island of Eriskay in the Outer Hebrides, very nearly became extinct

Highland ponies, from the north of Scotland are thick-set, hardy and were used for a variety of purposes. Today, although they are sometimes used for riding and driving, some are used for forestry work or by stalkers to carry red deer, which have been shot, off the hills in places where vehicles are unable to access.

Welsh ponies and cobs too are sturdy animals with a long history dating back to pre-Roman times and mentions of them can be found in medieval Welsh literature. They have been put to a multitude of uses during that time including farm and forestry work and serving the Welsh Militia in the 15th century as war horses.

A few Fell ponies can still be found living a semi-wild existence on the open fells of Cumbria. They are stocky, strong and hardy. The breed was once vital to the local economy serving both as a pack animal transporting goods across the steep rocky hillsides and as an invaluable assistant to the hill shepherd. Today they are used for riding or driving and for several years a Fell pony was the favourite mount of Queen Elizabeth II when she went riding.

The Dales pony is a very similar breed and was used by the lead mines of the Yorkshire Dales as a pack animal.

One of the most rare breeds is the Eriskay pony, once the mainstay of crofting life on the remote island of Eriskay, in the Western Isles of Scotland. Crofters used the ponies to collect peat they'd cut for fuel and seaweed which they spread on the land as fertiliser. In the 1970s the number of Eriskay ponies had dropped to only 20 but people stepped in to preserve them and at present there are about 200.

Today, native breeds of wild ponies are of little use other than as children's ponies. Mechanisation has made them redundant. There is no money made out of allowing ponies to live a natural existence wild on the moors but the moors would not be the same if it wasn't for their grazing. They are owned by farmers and people who hold grazing rights, but there is only a certain sustainable level, so numbers have to be managed accordingly. Left to their own devices, the population would get out of control.

DOGS

There are over 200 breeds of dogs recognised in the UK and even though pet dogs number more than 10 million, there are several breeds that have fallen right out of favour and are becoming rare.

The Otterhound, used for hunting otters until 1976 when it was banned, is the most vulnerable breed with only 7 being registered with the Kennel Club in 2020. Bloodhounds are another breed under serious threat.

Across the UK many local breeds of terriers evolved to control vermin such as rats and foxes. Some like the Dandie Dinmont, Glen of Imaal, Irish and Skye all face extinction.

The elegant English setter is at risk and Sussex spaniel numbers are very low. King Charles spaniels, popular as lap dogs since the 17th century, have recently lost their appeal.

Fortunately there are enthusiasts trying to preserve at-risk pedigree breeds who show their dogs and strive to maintain the breed standards. By doing so they are preserving a gene pool ensuring breeds won't become extinct.

PLANTS

Seed banks have been set up across the world to conserve old varieties, many of which are rare and might otherwise be lost forever. For scientific reasons, it is very important that a gene pool is preserved. Researchers collect the seeds by hand, which are then cleaned and dried before being placed in sealed, airtight containers, frozen and stored at minus 20°C. Most plant seeds can survive and remain viable for decades cached in this way.

Our cereal crops of wheat, barley, oats and rye have evolved over many thousands of years from what are known as 'landrace grains'. These originally grew as wild plants across the world and have been domesticated by farmers and, through selection, gradually improved. The plants themselves have adapted to suit local environmental conditions and to being cultivated. It wasn't until the late 19th century that scientists began crossbreeding different strains to produce hybrids which increased productivity and became widely used and improved during the 20th and 21st century. Progress continues.

Heirloom varieties of plants and trees, as the name suggests, are traditional ones. Many varieties have stood the test of time and are still popular today; some are even being grown on a commercial scale.

Brogdale, near Faversham in Kent, is home to the **National Fruit Collection** with more than 4,000 varieties, some of them rare.

Over 2,500 varieties of apples have been developed in the UK, with many local to different regions. There are 157 varieties in Gloucestershire alone. Bramley apples were first grown in England more than 200 years ago and Cox's Orange Pippin in 1830. Beauty of Bath appeared in the Victorian era and Worcester Pearmain was first recognised in 1873.

'Apple Days' are held in some places where apples from old trees can be taken to be identified using its DNA if necessary. Occasionally a variety that was thought to have been lost has been rediscovered by this means. Cherries were being grown in England before the 17th century. William pears date back to c1770 and Conference to 1885. Victoria plums were being widely cultivated by the 19th century.

It is not only fruits that are heirlooms but varieties of vegetables as well. Carrots have been cultivated since Elizabethan times and Savoy cabbages have been grown in gardens since the 17th century. King Edward potatoes, possibly named after Edward VII, were introduced in 1902 followed by Moneymaker tomatoes in 1913.

Runner beans were first introduced to Britain as ornamental climbers in the early 17th century. It was a hundred years later that they became regarded as food. One of the oldest varieties is Scarlet Emperor which for well over a century has remained a popular choice for gardeners.

Our future is so entwined with our past that it is of great importance that all aspects of our treasured heritage are safeguarded for future generations.

◀ Varieties of heritage apples are often on display at Apple Days usually held in October

ABOUT THE AUTHOR

Jill Mason has spent all her time living and working in the countryside. Now retired, she was employed for 30 years as one of the country's few women gamekeepers. She has written extensively for countryside magazines and is the author of several books. Her husband David Mason's beautiful photographs illustrate her writing. They live in a village in Norfolk.

INDEX

INDEX

INDEX